HQ

C

D0893423

"The Sex Side of Life"

"THE SEX

SIDE

OF LIFE"

Mary Ware Dennett's
Pioneering Battle for
Birth Control and Sex Education

CONSTANCE M. CHEN

THE NEW PRESS / NEW YORK

LIBRARY OF CONGRESS CATALOGING-IN-PUBLICATION DATA

Chen, Constance M.
 The sex side of life: the story of Mary Ware Dennett / by Constance M. Chen.
  p. cm.
 Includes bibliographical references and index.
 ISBN 1-56584-132-8 (HC)
  I. Dennett, Mary Ware, 1872-1947. 2. Birth control—United States. 3. Sex educators—
   United States—Biography. 4. Women social reformers—United States—Biography.
   5. Sex instruction—United States. I. Title.
 HQ764.D46C46   1996
 613.9′07—dc20

[B]95-44173
CIP

Published in the United States by The New Press, New York
Distributed by W. W. Norton & Company, Inc., New York

ESTABLISHED IN 1990 AS A MAJOR ALTERNATIVE TO THE LARGE, COMMERCIAL
PUBLISHING HOUSES, THE NEW PRESS IS A FULL-SCALE NONPROFIT AMERICAN BOOK PUBLISHER
OUTSIDE OF THE UNIVERSITY PRESSES. THE PRESS IS OPERATED EDITORIALLY IN THE PUBLIC
INTEREST, RATHER THAN FOR PRIVATE GAIN; IT IS COMMITTED TO PUBLISHING IN INNOVATIVE
WAYS WORKS OF EDUCATIONAL, CULTURAL, AND COMMUNITY VALUE THAT, DESPITE THEIR
INTELLECTUAL MERITS, MIGHT NOT NORMALLY BE COMMERCIALLY VIABLE.
THE NEW PRESS'S EDITORIAL OFFICES ARE LOCATED AT THE CITY UNIVERSITY OF NEW YORK.

BOOK DESIGN by Hall Smyth and Gordon Whiteside of BAD
PRODUCTION MANAGEMENT by Kim Waymer
PRINTED in the United States of America

96 97 98 99 9 8 7 6 5 4 3 2 I

For my dearly loved parents,
TED AND MARIAN CHEN,
whose support made this book possible.

I for one
Think the country would be better run,
If Mary Ware Dennett
Explained things to the Senate.

—*Ogden Nash*

Contents

Preface

Most biographies deal with unevenly developed folks, neurotic geniuses, single-minded zealots, and the like. Part of their genius has been to utilize their one-sidedness superbly, so that rightly enough, the world is indebted to them. But best of all are the people who are alive in all directions, and who have many kinds of faculties in use their whole lives through. They are less famous than the people of one idea, but in the long run I believe they add more to the value and joy of life.

— Mary Ware Dennett

IMAGINE a world in which a mother could not legally mail a letter to her daughter teaching her how to use birth control.[1] Or a high school in which a teacher felt obliged to close the window shades during a class about human reproduction.[2] Or a courtroom in which a fifty-seven-year-old grandmother was convicted on criminal charges for sending a sex education pamphlet through the United States Post Office. Such was America in 1929.

Mary Ware Dennett (1872–1947) was a mother, artisan, suffragist, peace activist, and birth control and sex education advocate who would fight three major battles in her life. The first involved her fight to hold together her family. Around the turn of the century, religion was being challenged as the arbiter of moral values and a new individualism was leading to a decline in social responsibility and the rise of a "rights"-oriented culture. Reacting against the repression of the old world, a major paradigm shift occurred as pleasure replaced duty and personality replaced character as the defining factors of the new belief system. The fall of traditional religion led to the rise of do-it-yourself philosophies whose only criteria were to please the self. This resulted in a general questioning and weakening of the institution of marriage, from which alternative lifestyles took root. In the midst of this, Mary's husband became convinced through the rhetoric of another woman that "free love" was the path to a "higher morality."

Mary's second battle took place during her Greenwich Village years, when she fought to make birth control legally available to all

Americans. Concerned about the lack of sexual ethics, Dennett would begin a crusade that opened up discussion about sex in Congress and pitted her against fellow birth-control advocate Margaret Sanger. Although Dennett and Sanger initially worked together, it was Dennett, not Sanger, who organized the first birth-control organization in America, and their divergent convictions about who should have access to birth-control information would lead to a bitter rivalry for the movement's leadership. Dennett stood firm on the principle that contraceptive information should be available to all—men and women, rich and poor. Generally uninterested in legislation, Sanger stepped into the Congressional arena only to block Dennett's work by presenting a "doctor's only" bill that would create an information monopoly among the male medical elite.

Dennett's third battle was over her groundbreaking sex education pamphlet, *The Sex Side of Life: An Explanation for Young People.* Dissatisfied with all other available material, Dennett wrote *The Sex Side of Life* as an essay for her two sons in an effort to demystify sexuality. Later published in pamphlet form, it became tremendously popular as doctors, parents, church leaders, social workers, camp counselors, and schoolteachers snatched it up by the dozens. The Bronxville public schools system and the Union Theological Seminary used it as the primary text in child care classes; even the YMCA, founder of the Society for the Suppression of Vice, sold *The Sex Side of Life* in its bookstores and newsstands nationwide.

Dennett hoped to eliminate fear and shame about sex. Not arguing for promiscuity, she wanted to use reason and good taste to create a more civilized society. The eternal idealist, Dennett wanted to give to her children the "self-control that is born of knowledge, not fear, the reverence that will prevent premature or trivial connections, the good taste and finesse that will make their sex life, when they reach maturity, a vitalizing success." In a world ravaged by extremes, Mary Ware Dennett sought to achieve balance and moderation in defining a new set of sexual ethics. Yet despite her success in bridging the gap between liberals and conservatives, she would be charged with obscenity in a trial that became a landmark case in censorship law. As debates over sex education still linger, Dennett's work is as timely as ever. Over sixty years later, Dennett's story continues to raise urgent questions about America's ongoing struggle with sexual morals.

Despite her pivotal work in the birth-control movement, Dennett's contributions have been long buried in the footnotes of American history. In a standard American history textbook, Dennett breezes by in a brief mention of the early twentieth-century birth-control movement.[3] In *Notable American Women*, Margaret Sanger, not Mary Ware Dennett, is mistakenly credited with the founding of the National Birth Control League.[4] In his book, *The Birth Control Movement & American Society: From Private Vice to Public Virtue*, James Reed footnotes Dennett as "Margaret Sanger's rival for leadership of the birth control movement after World War I."[5] In her biography of Margaret Sanger, *Woman of Valor*, Ellen Chesler mistakenly has Dennett mourning an infant daughter, instead of a son. And several books covering the subject of censorship and obscenity law, including *Obscenity and Public Morality: Censorship in a Liberal Society*,[6] *Censorship: The Search for the Obscene*,[7] *Law, Politics and Birth Control*,[8] *Suppressed Books: A History of the Conception of Literary Obscenity*,[9] and *In Defense of American Liberties: A History of the ACLU*,[10] refer to "the Dennett case" in a few sparse paragraphs, with one book, *Federal Censorship: Obscenity in the Mail*,[11] spelling Dennett's name wrong!

This unorthodox biography brings Dennett's extraordinary story to life. Hers is a story in which the personal and the political converge. Moving her from the sidelines to the center stage, *"The Sex Side of Life:" Mary Ware Dennett's Pioneering Battle for Birth Control and Sex Education* traces not only Dennett's life, but also the beginnings of several perenially relevant social and political movements such as birth control, sex education, and the fight against government censorship. It is a narrative, not merely analytical, but subjective and emotive. It is a story in which anyone interested in family life and relationship issues will unfailingly be drawn in.

Acknowledgments

EVERY book bears the mark of many people. This one is no exception. I am grateful to Radcliffe College, which awarded me two generous grants to encourage the use of resources at the Schlesinger Library, the Carol K. Pforzheimer Fellowship and the Schlesinger Library Research Support Grant. The Schlesinger Library also graciously granted me permission for the reproduction of various manuscripts and photographs from the Dennett Collection. Eva Moseley, curator of the manuscripts, was wise enough to allow me to continue using the original documents after having them microfilmed. Special thanks are also due to Kate Blatt (for always remembering to hold for me key number nine), Anne Engelhart, Diane Hamer, the late Patricia King, Sylvia MacDowell, the Board of Trustees of Radcliffe College, and the staff of the Schlesinger Library.

The Dennett family has also been exceptionally generous and helpful in providing private documents and photographs for the book. Carleton Dennett and Marie Dennett provided wit and good humor during the last months of their lives. Sally Dennett deserves special mention for providing constant notes of encouragement while maintaining impartiality in waiting to see the final product. Joanna Dennett, Nancy Dennett, and Margaret Chase Perry also provided warm friendship and hospitality throughout the research process.

No book can be completed without an army of helpful friends and readers to give support and feedback. This one benefited from the suggestions and comments of Jill Harrison Berg, Georgia Brian, Allan Brandt, Partha Chattoraj, David Chen, Marian Chen, Ted Chen, Elizabeth Coleman, Patricia Cooper, Katharine Ellen Day, Susan deGersdorff, Bruce Grover, Ann Melville LaCrosse, Molly Markert, Judy Norsigian, Joe Osterman, Sonja Muehlmann Schmidt, Mark Schroeder, Adrienne Stengel, Kimberly Syphrett, Gandhi Viswanathan, and the late Irving Zola.

This project never would have gotten off the ground without the support of Lindy Hess, who has successfully introduced so many young people to the publishing world through the Radcliffe Publishing Course. I am also grateful to my literary agent, Faith Hampton Childs, and to my editor, Dawn Davis.

More than anyone else, however, this book owes its existence to my parents, Ted and Marian Chen, and I can only hope that after reading this book they will feel that their sacrifices for and confidence in their daughter were all worthwhile.

Comstockery and the Origins of Censorship in the United States

Comstockery is the world's standing joke at the expense of the United States. Europe likes to hear of such things. It confirms the deep-seated conviction of the Old World that America is a provincial place, a second-rate country-town civilization after all.[12]

—George Bernard Shaw, 1905

"MORALS, not art or literature!" With this cry, Anthony Comstock carried Victorian sexual mores well into the twentieth century, giving them the full force of law. Boasting that by the end of his life, he had convicted enough people to fill a passenger train of sixty-one coaches with sixty people in each,[13] Comstock was a religious fanatic who stopped at nothing in his personal crusade for moral purity. Midway through his career, he stopped listing among his many "accomplishments" the number of abortionists, freethinkers, and other "smut dealers" whom he had driven to death or suicide. From the very beginning, he used signature traps of decoy letters bearing false signatures to lure his victims into arrest. But none of his work could have been possible had it not been for the law that bore his name.

Born on 7 March 1844 in New Canaan, Connecticut, Anthony Comstock was brought up on Bible stories from his mother and the fire-and-brimstone sermons of a stern Congregational church. As a volunteer in the Civil War, he attended religious services at least four times a week—and sometimes even eight or nine times— despite the fact that his regiment had no chaplain.[14] After the war, Comstock moved to New York City to earn his keep as a dry-goods clerk. Living in a boardinghouse on Pearl Street, he was appalled by the surrounding sinfulness. The destruction of the Civil War had left an aftermath of moral and physical chaos. Years of bitter fighting had ripped apart the social fabric, and society's dregs were floating to the top. Taking stock of the near-nightly drinking, gambling, and whoring of the young men around him, Comstock could only lament, "How rarely do they say they are going to a sermon."

Responding to conditions in the city, in 1868 the Young Men's Christian Association (YMCA) of New York effected the passage of a state bill that prohibited the dissemination of "obscene literature."[15] The same year, Comstock became severely distressed by the interest his peers showed in erotic books and pictures. Taking advantage of the new obscenity law, he went so far as to track down two book dealers and have them arrested. As a private citizen, Comstock made it his business to track down all dealers who offended his standards of morality. He scanned lowbrow newspapers and magazines for fraudulent advertisements. When he came across something that looked suspicious, he would send for it, often receiving a catalogue of "fancy books" as his reward. Yet too often, he found his poverty frustrated his efforts to wipe out vice.

Writing to the YMCA in early 1872, Comstock claimed that with a little money he could get at the stock of the dirty book publishers. Later, he would describe his mission: "In 1872, when I undertook the great and all-important work of suppressing by legal process this hydra-headed monster, what did I find? I found a business systemized and systematically carried on. I found newspapers teeming with the advertisements of these bold and shameless criminals. I found laws inadequate, and public sentiment worse than dead, because of an appetite that had been formed for salacious reading; and especially because decent people could not be made to see or understand the necessity of doing anything in this line."[16]

Morris K. Jesup, president of YMCA, happened to see the letter Comstock sent to the YMCA and, after paying Comstock a personal visit, mailed the crusader a check for $650. Jesup was a man of great wealth, keenly interested in science and education—in fact, he was president and founder of the American Museum of Natural History. With Jesup's financial backing, Comstock invited a New York City police captain and a *New York Tribune* newspaper reporter to accompany him to two local stationery stores. Upon entering the establishment, Comstock bought some books and pictures, which he immediately declared obscene. The policeman duly arrested six employees of the store on the spot, including two boys, ages eleven and thirteen; three adults were later convicted and sentenced to jail for terms ranging from three months to one year. The very next day, the *Tribune* published a story which brought Comstock, just a few days shy of his twenty-eighth birthday, out of obscurity.

Encouraged by his success, Comstock went further. Reserving a special hatred for anything that smelled of progressive thought, Comstock made the front page of *The New York Times* on 3 November 1872 when he brought about the arrest of two radical feminist sisters, Victoria Woodhull and Tennessee Claflin. In an issue of their paper, *Woodhull and Claflin's Weekly*, the pair had published a story about the alleged infidelity of Henry Ward Beecher, a highly respected clergyman of the time. The sisters, both professed free lovers, didn't mind the adultery but could not forgive Beecher's hypocrisy. Horrified by the indiscretion of the sisters, Comstock charged them with obscenity. It was a flimsy charge, but obscenity was difficult to define. He ran against a block in court, however: New York state law covered only dealers, and not publishers. Scornful of their accuser, Woodhull and Claflin churned out article after article in which they publicly mocked Comstock. The taunts of the two women only fired the man's wrath and zeal, convincing him that current laws needed more teeth.

In 1865, Congress had passed a federal obscenity law, responding to reports from the postmaster general that "great numbers" of "obscene books and pictures" had been sent to soldiers during the Civil War. To combat the flow of virulent material, the post office had asked for a federal statute authorizing any postmaster to seize obscene books and start criminal prosecutions against those who used the mails to disseminate such material, with sentences of up to one year in prison. In Congress, the discussion was brief and perfunctory, with little attempt to define obscenity. Vague mentions of censorship had wafted about and there was some objection to the thought of a postmaster snooping around, breaking seals of private correspondence. Vested with sole authority for regulating the mails, the postmaster general would gain unchecked power over the mails. Nevertheless, the law passed.

The 1865 law was not the first. Obscenity had been a concern in America in some form or another since colonial times. In 1712, a Massachusetts statute condemned "any filthy, obscene or profane song, pamphlet, libel or mock sermon in imitation or mimicking religious service,"[17] and in 1792, thirteen of the fourteen states that ratified the Constitution had statutes to cover the prosecution of libel, blasphemy, and profanity.[18] Despite concern about the perpetration of "bad morals," however, obscene libel was not really an issue until the 1815 case of *Commonwealth of Pennsylvania vs. Sharpless*, which charged "certain yeomen" with "being evil-disposed persons," indicting them with exhibiting in a private house "a certain lewd, wicked, scandalous, infamous and obscene painting ..."[19] and an 1821 case in Massachusetts which brought about the first reported prosecution of obscene *literature*.[20]

Yet censorship did not really become an issue until 1836, when anti-Abolitionists, led by President Andrew Jackson, voiced outrage that "incendiary" tracts put out by radicals could be disseminated in vast volume by the government itself—and especially in the south. This was the first and only time for a long period that Congress explored the question: "Can the government censor, on any ground, what it carries in the mail?" Indeed, early cases of obscenity were more concerned with the behavior of the person than with the material in question. The law lacked specific rules prohibiting the production of obscene *matter*.[21] It was not until 1842, when Congress passed a stipulation in the Tariff Act which barred the importation of obscene material, that customs officers were authorized to bring court proceedings to confiscate and destroy "prints" and "pictures" that were "obscene or immoral."[22] And over time, Congress broadened the 1842 Tariff Act to include "daguerreotypes," "photographs," "images," and "figures."[23]

Then in 1868, a landmark case was heard in England that was to carry over to the states and influence American obscenity cases for the next half-century. Lord Chief Justice Alexander Cockburn interpreted England's obscenity law in *Regina vs. Hicklin*, determining that each passage in a book could be isolated and judged separately from any other section of the book. If any excerpt, taken out of context, was obscene, then the book could be condemned—*even if the rest of the book was clean and the message and motivation commendable*.[24] Furthermore, Lord Cockburn also deemed that if the passage in question had the "tendency" to "deprave and corrupt those whose minds are open to immoral influences" and if it was possible for the work to fall into the hands of such a person, then such a publication was obscene. This ruling had two implications. First, the book did not actually need to bring about sexual misbehavior before its potential for corruption could be found; it was enough that passages could simply "stimulate sexual thoughts in impressionable minds."[25] Secondly, it assumed that any public work could fall into the possession of the young or others susceptible to lewd fantasies. This was "a class assumed to be large; and it was this kind of audience the law...was to protect by making criminal *all* circulation which *could* corrupt the corruptible, regardless of whether that harm actually had occurred"[26] (emphasis added).

By 1872, Anthony Comstock probably knew more about the evolving obscenity laws and their limits and capabilities than any of the lawmakers themselves. Turning to the YMCA, Comstock suggested a "cooperative drive" to lobby for a federal obscenity statute beyond the New York state law.[27] What he wanted was an all-inclusive statute without loopholes, which had guarantees for harsher penalties. Jesup agreed to the proposal and, along with other eminent New Yorkers, supplied Comstock with a salary and an expense account for the project.[28] With the best legal services at his disposal, young Comstock left for Capitol Hill as early as December 1872 representing the New York YMCA's newly formed Committee for the Suppression of Vice.

Comstock cut a curious figure. He dressed in dark, unpressed clothes, and no one would ever remember him in a hue other than black. Even in the summertime, he wore his black alpaca coat both in the street and in the office, and a black bow tie around the collar of his stiffly starched shirts. The nearest he came to colors was during the Christmas season, when he switched his black tie for white. A truculent, tense person, Comstock had a habit of drawing down his upper lip as he spoke, giving his face an expression of deep and passionate earnestness. A high, bald forehead topped a corpulent body, and his oft-caricatured muttonchop whiskers were ginger-colored in his early years, then white. Yet all year round, this somber-looking man wore red flannel underwear. His exterior matched his temperament. Underneath the black-and-white clothes was a personality so fiery that it would stop at nothing to attain its goals.[29]

By the time he arrived in Washington, D.C., members of the YMCA had secured for Comstock an introductory interview with Representative Clinton L. Merriam of New York and Senator William Windom of Minnesota. After impressing the importance of his cause upon the two men, Comstock was allowed to present his case before the House late in January 1873, accompanied by Representative Merriam. Carrying his special cloth satchel of books and pictures into the halls of Congress, the vice hunter remained on the floor nearly all day, displaying his special collection of pornography to all the lawmakers who cared to look. Designed to shock and horrify—and thus circumvent rational thought—Comstock's exhibits were the basest, most degrading specimens of obscenity he could find: gadgets purportedly designed to stimulate sexual potency; contraceptive and abortifacient matter; bogus sex literature; "fancy books" with titles like *The Lustful Turk, The Lascivious London Beauty,* or *Peep Behind the Curtains of a Female Seminary,* and other "abominations" sold through lowbrow publications and advertisements. Determined to seek out obscenity, he rarely failed to find it. His biographers would later quip, "But was not that a lucky break for Anthony Comstock that almost alone out of all the world he could have his cake and suppress it, too?"[30]

Convinced that children's names were being bought and sold on mailing lists around the country, Comstock fervently felt it was his mission to save children from traps set by Satan. A flood of vile traffic was corrupting the nation's children, Comstock insisted, and America needed a law to stop this "hydra-headed monster" of vice! Current laws just weren't strong enough. What the country needed was a law broader in scope and stricter in punishment. Tears flowed from his eyes as he addressed Congress. Indeed this man, a humble greengrocer, was at once so earnest and yet so self-righteous. Who could have foreseen that he would conduct a purity crusade so fanatical that it would one day result in a wholesale indictment against human sexuality?

Indeed, members of Congress were appropriately horrified. Comstock rushed back to New York with optimistic reports for the YMCA vice squad. Overjoyed when Committee members told him to return to Washington, Comstock hurried back to make a number of early-morning calls on prominent legislators, including Representative Merriam and Senator William A. Buckingham of Connecticut, a former war governor. This time, A. H. Byington secured the vice-president's room for a private viewing of the exhibits by the senators. Comstock spent an hour or two talking and answering questions, explaining the extent of the nefarious business. In his diary, Comstock recorded that all present seemed very much excited, declaring themselves ready to give him any law he might ask for, as long as it was within the bounds of the Constitution. There were many lawmakers present, including the vice-president, Henry Wilson. Comstock was exuberant: "All said they were ready to pass my bill promptly this session."

By this time, Senator Buckingham had promised to bring the bill before the Senate, with Representative Merriam introducing it in the House. At the time, two other obscenity bills were pending. The legislators decided to merge all three bills into one reconstituted and enlarged measure, which Comstock would thereafter refer to as "my bill." It was a lengthy bill, written in five sections, which prohibited the mailing of obscene matter within the United States and territories. The wording was designed to be careful and precise, in order to close many of the old loopholes.

The new bill contained several new points. First, instead of limiting itself to books and pictures as in the 1865 law, it included "every lewd, lascivious, or filthy book, pamphlet, picture, paper, letter, writing, print, or other publication of an indecent character." It also included "every written or printed card, letter, circular, book, pamphlet, advertisement or notice of any kind." And it did not leave out "any article, instrument, substance, drug, medicine, or thing." Now, virtually anything a diligent vice hunter might find offensive could be considered obscene. The penalty for obscenity was increased to a $5000 fine or a five years in jail or both for a first-time culprit, with sentences up to $10,000 or ten years in prison or both for repeat offenders. In addition, the new bill added a special clause: it became a crime to advertise or mail any information "for preventing conception or producing abortion."

How the birth control and abortion clause entered the obscenity bill is not clear, but one thing is certain: There was little debate about it in the halls of Congress. Instead, there was virtually no discussion of the provisions until after it was passed. Without taking a roll call in either the Senate or the House, there was an action for unanimous consent in the Senate and a suspension of normal procedure in the House. The Committee on the Post Office and Post Roads, which was handling the bill, did not make an official report. Sexuality contained such a stigma of shame that any sexual expression that did not lead directly to procreation was not only denied legitimacy but was pushed out of consciousness. The contraception and abortion clause, which would have dire consequences, was virtually ignored. For fear of appearing "lewd," "lascivious," or "filthy" himself, not a single politician dared speak out against the new obscenity bill. With great consideration shown to Comstock, the legislators wanted the bill passed immediately.

Back in New York, Comstock sat down in the YMCA rooms to write letters to ten abortionists, nine of whom advertised in the *New York Herald*. He looked forward to prosecuting them under the new laws. Yet he was cruelly disappointed: At first, the bill passed neither House nor Senate. There were many delays, and the bill had to wait. Then in the Senate, the revised bill was introduced and referred to the Committee on Post Offices and Post Roads.

Ever hopeful, Comstock spoke before the Committee on Post Offices and Post Roads, convincing them unanimously to consent to his bill and put it at once on the Senate calendar. Before long, though, the bill met with more delays. Forced to make his case again, Comstock conducted more interviews and put together more displays of his exhibits.

Then Senator Windom brought good news: The Committee on Appropriations had decided to set aside $3,425 for a special agent to carry out the new bill if it were passed, with the postmaster general promising that Comstock would be appointed. The Committee for the Suppression of Vice gave its approval to Comstock's activities, but also passed a resolution instructing Comstock not to take any salary should Senator Windom's resolution for his appointment as a special agent of the post office come through. Comstock was in complete accord: "This just meets my views of this question. I do not want any fat office created, whereby the Government is taxed for some politician to have in a year or two. Give me the Authority that such an office confers, and thus enable me to more effectually do this work, and the Salary and honors may go to the winds."[31]

As the bill bounced back and forth on Capitol Hill, Comstock had seven cases pending in Federal Courts. Forced to appear before a grand jury, he had to leave Washington until the following Monday. While in New York, the bill passed in the Senate. But there was a catch. In passing his bill, all indictments and prosecutions pending under the 1872 obscenity law would be quashed, including the eighteen to twenty cases with which Comstock was involved. Representative Merriam and Senator Buckingham were strongly opposed to another amendment, which would allow past cases to be tried. By this time, opponents of the bill were sending letters to Congressmen denouncing Comstock as a disreputable character and a perjurer. Attacks by his enemies and hostility from the press were beginning to create a feeling against him. To tack on another amendment now would be a terrible risk, but Comstock could not bring himself to invalidate past prosecutions and let the evildoers go free. He asked to go ahead with an amendment. The very same day, the *New York Herald*, which had carried the abortionist ads being prosecuted by Comstock, published an anti-Comstock article.

By Friday morning, 28 February 1873, Representative Merriam still had not introduced the bill. The next evening, Comstock sat in the House building, watching the proceedings with anxiety as the minutes ticked by. It was a Saturday, and Representative Merriam was supposed to introduce the bill, but he seemed to be waiting so long, irritating Comstock to no end. Before long, it was midnight, and Comstock realized that it was Sunday. Never having broken the Sabbath before, he was torn about what to do. Finally, at 12:30 AM, he left Congress so as not to desecrate God's day. Tormented all night, he needn't have worried. The bill passed the House at 2:00 AM on Sunday, 2 March 1873 with only thirty votes against it. On 3 March 1873, President Grant signed the bill into law.

According to the Comstock Act, the decision of obscenity rested with the legal advisor to the post office department, the solicitor. If material was determined to be obscene, the postmasters were notified not to accept it for delivery. If obscene matter was detected in the mail, then the postmasters were either to return it to the sender or destroy it.[32] In addition, the post office could request that the sender be prosecuted by the United States District Attorney. If the accused was acquitted and found not guilty of obscenity under the law, the post office nevertheless had the prerogative to stand by its original ruling and continue to refuse to send the material. The only relief for the accused was to file suit to force the post office to send the material in question.

On Thursday morning, 6 March 1873, Comstock received his commission as special agent from the postmaster-general. Taking the one o'clock train to New York, Comstock rejoiced. The New York *Journal of Commerce* printed a laudatory article about the bill's passage. By virtue of his commission from the post office, he could now enjoy the privilege of free transportation on all lines carrying mail. His job as special agent—his title would later be changed to inspector—vested him with special powers of arrest and made his work national in scope. The next day, 7 March 1873, he turned twenty-nine years old.

On 16 May 1873, only a couple months after the passage of the federal bill, Comstock had still more reason to celebrate. The New York legislature incorporated the Society for the Suppression of Vice, with Comstock as secretary. In the position, Comstock managed to toughen New York state law so much that it became a crime to give contraceptive information not only through the mails, but verbally as well![33] In addition, he gained special legal powers which allowed him to make prosecutions under New York state law.[34] Using unsavory methods such as decoy letters bearing false signatures, Comstock impersonated women and sexually depraved men in elaborate subterfuges to "get" sinners.[35] He tried to make his targets sell him forbidden wares, and afterward he would use the documentary evidence from the transaction to convict.[36] For example, Comstock sent the following letter to six different doctors on the same day.[37]

Washington, D.C., 18 March 1873
Dear Sir:

I am an employee of the Treasury and I have got myself into trouble. I was seduced about four months ago, and I am now about three months gone in the family way. The person who seduced me has run away and I do not know what will become of me if I do not get relief. I am a poor clerk and get only sixty dollars per month, and have to keep a widowed mother and a crippled sister, so that I send you all, in fact more than I can spare, hoping that you will send me something that will relieve me.

Now, dear Doctor, send it right away, and send it by mail, for I do not want any one to have a breath of suspicion about the matter. For God's sake do not disappoint a poor ruined and forsaken girl whose only relief will be suicide if you fail me.[38]

Enclosing twenty dollars in each envelope, Comstock sent the letters by registered mail so that the recipients would have to sign receipts before obtaining the letters.[39] Every physician who responded, even if with placebo only, was arrested and thrown into prison—their reputations destroyed and their families left impoverished.[40]

Sometimes, prison was not the worst of it. In one of his most infamous cases, Ann Lehman, more popularly known as Madame Restell, fell fatally into Comstock's hands. Comstock had called upon the sixty-seven year old woman, a former midwife whose practice had changed to contraception and abortion. By claiming his wife was in desperate need of her services, Comstock had wheedled out some medicine. With evidence in hand, he arrested her. Conviction seemed certain. An elderly woman who had saved many an aristocratic family from disgrace, Madame Restell dreaded the prospect of prison. Desperate, the night before her trial, she took a large carving knife from the kitchen and, while lying in her bath, slit her throat from ear to ear. All of New York was shocked. But upon hearing of her suicide, Comstock's only response was, "A bloody ending to a bloody life."

With little remorse, Comstock thought only of arrest. Indeed, he was not beyond altering his evidence to ensure conviction. In the case of Dr. Sara Chase, for example, Comstock obtained a "female syringe" by claiming to represent a woman who had attended one of Dr. Chase's lectures. A well-respected homeopath who lectured on physiology, Dr. Chase was also editor and publisher of a reform and health monthly, *The Physiologist.* Searching through the physician's private papers, Comstock found an article entitled "Foeticide," which advised against the practice of abortion. Trying to misrepresent her, however, Comstock reported to the New York *Tribune* that Dr. Chase had written an article called "Foeticide—When it should be done." Fortunately, the grand jury saw through his tricks and refused to see why Dr. Chase should be indicted. Indeed, one member of the grand jury asked Comstock if he meant to drive Dr. Chase to suicide as he had driven Madame Restell.[41]

Before long, Comstock had solidified a reputation as a sneak who tormented hapless souls by unfair and dishonorable means. On 30 May 1878, at a Boston meeting at which Comstock was attempting to organize an auxiliary branch of the Society for the Suppression of Vice, the Congregationalist Minister Jesse H. Jones rose to ask Comstock three questions: (1) "Did you ever use decoy letters or false signatures?" (2) "Did you ever sign a woman's name when writing a letter?" (3) "Did you ever try to make a person sell you forbidden wares and then, when you succeeded, use the evidence thus obtained to convict him?" When Comstock answered yes to all three questions, Reverend Jones announced to all present, "Mr. Comstock has been guilty of what would be considered disgraceful in a Boston policeman."

Not limiting himself to physicians and pharmacists, Comstock also went after the printed word—in every case tracking his prey under an assumed name. In one case, Comstock visited a bookstore, asking for a copy of *The Lustful Turk.* When the proprietor replied that he did not keep that kind of book, Comstock arrested him anyway, claiming that the man had sent him a circular letting him know where such books could be obtained.[42] In another case, Comstock wrote to a merchant for a set of pictures of ballet dancers in costume. When he received the pictures, Comstock substituted the original pictures with some that were clearly obscene. Committing perjury in court, Comstock sent the man to prison—from which he was only released at the point of death.[43] And in a third case, Comstock arrested a well-respected physician who had written and published a work on sexually transmitted diseases. The manuscript had been approved by the best medical counsel in New York state as well as by the district attorney and other legal advisors. No matter—according to the dictates of the Hicklin test of obscenity, the valuable medical work was condemned.[44]

Indeed, the passage of the obscenity law allowed Comstock to be very creative in seeking out obscenity. The streets of New York had been purged of almost all unseemly peddlers and shop windows cleared of indecent displays.[45] Forced to look elsewhere for material to ban, he put a small-town newspaper editor in jail for writing an editorial deploring society's treatment of the unwed mother; he seized a 1907 issue of the *American Journal of Eugenics* for advertising a book called *The History of Prostitution*; he prevented an official report on prostitution commissioned by the mayor of Chicago in 1911 from going through the mails.[46] As for literature, D. H. Lawrence, Anatole France, Apuleius, Aristophanes, Ovid, Boccaccio, Voltaire were among the many who produced work which Comstock found it necessary to censor.

The Comstock Act combined with the Hicklin test for obscenity were to be a lethal combination in the hands of Anthony Comstock. The problem, of course, was that Comstock's religious fanaticism, while well intentioned, exceeded all bounds of reason. The question of right or wrong became irrelevant. The result was an obscenity law so all-inclusive as to be practically unlimited in its domain and a legal precedent which allowed for the broadest possible interpretation. Under the Comstock Act, any article or thing could be found obscene; under the Hicklin test for obscenity, any passage could be taken out of context, judged against the tendencies of society's lowest common denominator, and, if available in the public domain, be condemned. These were to be the dual standards which would guard the morals of America for over half a century, until the arrival of Mary Ware Dennett.

THE EARLY YEARS

PART I

CHAPTER ONE

Old New England Granite

hen Mary Coffin Ware, blue eyed and bald, arrived in the world on the fourth of April 1872, the society she inherited was carefully circumscribed. Victorian mores were being codified into law. Men and women inhabited separate spheres; their very sexuality kept them apart. Discomfort surrounding the human body was so extreme that even piano "limbs" had to be properly covered. And heaven knows, few people would admit to knowing where babies came from.

The rigidity came from a moral foundation that was being shaken at its very core. Christianity, whose teachings had guided the nation's founders, had ossified and was breaking up into sects. During the mid–nineteenth century, several factions of millenialists had emerged—the Seventh Day Adventists, Jehovah's Witnesses, Mormons—all claiming that the fulfillment of Biblical prophecies was at hand. The Millerites went so far as to don white "ascension robes" in faithful expectation of the promised Return of Christ. Also responding to the potency of some divine force, Spiritualists, Transcendentalists, Unitarians, and others were creating new theologies celebrating the oneness and dignity of humankind. Mighty religious revivals produced the First Great Awakening and then the Second Great Awakening. A powerful spiritual force was shaking the land; the mood of the country was one of expectation and transformation.[47]

In the material realm, the technology of the machine age had fused together the nation's regional economies. Mills and factories had replaced the industry of the yeoman farmers. Manufacturing in mass quantities provided households with standardized goods. New railroad tracks connected north to south and east to west. Telegraph lines made possible instant communication across vast distances. And one federal currency replaced the old local bank notes. Through bitter fighting and enormous bloodshed, the Civil War had firmly established the unity of the nation so that even the most resilient Confederate newspaper would no longer say the United States "are" but instead, the United States "is."[48]

After the Civil War, it could no longer be ignored that an entire world order was embarking on change. Slavery had been abolished. The burgeoning suffrage movement was campaigning to give women equal rights. New economic theories were being spouted to end the unequal distribution of wealth in society. Reformers were working to create a system of universal compulsory public education. A new breed of pacifists wanted to end all wars and build a foundation for international arbitration. The progress that had always been recorded in dribs and drabs throughout human history had suddenly exploded in exponential fashion. For those with the eyes to see, it was the dawn of a new era.

Few could ignore the signs, but what to make of them? For the waning ruling class to which Mary belonged, the only clear truth was that an old way of living had passed. In the Northeast, progressive ideals had been put to the test. The bitter fighting of the Civil War had resulted in victory, but at great cost. Gone were the friends and relatives who had given their lives for a dream. Heavy bloodshed had ended slavery but not racial injustice. In their own midst, a flood of Irish immigrants was being subjected to a peculiarly Yankee form of intense discrimination. Quick to criticize the inequities of the South, northerners were unprepared to equate the end of slavery with the beginning of racial equality. Unwilling to rectify the prejudices of their own region, a growing sector of the blue bloods called out for restrictions in immigration. Instead of promoting unity and concord, they questioned the humanitarian standards that had been the hallmark of New England society.[49]

Massachusetts, which had served as a beacon of light for the most ardent reformers, dimmed in the aftermath of the Civil War. In its heyday, religion and education had converged to promote a broad sense of civic consciousness. The Puritan descendants had felt themselves to be stewards of God, members of a pious "elect." And indeed, the citizens of the commonwealth had championed many causes: temperance, public education, feminism, pacifism, as well as abolition. Bostonians, proud of the strong cultural influence they wielded upon the rest of the country, had declared their city the hub of the universe. But the destruction from the Civil War had challenged old feelings of permanence and security. The Puritan ethics that had stitched the community together were dissolving. Without its old spiritual values, the former ruling class descended into mediocrity.[50]

In these confusing times, many old-time Yankees began wallowing in the past, clinging to their lineage. Mary Coffin Ware was no exception. Her father could trace his name back to the landed gentry and yeomanry of Great Britain, some of whom emigrated to America in the 1600s and settled in Virginia and Massachusetts. One Robert Ware, who arrived in Dedham, Massachusetts, sometime before 1643, sired seven children—six of whom grew to adulthood—and later most New England Wares believed themselves to have descended from him. In Massachusetts, more than fifty Wares fought in the Revolutionary War, and the Reverend Henry Ware Jr. was a distinguished Unitarian divine and author in the early 1800s.

But it was her mother's ancestors who would prove to be the most spiritually inspiring for Mary. The Coffins hailed from Devonshire, England, where they had lived ever since the Norman Conquest. In 1642, Joanna Thember, widow of Peter Coffin, emigrated to Salisbury, Massachusetts, with three of her six children—about thirty-five years after her husband died. Generations later, descendant and namesake Captain Peter Coffin fought in the Revolutionary War. As Mary would later tell the story, his wife, Rebecca Hazeltine, was a stout American rebel who, when the Stamp Act was passed to tax tea, "resolutely put away the few ounces of tea in her caddy, and would not have any of it used until the act was passed." When her husband's company received orders to march to Bennington and two soldiers had no shirts to wear, Rebecca, who had a web partially woven in her loom, seized shears and cut out what she had woven, sat up through the night and provided two shirts in the morning—this only nine days before her son Thomas was born![51]

Mary loved that the blood of these old-time revolutionaries coursed through her veins. With her roots deeply embedded in Puritan stock, she was trained to value honesty, humility, intellectual rigor, and justice. Even while she decried the bleak reputation of her "deadly respectable forebears," yearning instead for art and beauty, her New England heritage gave her a strong sense of identity. Her entire life would be a struggle between the rigidity of her Yankee heritage and a free spirit that demanded release. Later on, exemplifying the upright character of her Puritan background, she would be criticized by her detractors for her firm adherence to law and order. Who would have guessed that this woman, known for her sobriety, would become a most determined champion of the controversial causes of birth control and sex education?

Her story began in 1861, when Mary's maternal grandparents migrated from Boscawen, New Hampshire, to establish an experimental frontier pioneer community at West Creek in Lake County,

Indiana. Only a few days after arriving, on 31 January 1861, her maternal grandmother, Elvira Coffin Ames, died, forcing Mary's mother, Livonia Coffin Ames, to give up her dream of attending Oberlin College—one of the first institutions of higher education to admit female students within its walls. At age eighteen, Vonie, as Mary's mother was called, had to attempt to fill Elvira's shoes, becoming "little mother" to her two younger sisters and younger brother. Before long, the experimental pioneer community failed, and the Ames family moved to the Chicago area, where Vonie met Mary's father, George Whitefield Ware.

Falling deeply into the Victorian contrivances of romantic love and marriage, George and Vonie considered themselves the embodiment of the middle-class ideal of true love and perfect union. When they married, they believed their union to be a genuine wedding of souls. In the nineteenth century, matrimony was not something to be taken lightly. Not only did the sentimentality of the Victorian era promote high expectations for romantic bliss, but the nuptial bond was also a carefully balanced economic arrangement that depended on equal cooperation from both partners. Victorian convention strongly enforced the notion of separate spheres for women and men. The angel of the house dared not venture beyond the domestic realm; the world yonder was a man's demesne. In the name of love, both husband and wife sacrificed personal interests to support the family: the man lost his place in the home; the woman lost her place in the world.

According to formula, the man fought for material sustenance while the woman provided the home with spiritual nourishment, guarding the family from the corruption of the outside world. In return for simple household work—cooking, cleaning, sewing, etc.—the nineteenth-century wife could expect to receive food, shelter, and a clothing allowance. Theoretically, it was a relationship between two complementary equals. Yet if a wife failed to perform her duties, she was the legal chattel of her husband—he could beat her, rape her, or divorce her as he willed. If a husband failed to perform his duties, however, the wife had little recourse, for a married woman was almost entirely dependent upon the generosity of her husband.

The notion of romantic love cushioned harder truths. Women were bound by laws but could not vote; they paid taxes but could elect no representative. A wife's property and earnings belonged to her husband, and her social status depended upon him as well.

Affection between husband and wife was an ideal, but it was not always realized. In a state of total social, political, and economic inequality, the idea of "love" simply meant a woman might willingly and even eagerly acquiesce in the selection of her future master. In 1861, John Stuart Mill became one of the first male feminists to speak out against the Victorian sexual code. "All men, except the most brutish, desire to have, in the woman most nearly connected with them, not a forced slave, but a willing one, not a slave merely, but a favourite."[52] He continued by pointing out, "Marriage is the only actual bondage known to our law. There remain no legal slaves, except the mistress of every house. . . ."[53]

Despite the rhetoric of love and romance, then, the reality was that marriage could often be little more than a elaborately orchestrated economic arrangement. Few professions were open to women. Teaching primary school was one of the few salaried positions available to an unmarried woman, but wages were low—much lower than for their male counterparts. Factory work paid slightly more, but the mind-dulling repetition and poor working conditions made long-term employment unappealing. Women in the lower classes might find work as domestic servants, but the Wares' social class tended to hire help rather than be paid as such. And the one profession that could be lucrative, prostitution, also lacked respectability.

Only very rich women of independent means could comfortably afford not to marry. Others, unable to find a man to offer them livelihood, were doomed to become "old maids." In the mid–nineteenth century, however, a small minority of women were beginning to reject marriage out of principle, rejecting the servile position that went along with it. Refusing to bow before a human master, they chose instead to endure long and lonely years of singleness.

Indeed, all three Ames sisters were quite independently minded. Vonie married, but only because she believed she had found true love. Both of her younger sisters carefully weighed their options and chose different life paths. Clara, the youngest, was a schoolteacher her entire life; she never married. Lucia rejected marriage for the first forty-two years of her life, choosing to support herself as a piano teacher in order to avoid the "dependent life." When she later won renown as an influential lecturer and writer on world peace and social reform, Lucia would often say she "profoundly pitied" unmarried women who relied on the income of a brother or father. Winning success with her most "unwomanly" mind, Lucia proved to herself and the world that women did not have to limit themselves to the domestic sphere in order to live. Greatly influencing her young niece, Aunt Lucia would imbue Mary Ware with a sense of strength and independence.

Yet it was in watching her own parents that Mary would come to develop her ideals about married life. Mary's father was a hard-working merchant who dealt in hides and wool. Guided by the high ideals of industry and honesty that had led generations of Yankees to success, he worked overtime to support their household. His business required constant traveling, so that even after they married, George was not able to spend much time at home. For months at a time, he kept a lonely room in a boardinghouse in the faraway South. It took him almost two weeks to make the train trek from Worcester, Massachusetts, to New York to New Orleans, where he would sail by ship to Indianola, Texas. Vonie sometimes accompanied him, but oftener than not, the funds just weren't there for them both to go together.

The couple hated to part. Yearning for one another's company, they wrote long and frequent letters. Vonie, especially, would long for her husband's kisses and caresses. Having married for love, not money, Vonie marveled to her husband about "how wonderfully our lives are blended together so that each feels incomplete without the other."[54] She was always ready with understanding reassurances when her husband met with financial disappointment. Like a good Victorian wife, she practiced frugality to make their money stretch as far as it would go. For his part, when George suspected company associates of being involved in foul play, he sent his funds to Vonie for safekeeping. Trusting his wife with his business woes, he turned to her for emotional support even when he was miles away from home.

Yet their forced separations caused neighbors to whisper that George had lost all his property or to speculate about how Vonie managed to support herself. Despite his sacrifices, George found that prosperity eluded him. The couple had to move often, renting apartments in one house or another. Foremost among his problems was the duplicity of his business associates. The expansion of the nation's economy was destroying the interpersonal connections of the smaller local communities. No longer was a gentlemanly handshake enough to close a deal. Increasingly, business was conducted between strangers and the increased anonymity was dissolving any sense of personal obligation.

Times had changed, and the post-war years were a period that contemporary Mark Twain would dub the Gilded Age. It was an era when greedy industrial and financial exploiters would not hesitate to cheat their associates.

> *Among American businessmen, there developed in these years the "Robber Baron," an unscrupulous, greedy industrial and financial type who competed ruthlessly with his fellows, exploited his labor force callously, bilked investors, and corrupted legislators and other public officials without conscience, all the while masquerading behind a façade of unctuous respectability.*[55]

Men like Cornelius Vanderbilt, John D. Rockefeller, and Andrew Carnegie started with ideas and built vast fortunes on the materialism of the industrial age. The new breed pledged allegiance not to God, but Mammon. Cynicism spread. The Yankee middle class, which had dominated American culture and politics for so long, was slipping from power.

The honest and the trusting would not have much luck in the new business world. George Ware's salary was enough to keep his family in the middle or even upper-middle class, but money worries never seemed to be far from his mind. Cheated of his money again and again, George was only one of many discovering that the high ideals that had guided generations of Bostonians to the pinnacles of success were no longer serving them. Struggling hard to earn a living, he was forced to consider whether he should cede to the low standards of a decaying society or uphold the high scruples of his ancestors—and risk financial failure.

The Puritan answer met with certain consequence. Vonie had to stretch out their income carefully to make ends meet. No longer could she take for granted tickets to a lecture. Strawberries on the breakfast table became a luxury item. At church, she gave up the family pew to look for cheaper seats. And it became difficult to pay the one servant girl she kept in her employ. But George Ware remained honorable until the last day of his life. By their very example, both George and Vonie would teach their children that no matter what the temptation, they were bound to serve high principles. The Wares were regular churchgoers. Vonie attended Bible-study classes after the sermon every Sunday; George started a Bible-study class among his colleagues in Indianola. Guided by religious values and a firm fear of God, the Wares would produce children of rare, unwavering integrity.

Still, they were married five years before the Wares gave birth to their first child. No doubt economic considerations played an important part in the delay. When the couple had married in 1865, Vonie was twenty-two years old. The ideal Victorian marriage consisted of more than just two people. In the eyes of many, marriage was not truly complete without children. Women made their social contribution by producing children. The mother raised and nurtured future citizens, imparting to them a sense of moral and civic duty. As the basic building block of society, the family unit gave marriage itself a broad social purpose.

But if George and Vonie wanted children, five years was a long time for a couple to remain childless. And their long years of childlessness were almost certainly not due to sterility, for after their first child, William Bradford Ware, was born in 1870, three other children followed at regular intervals: Mary was born two years after Willie; Richard was born a year after Mary and died in infancy; and Clara Winifred Ware, the youngest sister, arrived two years after that. Furthermore, after Clara's birth, the pregnancies stopped as suddenly as they had started—making it all the more likely that the Wares' five initial years of childlessness were by choice—not simply chance.

How did the Wares manage to space their babies so precisely? It is not clear, for they left no record of their methods in their letters and their documents. History, however, does leave us some clues. Let us look at what the Wares had available to them.

As part of the educated New England middle class, the Wares would have had access to Robert Owen's *Moral Physiology; or, A Brief and Plain Treatise on the Population Question* (1831). A standard nineteenth-century tract about population control, it only touched briefly on birth-control methods, but it was the first legitimate publication to give much information at all about ways to control fertility—under the guise of pushing a broader social agenda.[56] Recommending *coitus interruptus,* or withdrawal, it was only in a footnote that the author mentioned other devices, arguing against the vaginal sponge as ineffective and the condom as too expensive.

Better yet for the Wares would have been a bootlegged copy of Massachusetts physician Charles Knowlton's *Fruits of Philosophy, or, The Private Companion of Young Married People* (1832). The cost of this volume—from fifty cents to a dollar—was kept high to prevent purchase by the "immature." But *Fruits* was the first popular birth-control tract written by a physician, and its author had set out to invent a cheap and reliable method that would not involve any sacrifice of pleasure. What Dr. Knowlton recommended was douching with a spermicide—a suggestion no competent doctor today would rely upon—but in the mid–nineteenth century, the idea was a boon. With conscientious use, the method could double the interval between pregnancies and reduce conception by over eighty percent. And since birth control was not a polite topic of discussion in Victorian society, douching could be rationalized as simple feminine hygiene—a system for cleanliness instead of contraception. Finally, by placing birth control in female hands, where Knowlton believed it belonged, douching empowered women.[57]

Technically, however, knowledge about contraception was illegal. Knowlton was prosecuted three times for sales of his publication under Massachusetts's common-law obscenity statute. Once he was even sentenced to three months' hard labor. But more often than not the courts were sympathetic to Dr. Knowlton. Despite the illegality of birth-control information, there was widespread acknowledgment of its necessity. The first time he was convicted, the judge asked to subscribe to the next edition of the book. Additionally, the prosecuting attorney returned his share of the costs to Knowlton. And after the publication of *Fruits*, Knowlton became a respected member of the Massachusetts Medical Society and a regular contributor to the *Boston Medical and Surgical Journal* (now, *The New England Journal of Medicine*).

Knowlton was not all-knowing, however—he believed that sperm was absorbed through the walls of the vagina. It took another contemporary physician, Frederick Hollick, to explain that "the Animalcules can pass into the Womb themselves, by their own motions..., one of them creeps in, and thus effects impregnation."[58] Giving lectures around the country, Dr. Hollick spoke about women's diseases, general anatomy, and the functions and diseases of female and male sexual organs. His talks were so popular that he eventually published his own series of illustrated advice books. By the 1870s, his *Marriage Guide or Natural History of Generation* had gone through dozens of editions, becoming, in the words of one advertisement, "*household books*, so that not a house, cabin, nor a miner's camp can be found without them for hundreds of miles."

Hollick's tracts also discussed birth control, noting methods such as withdrawal, douching, vaginal tampons, and condoms. But he himself advocated a natural or rhythm system of contraception based on periodic abstinence. Hollick's advice was scientifically sound, and was repeated by two other birth-control proponents: Francis Low Nichols in *Esoteric Psychology* (1857) and William Alcott in *The Physiology of Marriage* (1855).

These marriage manuals were among the dozens of self-help books that were a growing trend in the mid–nineteenth century. As family and gender roles shifted in the ninetetenth century, the Wares would not have been unusual in consulting such literature. Many middle-class couples were considering the expedience of smaller families. The country had abandoned yeoman farming, and large broods of children were now a burden. The birthrate reflected these broad economic changes. From the beginning of the nineteenth century until its end, the fertility rate of white middle-class women in the United States decreased by half, from an average of seven children per family to just over three. By 1865 various physicians had publicly endorsed withdrawal, spermicidal douches, pessaries, rubber condoms, and periodic abstinence.[59]

Despite the drastically lowered birthrate, however, which might seem to imply a growing use of birth control, contraceptive devices were still taboo. Rubber syringes for douching were readily sold in pharmacies, but their supposed function was feminine hygiene, not contraception. Pessaries, a precursor to the modern diaphragm, were not intended for contraceptive use, but to support a tilted or fallen womb—to *promote* pregnancy—and were available by doctor's prescription only. Even condoms of the era were marketed "for medicinal purposes only." That is, instead of being acknowledged as contraceptive devices, they were to be sold as protection for *men* against venereal diseases which could be acquired from prostitutes.

According to the values of the day, the purpose of woman was childbearing. It followed that women were to engage in sex for reproduction only. Love was a chaste feeling, with no bodily base. Sexual restraint was considered the basis of social purity, and Victorian thought imbued feelings of sexual pleasure and desire with guilt. Taught to refrain from all vice, women were supposed to be completely passionless. In particular, some Christians had developed an idea of religious morality idealizing woman as man's moral guardian. The Christian concepts of an immaculate conception and a virgin Christ reinforced the idea that an active sexuality was anathema to religious purity. And as women became a majority in the churches of America, Christian values and virtues and "female" values and virtues became almost identical.[60]

Before long, the idea of "virtue" in a woman had spiraled down to the single virtue of chastity. And as sexuality came to be the cornerstone for how a woman's morality was defined, chastity developed an unnatural importance far out of proportion to its actual place in life. There was no logical reason for chastity to take higher precedence over the virtues of honesty or courage or intelligence. But as discomfort with sexuality grew, the other virtues were pushed aside. Morality for women began to mean almost nothing else but chastity. Women were increasingly valued for their reproductive functions, and functions not overtly based on biological sex were understood to comprise the essence of femaleness. No differentiation was made between sex and gender. For example, although childbearing was quite clearly a sexual function, cooking and housecleaning were not—yet the latter came to be viewed as definite sex-specific duties.

In such a sexually polarized society, prostitution became the socially accepted way of sustaining marriages. Victorian thought created the fiction that women had no sexual needs, feelings, or desires, and in fact, were averse to the thought of sex altogether. Women were the saints, the spiritual angels who would uplift the male of the species to a higher plane. "What is striking is that in the middle class, where the idea of women's engaging in sex outside marriage was viewed with horror, men's visits to prostitutes were almost taken for granted."[61] Male patronage of prostitutes[62] was considered a necessary social evil protecting marital fidelity. Indeed, prostitution was so rampant during the Victorian era that it even drew backing from upright professionals. "Prostitution had supporters among the police and the medical professions. Since they dealt almost exclusively with crime and disease as sanitary problems, morality was of only tangential significance.... Like the German burghers who had introduced municipal regulations in the Middle Ages, *they expected prostitution to ensure marital purity*"[63] (emphasis added).

The great tragedy of the double sexual standard was the havoc it could wreak on the bodies—not to mention the emotions and spirits—of chaste wives. It was no secret that the sexually promiscuous husband who contracted a venereal disease often passed on his infection to his faithful wife. Both were often too embarrassed to discuss the issue, which was problematic, not only because it highlighted Victorian sexual hypocrisy, but because such diseases also tended to be much more damaging to the female body than the male. While the effects on the man were generally minimal, many venereal diseases destroyed a woman's reproductive organs, making it impossible for her to bear children. And the sterility that could result caused immeasurable emotional damage in an age in which motherhood was glorified as a woman's highest, most sacred responsibility. Thus venereal disease,[64] which was little understood in the nineteenth century, destroyed both the chaste and the promiscuous alike.

Men and women alike rightfully faulted the unfaithful man who visited a prostitute for the spread of venereal disease.[65] One tactic for dealing with the problem of venereal disease was state regulation of prostitution. Beginning with the Civil War, the army set up a system of medical inspection to regulate and license prostitutes for their soldiers. Dr. J. Marion Sims, a prominent gynecologist and president of the American Medical Association, also recommended that regulation become the norm in American cities. Accepting prostitution as a necessary evil, doctors and others in the medical professions encouraged regulated prostitution as a public-health measure. Yet though the matter of state-regulated prostitution was brought up in several state legislatures, the open acceptance of marketed sex did not win widespread support. Many Americans found "state-supported prostitution" offensive. The clergy tended to see prostitution as a matter of sin rather than disease. Female reformers looked upon prostitutes as victims of male lust.[66] Indeed, government-regulated prostitution would have provided unlimited opportunities for extra-marital sexual encounters.

The prevalence of prostitution gave rise to a group of reformers who devoted their attention to the problem of "social hygiene." Embarking on a purity crusade, the reformers sought to create a single sexual standard for both men and women, championing abstinence as the best form of birth control. Nineteenth-century purity reformers foreshadowed the women's movement a century later in deciding that private life and ideals had to be matters of public concern. Politicizing sexual inequality, some female reformers sought to form a new system of values which would hold men and women accountable to the *same* standards of purity. For women, this meant a rebellion against being sex objects but not against sexuality itself.[67] In the 1880s, Grace Hoadley Dodge pushed purity reform into the Working Girls' Society with a tract called *A Bundle of Letters to Busy Girls*. A major step forward in sex education, it was the beginning of the destruction of a "conspiracy of silence" which "mystified sexuality by ignoring it."[68] By introducing a tabooed subject into society, the purity reformers played a significant role in changing American attitudes about sex.

At about the same time, a small group of women also began fighting for abstinence as the best way to control births. As new opportunities opened up for women and the move away from farming made large families economically unsound, some women began to realize they did not have to participate in the reproductive process. Childbirth had always been a dangerous proposition for women; now some refused to accept passively a life of perpetual pregnancy. Realizing for the first time that they could say no to unwanted sex, these women began to press for "voluntary motherhood." Empowering some women—predominantly white and middle-class—to negotiate with men's sexual demands, the voluntary motherhood movement was consciousness-raising and revolutionary. For the first time, there was a rhetoric which gave women the right to control their own bodies.[69]

Abstinence may well have been George and Vonie's choice when they were planning their family. Abstinence was the method recommended by the popular Dr. Hollick and backed up by two other widely available advice manuals. Among certain groups of feminists, the "insistence on female chastity was not seen…as oppressive but, with very few exceptions, as both natural and necessary."[70] Indeed, contraception was still considered somewhat deviant. After all, abstinence then, as now, was the only 100 percent foolproof way to prevent conception. But if George and Vonie were part of the movement toward "voluntary *motherhood*," their version may have been more aptly named "voluntary *parenthood*." For the Wares practiced a high degree of consultation and cooperation, and their daughter would later stress that parenthood was a jointly made decision by both mother *and* father.

In any case, George and Vonie did eventually produce three children. But soon after Mary's birth, the nation's economy took a turn for the worse. Between 1873 and 1879, the nation's business activity declined by a third, and the number of bankruptcies doubled. George was spending much of his time away from home, as he had to work harder than ever to support the family. When she could, Vonie traveled with her husband, but this meant leaving the children behind in Massachusetts with relatives. Striking a compromise, the entire family lived together for three years in Texas. But the Wares were a New England family. Unhappy in the Southwest, Vonie finally decided to tend the family home alone in

Massachusetts—where Mary spent most of her childhood with her two siblings, Willie and Clara.

From a very early age, Mamie, as little Mary was sometimes called, showed signs of a precocious intellect. By age two or three, she was a chatterbox, peppering her mother with incessant questions. In sibling squabbles, the little toddler was not afraid of her older brother, boldly scolding him for striking her, often quoting the Bible. As early as age five, she wrote her first letter to her father in Texas—less than two months after she formed her first writing character. And even at that age, her penmanship and diction rivaled that of her brother, who was two years her senior. Indeed, as a five or six year old, Mamie seems to have skipped the first grade, finding the second grade very easy, and showing herself smart enough to beat an eight-year-old boy in a spelling bee. A bold little girl, she was not easily intimidated. Bright and outspoken as she was, distinctions based on sex would never make sense to her.[71]

As she grew older, the child grew to develop a deep sense of her place in society. Living the first decade of her life in Worcester, a town that had only been incorporated as a city a generation earlier, Mary was immersed in a close-knit community heavily influenced by Protestant ethics. The Puritan inhabitants of the commonwealth had traditionally shaped all values. But in the course of a generation, an influx of Irish immigrants had flooded in to provide cheap labor for the mills and factories—which employed about half the workforce—and a new faith in machinery had led the city to hold a series of highly celebrated "mechanics fairs." Later, unimpressed by the ethos of mass production, Mary would feel that industrialization only degraded and exploited human workers while turning out shoddy commodities. She preferred the model of the native-born Anglo-Americans. A member of the class that had traditionally dominated local culture, she felt compelled to uphold the standards of a bygone age.[72]

Any class consciousness which developed in her was only reinforced by visits to her relatives. Only an hour or so from the capital by rail, Mary often called upon her great-uncle Charles Carleton Coffin, a journalist and author. A great character in Mary's childhood memories, Uncle Charles lived in a large four-story brownstone on Dartmouth Street in Boston, where he held children spellbound at his extravagant Christmas parties. Splendid in charades, he introduced his grandniece to Louisa May Alcott. Uncle Charles took Mary to her first Gilbert and Sullivan opera, *H.M.S.*

Pinafore, which delighted her immensely. He was at the Chicago convention that nominated Abe Lincoln in 1860. When the Civil War broke out he was sent out in the service of the Boston *Journal*, and one newspaper would call him the "most important and popular" of all the Boston war correspondents. Thereafter he wrote boys' adventure stories, which became juvenile classics, even though he and his wife never had children of their own. At the end of his life, he became a member of the Massachusetts legislature. Mary admired him enormously.[73]

If Mary was charmed by the genteel life of Boston, it wasn't long before she had reason to move to the city herself. Around 1880, George Ware lost a large sum of money when a shipment of goods he had invested in sank with the ship. Following on the heels of economic woe, home life took a turn for the outright tragic in 1882, when George Ware died of cancer. Mary, who was only ten years old at the time, lost her "blessedly good-humored" father. Her father's death at such an early age reinforced in her a lifelong determination for independence—and a realization that a woman needed to learn self-sufficiency. Mary's mother Vonie found herself in the same position she had been in when her own mother, Elvira, had died. Like it or not, Vonie was now faced with the challenge of raising a family on her own. For a woman, of course, work was scarce. Vonie had to be resourceful. As a temporary measure, she started by taking in boarders, a respectable thing for a middle-class family seeking extra money to do. Then she moved the family to Boston, where they could live near their relatives.

Before long, the widow hit upon a feisty and entrepreneurial venture. Toughened by her husband's death, she supported herself and her children by starting a business bringing young ladies on summer trips to Europe. At $1,200 per student, plus $200 for an optional extra month, the European tours provided the fatherless family with a reasonable income. And they provided the mother with a sense of adventure. On one tour, Vonie narrowly escaped death herself when one of the girls came down with appendicitis, forcing her to postpone their return trip. As it turned out, the ship they missed was the ill-fated *Titanic*![74]

While Vonie was away, the children stayed with their aunts. More often than not, Mary would spend time with her aunt Lucia, a piano teacher, reformer, and scholar. Aunt Lucia reminded Mary that all people, even those born female, were created to lead a purposeful existence. A popular speaker at clubs and colleges on subjects like suffrage and world peace, Lucia impressed peers, like Jane Addams, who would later write: "There perhaps is no one in America who is more thoroughly informed on the various aspects of international arbitration, and at the same time so competent to present it to her fellow citizens than Mrs. Lucia Ames Mead. She...has the power of making even the bristling war statistics interesting and graphic. I have...seen her hold the closest attention of even an antipeace audience...." A prominent social reformer, Lucia was Mary's mentor. Lucia planted in Mary the seed of civic consciousness; Mary would turn to her aunt for advice and support throughout her life.

During one visit to her aunt Lucia, however, when Mary was about ten, she overheard a conversation that would forever undermine her sense of self. Listening behind a door and not disturbed at all by "the crime of being an eavesdropper," Mary would overhear Edwin D. Mead (the man Lucia would later marry) tell Lucia "Mary is certainly about the most uninteresting, unattractive child imaginable." From then on, she was acutely conscious that even if she were "good," she would *never* be interesting or attractive; she would yet be lacking the only things she really loved and which she couldn't achieve by sheer willpower—"beauty and the joy of life."[75]

Unaware of the searing effects of these words, however, the aunt was actually impressed with Mary's mind. Willie, Mary, and Clara enrolled in the Boston public-school system. As she had been from early childhood, Mary was distinguished by her intelligence. Bespectacled, with long, dark blonde hair, she looked like a young scholar, receiving straight I marks. Very opinionated, she refused to be reined in by Victorian demands for female submissivity. In one school paper, she lambasted the "American habit of hurry." In another, she argued for her pet passion—cremation—displaying her top-to-bottom concept of reform: ". . . but to have cremation become a general custom, it must be introduced by wealthy and influential people, and, like many another reform, when it becomes the fashion, people will wonder why they did not adopt it sooner."[76]

She fancied herself an insurgent, but she was a rebel in the old Puritan tradition. Strict and disciplined, she wanted to effect radical social change—but only through established and legitimate channels. Indeed, her self-image was belied by her rule-following tendencies. She wore white gloves, was polite to the family's servant girl, and attended the Central Congregational Church in Boston. When one classmate threw a large party for the teen-aged girls and boys of Boston, Mary felt obligated to decline the invitation because of

Vonie's strict curfew. The other girls thought "it was awfully cranky of me to do as I did." In contrast, Willie went anyway and had a fine time.[77]

In 1887, Mary transferred to Miss Capen's school for girls in Northampton, Massachusetts. It was her first taste of independence. Bonding with her roommate, Katherine Ware (no relation), and some other girls, Mary developed what she would consider her life's work: "a mixture of rebellion and beauty-hunger." Graduating from high school in 1891, Mary enrolled in the School of Art and Design at the Boston Museum of Fine Arts. The museum school was a significant step in Mary's development. In deciding to continue her education, Mary Coffin Ware was vindicating her mother's old desire to attend Oberlin while joining the ranks of women pioneers opting for ultimate self-sufficiency. And by choosing art school over a more traditional college, she was attempting, in her own words, to choose "art and beauty" in conscious rejection of her "deadly respectable forebears."[78]

CHAPTER TWO

The Arts and Crafts Movement

he School of Art and Design at the Boston Museum of Fine Arts was the center of a new movement challenging America's religious and social norms. Addressing the three issues burning in the hearts of nineteenth-century American intellectuals—nature, religion, and art—the turn-of-the-century Arts and Crafts movement embraced an organic kind of spirituality, one which placed the dignity of the human being over that of the thing. Beauty was an *essential*—achievable only in a society in which all people could work, take pleasure in labor, and share delight in its results. In this paradigm, beauty was as necessary to human survival as food, shelter, and a living wage. No mere drudgery, the work of a craftsperson was to create individual pieces of handiwork that elevated the human spirit.

The utopian ideals were a far cry from the soul-hardening Christianity of Mary's upbringing. Born out of a revulsion for the industrialization that had taken over the modern landscape, the Arts and Crafts movement had originated as a direct reaction to the ugliness of the industrial age. The new ethos blamed the machine age for the "destruction of fundamental human values reflected in poverty, overcrowded slums, grim factories, a dying countryside and the apotheosis of the cheap and shoddy."[79] Rejecting the lack of individuality in mass-produced, standardized goods, it hoped to reinstate the old-fashioned values of handcrafted items.

Transplanted from England in the 1890s, the Arts and Crafts movement was particularly influenced by the thinking of John Ruskin and William Morris, two of its originators in Great Britain. Ruskin and Morris had a wide following in the United States: publishers reprinted their books regularly; societies, settlements, and university extension programs offered reading groups around their work; newspapers, libraries, and societies put out reading lists to let Arts and Crafts enthusiasts know where they could turn for enlightenment.

Laying the moral foundation for the Arts and Crafts movement, Ruskin stated that the fundamental principle of art was the "expression of man's pleasure in labour." He criticized society for making people loathe work, pointing to this as the reason people looked to the attainment of riches as "the only means of pleasure." A true aesthetic culture would develop feelings and tendencies leading to virtue, good manners, and even a higher faith. All people would want to work, and preferably for some time with their hands. The capitalist who lived in idleness off the interest of his money was a despicable sort—all the more so because he most likely exploited the workers whom he turned into inhuman "machine minders." In the world of Arts and Crafts, the people would realize that the best place to live and work was in the countryside, where the beauty of nature would inspire the soul.

The best form of art was the kind of public or decorative art that was created by and for the people—and not the elite "fine art" that was limited to museums. And architecture, which reached the greatest number of people, was particularly lauded as the most sublime form of art—above painting, sculpture, and decoration. In particular, Ruskin felt that architecture should be different from mere building in that it ought to sum up the aspirations of a people or a nature. It had to be spontaneous—the product of designers and makers, each showing their talents. Such architecture would lead to a higher morality.[80]

Ruskin united art with religion, claiming, "Religious faith is an essential element of true art." Addressing the traditional discomfort that Puritan America had with artistic expression, Ruskin assuaged the fears of those who recognized the power of art but feared it would bring down man's noble nature. True art, he asserted, elevated the human spirit and turned it toward God. His message found a receptive audience. Not only did ecclesiastics agree that John Ruskin was their ally in teaching art's morality, but the public found in his writing a means of reconciling art with religion. Ruskin's influence on the Arts and Crafts movement suggested a way to reconcile a distrust of art—still a part of the American evangelical middle-class heritage—with a desire for beauty.[81] On the other hand, William Morris took a materialist's approach to art. Believing that art could not flourish under conditions of economic inequality, he believed the implementation of the Arts and Crafts ideal meant a complete overthrow of the capitalist system. Handmade items required painstaking attention that was not cost-effective;

goods sold on a competitive market basis had to be produced cheaply and efficiently. While Morris himself did not reject machines outright, he felt that "men should be masters of their machines, and not their slaves as they are now."[82] In 1885, convinced that capitalism would inevitably lead to the degradation of art, Morris founded the Socialist League.

As personal friends and lifelong associates, Ruskin and Morris were united in their battle against what they called middle-class philistines, whose struggle for wealth through industrial commerce was causing a decline in sensibility. As the Arts and Crafts movement reached its peak in the United States between 1890 and 1910, reformers created works with deliberate social messages. Using art as a medium to heal social ills, they devised their own prescription for living. Art became an approach, not a style. Appealing primarily to the white middle class, the Arts and Crafts philosophy advocated a return to the simple life. Such a life was characterized by making beautiful objects in a bucolic setting, where activities such as calisthenics, drama, and music formed an integral part of daily routine and where profit-sharing contributed to spirit of comradeship.[83]

Encouraging the transmution of ordinary and common items into the beautiful, William Morris advised, "Have nothing in your houses that you do not know to be useful, or believe to be beautiful."[84] Arts and Crafts advocates hoped to reform the imitative fashions of the Victorian revivalist period: overstuffed furniture, over-ornamented surfaces, ill-suited textiles, and pretentious styles from Louis XIV to rococo.[85] Firmly rejecting aristocratic European precedents, which were believed to be unresponsive to human needs, American reformers felt they should look to their own heritage for inspiration. The message was that the art of any epoch had to be the expression of its social life. Decoration had to inspired by nature—not imitations of bygone historical epochs.[86]

Out of this concern for the home emerged an ideal crafts bungalow—one which invited rest, comfort, and family togetherness. Yet again, the individuals who lived within were the centerpiece—not the structure itself. Part of the Arts and Crafts philosphy was that art could only flourish when it came directly from the people—adapted to their way of life and reflective of their spirit. The reverence for the individual was central to the general Arts and Crafts love of handicraft. Proponents yearned for the "old American spirit...of independence, self-confidence and of ambition to rise in life by force of ability, intelligence and honesty."[87]

For young Mary Ware, the social and aesthetic goals of the Arts and Crafts movement were food for the soul. At the museum school, she immersed herself in its writings and gleaned from its theories the makings of her own philosophy. Her companions were all fellow enthusiasts looking for a new way of ordering life: Her sister Clara had been drawn into the movement by Mary's enthusiasm; Boston-area students Ralph Adams Cram and William Hartley Dennett were pulling together troops from the architectural ranks. Fashioning an alternative ethos out of Christianity, Gothicism, monarchism, anti-capitalism, craftsmanship, and a hatred of modern democracy, the circle of young artists and designers revolted against the evils of commercial America. Severe critics of hyper-individualism, their philosophy encouraged teamwork, collaboration, and close comradery. In an era when the fear of God was dying and human beings would accept no limits on the potency of their own minds, the ideas which emerged from the Arts and Crafts movement were quick to gain popular credence.

As in her previous arenas, Mary excelled at the museum school, earning first honors. After graduation, she studied with Arthur Wesley Dow, a painter and one of the most influential American teachers of the Arts and Crafts movement. One-time curator of Japanese art at the Boston Museum of Fine Arts, Dow was a great champion of Japanese design principles. He argued for abstraction in both decorative and fine arts, asserting that the basic elements of design were line, color, and *notan*—a Japanese term for the arrangement of dark and light. Incorporating the Arts and Crafts concepts of joy in labor, dignity of work, and utility in design at all levels of instruction, he applied his principles to painting and prints as well as metalwork, pottery, textiles, and woodcarving. Dow worked with music, exhorting his students to allow sound to enrapture them to produce nobler works of art, and he supported an aesthetic which drew its inspiration from nature. Students and teachers from all over the country came to study with Dow, leaving only to spread his design philosophy at their own institutions.[88]

After completing her studies, Mary was able to find a teaching position in Philadelphia at the newly-opened Drexel Institute of Art—quite a coup for a young single woman in 1894. Only twenty-two, she had been asked to keep quiet about her age—for she was younger than many of her students. The president of the Drexel institute, Dr. James MacAlister, had conducted an extended search for a teacher of design and decorative art. He intended to establish at the Institute the most thorough and comprehensive program for decorative art in the country. Mary was appointed head of the newly-created Department of design and decoration. Her duty would be to design a completely new course of study.

Mary left Boston to start the decoration class in late October 1894. The Philadelphia *Ledger* hailed her arrival, calling her "a distinguished graduate of the Boston Museum of Fine Art's School of Decorative Art" and "eminently suited to her new position." Mary's classroom would be one of the largest, most well-equipped spaces at the Institute. Textiles and other industrial arts products would be available for her use, as well as a collection of casts for the teaching of historic ornament.[89]

Her salary was to be $1,200 a year, allowing her to reach financial independence. Living in a strange city, Mary must have felt a strange exhilaration. Her sister Clara had decided to join her in the mission, and the two sisters shared an apartment. Life became an adventure. For Thanksgiving, the two invited a couple of other girls over for a turkey dinner cooked on a one-burner stove. On weekends, they spirited off with friends on jaunts into New York City. Devoted to art in all its forms, they both tried their hand in the local acting troupe. Clara entered and won poster contests, which Mary judged. And there always seemed to be another costume party which allowed the sisters to express their creativity.

Moving to Philadelphia to teach the principles of the Arts and Crafts movement, Mary was forging new ground. In unfamiliar territory, she envisioned the creation of a new world based on high ideals. What she desired was beauty, a spiritual beauty which would be manifested in the material realm.

Like her teacher, Dow, Mary championed abstraction, because it contained "the beauty of idea."[90] As she pointed out in the very first lecture of her course, "it is only ideas that live, not things."[91] As far as she was concerned, "Beauty, and art, which is the expression of beauty, should be a part of every one's life." Mary made clear her view that decoration was no mere exalted or artistic "industry," but a fine "art" applied to houses, books, utensils, and other common items. Well-decorated surroundings could confer peace to the soul and uplift the spirit. In her classes, she showed slides of beautiful courtyards, doors, gates, halls, staircases, and all such things. "The love of beauty and the longing for it is one of the eternal qualities of the human race,"[92] she declared. "Broadly speaking, art is an agreeable way of doing things that appeal to the senses, its aim being pleasure."93

Mary pointed out that from the beginning of time, every people had desired a kind of beauty which they could not find in nature. From the Assyrians to the Zuni Indians, Mary was extremely well versed in the cultures and histories of the world. Even the first human beings had decorated water jugs and war implements, Mary explained, proving that humans had always possessed an instinct to make their utensils beautiful—more than simply useful—to give them a sense of restfulness and permanence.

To attain the qualities of restfulness and permanence, she said, two things were necessary: simplicity and order. By simplicity she did not mean that a design could not be complicated, but that it had to have a unity of purpose. Decoration always had to have a point, that is, "interest and attention must be given mainly to one motive and then the secondary motives only enhance the beauty and value of the chief one."94 And something was not simple if it could not be expressed in few terms and easily understood. She explained success, "Your first feeling when you look at a work of art should be a glow of pleasure, at its beauty and perfection, not a wonder at the amount of work in it."95 Frustrated by people who were intrigued by complication instead of simplicity, she was often condescending. "A great comfort, under those circumstances, is that such people don't count, and perhaps you can do a little missionary work and help them to know better."96

A true Bostonian, she possessed an odd combination of snobbery and civic consciousness. For example, she called the Zuni Indians a "savage tribe," likening its people to children who had "only reached about the same stage of development as some of the pre-historic races" because they saw things in straight lines whereas "civilized minds" saw curves.97 Obviously brought up in an unquestioned Europhilic tradition, she could not laud the Greeks enough. "Looking at Greece, as compared with the Oriental nations, and immediately you feel a different atmosphere, an entire change of temperament, and national feeling. Their keen intellect, their fine physical development, their invigorating climate, all these affected their art."98 Lavish in her praise, she called Greek architecture and sculpture "surely our most valuable inheritance, and that means more than we shall appreciate for a long time to come."99 Clearly ethnocentric, she stated flatly, "Their works were perfection."100

Mary voiced strong opinions, for she wanted to educate the public and bring it out of a morass of ugliness and bad taste. Without an appreciation of fine art that was more broadly based, she recognized that her craft could not survive. She dreamed of a great art that was "not so much art for art's sake as art for everybody's sake."[101] She harkened back to a golden past when the environment bathed all people in beautiful art. "The finest buildings were the public buildings. The best could be enjoyed by everyone, and of course that meant cultivation of their taste. Their surroundings influenced their feeling exactly in the same natural, unconscious way that a child brought up by educated people will say "is not" instead of "ain't."

Pointing to an age when people made things for their own needs and uses—not to send halfway around the globe—she mourned the modern-day loss of individuality and special feeling. Art must come from and reflect the people, she said. Unbridled in her pride for her own colonial Anglo-American heritage, she seemed not to notice the immigrant roots of the New World. Mary explained to her students that "since we are neither French, Moorish, or Dutch, but American, nothing will ultimately suit us, but American surroundings.[102] Emphasizing her point to the point of provincialism, she stated, "just as no American can best express himself in French or any other acquired language, neither can he express himself by any borrowed art."[103]

In keeping with the spirit of the Arts and Crafts movement, machinery was her bane. In her eyes, machinery had invaded the world so that art no longer represented the people. "I would not have you think I undervalue the wonders of machinery, but machinery should be a servant to man, not make man its slave and attendant."[104] For while she worked for equality, she also feared mediocrity. "When some reformer appears who tells about the millennium that is coming, when all men will have equal opportunity and advantage, people get very antagonistic and rebellious, and say, 'We don't want a dead level of uniformity.' But that same dead level is exactly what we are drifting toward."[105]

Indeed, the millennial feeling was high during the late 1800s. Helping her students realize they were living in a new day, she emphasized that the world's outlook was drastically different from any which had ever existed before. In the art world, this meant the remarkably rapid progress of science and machinery was bringing about a separation between art and the masses. Art was becoming "a luxury only to be enjoyed by the rich."[106] The trouble was this: "We *have'nt* [*sic*] any life as whole. We are too individual and selfish, and are all split up into classes, the poor struggling to acquire wealth, and the rich struggling to acquire more, and what becomes of art in the rush?"[107]

She quoted Walter Crane in saying that true art was the "spontaneous expression of the lives and aspirations of a free people."[108] Said Mary, "All great art of the world has been the art of the people, and the trouble with our time is, that what art we have is confined to a very small class of people."[109] The only solution was to educate the masses to love art and demand beauty.

Incorporating these values into her lectures, Mary designed her class to alternate between lecture and hands-on design. A lover of classical music, she probably played music in the studio as well—following the guidance of her teacher Arthur Dow, who emphasized the relationship between music and the visual arts. She took her students to the Metropolitan Museum of Art in New York to let them drink in beauty for themselves. Her emphasis was always on the joy of discovery. She adamantly refused to line up her students in front of paintings, boring them with half-minute lectures.[110]

Beauty was the criterion against which Mary judged the labor of the world. Yet since beauty was a direct result of a "free person's pleasure in creation," it was impossible for a wage laborer, who controlled neither the nature of his work nor its reward, to create beauty. Nothing less than the reform of society would develop art. For "Arts and Crafts represented idealism with a material face, with the goal to rebeautify daily life and labor." Indeed, handicraft revival was supposed to be a democratic movement in which every man, woman, or child could be creative.[111] Mary assumed the tone of a moral crusader in her writing and her talks. Embracing the Arts and Crafts philosophy, Mary made the pursuit of art and beauty the basis of all her thought and action for the rest of her life.

CHAPTER THREE

Falling in Love

efore leaving Massachusetts, Mary had become good friends with fellow Arts and Crafts devotee William Hartley Dennett. Hartley, as he was called, was an earnest fellow with wavy auburn hair and a neatly trimmed mustache. A budding architect from a solid New England family, Hartley was a Mayflower baby.[112] His ancestral roots took him back to Saco, Maine, where his mother still lived in a sprawling Colonial mansion in the center of town. Considered quite fashionable and debonair, he was a founder and member of the Chi Phi fraternity at the Massachusetts Institute of Technology. After graduating from MIT in 1892, Hartley had enrolled at Harvard specifically to study with Harvard's renowned art professor and promoter of the craftsman ideal, Charles Eliot Norton. The extra senior year gave him a second degree and allowed him to matriculate with Harvard's class of 1893. Charming and fun loving, he had been one of Mary's free-thinking friends in Boston's Arts and Crafts community.

Adhering to the same high ideals, both Mary and Hartley disdained the robber barons of the Gilded Age who had made popular the look of wealth and ostentation. Both favored simple, handmade crafts modeled after nature and harbored a conscious dislike for display. When she first arrived in Philadelphia, Mary had written letters to Hartley in a quite formal and pseudo-professional tone. "My dear Mr. Dennett," she wrote from Philadelphia in 1894, "perhaps you can tell me where I can get Mr. Wackers decoration lectures..."[113] Masking any deeper intent, she also inquired about the whereabouts of a certain set of slides, asked his opinion on various architectural subjects, and shared with him bits and pieces of her classroom lectures. Never quite able to express her feelings—even later on, when their relationship grew more intimate—she would lament, "Shall I ever learn to say what is in my heart?"[114]

For his part, Hartley poked fun at Mary's formality. He would send the young teacher what she requested, but his impish nature couldn't help but tease. And Mary was an easy target, too, since she took everything so seriously. In exasperation, she would write, "Why don't *you* do something foolish so I can retaliate?"[115] But there were times when Hartley would relent and share his dreams of the future with her. Both yearned for the same Arts and Crafts ideal of the "simple life."

Together, they dreamed about life as farmers in the country, away from the ugliness of city sidewalks. In letters back and forth, they laid out a pastoral scene, with a big square house, great elms, a bridge, a creek, wide meadows, a beautiful clump of trees, a breeze, bees, ducks, geese, a fawn, and "two nice bow-wows."[116]

Living at a boarding house on 76 Pinckney Street in a bookish atmosphere, Hartley was trying his hand at writing—poetry mostly. In many of his letters, he began to include little bits of poetry, sometimes about life in general, and occasionally poems addressed to Mary.

> *Go, little book,*
> *Seek her out and say*
> *That long I have—Tell her how deeply—Nay*
>
> *Keep it yet secret: do thou simply be*
> *Aye near her, so be it she suffer thee;*
> *Turn, an thou can'st, some gentle thought*
> *Hither—my way—when she guardeth not;*
>
> *Prepare her to learn, dear, by and by,*
> *What we alone know now—*
> *Thou and I.*

Hartley was a true romantic, dedicated to love and sentiment. While he tried to find architectural work, he began to play with the idea of a literary career. With Mary's encouragement, he sent out his poems to *Harper's, The Atlantic, New England Magazine,* and a host of other publications. As the rejection notices for his literary efforts piled up, he continued with grace anyhow, practicing his rhymes with the diligence of a true dilettante.

In return for the charming poems, Mary began to send Hartley sample book covers she was drawing. Beautiful in design, they reflected her effort to hold up her half of the artful conversation. Sometimes her work would be an example of what she was teaching in class; other times it would demonstrate her thoughts on what was needed in the real world of bookbinding. Both supported and encouraged the work of the other, and neither side elevated his or her own position. It was a conscious acknowledgment of the equality of the sexes. In fact, by the end of October 1895, a full year after she had left Boston, Mary had dropped the formal tone of her correspondence. Instead, she was writing to "My dear Hartley" about a future day when she would be expecting great assistance from W.H. Dennett for a firm run by Mary and Clara, whose sign would read "M.C. Ware, C.W. Ware, Decorative Designers."

The shift to communication on a first-name basis went along with an acknowledged desire to actually spend time together. The pair began to arrange free weekends to see each other. They traveled to various museums to make sketches of artwork; they took a ten-mile photography trip together; they did color studies of Persian tiles, mummy cases, tapestry, Chinese vases. Hartley began to invite Mary to dinner regularly—despite the 500-mile distance between them—causing her to exclaim, "Don't invite me to dinner any more! I am fearfully homesick already!"[117]

The two began to speak of more serious subjects. Like many forward-thinking people in the last decades of the eighteenth century, they were rethinking the relevancy of the Christianity they had grown up with. Dissatisfied with traditional church hierarchy, even their elders were challenging established church doctrine. Mary's Aunt Lucia had already been denied membership in Shawmut Church, one of the oldest institutions in Boston, even though their renowned relative, Charles Carleton Coffin, had been inseparably associated with Shawmut. Lucia just couldn't accept certain literal "truths" like a personal devil and a spatial interpretation of heaven and hell. Joining the more liberal congregation at the Park Street Church, Lucia soon went a step further, switching to the even less orthodox Mount Vernon Church. Eventually, she gave even that up to attend Edward Everett Hale's Unitarian services. Aunt Clara, less intellectual than Lucia, had been accepted at Shawmut Church, but even she was asking questions and reading a dissertation on Episcopalianism.[118]

Confused about religion, Mary joked about her pagan lack of direction. "The trouble must be with me," she lamented, "I am not a Unitarian—that is one sure thing. I can't bear to *sit* through a whole service, or read doctrinal platitude responsively, or sing hymns to the tune of "Auld Lang Syne," and it doesn't feel like church when all the women come in, and have a regular sociable before service."[119] God was not the problem, it was the trappings of church. "Church is such a good place to think in," she pondered, "and the service is an excellent screen."

Hartley responded to Mary's questioning by encouraging her to explore alternative modes of thought. Excited by socialism, for example, he explained to her its "fundamental principle: 'From each according to his capacity—*to* each according to his needs.'"[120] Peculiarly *American* in its emphasis on the self, Hartley's brand of socialism seemed to emphasize the individual over the needs of society as a whole. Fashionably progressive, Hartley possessed other ideas as well. He believed in Henry George's single tax theory, which proposed to eliminate all taxes except the land tax. He also introduced Mary to homeopathy, explaining to her Hahnemann's principles of "like curing like."

As Hartley and Mary continued their correspondence, they began to inch cautiously toward a more serious relationship. Letters between them were flowing daily—sometimes even twice a day. Hartley began sending Mary bouquets of violets, explaining to her that violets "are the kind the cows like—and cows are the most poetical of animals."[121] On Valentine's Day, the two young people exchanged valentines—albeit apologetically, as if they didn't really mean to do so at all. Hartley sent a valentine poem that was full of whimsy and longing. And then another poem, entitled, "Hope," in which he supplicated his "Lady" in medieval troubadour style. As time went on, the growing romance between Mary and Hartley made their physical separation oppressive. In 1896, Hartley found interim employment at the Boston Museum of Fine Arts; Mary decided to spend the summer in Boston working alongside him. Together almost constantly, save for short stretches of time when Hartley was in his native Saco or when Mary was vacationing by the shore, the pair grew much more intimate. When they were alone, more often than not, they were at a loss of words.

Mostly they were very quiet, sometimes kissing, but each would comment later on how common it would be for them to simply sit together in silence. By the latter portion of July, Mary and Hartley had truly solidified their relationship. Not telling anyone, the couple secretly decided to get engaged.

The reason for the secrecy is not clear. Perhaps it was a love of romance; perhaps it was a desire to create a private and privileged world of their own; perhaps it was a simple question of economics. On Mary's part, the secrecy probably had to do with her Puritan desire for discretion—after all, Hartley would not be able to marry until he was more financially secure. On Hartley's part it was probably a love for romance—he seemed to thrive on the clandestine rituals they created. Whatever the reason, the two kept their decision private. The very secrecy of their engagement was to make their love for each other all the stronger. Mary would herself comment, "Nobody could have made me believe two years ago, or even one year ago, that I should be longing for my boy every minute of the time, when I had only left him twenty-four hours before."[122] Behaving as if they were defying all the world, the two gloried in the fantasy world created by their surreptitiousness.

Their little secret did not stay secret for long, however. The news seemed to leak out. By the end of August, the congratulations letters were flooding in. Mary's mother was overjoyed, for Hartley had taken care to spend much time with his future mother-in-law. Hartley's mother, Annie O. Dennett, was more restrained, writing in her congratulations letter to Mary, "let me say that she who loves Hartley will be very dear to me. What more can I say, except that I give up my baby to your keeping, hoping you will be as good to him as I know he will be to you."[123]

Hartley was considered to be quite a catch. Several people who had known him from boyhood remarked particularly on the excellence of his character. From The Rectory in Dover, Marcy Beard wrote, "[Hartley's] nature is so truly poetical or artistic and so thoroughly refined that he has almost a woman's insight into another's feelings and that is a rare foundation to build on in married love."[124] From the Grace Mission House in New York City, Theodora Beard reported, "I never have known a man or woman either with a more simple, unselfish, and truly and fundamentally *good* nature than has been given to Hartley Dennett."[125] And another old friend of Hartley's, Charles Horne, who had just become engaged himself, told Mary, "I honestly don't know a man who is so sure to be a true and noble husband as Hartley Dennett."[126]

Mary's aunts, however, voiced caution. Aunt Lucia, in particular, had a very curious reaction to Mary's "secret" announcement. Of course she offered the necessary congratulations: "The best thing that can come to any girl next to God's love is this dear, sweet human love which has come to you, and I rejoice with you with all my heart." Informed by Mary's mother that Hartley was a very "noble, true man" who had "shown courage and patience and a high purpose under very trying circumstances," Lucia welcomed

Hartley into the family, calling him "one of 'our kind' with the same
tradition and ideas and experiences." Protective of her niece, however, Aunt Lucia wanted to make sure Mary would be well respected
and appreciated. Congratulating Hartley, Aunt Lucia sent him a letter from Paris, saying, "I think you are worthy of her, and that is
saying a good deal." Continuing, she immediately added, "I don't
know of anyone who could be better adapted by temperament and
tastes to satisfy her nature and make her happy."

For despite her well wishing, Aunt Lucia intimated suspicions
about marriage. She wanted to make sure her niece would never
engage in matrimony for its own sake. She reminded Mary, "A life of
single blessedness...is infinitely better than any marriage that is only
a half marriage and leaves the heart unsatisfied...." Although she
herself had finally married Edwin D. Mead, a lifelong friend and
colleague, Lucia warned Mary about the sacrifices of the nuptial
vow: "I think of Clara with some commiseration. The little studio
you two were to have together can not be, and it must be very hard
for her to think of losing you." Particularly fearful for Mary's professional life, she claimed that even Mary's mother wanted to make
sure Mary wasn't making "a terrible mistake." Lucia just wanted to
make sure: "If you really know your own mind (and if you don't
now it will be the first time I ever knew you not to) then I am glad
you threw your theories and plans to the winds and set about making better ones."

Lucia was loathe to see her talented and strong-willed niece
swept into confinement. Apparently, Mary had once had misgivings
of her own about the institution of marriage. Lucia reminded
Mary of her former doubts: "I felt afraid at one time that you were
going to be a little cynical and suspicious of men, for indeed there
are not many who are all that a woman wants them to be, but
I think now you will have to recant your former verdict that 'all
men are conceited.'"[127]

But Aunt Lucia's hesitation was of little consequence. The
thoughts of the outside world had little impact on this couple in
love. With Hartley, Mary discovered for the first time that there was
a man she could understand. Throughout her life, most of her role
models had been women. The male influence in her family had been
minimal. Her brother Willie—never as intellectually inclined as the
rest of the family—had left Boston to live in the Midwest and
become a mechanic and a chauffeur, disappearing from the annals
of the Ware family's life.[128] Her Great-uncle Charles Coffin had

taken on such gargantuan proportions that he became more myth than reality. And her father, of course, whom she had adored, had passed away when Mary was ten years old.

Glorying in their alikeness, Hartley expended much energy in confirming for Mary their absolute compatibility. "But *isn't* it fine that we have so very much in common—that we have the same ideas on the aims of life and object of effort, that our tastes are so nearly identical, and our ambitions so unsmirched with 'society' and 'wealth.'"[129] The idea he aspired to was the Arts and Crafts–inspired dream of the simple life. Concerned particularly with the middle-class home, the key elements of this "simple life" were a bucolic setting, a family-centered environment, and a system of self-improvement achieved through beautiful surroundings. The work required to finance the home would come directly from the heart—anything less would be immoral. Hartley dreamed about their future together. "Home-life first—cheerful & devout labor—leisure rightly directed—it seems as if we ought to sing our way through any hardships that come up—arm-in-arm."[130]

Unable to contain overwhelming feelings of heady adoration, Hartley seemed to be totally beyond self-control. Encouraging Mary to share with him every feeling, and not to hide even the "smallest sadness," he would eagerly declare, "I love you just the same with all my heart—and I know full well that that isn't half as much as you deserve." He couldn't seem to say it enough. Expressing his feelings again and again, he signed his letters "Hart"—with a picture of a heart next to it. Then in his next letter, he would write with enthusiasm, "this time I *must* tell you that I love you, by way of relieving my self—, you know." And his lover's heart would fret, "Will you *always* love me, Mary?" A young woman could not help but be swept off her feet, Hartley was so insistent. "I do love you dear—and I hope you will always love me back. I grow a little happier right along. I think I shall be a mighty happy boy by the time I am ninety—I certainly shall if I can then have a happy little Mary-wife in my arms."[131]

Hartley was in love with the idea of love. Writing every single day, he chastised himself for defying the then-current lover's norm of three letters a week. Hartley charmed Mary—who was definitely the more practical of the pair. "The fairy tales are truer, when the wand (love) can turn the cottage into a glittering palace with a single stroke. The wand being the only necessary thing in fairy-land— and that is of course why our shortsighted worms don't believe in fairy-land. Let us, my dear, never lose faith in the magic wand."[132] Hopelessly idealistic and starry-eyed, he carried her letters around with him and stared at her picture until his eyes were strained. Certainly the more demonstrative of the two, he cherished her photos, but emphasized, "I like you best right in my own arms where you are safe."

She, too, lived off of pictures of him. But Mary, kept in check by her Puritan upbringing, began to wonder about the headiness of it all. "What right have we to be so happy—when other people can't be too—and people that deserve it twenty times more than I do! Happiness doesn't seem to be distributed like medals—does it?"[133] Trying to keep the correspondence level-headed, she wrote Hartley about politics and current events. She loved Hartley, but she warned him against excess. "Love me more and more if you can, dear. But don't forget that I am just plain Mary Ware and not an ideal girl at all, and whose whole heart is yours."[134] Over and over she reminded him, "I love you all the time my dearest, and I know you love me, but don't you idealize Mary, so you will come down with a thud at Christmas."[135]

The period between the end of summer vacation and the beginning of Christmas holidays seemed to wax endless. Unable to see each other in person until the Yuletide, they flirted with the idea of an unscheduled visit, counting the weeks, then the days, before they would be together again. They longed for physical contact. Defying Victorian mores, they expressed their desire. "*Pet* you? Lord I can—and does Mary doubt it herself…? Pet & get petted is my motto now—, I don't believe it does any harm when it is two sided, do *you*?" Hartley insisted, "You see your old Hart needs a lot of petting (you wouldn't feel that he might need to be disciplined, like Miss Webster, would you dear?) and he needs his Mary girl to pet, which is as necessary as being petted."[136] Forthright about his needs, he thanked her for sending kisses, saying, "I need them— and I am pining for some real ones from you."[137]

To keep their bodies busy, each turned to sport and exercise. Mary was not particularly physical—she was much more cerebral in her inclination—but she dutifully bicycled and exercised at the gymnasium to please Hartley. No doubt part of her hesitation came from her nearsightedness. She wore spectacles to see clearly—eyewear which she would later trade in for pince-nez—and when she worked out at the gym, she had to be careful to keep her glasses on her face. "I can't play basket ball on account of my glasses—can't see without them—and can't keep them on. I tried it this afternoon—and bang they went on the floor—but didn't break—this time."[138]

Undeterred by Mary's excuses, Hartley was insistent. Unlike Mary, who felt that one's body could be ill while one's spirit remained healthy, Hartley was part of a new trend that preached the all-consuming importance of physical health. He wrote to Mary that physical health was "the first essential to happiness," saying, "You ought not to be 'tired anyway'—It may not be overwork, but it is certainly under-exercise, that makes you tired—If the muscles arenot [*sic*] properly agitated the nerves don't get nourished, & then we get tired & fretful & disagreeable."[139]

But Mary's interests were elsewhere. In keeping with the millennial fervor, Mary was still looking for the right religion. She "shopped" various churches—sampling their theologies—but she never seemed to be satisfied with what she found.

> *We went to church today. We thought we would sample a Presbyterian one this time since the "woods are full of 'em" here. It was dreadful—I never shall go there again. A silly weak lot of primary class platitudes for a sermon—and a dry almost irreverent kind of service—the kind where the congregation sit down to sing hymns. There was a little baby baptized—and I really didn't know there was that kind of a service in these days—the minister said "this child is born sinful—just as you are sinful"—and then explained that the blood of Christ would wash the sins away. I wanted to stand up for that little white soul and tell him it was nothing of the kind. Do you know I really don't understand baptism yet. I hate to expose such ignorance—but I have never seen a service that seemed intelligible to me—from any reasonable standpoint. I can imagine such a one—but have never seen any. What does it mean to you? I feel sure that there is a beautiful idea in it—but do most people find it—and just what is it anyway?*[140]

Exasperated by a religion overtaken by human-made rituals, she decided to turn back to original Scripture. "I think I will read some Bible now. I haven't for some time." Finding church boring, especially the long-winded sermons, Mary's mind wandered to a little country church she longed to remodel in Alstead, New Hampshire.[141]

Meanwhile, Hartley had taken an active interest in the free-spirited quality of Unitarianism. With its noble belief in the essential unity of all peoples—despite its predominantly white, upper-middle-class make-up—Unitarianism was right in line with the spirit of the age. Embracing all the various progressive thoughts of the day, it seemed the perfect way to keep an open mind while remaining comfortably Christian. As well as fulfilling the basic human need for spiritual connection with the universe, the tenets of Unitarianism would not conflict with an individual's personal plans or involve submission to a higher will. Appealing mostly to intellectuals, the doctrine accepted the social principles of a new era while staying under the familiar name of Jesus Christ. The sort of thinking that attracted Bostonian tastes, Unitarianism was really taking hold in New England. While Mary was still searching, Hartley was hoping to gain admittance into the Unitarian Church and was awaiting the committee vote. Excited by its tenets, he encouraged Mary to accompany him to Everett Hale's sermon on the very first Sunday upon her return to Boston.

When she returned to Boston for Christmas holidays, Mary did attend Everett Hale's sermon with Hartley. Indeed, the two spent their entire Christmas together. Mary encouraged Hartley to bring his mother down from Saco to Boston, so that Annie O. Dennett would not feel excluded from her son's Christmas plans. After all, it was still Annie O. Dennett who controlled Hartley's purse strings. Unable to find a commission in his chosen profession, Hartley was having an exceedingly difficult time finding work. Alas, all the architectural jobs seemed to disappear almost as soon as he heard about them. His inability to make a living was starting to make him feel "blue," as he began struggling with the type of depression that seems to work its way into young people whose promise still lies entirely in the realm of potential. The heavy burdens weighing in his consciousness were most likely not helped by the knowledge that Mary was comfortable in her success, at the age of 4, as head of the Department of Design and Decoration at the Drexel Institute.

In an effort to address the problem, Hartley had decided to make a grand tour of Europe which would begin in February. A budding architect, he wanted to study the styles and details of the buildings and structures of the Old World. Making plans to tour Europe with his mother, Hartley considered the trip time conceded to her. Most likely, he had little choice about his maternal travel companion. Yet if he was to spend several months in Europe, he wanted his sweetheart to be with him too. Urging her to follow suit, he convinced Mary to make similar plans with her sister Clara. Mary was a fellow artist, and he was sure such a tour would help them both professionally. He tried to inspire her with images of the great architecture, the great artwork, the great culture of the Old World.

His argument must have been persuasive—or perhaps Mary could not bear the thought of continued separation from her beloved—for she decided to leave her post at the Drexel Institute to accompany Hartley to Europe. When she went back to Philadelphia after Christmas, news of her impending departure had already spread. Mary was appalled. Her Bostonian nature sought discretion. Mary was concerned about "the gossip of the students"; all she wanted was "to quiet down for the rest of the year."[142] But at least she had the future to look forward to. She consoled herself with the thought, "if I work hard [it] will soon be over. Then we will live happily ever afterwards."[143]

By her second day in Philadelphia after the holidays, Mary was already buying clothes for Europe. After spending Christmas together, she was finding the distance between her and Hartley harder than ever before. She wanted to see her "bonny lad." Only the thought that the separation would end could keep her cheerful. Longing for her beloved, she begged for some photographs, some tangible memento to keep her going for the next several months. The isolation seemed unbearable, as her attitude toward the European trip changed drastically. "For the first time I have the European fever *hard*. I can't wait to go now. And before I have actually dreaded it."[144]

At the beginning of February 1897, Hartley left for Italy—the first of the two five-month long tours which he was to take with his mother. Mary sent him off at the harbor. The minute his ship actually set sail from New York, she found hidden anxieties welling up inside her. Even though she knew Hartley was leaving for the good of his career, a fear of abandonment crept in.

Mary began to worry he was only leaving her to assuage the demands of his mother. Doubts seeped into her mind about the advantage of such a long, wandering trip covering so much ground. "Won't it be like a dinner with too many courses?" she asked. Not wanting to seem jealous or clingy, however, she tried to ignore her feelings. It was her childhood fears of seeming plain and unlovable that came back to haunt her. Of course Hartley would come back, and of course she would join him shortly. The Arts and Crafts ideal was one of freedom, after all. Who was she to put a damper on the freedom of her beloved? Like many other women before her facing forced, unwanted separation, she tried to pretend it didn't matter.

"Of course an outsider would say—'Pooh—Mary is only arguing because she wants him to come home and play with her, without padding around'—but you know me, dear, and so you know I want you to do what is the very best thing all round—for the present and future and that if you decided to be gone *three* years—and visit Hong Kong and Kamskathka [?] I should say Amen and be happy—"[145]

She needn't have worried. On 10 February 1897, eleven or twelve hundred miles out in the sea on the SS *Fulda*, Hartley was already pining for his beloved. He was seasick, constantly lying flat on his back in his berth. His appetite was gone. The deck was a place he hardly frequented, and only with great effort, along the way. The only activity for which he had energy was the correspondence of his beloved. "I *have* read your letters every day.... Even now reading & writing makes me feel a little queer." Mary was the first person he attempted to write—although it did take him a while to get around to it. But he reassured her, "I love you, my heart. If I haven't written, I have thought of you constantly—and, Mary, the *seasickness did not interfere.*"

With the help of the postal service, they read poetry together: Elizabeth Barrett Browning, William Shakespeare, Christina Rosetti. They were trying to find different ways to express their love. Hartley insisted, "I love you, Mary, as never before. And I ever more & more realize how much I must struggle to be good enough & to nearly satisfy you. If only you are here, to be with me in my work & play. I *must* do something. Then afterwards *we* must do something worthy of our love. Now Goodnight and sweet dreams and a kiss from your boy." As soon as he arrived in Naples, Hartley wrote to his beloved, "I love you, my Mary—and I shall bust if I don't get a letter pretty soon."[146]

Describing sights, smells, and colors, Hartley tried to share his discoveries with Mary. He was drawn into the foreignness of Italy, different from anything he had ever known before. He visited the aquarium, the opera house, the ballet, the market, the monasteries, the museum—brushing up on his Italian all the while. He improvised a dialect of his own, "part French, part Italian, part Latin, and a very extensive propping of gestures."[147] Unaccustomed to the habits of the Old World, he found the hotels he stayed in dirty and inadequate—"a high-sounding name for a high-smelling dive."[148]

And in this papal land, religion was to be found everywhere. "There are churches here thicker than flies—one can stand almost anywhere and turn about and see anywhere from three to ten. Of course most of them are little ones, just like those in the scenery of the Italian opera, and a good many of them have no roofs, or even have holes cut through them and a charcoal shop or a small lodging built in."[149]

Describing the festivals in Italy, he remarked on the theatrical quality of the worship. "The only difference I know of between a Feste and any other day is that on the Festival the Museum is always closed. And the church services are more magnificent. Yesterday we went to church at the Palace Chapel—the whole thing was perfect—the faultless chapel, the gold and silver robes—full clergy—incense—beautiful organ—and all; the people strolling in and out, crossing themselves and all the other things. It is too bad that it all seems so much like a play."[150]

With all of his sight-seeing, Hartley had to discipline himself to work—ostensibly, the reason for his visit. He traced mosaic patterns from an 1142 Norman church by rubbing black wax over tracing paper and then taking notes on the color combinations.[151] He described the catacombs with 8,000 or so embalmed remains of Italian nobility, affirming Mary's support of cremation: "Wouldn't it be great if cremation could come in, and bring with it again the pottery art and the making of those nice little terra cotta and marble or even bronze memorial tablets! And architecture, too—crematories with chapels, and great public storage palaces for the ashes. Ah—then we might all have a job."[152] By gathering ideas for the necessary details that would go into his future architectural designs, he was studying the art and architecture of the old world and rounding off his technical education.

Separated from her loved one, however, Mary began to worry yet again about the practicality of a long-distance relationship. She feared, fretted, and dreaded that Hartley might be falling in love with a fantasy rather than with a real live person. It was the skeptical voice inside of her saying, "Impossible, it *can't* be true, I wouldn't if I were he, it's *love* he loves,—not me."[153] Hartley kept trying to reassure her, "I don't see how I can help idealizing you, but there is no danger of my getting ahead of you yourself."[154] Nevertheless, he was very apologetic about his letters: "I wish I *could* write nice long letters—but I've been so used always to just *thinking*, that I don't know how to chatter. And then I fear I have no faculty for talking to develop. But we *must* talk—everybody *does*." But when it came down to it, he did feel that "women were meant to talk more than men."[155]

The difficulty of a romance by mail would eventually lead to a closer relationship. By the end of May 1897, as the school year ended at Drexel, Mary was preparing to leave Philadelphia permanently. The decision had been made easier by her frustration with her post. Her original plan to spread the high standards of the Arts and Crafts movement was going nowhere. Philadelphians seemed to be hopelessly bogged down in the machine-made products that she detested. Driven to take one of her classes to visit a factory, she complained, "It always makes me doleful ... to see machinery perfected to such an extent, all for the purpose of grinding out wicked trash, for people to buy. They know it themselves, the manufacturers that it is bad stuff—for they say good work does not pay, and they can't afford to educate the public against its will."[156]

If that wasn't bad enough, she had been frustrated with the students in her classes, calling some of them "too hopelessly dense." Her experience only led her to believe the best thing to do was to inform Dr. MacAlister that if he wanted a class in decoration, the students had to have "at least the *average* amount of intelligence." Privately, she had noticed that there was a great falling off in the art department, and she had come to the conclusion that an art school could never flourish in Philadelphia.

By 7 June 1897, she was on the train writing frantically to her beloved, thrilled at the thought that she need never go back to Philadelphia. "Well—it's all over—my three years away from home. I love Boston as I never did before. Let's never go away from it for long at a time. We have had our last deviled Crab at the Broad Street Station—now we are going home again home again."[157] By mid-June she was sailing for Spain and Italy, prepared to spend three months reunited with her beloved and studying the art of the Old World.

As she made plans to meet Hartley in Florence, he informed her that he had just turned down the offer of a fellow architect to set up shop with him. Instead, asked Hartley, would *Mary* become his business partner? With his architectural skills, and her decorating talent, the two of them could work *and* play together.[158] She would decorate the interiors of the homes that he built. It was the fulfillment of the Arts and Crafts ideal.

Once she arrived in Europe, Mary and Hartley were heady with excitement. They traveled and spent almost all of their time together, much to the dismay of Annie O. Dennett, who felt ignored. Hartley's mother had already become slightly resentful of Hartley's relationship with Mary. After the holidays, she had never failed to notice and comment that his letters to Mary were much longer than the short notes he wrote to her. She offered many statements of her misery, flatly stating, "you are simply killing me."[159] Her jealousy bothered him. But instead of changing his behavior, Hartley only became all the more adamant about his right to freedom. Putting the blame on her, Hartley told his mother, "the meagerness of my letters is a condition you have forced upon me." He insisted upon maintaining his free will and autonomy: "Love means glad sacrifice, it does not mean asking the other fellow to constantly prove his love by sacrifice."[160] He even enlisted Mary to write on his behalf, "Hartley & I are bound to be happy... & it would add immeasurably to our happiness to feel that you were with us & *for* us..."[161]

Yet Mary soon discovered something else which caught her attention. The sights of the Old World were filling her with excitement. At the Palazzo Vendramini in Venice, Mary came upon an antique type of gilded Cordovan leather wall-hanging, called a *guadamaçile*, which captured her fascination. Intrigued by its artistry, she researched its origins further. Guadamaçiles, which had been introduced into Spain by the Moors in the eleventh century, had been very fashionable in Europe in the fourteenth and fifteenth centuries. Among the aristocracy, the *guadamaçile* had been in high demand. But with the general decline of art throughout Europe, it had degenerated until it finally disappeared in the eighteenth century. Mary was disappointed to find that the craft had dwindled to the point where there were no longer any craftsmen engaging in its production. Eager to learn more about the beautiful art, Mary carried around pocket-sized sketchbooks with her which she filled with drawings of the *guadamaçile*. She also used her money to acquire several samples of the leather. Hoping to learn how to reproduce the beautiful gilt leather, Mary engaged in extensive research until she finally discovered two books about the ancient craft which existed in Old French. When she returned to Boston, she investigated the libraries of Harvard and MIT and wrote to the Boston Public Library, trying to find some institution which might be able to track down the books. Finally, after much diligence, she was able to obtain copies of the books and translate them to unravel some of the technique. She had die stamp tools made and did some experiments to work out the original process. She began creating her own *guadamaçiles*, teaching her sister Clara along the way. Before long, Mary had almost single-handedly revived a lost art form.

Meanwhile, she and Hartley had plunged right back in the midst of the burgeoning Arts and Crafts community in Boston. In the spring, a small group of architects, educators, craftspeople, and collectors organized the first crafts exhibit to be held in the United States. The work of more than a hundred exhibitors was featured. The success of this first exhibition seemed to justify a permanent organization. Before long, Mary and Hartley found themselves active in organizing the Society of Arts and Crafts, the first of its kind in the country. Modeled after the Arts and Crafts societies of England, the purpose of the Boston Society was "to develop and encourage higher standards in the handicrafts." Hartley's professor at Harvard, Charles Eliot Norton, praised as "dean of fine arts in America," was elected first president.

In the membership roster, Mary was listed as an embroiderer and leather worker, Hartley was down as an architect. Soon Clara joined as a leather worker, and a few years later, Hartley's brother, Vaughan J. Dennett, enlisted as a cabinetmaker and furniture designer. As Mary devoted herself to her leather work, her technical proficiency began to win her a loyal following. In 1899, she and Clara held their own showing at a gallery on Clarendon Street in Boston; they exhibited at an Arts and Crafts exhibition in Chicago; and their work was prominently featured at the Boston Arts and Crafts Exhibition. Mary began to receive letters from fans drawn in by the beauty of her work. And as Hartley waited for his own client list to build up at his Joy Street office in Boston, he helped the two sisters run their business—just as they had planned. As the sisters were becoming successful, Hartley's architectural practice also started to pick up. Feeling financially secure enough to afford a family four years after their initial engagement, Mary and Hartley were going to be married, finally fulfilling the sentiment expressed in this poem, written by Hartley to Mary:

Who made my heart go pitty-pat?
Who made your heart go squeaky-squee?
San Valentino di Lovidov
Let us not doubt that it was he.
Who moved my lips to speak my heart?
Who moved your lips to whisper Yes?

Amid the crowd of panicky thoughts,
  Sweetheart, he was there too I guess.

Now who is the nicest girl on earth?
  And the happiest boy (and wus and wus)?
Who owe the most to San Valentin?
  Why, my wisdom & comfort, that is US![162]

CHAPTER FOUR

Building a Family

O n 20 January 1900, Mary Coffin Ware and William Hartley Dennett were married in a very simple ceremony at King's Chapel in Boston. Taking their wedding vows as set forth in the Anglican prayer book, they pledged themselves to love and honor each other—but decided to omit the word "obey." For freedom, not obedience, was the Arts and Crafts way. Mary believed that marriage was in essence a spiritual union, not a legal contract. Marriage vows were a private matter between two people; formal recognition by the state had little to do with its reality. For what difference was a piece of paper when it came to love? By the time they were married, Mary was twenty-seven years old and Hartley was twenty-nine. As thinking adults, both felt mature enough to embark on a new life together with their eyes wide open.

As was customary at the turn of the century, Mary and Hartley went on a "wedding journey" after the ceremony. They stopped at the homes of friends along the way, among them Mary's roommate from the Capen School, Katharine Ware, who herself had since married George Smith. The honeymoon was brief. Returning to Boston in February, Mary and Hartley found a small apartment at 14 Ashburton Place, where they were at home to receive visitors on Thursdays.

The two seemed to be of one mind. Hartley would later recall, "Our esthetic tastes, our religious beliefs, our social theories, our interpretations of society's discourses, our political opinions, were wonderfully alike. We read with unanimous approval the thoughts and experiences of the greatest poets and philosophers of freedom, of the revolutionists of the past—including Jesus the greatest of all—and of the radical economics of our day. We loved together to review the phenomenon discovered all through history—of the lowly birth and despised associations of every new phase of truth; of the everpresent Pharisee with his investments all in the dying order; of the necessary sacrifices for truth, and its certain victory." As they liked to quote, "One with God is a majority."[163]

In June 1900, only a few months after they were married, Mary and Hartley decided to buy a farm in Framingham, Massachussetts. Buying the place with money left to Hartley by his "Cousin Ann," an old relative he had been fond of, the young couple were giddy about their purchase. Cousin Ann had disapproved of Hartley marrying until he was financially secure enough to do so without worry. So once they were married, Hartley and Mary felt justified in spending her money on something they felt was permanent and for the future. It was an Arts and Crafts dream come true. The new Dennetts declared themselves "farm-mad."[164]

In 1900, Framingham was a lovely village. Their land was about seven minutes away from Framingham Center by trolley car, and the car stop was about five minutes from the house by foot. There were twenty-eight acres on a hillside, about two-thirds of which was wooded with beautiful oaks, chestnuts, and birches. In addition, there were fruit trees galore: twenty apple trees, seventy-five peach trees, a dozen pear trees, three or four cherry trees, plum trees, some grape vines—and some good hay and pasture lands full of blueberries, raspberries, violets, and columbine. The house itself was "nicely out of sight and hearing" and "*very* countryfied, it might well be in Maine or New Hampshire." There were three good wells for water. Overlooking a beautiful pond that was a part of the Metropolitan Water System, the house afforded a fantastic view of the distant hills. Little ledges and dales went up and down the property. There was a "*mean* little house, a fine barn and a quaint little shop—and a *magnificent* hen-yard—the most secluded and inoffensive one I ever saw."[165]

With a little cleaning and knocking down of partitions, the young couple saw the little house as a good camping place for a few years until they could afford to build a more substantial year-round house to suit them. The previous owner had been a "shiftless individual, who dropped old clothes and tin cans and broken china anywhere he happened to be—and he was anything but tidy in the house."[166] But they hoped to clean it well enough to use by the following summer. Every weekend during the first summer, they went to clean up the place with the help of some neighboring farmer boys.

With very little money, the Dennetts managed to make their farm scheme work. Most of Cousin Ann's money went toward the down payment—with a hundred dollars set aside for repairs and such— and the previous owner had prepaid taxes for a year. Friends of theirs agreed to buy their hay crop—the sale of the hay alone

would almost pay for the interest on their mortgage. And a neighboring farmer offered the young Dennetts fifty dollars to use their
land the first year—throwing into the deal all the fruit they could
carry back with them for the winter as well as a separate little
kitchen garden of their own. They planned to build their home in
Framingham together, with the title in Mary's name, as was traditional in New England families. With excitement, Mary exclaimed,
"So you see we have not had a penny of expense about the place
for this year—and if we spend anything it will be toward some old
duds to furnish the house just enough to camp with—beds, chairs
dishes etc. Isn't that pretty fine for poor folks!"[167]

Meanwhile, defying the convention that kept ladies penned into
their homes, Mary was building a reputation lecturing and writing
about Arts and Crafts. Described as "a visionary whose concern lay
with the future of the Arts and Crafts movement, rather than with
the present,"[168] Mary called for a general restructuring of society.
Influenced by Leo Tolstoy and Russian anarchist Prince Peter
Kropotkin, she advocated combining crafts work with agriculture—
calling to mind the American Colonial lifestyle, when people cultivated land during the summer and created masterpieces of
craftsmanship during the winter. Such variety, she believed, was the
secret to creativity. Her idea was that each craftsman should be
given an annual salary of $5,000 and "enough leisure to work
with spontaneity and joy." And she was convinced that useful and
beautiful objects could be produced only if the lives of craftsmen
were enhanced by those "blessings" which their patrons enjoyed:
"education, refinement and leisure."[169]

According to Mary, connoisseurs and humanitarians—the former
was concerned with the object; the latter with the maker of the
object—would have to be united, along with the large majority of
the noncommittal masses, to produce any noticeable change in the
handicrafts. Mary's own sympathies lay firmly with the humanitarians: She believed ethics far outweighed aesthetics in importance. In
an article she wrote, entitled "Aesthetics and Ethics," Mary
addressed this split between the aesthetes and the humanitarians.
Too many Arts and Crafts societies, she felt, placed too much
emphasis on the aesthetic and not enough emphasis on the ethic.
She wrote, "the Arts and Crafts Problem is at bottom, not an educational, so much as an economic, moral and religious problem."[170]

In Mary's time, economics, morals, and religion were all burning
issues. For Boston intellectuals, the place to explore such questions

was Greenacre, a summer institute in Eliot, Maine, founded by one of Mary's distant cousins, Sarah Jane Farmer.[171] Given its name by John Greenleaf Whittier, Greenacre was the turn-of-the-century equivalent of Bronson Alcott's mid-nineteenth century Concord School of Philosophy and Literature. Its purpose was to foster the independent investigation of truth, and the first principal of Greenacre was that no system of thought would be excluded. Edwin Doak Mead, Aunt Lucia's husband, Mary's uncle, and Director of the World Peace Foundation, was a frequent lecturer; "Ah Loo" (as Hartley called Lucia) gave talks there as well; Mary's teacher Arthur Dow was another regular speaker; Charlotte Perkins Stetson, the rising feminist, spoke about women's issues; and even Mary herself gave lectures at Greenacre about Arts and Crafts.

Greenacre was a prestigious place to speak. In 1893, Sarah Farmer had attended the Congress of World Religions in Chicago. While she was there, she had developed the idea of creating the Monsalvat School of Comparative Religions at Greenacre. Before long, Mary and Hartley were exposed to talks at Greenacre not just on Christianity, but also on Hinduism, Buddhism, Judaism, Zorastrianism, Islam, and a new religious movement, the Bahá'í Faith, listed in the program as the "Revelations of the Báb and Behá'u'lláh[sic]."[172] From the Greenacre program, Hartley cut out for his collection of quotations the following Words of Bahá'u'lláh translated from Arabic:

> *O Son of Spirit, I created thee rich: how is it that thou art poor? And made thee mighty: how is it that thou art powerless? And from the essence of Knowledge I manifested thee: how is it that thou seekest some one beside Me? And from the clay of Love I kneaded thee: how is it that thou occupiest thyself with some one else? Turn thy sight to thyself that thou mayst find Me standing in thee, Powerful, Mighty and Supreme.*[173]

The new religion, emerging from Persia (now Iran), was not a sect of any other religion but an independent world religion which made the earth-shattering claim to be "the fulfillment of all previous religions." Every Wednesday at 10:30 AM, curious seekers could gather under the pine trees to hear a Persian scholar talk about the Promised One of all ages, Bahá'u'lláh. Before long, Sarah Farmer herself had become a dedicated Bahá'í, and Greenacre was transformed into the first Bahá'í school in the United States.[174]

Although the social principles of the Bahá'í faith would bear an uncanny resemblance to Mary's own belief structure for the rest of her life, she and Hartley had more immediate concerns. By mid-August 1900, Mary discovered she was pregnant. Until this time, she had continued making her *guadamaçiles*. Realizing the pregnancy would mean a "quietus on leather and lectures and such things," Mary decided her primary concern would be to "think harder and plan faster to get the leather work into somebody else's hands, if possible, and to keep it alive."[175] For having rediscovered the craft, Mary and her sister Clara believed themselves to be the only artisans in existence who knew how to make *guadamaçiles*. And on 27 June 1900, Clara had married George Hill in a simple ceremony, like Mary, at King's Chapel. The sisters could only expect that Clara, like Mary, would soon have to stop as well.

Mary wanted to continue with her love of creating *guadamaçiles*, but she gave birth to her first child just as her leather work came to the stage where she was able to hold her first big public exhibition. Carleton Dennett was born in the middle of the afternoon on Sunday, 23 December 1900. The infant was delivered by a Dr. Wesselhoeft— "after a very long serious time." It was a very difficult birth—nearly fatal. Worried about his wife, Hartley consulted doctors soon after the baby was born. As early as January 1901, Mary was already so ill that she couldn't even breast-feed, and little Carleton was given "artificial feeding."[176] Yet the two new parents were delighted with their newborn. Hartley dashed off a note to his mother the very night Carleton was born to let her know of the good news. A little while later, Mary wrote to her mother-in-law—with Hartley interrupting his wife's letters as she wrote to make his mother think the handwriting change was due to Mary's having a fit: "It's good to be at home," wrote Mary. "What is home without a mother?" "(& a grandmother)," scribbled Hartley. "& a small boy!" added Mary.

From the very beginning, Carleton was a mischievous baby— grabbing at hair, kicking and sticking his heels up in the air. But his mother described him as "quite a beauty," saying, "He looks like a regular advertisement baby—If we love him much harder, I'm afraid something will explode." His eyes were a clear sky blue and his cheeks a healthy pink. When his hair grew, it proved to be very fair and light, and hung down on both sides of his chin. If he cried when put to bed, Mary explained it was "just because he hates to stop playing—but it doesn't last long, and then he doesn't get any more attention till morning except a drink of water about 3 o'clock."[177]

Mary loved company—especially after Carleton was born. Despite her illness, she declared, "I have never taken so much pleasure in my friends before."[178] She called Carleton a "remarkable show-off baby" because he never seemed to cry *at* anyone nor was he ever afraid. And when anyone paid attention to him he usually burst into a "beamy smile."[179] Declared his mother, "I couldn't imagine a better natured baby."[180] Indeed, both mother and father were fascinated by their first child. When Carleton rocked himself back and forth, flapping his arms and legs as fast as he could, Hartley tried the same kind of exercise himself, just to see how it felt. Mary laughed that Hartley "was all played out in about two minutes."[181]

The Dennetts found Carleton a nurse named Lüna, and the domestic help allowed Mary to continue with her interest in the Society of Arts and Crafts. Initially, the Society's new president, Arthur Astor Carey, was of one mind with Mary when it came to the social ideals of Ruskin and Morris. Disregarding her own position of privilege, which afforded her a country house and a nanny, Mary sat on the governing board of the society and called "*all* special privilege" the "craftsman's enemy." What she had in mind was the category of special privilege that included monopolies and trusts, corrupt legislatures, and a "weighty" military establishment. For this reason, Mary believed, a craftsman and his friends had to fight for industrial democracy—that is, economic parity—as the first step toward transforming the look of daily life. Mary was earnest. If a factory could imitate art, it would be nearly impossible for the crafts worker to make an adequate living. Indeed, counseled Mary, the greatest possible service the Boston Society of Arts and Crafts could perform was, first of all, to work for the industrial independence of the craftsman—and to do this with unerring persistency—even though it might mean temporarily discarding all thought of aesthetic excellence![182]

In response to Mary's cry, in 1901 the Society of Arts and Crafts developed the Handicraft Shop. Based on communal ideals of the Arts and Crafts movement, the Handicraft Shop allowed independent craftsmen to labor in a cooperative setting, avoiding the debilitating isolation they might experience in a typical factory. Located in Wellesley Hills, the natural surroundings were supposed to bring to the crafts workers wholesome benefits denied to them by city living.[183] Given an escape from specialized mass-production processes found in factories, crafts workers had opportunities to collaborate with others in creating objects from start to finish.[184] With a nonprofit salesroom on Beacon Hill,[185] the shop only carried objects that had been judged worthy of sale by a jury. Originally producing work in wood, leather, and metal, the shop would eventually concentrate exclusively on handwrought silver, copper, and brass and enamelware.[186] Arthur Carey provided financial support for the venture. Mary was director—as well as leading spokesperson for the craftsworkers. One of Mary's former Drexel students, Mary Catherine Knight, worked as supervisor. And Miss Knight used Mary's leather working equipment to produce tooled ornamentation on silver.[187]

From 1902 to 1904, the society also began to publish an influential monthly called *Handicraft* which printed essays, book reviews, exhibition announcements, lists of craft services, and quotations from works of Ruskin, Morris, Ashbee, and Emerson—a combination of theory, practical information, and exhortation characteristic of all turn-of-the-century craft magazines.[188] Several of Mary's articles appeared in *Handicraft*. She also wrote an article about the *guadamaçile* for *The Craftsman*. And she continued to give her lectures "The Relation of Art to Our Homes" and "The Relation of Art to Manufacture" at a variety of places including the Boston School of Housekeeping, the Brooklyn Institute, and Greenacre.

The young family was devoted to living life according to their highest ideals. They were playful, always helped out their neighbors, gave generously to friends in need, had similar tastes, were interested in the same things, and had a deep affection for one another and for their children. Their married life was an ideal one. Hartley was becoming increasingly successful in his chosen profession, and Mary lovingly assisted him in his work. As they had planned, the couple had already extended their personal relationship into a professional one. While Hartley designed and built homes in the Boston area, Mary worked alongside him as a home decorator. They consulted with each other on all decisions—but as each had such an intuitive understanding of the other, their harmony of spirit rarely required them to settle major disagreements.

Besides the Society of Arts and Crafts, the Dennetts were also quite active in the progressive politics of the greater Boston community. They were active in several reform—but no charitable—organizations. They belonged to the Free Trade League, the Anti-Imperialist League, the American Peace Society, and Hartley was secretary of the Massachusetts Single Tax League. Mary was also interested in the suffrage movement. Socializing at various meetings, dinners, and lectures in the area, the Dennetts became noted for their openness and generosity of spirit.

Mary and Hartley attracted like-minded people in the greater Boston area, and their closest friends were all very active in various social movements. Frank W. Patch had been president of the Massachusetts and National Homoeopathic Society and was now a professor at the Boston University School of Medicine. Anne Withington was the head of women residents at South End House, head of school gardens, secretary of the School Voters League, and a prominent social worker on the executive boards of various organizations. Their relatives, too, were prominent in working for progressive causes. Aunt Lucia's husband, Edwin D. Mead, whom both Dennetts called Uncle Ned, was formerly editor of *New England Magazine* and was now director of the World Peace Foundation. After marriage, Aunt Lucia had dropped all her other activities to devote herself full-time to the peace movement. Both Uncle Ned and Ah Loo, as the Dennetts called her, had known Mary for her entire life, because Ned had been good friends with Lucia and her siblings for over twenty-five years before they were married. Now Uncle Ned and Ah Loo visited the Dennett home very frequently. Illustrious Bostonians both, the Meads' social circle included Phillips Brooks, Andrew Carnegie, Booker T. Washington, and Woodrow Wilson, among others.

In addition to her public work, Mary was kept occupied at home on the farm. She sewed new clothes for the baby, Hartley, and herself. She also weeded the garden, cooked the food, painted the walls of their house, and attended to all other domestic matters. As a woman vested in her family, her husband's business, and the Arts and Crafts movement, Mary was busy. But she was well-appreciated. Hartley was constantly writing adoring bits of poetry to his wife, and in 1902 he wrote a Valentine's poem entitled, "To Mary the Mother of Carleton."

> *Red-Heddiwiggi's Valentine*
> *Was Roly-poly Molly Wogg*
> *Before the Earth was Land and Sea,*
> *But only soft and squeezy Bog.*
>
> *Now there's a Little Sonni-Wogg,*
> *A weenty-teenty Heddiwigg;*
> *And all are each others' Valentines—*
> *Little, Sweet Middle, and Might-Big!*[189]

The following summer, Mary and Hartley continued working on their farm project. They hoped to keep some cows in the old barn—although they felt they would have to wait until they were ready to be year-round farmers. Until the young Dennetts felt their income was more secure, they did not even dare purchase a "hoss" with which to drive a carriage. Laying out their plans, they learned all they could about farming, getting the buildings improved, "and having a bully time."[190] The farm turned out to be a "splendid strengthener for Mary" and a "necessary playground for Carleton."[191] Hartley was exuberant about the peace and fresh air and exercise it gave his new family. As he tried to build up his architectural practice, Ah Loo asked him for professional advice on a four-story town house which she and her husband Ned were considering buying.[192] Later in the year, Mary's cousin Sarah Farmer asked Hartley to submit a design for new buildings at Greenacre.[193]

Before long, Annie O. Dennett decided to give the couple money to renovate the Framingham house so they could live in it year-round. Hartley and Mary were ecstatic. Aspiring to the "simple life," they were passionate about the prospect. They decided to build an entirely new structure on the Framingham property. It would be their dream house, their pet house, their life and their project. Both were very happy about the quiet and cleanliness and health that life in the countryside would mean. Already, their summer experiments were very cozy—much more satisfying than either had ever dreamed. The move from their tiny winter apartment in the city to a permanent residence in the countryside was a daring plan, but they believed it was "a good thing for both Mammon & his worshipper."[194] After all, although it would be far from the commercial life of Boston, their property was still quite close to the Boston and Worcester car lines. And Boston was only a forty-minute train ride away.

In May 1903, the couple found out that Mary was pregnant again. Although the discovery took them by surprise, they were excited, expecting a daughter for themselves and a sister for Carleton. Touching up the existing house while erecting the new house, Hartley and his builder-friend Harry Adams put in hard labor to slap nine dollars' worth of white paint on the old house. Redoubling their efforts for a growing family, by the end of July 1903, they had the new house ready for plaster. Mary had a beautiful flower garden which was transplanted to the front of the new house. Two Italian masons cleared the stone from the front yard and built it into a wall along the road. A pretty scheme of shrubs and grass filled the garden space. And the view from the bedrooms and Hartley's office in the new house was magnificent—it overlooked the ponds and the hills all around their property. Annie O. Dennett lent the couple about $2,000—and Hartley was eager to accept more. As he put it, "it is hard to stop when yr pet house gets going—and it will be quite a gem of a house."[195]

Meanwhile, Hartley's architectural practice was growing. Mostly designing residences, Hartley had a "functionalist" bent toward architecture. That is, he created designs only after the most thorough and sympathetic study of the needs of his clients: their manner of living, their habits, their possessions. Hartley's kitchens were innovative in design, precursors to modern kitchens: small, "with a system of built-in cupboards, ice box, sink, etc. carefully planned to make easy and efficient all the household tasks."[196] He used delicate moldings, small window panes, outdoor sleeping piazzas; he also tried to persuade clients to have their servants' rooms nicely finished with the same pretty details. Hartley worked hard with his clients to determine how their needs and tastes were going to develop, for he wanted to make sure a house would suit its inhabitants ten years later as well as when it was built.[197]

But trouble was brewing in the Society for Arts and Crafts. In November 1903, Arthur Carey resigned as president because of ideological disagreements with the Society. Both Carey and Mary had led a faction that felt that the status and financial well-being of the Society was being emphasized at the expense of some of its original ideals. Mary was adamant. She insisted that the "great work to be done [is] the study of the conditions that underlie the production of artistic things." According to her, the "work of the Society is educational and social first, aesthetic and commercial second."

To add to the general turmoil, on 11 December 1903, Mary gave birth to a little baby boy. His parents named him Appleton. Again, the delivery was hideously difficult. And this time, the baby had a hard time as well. Not only did Mary become very ill, but little Appleton died of starvation at three weeks of age. Years later, Carleton would love to say of his baby brother, "when he found out his name, he decided to go back to where he came from."

The personal tragedy was accompanied by Mary's growing dissatisfaction with the Society of Arts and Crafts. By 1905, the society was being run more like a business than a reform organization. Led by a new president, an architect and Harvard University professor, the membership chose to separate improved standards of craftsmanship from social reform. The life of the craftsworker would now be of no concern—a craftsperson would be judged solely on the merits of the product. Embroiled in the dispute, Mary ignored the rules of consultation. Perhaps her views were right, but her rigid inability to compromise—or to fully support the majority even if it was wrong—was a trait that could only lead to discord, division, and ultimate defeat for all. As the society split between its commitment to the ideals of craftsmanship and the improvement of working conditions, many reformers would consider the conflict to exemplify the failure of the Arts and Crafts movement in both Britain and America. Concluding that "good Art cannot come out of fundamentally bad conditions," Mary resigned.[198]

Mary's departure from the Society of Arts and Crafts coincided with her redoubled attention to her family. By this time, she and Hartley had built a large white cement house with a red tile roof and a pretty garden enclosed by a wall. There were ten rooms besides the kitchen and bath, all heated by hot water. Hartley kept two offices, one at home in an upstairs tower and another in town. The property had a stable made of cement, and the Dennetts were finally able to fill it with a horse and carriage. Nearby, there was a six-room cottage, and in 1904, the Dennetts took in tenants, Mr. and Mrs. Addison B. Le Boutillier.[199]

Hartley and Mary were working very hard to build a perfect house and family. At its peak, the Dennett home was described as "one of the most beautiful homes I have ever known, perhaps the most beautiful, the relations not only of Mr. Dennett and Mrs. Dennett, but their relations towards their friends and towards the community. It was, I think, to everyone who knew them a singularly blessed spot."[200] Mary and Hartley Dennett distributed a quote from Phillips Brooks to their friends as a Christmas message in 1904:

> *We see the greater glory of the new miracle—the miracle of the advancing civilization, where purpose is not to do away with struggle but to make the conditions of struggle fair and the prospects of struggle hopeful. Into the spirit of that miracle we cast ourselves, not expecting to see the world's misery suddenly removed, but sure that at last the world, in and through its misery, will triumph over its misery by patience and diffused intelligence and mutual respect and brotherly kindness and the Grace of God.[201]*

Life seemed ideal. In February 1905, Mary was pregnant again. Hartley wrote her a special poem.

Lady-love, Lady-love
Say you are mine:
Lady-love, Lady-love,
My Valentine!

Once you did say it:
Who would now dare
Think 't was not Heaven
Made us a pair?

The Warmth of your Spirit
Is as Sunshine to mine,
Lady-love, Lady-love,
My Valentine![202]

On 12 May 1905, the Dennetts' third child, Devon, a baby boy, was born. Again, the mother emerged in gruesome shape. But this time she did not heal. After Devon's birth, the doctors said the Dennetts should have no more children. Not one doctor, however, offered the slightest information about birth control. For the Comstock laws had resulted in the complete banning of contraceptive information. By the turn of the century, many states had restricted the sale or advertising of contraceptive devices. The threat of imprisonment had encouraged many writers to eliminate sections on contraception in marital advice books. Furthermore, due to Comstock's ceaseless crusade, large sectors of the medical profession were against artificial methods of limiting fertility. Birth-control information had been driven virtually underground.[203]

Indeed, Mary would later mourn the Victorian silence. "I was utterly ignorant of the control of conception, as was my husband also. We had never had anything like normal relations, having approximated almost complete abstinence in the endeavor to space our babies." The last two babies were "both wanted, but both accidental."[204] Now, the medical men were adamant; another pregnancy would kill her. Threatened with the specter of death, Hartley and Mary stopped making love.

After Devon's birth, Mary was continuously ill for two years. For the first time in her life, she had to give up her professional work entirely. Despite careful precautions to avoid lovemaking, her body was completely broken. She simply could not fully recover from Devon's birth. It was agonizing. The nature of her symptoms was not discussed. It was considered "impolite" in those days. But Mary had to go away for frequent rest cures, which left Hartley feeling terribly lonesome. While she was gone, Hartley used to send his wife sweet notes to let her know how much he missed her.

*Marimine—This is just a billy doo to tell you how I lovvy yoo. When I
stay home and you, dear, go, the house and garden aren't the do. The
apples falling on the ground have now at night a dreadful sound. Like
Burglars [sic] lifting up the screens or getting in by some other means.
When you're near by I feel so safe, and brave—and then I like your cafe.
The above bit of song middly expresses the 1000 feelings that well up as
I think of you away off in Norfolk. I hope you are having a good time & a
good rest. Love to Carleton & to the hillsides.*

If Mary were to go away for as long as a day, he would send
her notes.

Beautiful Bunch: I am Lonesome: *Please come home right off. You never
made me hurry for a train—you never forgot yr umbrella nor anything.
You are the Only the Beautiflest. [sic] My Complete Satisfaction.*"[205]

He even wrote poems while he was at work.

*O Mary I wish I could write you a poem
But I can't think of aught but I want to get hoem.
Just think of the miles that are lying betwixt us—
Yet I'm not off my end of the shaft that transfixed us!
And the quiver you give to yr end of the arrow
Sends violent twinges right into my marrow.
Do you feel my pitty-pats shaking the line?
I love you more stoutly today—Mary mine.*[206]

Indeed, Hartley's own relatives used to make fun of his "docility" in
the face of his strong and independent wife.

But even the strongest of wives were only mortal. In December
1906, a New York City relative, Dr. Spencer Carleton (after whom
Carleton was named), finally discovered that Mary's illness was due
to an internal tear left from Devon's too rapid birth. Somehow, the
laceration had escaped the notice of the local doctors. For the unique
experience of childbirth meant that women were susceptible to certain infirmities that men were not; at the turn of the century, few
medical schools had courses emphasizing women's health. Dr.
Carleton told the Dennetts that the rip had been keeping Mary down
and would continue to keep her down until she had an operation.[207]

Meanwhile, in the summer of 1904, the year before Devon was
born, Hartley had been commissioned to build a house for Dr. Heman
Lincoln Chase and his wife Margaret. The Chases had seen another
of Hartley's houses in town, and had become very interested in his
approach to architecture. They appreciated they way he fitted a

house for its occupants and especially kept in mind the ease of accomplishing work in the house. When the two families met, they discovered they had much in common as well. Both husbands were graduates of Harvard College, both wives were interested in the suffrage movement, and both couples belonged to many of the same progressive reform organizations. Over time, they saw each other at various meetings, dinners, and lectures, and became fairly well acquainted.

Once construction began, however, Dr. Chase decided he really did not have enough time to oversee the house-building operation. Besides his private practice, he was health officer of Brookline, general medical inspector of the schools, and superintendent of the Contagious Hospital. When the time came to erect the structure, he told Margaret she would have to be the "building committee." Margaret was thrilled. Hartley was dashing and entertaining; her own husband was deadly dull. Immediately, Margaret was heady with adoration for Hartley.

The construction of the Chase house took quite a bit of time. By 8 January 1906, the Chases were able to move into their new house, but well into the summer of 1906 parts of the building were still not finished. Margaret began coming to the Dennett household quite frequently. She consulted with Hartley about the work at his home office. When she visited, she usually stayed for luncheon or tea or something else of that nature. She would later say, "I can truly say that I felt profoundly the influence of this man's spirit, as shown in his way of working, and I believe that to most of his clients, exactly the same experience comes."[208] After all, Dr. Chase was exceedingly busy, and he was not particularly interested in the construction of the house. And Margaret was exceedingly interested, and grew more so as the project went on. Margaret was working very closely with Hartley, and their friendship progressed rapidly. Since the Dennetts' marriage, the Chase project was the first piece of work that Hartley had ever done without his wife—as Mary was simply not well enough to take part.

It was "inevitable," Margaret would later write, "under the circumstances, that a comradeship—open, sweet and wholesome, strong and close, should develop between Hartley and me. I did not analyze it at the time, nor realize its approach until it was an accomplished fact, but I gradually came to feel that his way of meeting life, was the answer to our most eager questioning."[209] Margaret was impressed. "To me who dreamed of 'democracy,' the coming of the brotherhood of man, as something greatly to be desired, yet unattainable except through the long and painful processes of 'reform,' it could not but have a profound influence to associate with one who in the business of earning his daily bread coming into daily and hardy contact with the system of organized and unorganized greed, in which the world is wallowing, was inflexible in purpose, yet was unfailing in kindliness, gentleness, and courtesy."[210]

Margaret lauded Hartley, presenting him as the essence of nobility and virtue. Clearly, he was approaching sainthood in her eyes.

> *For two years I saw this man going in and out, doing his daily work, no strikers or watchers or foremen or draughtsmen to the 'menial' tasks, no buffers to stand between him and petty annoyance, or to divert from his own head, the consequences of any mistakes he might make—meeting each question to be settled, each man on the job, each clerk in the shop, and each client who employed him, simply and humanly, as having each, his or its own individual claim on him, belonging as much as any other belonged, and receiving, without assumptions of authority, or superiority, or any kind of aloofness, the attention each seemed rightfully to demand.*

Emphasizing that her own soul had been rejuvenated through his example, she made the house building a metaphor for her spiritual growth—indeed, a metaphor for the spiritual growth of all humankind. Clearly, she recognized, a new age had dawned.

> *I saw my own dim and crude vision of what a home should be, gradually enlarge to something more than the setting of an exclusively daily life, however virtuous, something bigger than a private possession, however benevolently held, and I watched, and helped as far as I saw, the vision take form and grow, under the loyal, patient, devoted purpose of its master craftsman, into a real home, capable by its very plan and structure of helping those who might live in it, to reach out toward the daily exercise of the spirit of democracy. The effect of this 2 yrs association on me, had been mostly unconscious as I can see in looking back. I should say it was chiefly that the sense of separation between myself and the mass of my fellow men had begun to melt away, and that within me had begun to grow a dim realization of the fact that differences in people because of birth, culture, education &c are merely superficial, that we are all first folks, and that without waiting for the effects of juster laws or better education, or more diffused culture or "advantages," each one can put what he has of faith, of sincerity, of purpose, and of brotherly love into his daily life.[211]*

She added, "I may add in passing that during this time there had been no thought of a personal friendship between us, nor was there until the spring of 1907, nearly a year later still."[212]

Meanwhile, Mary's health was deteriorating. In mid-July 1906, Mrs. Chase invited Mary and Devon to go with her to the Chase log cabin on Sunset Hill in East Alstead, New Hampshire. It was the beginning of a personal friendship between the Dennetts and the Chases. Hartley sent frequent notes to his beloved wife from his Boston office. "Molly wolly good & true, I am awful fond of you."[213] He gave her encouragement, "A bear hug for you & a cub hug for Devon."[214] And he addressed envelopes to "Mrs. Mary Ware Dennett," explaining, "I always feel so like an economic superior when I wrote you as Mrs. H that I feel easier that way. To be consistent I am doing Mrs. Chase same way—I hope she is strong minded enough to stand it."[215]

During this two-week visit, Mary told Margaret of her withdrawal from the Boston Society of Arts and Crafts because of a fundamental disagreement about the true function of Arts and Crafts. Believing all Arts and Crafts societies had to dig down to the roots of the economic conditions surrounding craftsmen to give real assistance to the development of craftsmanship, Mary planned to form a committee to study these very economic questions. Mary wanted the committee made up of "women willing to go to the bottom of the question, brave enough to face what they found, and big and wise enough to present the results in such form as to compel the attention of thinking people." The Economics Committee was to be formed out of a subcommittee of the Committee of Arts and Crafts of the Massachusetts Federation of Women's Clubs. Mary invited Margaret to be one of its members.[216]

Indeed, by 1906, the Arts and Crafts movement had mushroomed. Americans everywhere were subscribing to dozens of periodicals, joining hundreds of Arts and Crafts societies. There were classes available at a countless variety of summer schools, night schools, design schools, and settlement houses. And craftsmen showed their work at international expositions and exhibitions sponsored by societies and schools.[217] Most of the Arts and Crafts societies patterned themselves upon Boston, which itself patterned itself upon the Arts and Crafts Exhibition Society of London.[218] Besides selling crafts, the societies brought crafts workers, amateurs, and enthusiasts together for talks and exhibitions. Societies were important factors in improving taste and encouraging artistic design. Only the more radical members, like Mary, hoped they would help transform conditions of labor.

That autumn, the Dennetts decided to buy some pasture property adjacent to the Chases' log cabin in Alstead, New Hampshire—most likely with money saved from Hartley's growing architectural practice. Margaret was beside herself with excitement. She quoted a friend who said the purchase would be a "good investment for your children and grandchildren if you can let it alone for twenty or twenty-five years."[219] Acknowledging the pasture was most beautiful in the area farthest away from the Chase property, she fretted and worried, declaring herself "desperately afraid you'll decide to put your house there instead of over here when you get it."[220] She was even on the verge of asking her husband to pay for half the cost, saying, "I'm ready to beg Dr. Chase to go halves and buy the other end if you want to..."[221]

In November 1906, Mary's Economics Committee began its study. Meeting once a month at the homes of members, the women had lunch, discussed assigned reading, and made plans for the future. Books were read in common, or, if read individually, the reader would sum up the contents for the others. Focusing on topics such as sociology, economics, education, philosophy, and religion, the women discussed all subjects.

At one committee meeting, Mary told her friends about how five-year-old Carleton had asked his mother a series of questions about the origin of his life. Carleton had asked, "Mother, who made me?" And Mary had answered, "God." The little boy then inquired, "Where did I come from?" And the mother answered, "Heaven." According to Margaret, Mary related a half dozen such questions and answers to the group, "laughing as at a huge joke," and the answers, "starting from that false first one, had involved the Mother in a more and more impossible situation." To Margaret, Mary's early approach to sex education was "revolting." Disapproving of the way Mary had handled the situation, Margaret felt that Mary had been less than "truthful."

> ... *as a child I had been lied to by my mother, about these things and had had to get the knowledge of life's beginnings through the usual distorted and impure channels; and when I was mature enough to realize the dire meanings and consequences to human lives of that "impure hush," I had vowed that any children I should ever have should have their questions answered straight.*

Without any other comment on Mary's story, Margaret told Mary that four years ago, the oldest Chase child had begun "questionings" at age three, and that "simple truthfulness" in her answers, then and in later conversations, had paid off in a growing bond between Margaret and her daughter. As a result of this approach, Margaret reported, her daughter had developed a "glad and reverent interest in God's care for the beginnings of life."[222]

Margaret's own interest in God came from a nervous breakdown she had experienced ten years earlier. After much "soul-searching and mind-rocking," and after trying the usual "change of scene," she had come to recognize that her need was "primarily spiritual." Margaret had been a traditional Christian for many years, with the "usual belief" in God and a hereafter. But in the "strain and stress of this storm," she reported, such beliefs, however beautiful, "could not hold." A self-described "soul adrift, alone—with nothing to cling to in all that terrible waste," she found her way to a Christian Science teacher.

> *Patiently, sympathetically, lovingly, that man led my sick spirit, through the mazes of its selfish sorrows, to a living spring—the source of all Good. He showed me that people, friends, children, wives, husbands—or circumstances, are agents, channels through which that "good" finds its way to us, but that there is but one Source, and it is to that Source we must look—not to any of its channels, in our need.*

She continued:

> *. . . It gave me a rock upon which to stand, and although in the intervening time it had often grown dim to my sight, and its affliction often lost sight of, still I had never forgotten the wonderful experience of finding a real live God, nor let go the truth that there is a straight path from each soul to him, and that in any situation, to realize this truth, is one of the ways of seeking first that kingdom, after which the other things shall come in their order.*[223]

Given her worldview, Margaret would later have trouble accepting the premises of Mary's committee. Mary was convinced that since society was the wrongdoer, society alone could undo the wrong. Fond of quoting John Hobson's statement, "Social wrongs demand a social remedy," Mary possessed a philosophy which was to agitate, educate, and then finally change the laws. But this did not satisfy Margaret's spiritual instinct. Something within her rebelled. Mary's reply did not speak to Margaret's experience, which sought a deeper spiritual remedy for external social ills. And while she could not state her feelings clearly, it was evident that there was "a more or less clear line of cleavage between my understanding of life and Mary's."[224]

Indeed, while Mary and Margaret were both active members of the Economics Committee, they began to diverge in approach. In the committee meetings, Margaret expounded on "a wholly new understanding of human relationships" that required "certain definite reforms...more fundamental" than any she had worked for before. These reforms would deal with changing the way human beings related to each other at a fundamental heart-to-heart level, rather than focusing purely on the effects of "maladjustments which we all see and suffer from." That is, Margaret wanted to deal with the cause of social problems—the underlying spiritual malady—and not just the external symptoms—the social problems themselves. To Margaret, the social problems they had been discussing were very real wrongs, but the materialistic solutions they proposed didn't see life "whole"—the answers didn't have "a message that satisfies either its writer or her hearers."[225] Hartley was deeply interested in the work of the committee, and he was impressed by Margaret's point of view.

By January 1907, Mary was making her first preliminary visit to Dr. Carleton to prepare for an operation. When she went in for surgery, in May 1907, Mary had to stay for a little over three weeks at a homeopathic hospital called the Hahneman Memorial Hospital in New York City. Her husband accompanied her some of the time, but for the most part, Hartley was forced to remain in Framingham to attend to business.

CHAPTER FIVE

Domestic Unraveling

ary was in very bad shape. Dr. Carleton told the Dennetts that if she had gone untreated for another year, she could not have been saved from complete invalidism—with internal cancer following a few years after that. The repair procedure for the laceration was very expensive, about $200 in all, but the young couple could only be thankful that they had discovered the problem in time. Paying the bills from Framingham, Hartley sent daily letters of encouragement to his wife, cautioning her to take as much rest as she needed until she was completely healed.[226]

Hartley had to work quite hard at his architectural practice to keep financially afloat. While Mary was in the hospital, Hartley kept her up to date on his projects. He was constructing a gymnasium and working on at least one residence. At home in Framingham, he was continually making improvements on their own dwelling place. His brother Vaughan was building a new awning in the back of the house to make into Devon's play yard. Hartley also envisioned the area as a place where Mary could spend a large part of her day getting stronger once she returned.

Three weeks was just about the longest time in his married life that Hartley had ever spent wifeless. Unlike the short rest cures she had taken earlier, Mary's present hospital stay required that Hartley make some real adjustments in his living habits. Without Mary there to cook, clean, and look after the children, Hartley had to learn how to take care of himself.

To help him out, Mrs. Chase began coming over to Framingham with increasing regularity. Spending time with Hartley and the children, Margaret read Kipling's *Just So Stories* to little Carleton; Margaret and Hartley took walks with Carleton and Mary Sunshine (Margaret's own little girl, who was about Carleton's age); Margaret and Hartley planned picnics and bonfires. One night, Hartley even insisted that the Chases stay overnight to sleep outdoors with him on the Dennett family sleeping porches—for he was trying to bring himself closer to nature. Margaret and Hartley began to share long outdoor lunches together too, enjoying quiet talks—just the sort he and Mary used to have, as Hartley reported to his wife. Sometimes Margaret's husband, whom Hartley referred to as "the doctor," accompanied Mrs. Chase, but more often than not, it was just Margaret herself. Before long, Margaret was such a frequent guest at the Dennett home that Hartley felt obliged to pay half her carfare from Brookline to Framingham just to be "fair."

Mary was always a frequent topic of conversation—Hartley missed his wife—but over time, Hartley began to enjoy Margaret on her own merits. Hartley wrote to Mary with excitement, "Mary, Margaret's feeling for us is deep and wonderful—and we must not let it drop off from neglect—I feel sure that she is the most raw & sympathetic friend to us, individually & as a family unit that we have found, and it must inspire us & encourage to rise higher & live more & love more—hoping that our sprouts will catch the spirit and do likewise."[227] Apparently, Margaret had told Hartley that once she had met Mary, she had told "many people that here was one of the rare cases where a good man had a wife as good as himself."[228] Hartley demurred, saying he knew he was only a quarter as good as his wife, but nevertheless, he was overwhelmed by Mrs. Chase's praise.

As time went on, Margaret began to talk to Hartley about her "sunshine factory," saying the "Dennett spirit" had completely turned her around and given her a "new lease on life"—just when she had been feeling herself become "hardened and more rationing & selfish." Claiming she was taking the lesson to heart, Margaret exclaimed that it was making her attitude toward all people "sunny and life-giving."[229] Flattered by Margaret's approbation, Hartley started to believe it. He wrote to Mary, "Now, bunny, doesn't that make you feel as if it is worth while to live—and a bit humiliated that what in us seems sometimes hardly to glow, should mean so much in kindling & warming others? I must say I feel like making a spurt & trying to be monstrously true to our light.... To think of it makes me feel as if I was in the Church of our Dreams."[230] In fact, Hartley *was* in the church of his dreams. Margaret was the only parishioner; he was the false idol.

Hartley was just beginning to feel the effects of Margaret Chase's influence. Before long, his letters were full of Margaret from beginning to end. Margaret worshipped Hartley. And in turn, Hartley's sense of self grew. He began to think quite highly of his new-found flatterer. He voiced his wish to Mary that she might spend more time with Margaret. For in his eyes, Margaret's influence was the best thing he had come across in a long time. Hartley adored being told how wonderful he was. He encouraged Mary to be as loving, "It makes me young & gay to have you say you think I am a good fellow—can't you cultivate phrases of that kind in my behalf now? Only don't you say a word that you don't mean."[231]

Part of what impressed Hartley about Mrs. Chase was her concern for the "spiritual." He advised Mary, "Put all yr thoughts into spiritual things and when you get back we'll together show folks how to make a health snap with the higher life."[232] Margaret told Hartley about her conversion experience, and Hartley described to Mary the "philosophy of life" that Mrs. Chase had worked out, saying, "she certainly is even more staunch & noble than you have estimated her." An inspirational speaker, Margaret painted herself as one who had suffered and triumphed. Continually alluding to her ordeals—but never giving any details—Hartley was awed by the "vigor" with which Margaret had "faced her problems" in the face of "some pretty uncompromising situations." His heart was stirred by her stories of how she had come through with a "lack of warm hearted sympathy." Indeed, all her talk of God must have made his association with her seem especially holy. To Hartley, Margaret's tales of suffering were "something great."[233]

And what particularly pleased him was Mrs. Chase's claim that it was Hartley and Mary's life together that had "deeply stirred" her and that it was "from me," exulted Hartley, that "she feels as if she had got something she sorely lacked."[234] Yet not wanting to seem envious or dissatisfied with her own situation, Margaret said she was filled with certainty about the strength of her own marriage—about Dr. Chase and "his devotion to her & her own devotion to him." Moved by Mrs. Chase's words, Hartley began to feel shame that he might have ever seemed to "lack faith" in Mary's interests "in any detail." Margaret's picture of the Dennetts' marriage was so hyperbolic that reality could not help but fail to measure up. Wrote Hartley, "Molly dear, I am going to be a better husband, & you can thank Margaret in a Transcript 'card' for making me ashamed of my complacency in noting on the satisfaction that you & I are ideally mated & therefore have nothing to strive for more ideal."[235]

Margaret and Hartley were becoming such good friends that they began to speak about what would happen once Mary returned.

Once he no longer had to write to his wife, Margaret suggested, perhaps Hartley could direct his daily letters to her instead. She would welcome any correspondence and she was "more than willing to read the tiniest size."[236] She called their growing relationship "a provision of Providence."

> You *needed an appreciative listener; Mary was ill and needed a rest; I was becoming all dried and hardened for lack of this very commodity which was a drug in your market. The fact that we wanted a house and you built it for us was only the neat little way Providence had of bringing about this larger result. The process is to* continue *until Mary is restored to her old strong jolly self and then I suppose that "sacred institution" the D. Family will retire unto itself and put up the bars. That will be hard on some of us, but as you have given me such a splendid start, I am opening a sunshine factory of my own any way, and you may, in future,* sometimes *want to exchange products, so we may meet, say once a year, the Chases and Dennetts, for this purpose.*[237]

Painting the situation to make it look like she was being unfairly shut out, Mrs. Chase gave herself victim status. She triggered Hartley's sympathies. She compelled him to question what he had always been taught about the sanctity of his family, that "sacred institution."

Like many others before and after him, Hartley was put to the test. If two people were not doing anything "wrong" (that is, not engaging in illicit sexual relations), and if, in fact, they were even doing something "right" (for what could be more right than discussing God?), why shouldn't two married people of the opposite sex (but not married to each other) spend extended periods of time alone together? When Hartley was unable to answer this question, he came to what he would consider to be a revolutionary new conclusion: there was no reason. Full of hubris, lacking intellectual humility, he was prone to easy rationalizations. Without faith and too arrogant to admit the limits of his own mind, he failed to understand that just because he could not come up with an answer to his question it did not mean that an answer did not exist.

Hartley had already lacked the moral vigilance to resist succumbing to Margaret's flattery, and now he proved lacking in other areas as well. Naive, he failed to acknowledge that relationships develop imperceptibly, step by step. Ignorant, he failed to recognize the unwieldy nature of the human heart. And selfish, he failed to realize that actual sexual infidelity is of little importance when it comes to marriage—casting even the slightest shadow of a doubt in a partner's mind is enough to destroy a marriage. Jealousy is a moot point when it comes to building trust. For the relationship between husband and wife is an organic one that must be carefully tended—even the strongest of marriages is infinitely fragile. The answers to his question "Why not?" were clear, but Hartley refused to open his eyes.

By the end of June, Mary was finally ready to leave the hospital. Hartley went down to New York to pick her up—asking Margaret to come along with him. But the very day Mary returned, she discovered Mrs. Chase would not leave the house—even though Mary had not invited her to stay. As Mary would later recall, it was "at a time when I would have distinctly rather not have had anyone there at all."[238] But as Mrs. Chase spent the day, it became perfectly obvious to Mary that her whole life had changed. Hartley had become completely absorbed in another woman.

Hartley's conduct toward Mary was different. As Mary would later recall, "It was as complete a reversal of his previous attitude as could be imagined."[239] Mary was confined to the sickbed for recovery. To begin with, the doctor would only allow her to sit up for two hours a day, and it would be a long time before she could stand on her feet. While she was recuperating, Hartley continued to "entertain." He seemed to glory in playing host to Margaret Chase. Mary began to view Mrs. Chase with a new eye.

Mary and Margaret were still friends. Margaret claimed to be as impressed with Mary as she had been with Hartley, and she would later say she saw "nothing to indicate any moral divergence between them."[240] Indeed, Margaret noted, "Hartley had always spoken of their [Mary and Hartley's] aims and purposes as being singularly unanimous and certainly during the time of the building up of our friendship, when we were plunged deep in an earnest and enthusiastic and purposeful study of the social, and economic questions of today, Mary's understanding of principles and her attitude of mind seemed to me to be identical with Hartley's."[241]

> *Especially I was impressed with the fact that she seemed at one with him in his way of conducting his business—never seeming to entertain the thought that he could compromise with his conscience where prestige or any sort of advantage might seem to be gained by doing so, and apparently without thought of any other possible course, sharing with him whatever loss was involved in his loyalty to principle.*[242]

But unbeknownst to Mary, Margaret never failed to let Hartley know how much she cared for him—masking her personal affection for him alone under the guise of affection for the entire Dennett family. In one letter to Hartley, Mrs. Chase went on for a page and a half listing all the dreary domestic chores she should have been doing. Instead, Margaret pointed out, she was writing to him. Making herself out to be more fun and carefree than his own wife, she flirted, "I shall write to Mary but shall not mention all these things, because being a woman and the mother of a family she would be distressed that I was neglecting so many important things. But you, being a mere man will I suppose simply feel that such sacrifices are only right and proper as a means of showing how much I care for the D—Family. And perhaps after all, you're right."[243]

Three years older than he, Margaret appealed to Hartley's boyish nature. Emphasizing her maturity, she said being with him and Mary made her feel "like an old horse who finds herself racing along forgetful of her age, in the wake of two frisky colts. Well I like it!"[244] When the Dennetts invited her over for a "frugal lunch" soon after Mary returned, Margaret was overjoyed. Lacking any shame or conscience whatsoever, she wrote, "I'm so joyful inside that I feel fairly heartless, and think I might even guggle *[sic]* at the invalid and her present woes."[245]

Before long, Margaret was finding any pretext she could to have as much contact with Hartley as possible. While Mary was bedridden, Margaret asked Hartley to bring her some beads, saying that her niece was about to graduate. In a letter to Mary, she said, "I'll meet the car he goes on if he can't stop, though it would give me joy to have him walk into my parlor for a visit of an hour, a day or a week."[246] Asking the young couple if they couldn't use her oven, washbowl, pitchers, and soap dish in their tent over the summer, Margaret thrust herself into the Dennetts' life on every occasion. Mrs. Chase would make her presence felt no matter what.

That summer, Margaret wanted Hartley and Mary to spend the season with her and Dr. Chase near the Chase summer camp in East Alstead, New Hampshire. After all, the Dennetts had bought a tract of land adjoining the Chase property with the idea of spending summer vacations there. Hartley could have his long-needed rest, and Mary, too, would have a chance to recover. Although Hartley was not sure whether or not Mary would be strong enough to go, Mary agreed to the plan, as it would be a pleasant way to recuperate. And besides, the Dennetts would not go until August.

By mid-July, Mary was making improvements. She could only stay up eight hours a day, as ordered by the doctor, and of course she tired easily, but wanting to make the best of things, she claimed that she was now much better in mind and body than she had been for years. At Hartley's insistence, both Dennetts were sleeping outdoors on the sleeping porch—although Hartley enjoyed it more than Mary, for she didn't like the brightness of the early morning sun. But Hartley was firm on the benefits of nature. When it rained, they could sleep in the living room.

Margaret went to East Alstead early in July 1907; Mary and Hartley were preparing to arrive in August. They wrote to Margaret warning her that they planned to wear their bathing suits the entire time at camp. Hartley was caught up in the benefits of dress reform—particularly for women. Dress reform was part of the ongoing Arts and Crafts trend, and adherents felt that a concern for functionalism as well as physical well-being could only mean the rejection of the tightly laced corset. Oscar Wilde, a staunch dress reformist and champion of the tea gown, urged women to return to classic principles of drapery, with costuming hung from the shoulders rather than impeding the waistline with cumbersome bulk and weight.[247] While Mary had been in the hospital, Hartley had been emphatic.

> It would make me orful happy to get you to the point of enjoying pejammers & sleeping bag & no corsets! Damb the corsets—I am madder & madder at them every day. The man that invented them (I am sure it was a man) should be in Hell now & forever more. I hope you will join me in a serious and scientific & eager endeavor to make yr dressing delightful & sensible. You are just the genius to make a 10-strike if you will be so good to yr hunnybunch as to pitch in. I'll work harder to raise the money necessary.[248]

By now, according to Hartley, Mary was "full of zest for camping, and quite astir for the simple life." Hartley wrote to Margaret that Mary "has declared to me that she thinks she will live mostly in her bathing suit,—I am afraid you will not want to associate with your unconventional neighbors."[249] Indeed, said Mary, "If bathing suits are decent then why can't we wear them?"[250] And Margaret replied, "If hot collars are damnable, then why *must* we wear them? It is a tie!"[251] So Mary brought a bathing suit for Margaret also, and Margaret would later say she found the absence of a long skirt a "great convenience" in doing the housework.[252]

Indeed, the environment at Alstead was about as different from Boston city life as could be imagined. For starters, the Chase camp was simply magnificent. It was called a camp, but it was rather a luxurious camp. With six rooms including a spacious living area, it was really a beautiful log cabin filled with modern conveniences. Nearly everybody knew it for miles around. One simply had to ask for the "log house." One and a half miles from the East Alstead post office, on the road from East Alstead to Alstead Center, the house was situated several miles from the railroad up in the mountains. And from its windows, the view overlooking the country scenery was spectacular.

Not a building could be seen, only creations nature had wrought. For almost half a mile, a luxuriant pasture spread thickly down the hill. Bordering it were groves of lush young hemlock and pine, their leaves mingling in the treetops. And all around the countryside was a broad expanse of green: "little patches of grass and ferns at cozy spots in the woods."[253] Here, the elements of earth and air met in peace. Gorgeous flowers and vegetables filled an abundant garden. It was East Alstead in the full bloom of summer.

When the Dennetts arrived, bathings suits were indeed the perfect vacation garb. As a means of expressing their desire for freedom, both families wore them more or less throughout the summer, especially on the long walks over the hills. Devoted to the outdoor life, they all customarily slept outdoors as much as possible. The log cabin had outdoor sleeping porches. Mary and Carleton slept in a little tent with wooden floors; everybody else slept in a big tent, with Hartley sleeping on the tent piazza.[254] They enjoyed bonfires and when not frolicking, they dined on picnics of roasted corn and other garden delights. Often they had weekend guests, and they socialized with the rest of the Warren Pond Colony.

While Mary slept late in the morning—perhaps until seven — Hartley and Margaret took daily morning walks up into the high ground behind the camp. Before the others were astir, Hartley and Margaret would be "starting the necessary morning work."[255] By the time Mary and Dr. Chase and the children awoke, Hartley and Margaret would return—just in time to get breakfast.

Before long, Mary began to realize that her husband scarcely appeared except at meal times—and sometimes not even then. For he devoted the bulk of his days to going off on long daily tramps with Mrs. Chase. Indeed, even Hartley had to admit that he and Margaret did go off for extended periods of time together. One time, he confessed, he and Margaret walked to the adjoining town early in the morning to get butter for both families. And on another occasion, he would relent, he and Margaret walked to the post office to start off Dr. Chase and his friend on a walking tour. But Hartley claimed he always returned "promptly." He insisted, "At all other times during the 2 1/2 weeks in which I was at the camp I was at hand, and only with Mary either alone or with other members of the two families. We had meals in common and did much reading aloud in group."[256]

But to Mary, Hartley and Margaret were together far too much for comfort. Mary was still in a state of semi-invalidism, and she was beginning to feel practically abandoned. She felt that they were there so that she could recuperate from her operation. And she was spending the entire vacation alone. Finally, Mary felt she had to speak up. One night, Mary asked Hartley if he knew what was happening. Picturing Mary's misery in a way that "excited my pity to the highest point," Hartley expressed his "regret for what she made to look like utter selfishness on my part."[257] Remembering the session as a "stormy night," Hartley would later say the "violent objection" took him by surprise. Startled, he immediately apologized. "Mary, I have been a brute—can you forgive me?"[258]

The next morning, he reported to the Chase cabin as usual to do his morning chores. Mary remained in the Dennett tent, believing Hartley would tell Mrs. Chase that he had come to his senses. Indeed, when he arrived at the cabin, his distress was obvious. Hartley explained to Mrs. Chase that he had "been knocked down by the discovery of Mary's feelings about our morning walks."[259] But according to Hartley, Margaret's only caution was that perhaps Mary and he did not have a "uniform understanding" of their purposes. Hartley claimed, "As has been Mrs. Chase's custom she did not intrude in the affairs between Mary and myself."[260]

Mary believed differently. Margaret was a forthright woman with a very convincing way about her. From Mary's perspective, Hartley was gone for several hours. When he finally came back, he had completely changed. Instead of his earlier remorse, Hartley announced that he had reversed his judgment of his actions entirely. Speaking with much excitement, he declared that he had not seen it aright—that it was really the beginning of a great new era. He had seen a vision of what his life ought to be and now he was going to work it out—and he needed Mrs. Chase for completion. Very gallantly, he told Mary that while it might perhaps seem hard for her at the moment, that doubtless she would presently see the vision also. Telling her that he and Margaret needed to be alone, he went on to explain that there were times when Mary's presence or Dr.

Chase's could rightly be considered an *intrusion*.[261]

Mary was stunned. She did not want to be a nuisance, but they were supposed to be in Alstead so that she could rest in the country air. But Hartley was deaf to her protests. Sometime thereafter, he left for Boston for a few days to take care of business. While he was gone, Dr. Chase made the same appeal to his spouse that Mary had made to hers. Approaching his wife with an attitude of broken-hearted despair, he made an indignant protest. But again, Margaret's arguments brought about an incredible transformation.

On what she would later describe as a "phenomenally still summer evening," Mary overheard their conversation. Mrs. Chase persuaded her husband by appealing to his *religious* convictions. She began by saying that no man in all the world had ever before had this wonderful opportunity to be the pioneer of a new era—of "brotherhood" and the "oneness of mankind." She explained that many would misunderstand, but that the discerning few would comprehend and admire. She reminded him that his own happiness depended upon his being able to reach the sublime point from which he could purge his heart of all earthly feelings and have faith in this new vision that had divinely come into their lives. Margaret was liberal in her use of high-flung phrases, but she would not explain precisely the *meanings* of what she was saying—her words could mean whatever the hearer wanted them to mean. Using the language of religion and philosophy to suit her own purposes, she made her case with great passion. Gradually, her husband yielded to her eloquence and echoed her teaching, and Mary heard her say, "Lincoln, the time has come for you to rise to the heights—I know you can do it." And her husband answered, "Yes, Margaret, I can."[262]

In spite of his adoption of her plan, however, the very next week Dr. Chase requested Hartley not to sit quite so near to Mrs. Chase, not to kiss her quite so often, and Mary repeatedly saw Dr. Chase signal to Hartley not to be so demonstrative with Margaret. And always, Hartley laughingly acquiesced.

Meanwhile, Hartley and Margaret were beginning to write clandestine verses of poetry to each other. They were mostly songs of love, and very sentimental. Referring to themselves in the third person, they used false names to masquerade their identities, not quite daring to speak out their feelings. Clearly, Hartley was caught up in Margaret's vision of the "new world." In one poem, he expressed how the "resurrection" of his "soul" demanded the dismissal of "youth's affection." Life without his "new love" could only be

"happy, somewhat grey"; "growth" demanded a new freedom—
anything else was "asphyxiation."[263] In other words, he considered
his relationship with his wife to be a childish crush he had now
outgrown.

For her part, Margaret wrote a short story to express her guilty
feelings of pleasure. All of nature was watching and supporting her,
she felt—the "little woodmouse," the birds, the cattle—and she herself was the "Day," sunlight personified, come to enlighten the rest
of the world. Symbolizing harsh reality, however, "Mother Life"
entered the picture. To this, Margaret responded with false piety,
portraying herself as the fair and helpless victim.

> *Mother Life was not pleased and she reproved the Day sternly. "I know,
> dear Life," replied the Day, "that you have some burdens and you can
> scarce believe in Love since your children seem so to live in hate. Yet ever
> and ever some have striven to find the better way and over their pros-
> trate lives all men have marched to something better." "But these will
> not," said Mother Life in anger; "they have chosen a path more perilous
> than any before them." A tiny cloud passed over the face of the Day, and
> she raised her beautiful eyes to Life, and Life saw the sadness there. Then
> Day said, "They did not choose the path. Love came and found them
> there. They cannot choose but walk in it, and though they fail they mark
> a way all men shall sometime tread; and then dear Life, ah! think what
> you will be in that sweet day, when all men walk in love, and none
> within or out to say them nay." And for a blessed moment Life saw the
> vision; his sad stern face grew tender. Softly she passed on. Not until the
> vision faded did her tread grow loud and harsh on the stony way.*
>
> *The Day whispered to herself a blessing and a prayer, and the wood-
> mouse felt the throbbing of her heart as he nestled close in the hollow of
> his breast.*

Margaret ended her story, "The Day, and the pilgrim, and the
woman, knew."

Hartley and Margaret rationalized that their feeling for each
other was a higher, purer, spiritual love. After all, their relationship
was based on talk about religion. But they obeyed no god but that
of their own vain fantasy. For Christianity had been permanently
shattered. Although its spiritual teachings would reign eternal, its
outward forms had been so distorted over the centuries that it
demanded a new manifestation. Avowed followers were drifting dis-
illusioned in a topsy-turvy state. Picking and choosing what elements they pleased from the remnants of old and familiar religious
traditions, Hartley and Margaret were able to create their own

unconventional faith. Vicariously reliving the romance of an ancient and bygone age, they prepared themselves for societal disapproval by studying the great sacrifices of martyrs in the Bible.

> *Behold, I send you forth as sheep in the midst of wolves: be ye therefore wise as serpents, and harmless as doves. But beware of men: for they will deliver you up to councils, and in their synagogues they will scourge you; yea and before governors and kings shall ye be brought for my sake, for a testimony to them and to the Gentiles. But when they deliver you up, be not anxious how or what ye shall speak: for it shall be given you in that hour what ye shall speak: for it is not ye that speak, but the Spirit of your Father that speaketh in you.*
>
> *And brother shall deliver up brother to death, and the father his child: and children shall rise up against parents, and cause them to be put to death. And ye shall be hated of all men for my name's sake: but he that endureth to the end, the same shall be saved. But when they persecute you in this city, flee into the next: for verily I say unto you, Ye shall not have gone through the cities of Israel till the Son of man be come.*[264]

Meanwhile, the tension between the entire group grew. Mary used to make fun of Dr. Chase, an easy scapegoat because nobody was particularly fond of him. Mary's upbringing had taught her to be a good sport, and she wanted to let her husband know that the Dennetts still shared the same views on all matters. "Wouldn't he make a great mechanical toy himself! I believe I will poke under his coat someday and see if I can't find the key." Apparently, he was less than dashing. But, not wanting to seem jealous, Mary tried to be gracious—even sympathetic—toward Margaret.

Mary need not have been so considerate with her rival. Hartley's vacation was fragmented as he had to go to Boston often on business. When he returned, Margaret would meet him at the train station at Walpole, New Hampshire, ready with a picnic lunch. The pair would walk the twelve miles back to camp, stopping to lunch under a pine tree on the way. Hartley and Margaret spent hours and hours of time together. Over time, Margaret even began to wear Hartley's clothes.

While Mary tried to regain her strength and recuperate from the operation that had saved her life, Hartley felt no pain. He wrote letters to his mother undated, putting where the date should have been, "I don't know what day of week or month—they are all alike & all very nice."[265] If he referred to his new companion at all, it was only as "Mrs. Chase"—only letting slip once that he really knew her by the more intimate and familiar "Margaret."[266] Life was wonderful, he felt carefree. "I can truly say, anyway, that I was never so sharp & well in my life as I now am: I feel fairly like a balloon, as far as the poise of my 160 lbs. is concerned."[267]

Hartley did try to spend some time with his wife. On one walk they took together, he would remember Mary generously telling him that "merely in the pains and problems of the summer" she considered the purchase of their land "well repaid."[268] And in an effort to charm her, Hartley penned a little ditty to his wife.

Mary mine—
  This is a little billy doux
Just to say that I love youx
(And I don't care a single soux
Whomsoever you might tell it toux)
Before we've lived our life throux
Let's take a week to bill and coux
And mutual plight of faith renoux.
Love me harder, do! di doux!
And tell me of it just a feux!

By mid-September, Hartley and Mary had returned to Framingham. According to Hartley, the vacation was a great success. "Mary and I both feel very gratified with our experiment at a summer vacation—We both have much strengthened in all ways by it . . ."[269] Hartley managed to convince himself that Mary had enjoyed the summer as much as he. He wrote to his mother, "Mary is much better—especially in spirit. The Alstead time was a great thing for her."[270] Regrettably, this too was fantasy.

CHAPTER SIX

Playing to Win

lthough she had done her best to keep cheerful, the summer in Alstead had been a miserable experience for Mary. Unhappy about the situation, Mary decided it was time to speak to Margaret. With wide open arms, Margaret emphatically declared that she welcomed Mary's story.

Your wish to tell me something of what the summer's experiences has been for you makes me glad. We,—you and I—should be able to talk freely and openly together! Are we big enough and true enough to do it? Fear, pride, the inborn desire for monopoly, all our miserable contrivances for shutting people out,—all the conventions,—are against us when we try to say and act simply the things that are in our hearts, even when those to whom we would show them have shared our thrilling experience. And yet I am sure that open and direct expression of the truth is not a question of method in meeting life but is the question of life itself. To be ourself without pride or fear and to touch simply and reverently each life we come in contact with, with the truth that is in us!—makes life indeed a thing to be looked upon with joy. And how such a picture lets the sawdust out of the thing called "social intercourse." Would you build the holy city? Come let us take our kit upon our shoulders and go out and do it now![271]

Strangely righteous in sentiment, Margaret seemed to speak in a foreign language. Not easily convinced by rhetoric, Mary recognized that despite the high-flung phrases, Margaret was not saying anything of substance. Unaffected by Margaret's soul-stirring speeches, Mary's immovability made any real communication difficult. Never having met a person with such a distorted view of life, Mary did not know how to respond to Margaret's meaningless words. Mary only tried to believe that somehow Margaret—like herself—did, indeed, intend the best.

In October 1907, Mary, still trying to give Margaret the benefit of the doubt, returned to East Alstead for a picnic meeting with the Economics Committee. The committee elected Mary to stay behind to do some extra research, but Margaret took Mary aside for a private conversation, explaining that Dr. Chase would be coming up for a few days. Mrs. Chase asked Mary not to stay, as she wished to be alone with her husband. But just after Mary left, Hartley arrived. The doctor was there, but so was Hartley. Dr. Chase was only in Alstead with Margaret for the weekend, while Hartley stayed for a week.

Hartley insisted upon remaining true to his heart—by spending as much time as possible with Margaret Chase. Mary was disturbed to see her husband spending a good portion of his time with another woman whom he professed to "love deeply." Naively, even stupidly, Mary tried to remain supportive. She refused to believe that such a complete absence of conscience could be possible. Her upbringing had taught her that if given the chance, all people would rise to their noblest natures. In response, Hartley said he refused to compromise his "ideals." He called Mary's request for undivided love and attention "selfish" and "unworthy." He would be a "coward" and a "liar," he said, to give up the newfound sunshine in his life, Mrs. Margaret Chase.

In the fall and winter, the intimacy between Hartley and Margaret increased. In the name of freedom, Hartley refused to be told when he could come and go from his own house—so he would leave for days and even weeks at a time to live at the Chase home in Brookline. When Margaret called him on the telephone, Hartley would leave suddenly—even if he had just mentioned that he had a busy day. Starting off at once, he would say, as he went out of the house, "I shall probably be home tomorrow."[272] Sometimes he would not be back for two or three days. Sometimes, he took Carleton and Devon with him. Sometimes he would stay away without giving anyone in the family any knowledge of where he was. When people telephoned to ask where Hartley was, Mary had to say she did not know—he went to Brookline, and that was all she knew.[273]

Mary and Margaret continued their efforts to stay friendly with each other, but Margaret had a tendency to use words like "true" and "just" and "honest" in situations that seemed particularly false and unjust and dishonest. Mary was defenseless in the face of utter shamelessness. Starting with old, established truths, Margaret had a funny way of giving them a new twist so that they would serve her own needs very well. Always taking the moral high ground, Margaret would never admit to wrong. Indeed, Margaret seemed to rejoice in trampling on Mary's spirit. In her letters to Mary, Margaret often included little notes to Hartley as well (saying she didn't want to waste space), in which she would write little terms of endearment.

Margaret seemed to have completely trained herself to become inured to any feelings Mary might have. Forever inviting Mary to join her and Hartley in some of their various activities, Margaret liked to appear generous. "Please don't let my invitations get on your nerves, Mary, nor bother you in any way. I am glad when our home can offer convenience, to be sure, but even at such times my realist [*sic*] reason for asking you is the genuine happiness of having you come, and you know what a great joy it is to us to have Hartley here."[274]

At the beginning of February 1908, Mary and Margaret engaged in a long talk in which Margaret told Mary that if she followed her "own dearest wish, she would spend the *rest* of *her life* with Hartley."[275] Margaret said she loved Hartley in every possible way—as "friend, mother, daughter, and wife."[276] Margaret went on to assure Mary that she loved her own husband no less for that and did not wish to change relations with him. But Mary was appalled. She asked Margaret to try an experiment of letting Hartley alone for a year. After such a hiatus, perhaps Mrs. Chase might feel differently? Margaret refused. Her rationale was that in order to end her relationship with Hartley, she would first have to be convinced that she was doing something wrong—and she knew she wasn't.

Mary did her best to hold up under the circumstances. She attempted to be civil and even friendly, even though Margaret's "kindnesses" often put her on the defensive. Wrote Mary to Mrs. Chase, "Please forgive me for being so uneven. I don't keep my balance well at all, and I am sorry. In most things, my wish to please Hartley and my instincts are at one, but where they are not, as in times like this, the hurt will show, in spite of me." Doing her very best to hold Margaret in high esteem, Mary told Mrs. Chase she realized "both of you are too fine to go on a single instant doing anything that you *know* to be wrong. It is exactly because you sincerely believe you are right that I respect you. And it is that same respect that I have for Hartley (my love for him I can't help) that makes life under these circumstances endurable."[277]

Thus Margaret—and Hartley—discovered that "honesty," "kindness," and, most of all, self-righteousness were their most effective weapons. Over and over again, as Mary recorded in notes she made for posterity, Hartley and Margaret told Mary that she was "hypocritical in doing social work to uproot social privilege, and at the same time wishing special privilege for myself in my personal life—that I represented 'monopoly'—And that no woman should expect the monopoly of her husband's affections."[278] When Mary responded to this in a detailed, eleven-point letter, Margaret was stung. Margaret painted herself as the supreme woman of sacrifice, saying she was trying to advance "a system in which each person stands independently on his own feet, with simply a fair field."[279]

Speaking of her "cause," in which love knew no ownership, Margaret wrote, "if you are to stand for such a reform as this you must be ready not only to make a sacrifice of personal advantage, but what may be much harder, to face the misunderstanding, pain and sorrow of dear friends whose confidence and affection are very precious."[280] In March 1908, Margaret wrote Mary a letter which Mary would refer to again and again in the future.

> It is true that I love Hartley,—deeply,—sincerely.
>   It is true that he loves me.
>   It is absolutely untrue that either wishes, or has ever wished, the other
> to be disloyal to any other person, or in any other relation of his life.[281]

Margaret explained that she and Hartley believed "that the gift of a pure love is a priceless treasure,—and a light, *not* to be hidden, but to be shown."[282]

Margaret also expounded on the marriage relation. "Marriage was made for man, and not man for marriage," she declared, "and when that, or any other institution, forbids the free expression of the spirit in any direction, there can be no question as to what must be done. If to preserve any institution, men must cover up their own hearts and thus become cowards and liars, then that institution must go."[283]

Mary did try to be frank and honest. Again and again, she attempted to outline exactly what was wrong with Margaret and Hartley's ideas. In her eleven-point letter, she pointed out the flaws in Margaret and Hartley's arguments in a clear and articulate manner.[284] Mary, however, should not have bothered addressing their arguments with any degree of seriousness. Margaret and Hartley were impervious. It was useless to try reasoning with people who had already settled upon the rightness of their theories.

Nevertheless, Mary was Panglossian in outlook, the eternal optimist who insisted upon holding Margaret in good faith. Wrote Mary:

> I have been discouraged about even trying to answer your letter—and
> so have let it go these several days—but I suppose I ought to keep on try-
> ing even though it is so evident that I speak a language you don't under-
> stand—for in spite of the fact that you say I present my point of view

*vividly—you really miss the whole point—and that being the case, you of
course can't do anything else but call it "misconstruction" and "false idealism." However, I am willing to try once more—and as many times
more—as it seems necessary.*[285]

The situation with Margaret was a difficult one because Margaret
was so unrelenting. With short brown hair and a determined look in
her eyes, her very appearance was that of immovability. Mary, with
her soft blonde hair and genteel demeanor, was more traditionally
beautiful. But Margaret's charms were not so much physical as
mental and intellectual. Like a political tyrant who grew more
resilient, determined, and self-righteous in the face of opposition—
and who only took greater advantage from appeasement—Margaret
stopped at nothing. Yet whereas the despot only wanted to possess
land and nations, Margaret Chase was attacking the world order at
an even deeper level. After a few generations, such dissolution of the
family could only mean the ultimate disintegration of civilized life.

On Valentine's Day that year, Hartley wrote Mary the following
verses:

*"The World all looks so black!" you cry.
Ah, dear, the lily may despair
Of life itself when it must lie
Buried from warmth and light and air.*

*Yet may it not so live God's will
That it can feel, and understand,
Amongst the death-pains some wee thrill
Of that new birth so near at hand?*

*Pray, dear, with me that we may keep
So close to Nature's ample breast
That though we lie ten fathoms deep
We may be sure we Live,—and rest.*[286]

The lover's poems to his wife were changing. By this time, Hartley
and Margaret were gleaning their "spiritual" ideas from the
Overbrook Farm in Wellesley, Massachusetts.[287] At Overbrook,
Frederick and Rachel Reed had opened up their home to Boston-area
spiritualists. A former Harvard classmate of Dr. Chase and a member of the faculty of the prestigious Boston Latin School, Mr. Reed
was also a member of the Spirit Fruit Society, a utopian group
founded by Jacob Beilhart whose philosophy revolved around the
principle of Universal Life.[288]

Beilhart's primary teaching was the evil of the self. In capital letters, he proclaimed, "NO ONE WILL EVER GET INTO SPIRIT WHILE THEY SEEK TO POSSESS ANYTHING."[289] Even the exclusive relationship of a "Soul-mate," he explained, would "shut out what is in the Universal." Making an analogy between string tied around a finger which cut off blood from the rest of the body and exclusivity in human relationships, he wrote, "So long as you possess exclusively, any thing you count your own; even to your 'Soul-mate,' you have a string around the passage between you and Spirit Universal." Like any warped interpretation, Beilhart's twist on the ideal of selflessness could only result in ultimate and utter destruction.

> *If you Will to have things all your very own, and will to cut them off from full liberty in Spirit, then you must put up with lifeless things until you are willing to count nothing as your own, but all things as in Spirit Universal and yourself in it as well. Then you will have no care, no husband, wife, child, friend, home, knowledge, or even a soul-mate to look after, for you will be free to let Life possess you and live in you as it Wills and also in all others you once called your own.[290]*

Beilhart explained, "no Self is so great, no two who are soul-mates or husband and wife are so great that they can afford to live apart from this free opening to the Universal Spirit in all. It is only by free receiving and giving on all planes that life is kept up. Circulation without restraint, is essential to perfect harmony."[291]

Hartley felt that the Spirit Fruiters embodied the "true spirit of Christianity."[292] Drawing upon Spirit Fruit, Hartley developed new ideas about marriage. Using the rhetoric of Arts and Crafts, single tax, socialism, and other progressive causes of the day, he became convinced that the institution of marriage could only result in an unjust "monopoly of love." Unable to see the superficiality of his words, he convinced himself that the "struggle against monopoly" was a "dogged day-to-day" in the "combat of the spirit of freedom against the spirit of bondage." Hartley deeply believed, "There is no possible peace short of the annihilation of the monopolistic spirit...."[293]

Yet as attracted as he was to the misguided ideas, Hartley would never actually become a Spirit Fruiter, for his desire for complete freedom repelled him from adhering to any organized belief system. Without Hartley realizing it, his concept of "freedom" only enslaved him in the prison of self. Believing only in himself, he assiduously copied down the "Creed of the Vuil St. Church":

This church has no creed. It does not ask its members to subscribe to any statement of belief. It does not tell men what to think. It tells them to think. It says to each member: "Write your own creed. Revise it as you go. Respect the right of your fellow members to do the same."

Again starting with a basically sound idea, Hartley took a wrong turn. While the advice *"to think"* was sound, the do-it-yourself mandate of the Vuil St. creed appealed to egotism. For such a creed recklessly ignored the limitations of human knowledge. By definition, self-made creeds prevented the coordinated development of any kind of ordered society. Even with the best of intentions, such spiritual anarchy could only end in chaos and social collapse.

In May 1908, Hartley went up to Alstead for two weeks with Mrs. Chase alone. Mary offered to go with him, but he told her he preferred to go without her. Mary objected. She made the most earnest entreaties, begging him to stay home. Annoyed by her clinging, Hartley stuck to his new beliefs. Like the convert that he was, he told Mary with no qualifications whatsoever that he would even consider it perfectly right, if he chose, to have a child by Mrs. Chase; no one but himself had a right to judge as to whether it would be right or wrong. Although he thought Margaret's health would be impaired by having any more children, that was mere circumstance. He stood firmly by the principle that his own individual choice in any matter should be his only guide. In his mind, "true love" respected entirely the freedom of another person. No boundaries could possibly exist within "true love."

Hartley saw the trip as another way to test Mary, as well as a way to prove to her that he truly loved her and that his intentions were "pure" and "true." Confidently, he wrote to her from Alstead:

You must know that I could not lightly, or for purely selfish reasons, refuse to do what you askd [sic] in behalf of your happiness, regarding this vacation. I simply could not with self respect admit the motives you ascribed to me and the meaning you put upon the matter. I don't believe you want my love for you to operate in ways incompatible with self-respect, and I implore you, for your own happiness as well as for my own opportunity to rightly show my love, to seek for good rather than for evil in my life as it goes on from day to day, and not in your distress deny the love that is in my heart, so true that it can see you unhappy rather than betray you with false kindness, and ever ready to work with you and for you according to the truth as it sees it.[294]

When he didn't hear from Mary for several days, he became worried, sending a note saying, "perhaps today a letter will come."[295] He sent flower blossoms, brought home a present, and always signed with "tender love" or "true love."

But Hartley's refusal to stay at home had pushed his wife to her limit. When Hartley returned from Alstead, Mary formally cut off all social intercourse with the Chases. She told Hartley and the Chases that she thought the two families should stop their social relationship and confine themselves to business. Margaret continued to invite Mary to her home for reasons which were more and more "flimsy," but Mary refused.

> *The time has come when you ought to realize that the kind of life you and Hartley are leading together can have absolutely no countenance or co-operation from me. The fact that your activities together, are along the lines of general good, does not disguise the wrong you are doing, nor palliate it in any way. It serves only to blind your eyes and dull your conscience and befuddle your philosophy.*
>
> *You are yielding to the same temptation that has blackened many another's life before you—and simply because the temptation is not in a gross form, it is no less a real temptation—and your yielding to it—no less a sin.*
>
> *My decision not to have any more social relations with you is merely registering my protest against the wrong you are doing; it would be no help to you or Hartley or anyone if I should make your downward path as frictionless as you would both like to have it.*
>
> *If you want to do this thing, and still delude yourself into believing that you are right—you must do it alone—and not expect support or co-operation from me—or anyone else.*
>
> *The kind of co-operation you have to offer is very much the same sort that is offered by any individualist in the business world, who want amicable relations with those on whose backs he is supported—but insists that those amicable relations shall be in terms of his own privilege and their loss. . . .*
>
> *. . . I earnestly hope your inert heroism will rise to the point of noble action, before you waste much more of life in this vain attempt at happiness. It is a card-house—this that you have built, and I trust you will begin to see it, in time to avoid the certain ruin.*[296]

Mary's tactic did not work. Hartley simply told Carleton and Devon that the reason Mrs. Chase had stopped coming was that "mother objected."[297] Mary's sense of desertion grew, and "the elders" stepped in.

Vonie, Mary's mother, had written Hartley a letter before his vacation with Margaret in Alstead. Mary had confided in no one else before this. When Hartley received the missive from his mother-in-law, he agreed to meet with her in person. Speaking for a little over an hour at the Mead's house—for Vonie was living permanently with Aunt Lucia and Uncle Ned—Hartley tried to justify his affection for Mrs. Chase. When he saw that he was making no impression at all on her, he said, "I want you to talk with Mrs. Chase. Will you put on your hat and go to Brookline and talk with Mrs. Chase?"[298] Vonie refused to go, saying she had nothing to say to Mrs. Chase—she had said all she had to say in the letter. The conversation ended very soon after that.

With Vonie's failure, Aunt Lucia and Uncle Ned took it upon themselves to serve as Mary's support system.[299] Each had long talks with Hartley which, for the most part, were unproductive. Hartley frankly confessed his love for Mrs. Chase, declaring it "profound and unalterable." Uncle Ned asked Hartley whether or not his feelings were "no more than a very strong or sublime friendship."[300] For if it were, he said, he and Ah Loo would step out of the picture, since nobody could be more tolerant of friendship than Mary.[301] But wanting to get at the "real nature" of the matter, Uncle Ned asked Hartley if he would prefer to marry Mrs. Chase if he were free— and Hartley answered he might do so.[302] At this, Uncle Ned informed Hartley that his private vacation with Mrs. Chase was "a scandal and an abomination."[303] Taciturn and silent, Hartley claimed he had to be his own judge in those matters.

Bringing in the Chase family, Hartley told Uncle Ned that he believed if Mrs. Chase were unmarried and could choose freely, she, too, would marry Hartley over Dr. Chase. Furthermore, Hartley claimed, Dr. Chase approved of the entire situation. Uncle Ned warned of impending disaster. "If Mrs. Chase's feeling is what you believe—a belief which I pray may be absolutely false—it is inconceivable to me how a mature and experienced woman of the world like her, a wife and a mother, can fail to see it."[304] Warned Uncle Ned, "I only submit that your understanding with Dr. Chase should be a real one—and that you let nothing tempt you to the risk of working wrong to a sacred home, by entering it under any mask."[305] Uncle Ned then sent a copy of his letter to Hartley to Dr. Chase.

In reply, Hartley sent a terse note to Uncle Ned, saying that the "exact quality of the feeling is and has been fully understood by Dr. Chase: Mrs. Chase is wholly frank with him and wholly loyal to him and their home, as is surely my purpose."306 After doing this, he wrote a short note to his "dear Margaret," saying that that was the last he had to say to "the relatives." In the future, he said, obedient to his guru, he would refer anything from the Meads to her. He asked for Margaret's approval. "If I have said anything you don't approve of my saying for you, please forgive me, and correct it either direct to him or through me."307

Before long, Dr. Chase came in to Edwin Mead's office for a careful talk on the whole subject. As Ned would later remember it, "He was perfectly heartbroken."308 Dr. Chase himself recognized that Hartley was infatuated with his wife and, according to Ned, he "made no bones in talking about it."309 But once he returned home, Dr. Chase allowed his name to be signed to a letter written in Hartley's handwriting, "If all of the four persons most concerned will remember the *facts*, and will act toward each other *faith*, *love*, and *respect*, there must surely soon come a reconciliation where now jealousy and selfish pride (more or less) hold sway. This change for the better I confidently hope and expect to see. If we can so act I believe a more real happiness than before can result in both homes."310 And indeed, to a friend, Dr. Chase confided, "I do not intend *to win*, but I do intend *to be true*."311

By this time Hartley was practically living in the Chase home in Brookline. Hartley claimed he was miserable because Mary had put him in "social quarantine" and made the atmosphere in Framingham so chilly that he was frozen out. In a telephone conversation with Aunt Lucia, Dr. Chase told her that Mary ought to be willing to forgive "even your enemies." Ah Loo pointed out, however, "that even God could not forgive one who did not repent, and that it was not a question of forgiveness."312 She stated that "the only absolutely new feature to a somewhat common situation was [Hartley's] own stultification of his instincts and his heroic self-effacement."

Lucia pointed out the fundamental flaw in Hartley and Margaret's reasoning: that if their "principle" were to be "lived up to by humanity in general," it could only result in "spiritual anarchy and chaos."313 Speaking of Hartley and Margaret, she stressed that "those two had never made any sacrifice in this matter but asked others to do all the sacrificing." Hartley and the Chases were all scandalized. Without exception, all of their former friends and acquaintances had shut them out. When Dr. Chase tried to say they had "sacrificed" the esteem and approval of such friends as the Meads, Lucia rejoined by pointing out that such a loss was "simply a logical consequence and not a voluntary sacrifice."

Lucia insisted that Hartley and Margaret's actions amounted to an "unwillingness to sacrifice." Dr. Chase offered an insight, saying he felt that "the only way to bring [Hartley] to his senses was to treat him in a friendly way and not as if he were a moral leper." Dr. Chase apparently felt "that the quickest way to end passion is not to oppose it but to give the afflicted victims a chance to see enough of each other and let it burn itself out." For her part, Mary continued to do her best to be kind; she had even baked Hartley a cake for his birthday—a fact that seemed to surprise Dr. Chase. Aunt Lucia told him that Mary's "heart would melt" and Mary would do her "utmost" to show her appreciation if only Hartley would make "a voluntary effort to deny himself and do right." Said Lucia, "it was rather weak and cowardly for H. to expect to 'eat his cake and have it' and to complain when the logical result of his refusal to stay with [Mary] last spring was now coming home to him."[314]

In the summer of 1908, just a few short weeks after his May trip, Hartley went again to Alstead. Spending the summer there with Margaret, he took Carleton with him. Mary did not go. Although Margaret invited Mary up to Alstead for a repeat of the previous summer, Mary had had enough. While he was in Alstead, Hartley sent frequent notes to his wife. But even though he signed his letters with "deep love," entirely gone was the loving tone of old. Instead, his letters seemed to reflect a feeling of resigned duty—"Dear Mary—I have spent the day doing nothing but write letters, and now I must sleep or bust."[315] Sending checks to pay the bills, reporting on his and Carleton's activities—the letters were entirely mundane and lacking in interest, wit, or charm.

Mary's letters, too, were entirely lifeless. A tired feeling permeated the weary reports of friends and relatives who were sick, troubled, or even nearing death. Physically, her own health was much improved, but she was emotionally depressed. Like a mother hen, she counseled Hartley with dos and don'ts for Carleton. With no effort to be entertaining or amusing, by the end of August, her notes were *extremely* brief and superficial—sometimes only a sentence or two long. One merely said, "There is nothing in particular to report today."[316]

But her enthusiastic letters to Carleton exhibited all the attributes of a living relationship. Imaginative, encouraging, full of love and energy, she thought up games for him to play and told him stories about Comrade, his puppy at home. She wrote of "new big shining spoons"[317] she had bought the children for their sand pile—tied to the railing with long cords so they wouldn't get lost. Too proud to communicate her hopes and feelings directly to Hartley, she asked seven-year-old Carleton to pass veiled messages to his father about various flowers and roses in her garden—ones she and Hartley had thought would not bloom or had been on bushes that were dying—which had flourished gorgeously and lived.[318] By the end of August, she was missing Carleton with a "hard ache."[319]

And Carleton desperately missed his mother and younger brother. Through Hartley, his faithful "personal secretary," Carleton wrote, "Dear Mother—I am coming home day after tomorrow. I wish I could come home this minute. Mother dear how is Devon?"[320] "Dear mother—why don't you come up here? We are having a dandy time."[321] "Mother I hope you will be very happy but I am missing you terribly."[322] "Mother I wish you could have a picture of me to look at while I am gone: Then you will think of my face. I want a picture of Devon to look at because I miss him terribly. Has Devon been a good boy while I have been gone?"[323] Of "Auntie Chase & Lincoln" and the two Chase children, Carleton merely reported, "Aunt Margaret wears her bathing suit nearly all the time."[324]

When Hartley and Carleton returned from Alstead, Carleton was full of stories. He described to his mother a friend of the Chases and Hartley, who had become attached to another woman who was the wife of a Pennsylvania man at the time. These two people, a man and a woman, occupied the tent that Hartley and Mary had formerly occupied the year before. They were not married to each other. Mary was shocked. Questioning Carleton further, she asked her son to be very explicit. He simply replied, "Why, yes, father and I had the little tent, and they had the big tent." Mary asked him, "Do you mean they did that regularly, was that the way they planned things all the time?" Carleton answered, "Yes." Not wanting to impress upon Carleton the illegitimate nature of the circumstances, Mary did not enlighten him at all.

Not at all a singular occurrence, Hartley and Margaret had frequently hosted houseguests who came up to try out their free-spirited living arrangements. Even though Hartley was not a Spirit Fruiter, Frederick Reed of Overbrook now wanted to spend a day together with Hartley, suspecting that they had "much in common in ideals and purpose, the assurance of which would give us both joy and strength."[325] In his poems, Hartley expressed his rebel-

lion against the puritan conformity of New England, painting himself
as the last hope for Christianity. Drifting further and further away
from his old life with his wife, Hartley was changing his identity.

By the fall of 1908, as Mary began to confide in close friends
outside the immediate family circle, her old Capen School roommate,
Kate Ware Smith, suggested to Mary that she attempt to "express
more affection than [she] felt" so that she could "will" herself to
love. In Kate's opinion, "there can be no winning him back and no
modus vivendi involved if you are strong." Aunt Lucia agreed,
saying Kate's suggestion was worth considering—although Lucia
pointed out this would only be "a return to somewhat the same
methods which you tried last year." But Hartley was impervious. No
matter what Mary did—whether she was gentle or strong—her husband stayed away from home. Gone at least half the time, he came
and went without saying where he was going or when he was
coming back.

In Brookline, Hartley was helping Dr. Chase put together a circular for young men on sex hygiene. Margaret was firm on the ideal
of chastity. Some years ago, she had come to the conclusion that
sexual intercourse was only justifiable if accompanied by the deliberate hope of bringing a child into the world. For if it was justifiable
without this intent within marriage, then logically, it would follow
that it was justifiable outside of marriage as well. Left struggling
with his sex impulse, Hartley wrote lengthy treatises on the subject.
Only in man did "unnatural" economic conditions exist which led
to the "prostitution" of pleasure beyond a "natural limit." Only
through chastity could a man build up "a feeling of respect for the
desire" and look upon "women as having the same desires and the
same self-respect." Only by restraint could he find "a dignity and
purpose" "in his own body, and in that of woman" that would
make his body "a fit house for the noblest soul, a house that may be
looked upon without shame."[326]

Scorning the men whose lives led them to easy indulgence,
Hartley pondered sex in his mind. He wrote, "Desire unfulfilled, if
acknowledged and given place and honor in our hearts and lives,
may by the pressure it exerts upon all our acts, be a means of
strength and grace that it could not be if it led by the straight road
to easiest fulfilment."[327] He insisted that the "low plane" of physical
gratification could exist in many environments—"self-manipula-
tion," brothels, concubinage, and even legal marriage. Intertwining
passion and puritanism, Hartley decided marriage itself was Puritan

hypocrisy when it hid non-procreative passion. By this reasoning, two unmarried soulmates who shared a "spiritual" love untarnished by sex were operating on a pretty high plane—certainly superior to that sort of sexually-tainted relationship that was supposed to exist between husband and wife. In the minds of Hartley and Margaret, then, any "insinuations of impurity" that might be thrown upon their life were unfathomable—for they felt they were standing on the highest ground of the "purity Commandment."[328] Playing with the sanctity of marriage, Hartley had fallen completely under the spell of Margaret Chase. And Mary resented it.

On Christmas Day 1908, Margaret sent Hartley, her "dearly Beloved," a gift and a note and a blessing. Quoting from holy scriptures, she reminded him to remain steadfast.[329] Then, on New Year's Day 1909, Margaret penned the following message to Hartley:

> *It is the New Year, Beloved. Let us play the whole world's new. Let us play that all about us is warm pulsing life—aching and pressing to express itself through us. Let us play that we can open ourselves to this life and with it build new bodies, strong and free and beautiful. Let us play all things are possible—that nature is undead plastic to human desire. Let us play that God is love, and joy is ours and all is well. Let us play that we are free, and*
>
> *Let us play to win.*[330]

CHAPTER SEVEN

Life Changes

As her relationship with Hartley grew worse, Mary put up a brave front. She refused to pine away at home for a wandering husband. Turning to her women friends, she began to cultivate an interest in feminism to take her mind off her marital troubles. "Women are people. That is perhaps the shortest possible explanation of what feminism stands for." She wrote: "Feminism is for women the same idea and the same program that men would surely adopt, if it so happened that men for centuries had been recognized by the world for the most part as some one's husband, some one's father, some one's son, or some one's lover... they would also insist most emphatically that these interests and obligations are not the whole of life, and should not represent a man's only claim to recognition . . ." She defended her brand of feminism as one based on *equality* and not *exclusivity*: "Feminism is not the lining up of women against men. Feminism does not imply that women want things as women. They only want to do things, have things, and feel things as people, as half the human race, on equal terms with the other half."

In response to Mary's moving on with her life, Hartley began to feel sorry for himself. It was January 1909, and he began to draw inspiration from Henry David Thoreau and poets Ernest Crosby and Walt Whitman. Twisting the words of Jesus of Nazareth to suit his own purposes, he rationalized family division in the name of "truth."

> *Think not that I came to send peace on the earth: I came not to send peace, but a sword. For I came to set a man at variance against his father, and the daughter against her mother, and the daughter-in-law against her mother-in-law: and a man's foes shall be they of his own household. He that loveth father or mother more than me is not worthy of me; and he that loveth son or daughter more than me is not worthy of me. And he that doth not take his cross and follow after me is not worthy of me. He that findeth his life shall lose it; and he that loseth his life for my sake shall find it.[331]*

In February 1909, just nine years after they were married, Hartley proposed to Mary divorce by mutual consent. In a grand act of magnanimity, he suggested that they "divide the children, one each." Mary objected to both ideas. Hartley's selfishness was unbelievable, as was his absolute disregard for the children. Carleton and Devon were absolutely devoted to one another—to separate them would be an untenable cruelty.

Furthermore, she did not think that Hartley's lifestyle was a good influence on the children. She could not accept "that it was possible for a child to live in association with the kind of thing going on in that camp and grow up with the idea that it was a perfectly permissible and sane kind of life." Mary still hoped to salvage the family.

That spring, at Mary's suggestion, Kate Ware Smith had a long talk with Hartley on the top floor of his office building in the Twentieth Century Club. Hartley told Kate that his love for Mrs. Chase was a "great reality in his life which he had no right to deny. …The marriage contract…did not preclude growth; this had come to him in the line of growth and had to be recognized and accepted."332 When Kate asked him if he acknowledged any "limits past which he had no right to go in the expression of his love with Mrs. Chase," he said he "thought not."333When Kate asked if he had a right to have a child by Mrs. Chase, Hartley said the question had not arisen but if it should he thought very likely he might feel that he had the right. Hartley scorned the idea of using the expression "platonic love," saying it was "ridiculous, there was no such thing." He said that "of course love involving the whole being—you could not separate it, you could not lack any element, it is not possible,—love was the whole thing, love was every part of you."334

Yet repeatedly, Hartley insisted that his love for Mary was as strong as it ever had been. So Kate asked Hartley if he would not at least acknowledge to her that perhaps his relations with Mrs. Chase might stand in the way of his ever assuming the husband's relations with his own wife and he said "very probably."335 Later, Kate would say that perhaps the problems would not have happened had both Hartley and Margaret "held to their old faith, that their emancipation from dogma has made it easier for them to accept new views of duty in many new directions." Having abandoned his old sensibilities so completely, Hartley was now without any recognizeable moral signposts whatsoever. He made up his own values to suit himself as he went along.

On another occasion, Anne Withington, a prominent social worker and personal friend of both Dennetts, tried her hand. She reminded him that his "personal pleasure" would mean that he could no longer be of service in various causes of reform. With much emotion, Hartley said that he had faced the fact that devoting himself to his love for Mrs. Chase meant that he might be lost to everything—his family, his influence. But he declared himself prepared to go on even if it meant his ruin—even if it ultimately meant death! Rambling on, he said that only he could judge his own standards of morality and dismissed her position as the "conventional view of morality." Anne left thinking the conversation "perfectly flabby." She commented, "You could not get anything from it."336

At the end of April 1909, Mary tried another tactic. Her lawyer, John Merriam, himself visited Dr. Chase in his home two times. Each time, he pointed to the unhappy condition of Mary's home, saying that Mary "objected strongly to the continued intimacy of her husband with your wife," and that the association, if continued, "was likely to wreck the Dennett home," and that "it was likely to wreck your home too." Mr. Merriam suggested that Dr. Chase take Margaret away. He told Dr. Chase of Mary Ware Dennett's "solicitude for her children," "her fondness for her home," and "the happiness that there had been in her home prior to Mr. Dennett's acquaintance with Mrs. Chase."337 The lawyer's efforts were futile.

As the efforts of her friends were obviously doing no good at all, Mary decided that marriage was indeed a "spiritual bond" and that theirs had been broken. She turned a cold shoulder to Hartley. In April 1909, arguments at the Dennett home reached a head. Hartley moved out. Moving into his brother Vaughan's shop, which was about a ten-minute walk from the Dennett home, Hartley took with him his architectural equipment, his safe, and quite a bit of furniture. He also closed down his home office. Meanwhile, Margaret came to Framingham a great deal. At all hours of the day and night Margaret could be seen looking out the windows of Vaughan's shop, walking down the driveway, and sometimes even going to Mary with a bundle and a check from Hartley.

Margaret could also be seen visiting the Tuckermans, who lived in the cottage across the lawn on Mary's property. For various reasons, the Tuckermans were under heavy obligations to both Hartley and the Chases. When the Tuckermans were financially strapped, the Dennetts had loaned them the cottage rent-free. And as Gus Tuckerman had been a Harvard classmate of Lincoln Chase, the Chases had done innumerable beneficial things for the family as well. The Dennett children and the Tuckerman children played together constantly. The Tuckermans were indebted to Hartley and the Chases. As a result, the Tuckermans sided strongly with Hartley, and they discussed the whole situation with the utmost freedom before their own small children. Despite Mary's utmost precautions to the contrary, Carleton and Devon were dragged into the discussion at intervals. And Hartley, Margaret, and Mrs. Tuckerman told Mary "very distinctly" they would always do this.

In late spring of 1909, Hartley had a long talk with Carleton, after which Mary found her son in tears. She asked him what was the matter. In a terrible state of nervousness, Carleton said, "I don't know what to do; father tells me all about how wrong you are and you don't say anything and I don't know what to do." According to Mary, Carleton said, "I wish father would not talk to me, and I don't know what to think." He was terribly worked up about it. Mary told her son that he should not have to think, that it was not fair to ask him, that he was too little to try to understand things which no child could understand. She suggested that he try to put it out of his mind and be as happy as he could. He could think it all out when he was grown, she explained, for that was the time when he could understand. Soothed by his mother's words, Carleton agreed.[338]

Yet Hartley continued to expose his children to Margaret. Carleton and Devon frequently joined the four Tuckerman children, the two Chase children, and the two Vaughan Dennett children at luncheon picnics held at "the headquarters" of what Hartley referred to as his "farming operation"—*i.e.* his brother Vaughan's shop. Invitations to Mary, however, had ceased. For Mary was against the picnics, protesting every time. Mary would later recall, "I did notice a definite effect on the children after each one, a perfectly reportable effect." Every single time Carleton and Devon came back, they would be full of questions—"questions which showed that there had been an attempt to appeal to their sympathy, to place the whole subject before their judgment." Although Mary conscientiously refused to speak ill of either Hartley or Margaret, the children would inevitably come back and ask her, "Mother, why don't you like Aunt Margaret?" And Mary would answer, "Why, who said I didn't like her?" At which point her children would respond, "Father did, and he said you *ought* to like her, that she was the best woman he ever knew, and mother, she *must* be good, because she made the loveliest party for us. . . ."[339]

Her patience finally exhausted, Mary decided the time had come to remove the children from Hartley and Margaret's pernicious influence. Her husband had lost his senses, and he had been brainwashed by another woman. Mary obtained a temporary order for exclusive custody. Hartley was furious. He had not been given notice until after the order was in effect. And then it was too late. The probate judge told Hartley that it was customary to grant such temporary custody without hearing until the subsequent session of court. Resenting Mary's action, Hartley regarded it as a great injustice. After leaving his father's company by court order, four-year old Devon had forgotten his boots at Vaughan's shop. It would be the last time Hartley would have free access to his children.

In response, Hartley decided he no longer had any responsibility for the family's bills. Mary continued to charge groceries to the family grocer and goods for the children and the home to the Jordan Marsh Company. Receipts accumulated. Several others bills piled up as well. Using the debts as ammunition, Hartley refused to pay them. He offered Mary "gifts" of money to help her out. But she refused. Insisting that Hartley recognize his responsibility as a father, she would not accept a "single cent" otherwise. That summer, he had all the family charge accounts changed from his name to Mary's. John Merriam, her lawyer, became indignant and, on Mary's behalf, took the case to the Middlesex Probate Court. After a series of hearings, in which Hartley refused to cooperate, a warrant was issued for his arrest. With the constable after him, Hartley retreated to Alstead.

At the beginning of August 1909, a disinterested observer, A.A. Merrill, took a closer look at Spirit Fruit and reported back to one of Mary's friends, Mr. George Page. Mr. Merrill discerned that Beilhart's doctrine implied the complete renunciation of individuality. Wrote Mr. Merrill, "This I do when I am asleep, and when I die I expect to renounce my individuality, but not before."[340] Delineating "the difference between the 'Spirit Fruiters' and sane people," he called their belief "delusional insanity in a wild form."[341] Said A.A. Merrill, "It is very evident then that the practical effect of these teachings is determined by the nature of the impulses in the believers. Those who have good impulses will be moved by the Spirit (as they say) to do good things and vice versa."[342] He continued, "Of course the complete renunciation of individuality is repugnant to me, one might as well bury oneself and become a vegetable at once, Beilhart not seeing any difference between the animal and the vegetable kingdom.

Nevertheless there are many who hold the fundamental beliefs of 'Spirit Fruit' and are only saved from absurdity by their common sense which will not let them carry their belief thru to its logical conclusion."343

After giving his opinion of Spirit Fruit, however, Mr. Merrill said he failed to "see how these teachings can have had any influence on the tragedy we spoke of. The party of the first part is a person of the strongest will & any renunciation of individuality here would be laughed at. It is possible that the "Spirit" might be invoked in order to dodge responsibility but not I think without an exhibition of hypocrisy such as any judge would fathom immediately."344

> *I really feel sorry for Mr. D. He seems to me to be a weak affectionate man hypnotized by an unscrupulous woman and he has failed to see that when he allowed Mrs. C to monopolize so much of his time & attention, he was injuring Mrs. D. quite regardless of any action which would give statutory grounds for divorce. This alone constitutes crime enough. As to Mrs. C's position it is a vicious one. Her claim is that if other people suffer from acts which, done to us would not cause us to suffer, their suffering is unreasonable, and hence may be ignored whenever we ourselves can gain thereby.*
>
> *Do your best to read this stuff and let me know what you and Mrs. P. think of it. It is, to a certain extent like a picture puzzle before it is put together but their [sic] is nothing here that has not been better said elsewhere and Beilhart could not put the pieces together to make a decent picture if he tried forever.345*

Meanwhile, Mary continued running the Dennett household alone—for without her husband's income she could not afford domestic help. She ran the pumping engine for the water supply, took care of the two gardens, and did what work she could to earn money outside of home. As a result, she fainted on the street several times, struggling very hard to keep going. Most likely, overwork combined with emotional stress were taking their toll. Mary's health was suffering again. Throughout it all, however, Hartley's manners were lofty, as he claimed that he was operating from the highest motives and that he himself should be the sole judge.

As the Dennetts's large circle of friends discussed the issues Hartley put forth, sympathy was going overwhelmingly toward Mary. Frank Patch, one of the Dennetts's most intimate friends, spent two or three hours on one day in most earnest conversation trying to bring Hartley to his senses. No luck. The Beard family, who had watched Hartley grow up from boyhood, cut off all contact with him.

Even Hartley's oldest friends were deserting him for Mary. Before long, his only brother, Vaughan, turned him out of his shop.

Beyond their own circle of friends, Mary's personal troubles were beginning to attract the attention of people she didn't even know. In August, Mary received a letter from Margaret's mother, Mrs. George Everett, who had gone up to Alstead for two weeks, to give Hartley and Margaret "some very plain facts." Carefree, walking around "scant of clothes," Hartley and Margaret had been enjoying their summer months in Alstead. Having eschewed "formal outdoors interests (like golf)" in favor of "walking, talking... and treepruning, etc.," Hartley attributed his growing sense of physical robustness to this "simplified and deepened life and thought."[346] Ignoring the restraining order, Hartley fantasized about having Carleton and Devon with him to work on "the farm." Margaret's mother told Hartley that she "was sure they wouldn't leave a *decent* Mother for such a Father." Very severely, Mrs. Everett told Hartley that he had "better ask [Mary] to forgive him & take him back, & try to live a decent life for the sake (if nothing more) of his children & the woman he promised before *God* to *love* & *protect* . . ."[347]

Mrs. Everett then took a walk with her daughter to remonstrate her for breaking up the Dennett family. Margaret responded, "But mother, I love him." To which her mother replied, "Nonsense—you just think you do!" She wrote to Mary emphatically in protest. "I do not *even try* to *shield* my own child from the severest criticism, which belongs to her & also to her husband for allowing it. Now do you feel free to tell me what you think better be done to break up the whole thing. I do not know the laws of N.H. but there must be some way to reach this *disgraceful* life. I feel so badly for *all the children* if I could only see you we would understand each other. Can't his parents do anything to yet save further *disgrace* & *sin*. Now I shall hope to hear what your opinion is on this matter." She signed as a *"friend."*[348]

On September 22, 1909, the Dennetts's custody hearing went to probate court. But Hartley refused to cooperate with the questioning. Insolent from the very beginning, he avoided straight answers for even the simplest questions. When asked, for example, where he resided, he responded, "I don't know what you mean by my residence . . ." And in a custody battle for his own children, he couldn't even manage to remember their birth dates![349] When questioned about his relationship with Mrs. Chase, Hartley recoiled. Judge Chamberlain advised him to answer the questions. But Hartley insisted that Merriam's questions were "impertinent." Unwilling to allow anyone else to represent his ideas, Hartley had refused to hire a lawyer.[350] At every question he balked. Hartley was finally told by the judge that he was not being "proper." At this, Hartley circumvented all other questions by saying that he couldn't "remember," that he didn't "understand," admitting to things which were "technically" true, but insisting on explaining his philosophy behind it. When Mr. Merriam read from Hartley's testimony from an earlier hearing, Hartley would not even admit to having said what was clearly on the court record.[351]

But John Merriam was persistent. He asked Hartley about Mrs. Chase, Spirit Fruit, Hartley's philosophy of marriage, his treatment of Mary, his non-payment of family bills, his income—the list went on. Hartley dodged question after question, insisting that Mr. Merriam was not after the "truth." Hartley insisted that his love for Margaret was a higher, purer "spiritual" love—and that he loved his wife as much as he ever did. Merriam asked whether or not these were all things he would teach his children. Hartley would only say that he and Merriam could not speak in the "same language" and that his marital troubles with Mary were simply due to an "essential spiritual difference."[352] Mr. Merriam tried to be more clear, by asking Hartley whether his marital difficulties had "to do solely with your relations with Mrs. Chase?" Again, Hartley would only admit, "Those [Mrs. Chase] are the terms under which this spiritual struggle is being fought out. It is unfortunate that it should be in such an uncomfortable phase of our life."[353]

Shortly after the trial, John Merriam assured Mary that her friends were "legion" and that they saw the matter in the "right light."[354] For by now, the private squabbles between Hartley and Mary had drawn widespread media interest. Front-page headlines covered the Boston newspapers. The lead article of the *Boston American* proclaimed in large bold letters: "SISTER-IN-LAW SAYS SOUL MATE HYPNOTIZED DENNETT." The front page of the *Record* declared: "'SOUL LOVE' DEFENCE OF HARTLEY DENNETT FAILS TO MOVE JUDGE." And emblazoned on the front page of the *Post*: "DENNETT LOVES BEST FRIEND'S WIFE, HE SAYS: COURT STARTLED, BUT DR. CHASE, THE HUSBAND, DECLARES IT PERFECTLY PROPER—ADMITS THEY KISS EACH OTHER IN PUBLIC."[355]

Dr. Chase seemed to be happy to do most of the explaining for Hartley and Margaret. Defending the pair, Dr. Chase said Mary "would monopolize the love of her husband simply because she was married to him." Claiming that Hartley was "clear sighted, an idealist and an upright and fearless man," Dr. Chase sanctioned the "friendship," declaring, "This love between Mrs. Chase and Mr. Dennett is pure. All the great teachers, Jesus, Emerson, taught that love is boundless. Mr. Dennett should have the right to show affection for women other than his wife." The doctor continued, "Mrs. Dennett is surrounded by ultra-conventional friends. They could not properly interpret the bond of sentiment that existed between my wife and Mr. Dennett."[356]

As a result of the trial, Mary's temporary custody order was made permanent. In addition, the judge ordered Hartley to pay child support—or at least the family bills which had been created before he had moved out. The case was so clear-cut, in fact, that the judge made the following statement:

> *Mr. Merriam, you need only discuss to me the question of how much he should contribute toward the support of his family. I have no other course than to decree the custody of the children to the mother. This respondent has not shown me any excuse, legal or moral, for the present estrangement between these two. He has not sought to and I do not believe he can. I will hear you on the single question of how much he should contribute to the support of those children that have been placed in the custody of the mother.[357]*

But when Hartley was asked about his income, he professed ignorance, saying, "I am not in the habit of balancing my books."[358] He claimed to earn only $25 a week. Having worked as his partner, Mary begged to differ. She knew that her husband could and did earn up to $5,000 a year—almost four times more than he claimed. When pressed again, he admitted that he might have made $5,000 one year, but said it was probably something like five years ago. He claimed that his gross income was now only about $2,500—estimating the cost of supporting his home at between $150 and $200.[359] Just a few months earlier, however, Hartley had won acclaim for remodeling the house of Harvard president Charles Eliot, and in architectural circles he had developed a reputation building houses for Dean Briggs, Dean Hurlbut, the Reverend Howard Brown, and other clients with elegant—and expensive—tastes.

Without custody of the children, however, Hartley was adamant. By mid-October, Mary was forced to pay the telephone bill in order to keep the telephone in her home.[360] Mr. Merriam arranged an agreement with Mr. Mundo, the head of the Collection Department of Jordan Marsh, to recognize Mary's right to purchase up to $100 in usual family necessities—and Mr. Merriam changed the account back to Hartley's name.[361] He then asked Mary to send him a list of all bills which Hartley "declined to pay."[362]

Indeed, Hartley's refusal to pay his family bills turned almost all public opinion against him. Friends flocked to Mary, offering emotional and financial support. Hartley was called "faithless," "dishonorable," and "pitiful." A few questioned his sanity. One of his former friends sent him a letter:

> *Your case is considered, as you doubtless know, a monstrous and unnatural one. I have heard it discussed by all kinds of people, people who know you or Mrs. Chase, or people who did not, and never once have I heard anything but indignation and contempt for you three [Dr. Chase]. Before I knew of your last act, I had a lingering hope that I should hear, in the general discussion, some voice raised to justify you, or excuse you. I even consulted experts in sociology, like Ms. Gilman, hoping that persons so radical could offer some explanation that would place you and Mrs. Chase in a better light. The verdict has been unanimous against you.*
>
> *Mary Hutcheson Page [signed][363]*

The Boston *Record* published an editorial:

> *The plane of "love" existing between Hartley Dennett, husband of Mrs. Hartley Dennett, and Mrs. H.L. Chase may be idealized and purified to the degree taught by Emerson, as agreed by the affectionate pair and the extraordinary husband of Mrs. Chase. But the court takes the matter-of-fact view that when a husband's affection is bestowed so baldly in other directions there is no question that the children belong to the woman who is deserted on this puerile basis. Breaking up a home in this fantastic way is without legal or moral excuse, and the judge properly penalized it so far as he could.*

Then Carleton came to his mother again. As Mary recalled, this time he was "trembling all over and so white I thought he was about to faint."[364] He had been with the Tuckerman children again. The whole family had just had a long talk together, with all the children there, and Hartley had been there as well. They had told him that Hartley was going to be sent to prison and that it was Mary's fault. From what her son told her, Mary realized that the discussion had revolved around the penalty for contempt of court. But Carleton could not be calmed down. He was in such a worked-up condition that Mary was forced to telephone a friend down at the seashore so she could take Carleton away with her that same day. That night, after he was put to bed, he was hysterical, screaming for hours. As Mary later recalled, Carleton would sleep a few minutes, and then wake up screaming, and then sleep again. It was midnight before Mary could quiet him down again, but gradually, Mary worked the fear out of him. Mother and son spent two weeks away, but it took months of careful guarding to prevent his fears from resurfacing. Understandably, Mary asked the Tuckermans to leave.

Mary wrote to Hartley, assuring him quite emphatically that she was not planning to take any legal steps against him that would result in his imprisonment.[365] She did let him know, however, that her health prevented her from doing the sort of work which would allow her to support the children. And as work for women was hardly plentiful, all she could find was a "possible position for part-time service." Without a "reliable assurance" from Hartley that he was willing to "meet his family obligations," Mary explained, she would have to give up their house and pay all bills pending with what was left in the bank—leaving her without "a single cent in the world." She stated, "I beg you, in all fairness, to be explicit about these things, for the very best I can possibly do by the children, alone, is so little, that I need all the help you can see clearly enough to give, and need it *now*."[366]

In answer, Hartley attempted to place the burden of guilt back on her: "If . . . holding me true to your conception of my responsibilities is what you think is your duty, do it with all your might. Be willing to starve for it...don't teach [your principles] to the children or recommend them to others so long as they don't work for you."[367] He continued, "I shall try not to let your action in that work compel me into anything that I don't think right, and insofar as I succeed in this I shall be able to take the knocks without resentment."[368]

By the end of October, Hartley cashed in his life insurance and used the money to wipe out the mortgage on the Dennett home. Of the small balance remaining, he used half for a "wise provision" for his own future, and turned over the other half to Mary for her future. "This latter, for the sentiment of it, I had in mind to deposit in a savings bank for you, but that appears to be a thing for which your own signature is needed; and anyway I guess it is a better sentiment to leave it all to your choice."[369] He enclosed a check for $250.

Thinking the matter settled, Hartley was irritated when John Merriam continued to send him bills. By 4 December 1909, Hartley decided that his "conscience" would no longer allow him to send any money to his family at all. He wrote an angry letter to Mary, which would later be used as a court exhibit.

Dear Mary—

I have received from you, through John Merriam, two of the bills I had returned to you; and I return them again; and again ask you to contract no further debts in my name—It can only bring annoyance and contention to you and me and the dealers. . . .

You suggested that I should like to have you "whitewash" me. It is not so. I want you to be morally firm, and I want the children to have the example of whatever sincerity and vigor you can put into your life. But I want my own moral life, and the children have an inalienable right to my life and teaching;—and you are not to be judge of my soundness any more than I am to be of yours. It must have been for some purpose that our children were born to you and me. You need not—you ought not—stand for or take part in any action of mine which you cannot honestly accept: But I belong, no less than you. I have a charter by which I exist and grow, as valid as your own. I want that respected, and it is to you a moral necessity that you respect it. I want no "whitewashing. . . ."

We can never now build up together the domestic life that was open to us before the persecution of me began; it is not probable that we could have done it out of the experience we then had (For it seems as if the agony attending our becoming independent of one another must be the measure of that spiritual need of independence, & I am sure that not until the agony is gone out of it will its work be done and we be free to love each other rightly, in equality.)—but we can at anytime begin to have a right relationship, with more love and more sympathy for each other and our fellows than we have ever had. There need be no recriminations and no regrets. No such relationship is possible without mutual respect, and respect and censorship are not compatible. So long as you look upon me as a bundle of qualities responsible to you by any agreement whatsoever, some of which you may call good because you happen to understand and value them, and some bad because your experience does not include a knowledge of them; and upon yourself as obliged to kill those you have named evil—so long as you have that irreverence for a life that has responsibility to God as imperative as your own, you will block the way to such co-operation, and to yr own possibility of happiness. . . .

With steady love,

Hartley[370]

That was it. Mary had had it with Hartley. She had no time for his self-righteous letters. She penned a response:

Hartley—

I have not had time to answer your letter of Dec. 4, till now, and I shall never again take the time from useful work to answer such rubbish. These things, however, you need to know, now.

The attachment of your bank account for the payment of the dry goods and grocery bills of the past few months was done entirely by the firms concerned, and I had absolutely nothing to do with it. That is now a matter between them and you.

I shall never again ask you to pay a single bill for myself or the children. The obligation is still yours, but there will be no demands upon you, except from your own conscience, neither shall I receive any more of what you call "gifts."

You can get no satisfaction whatever from attempting to believe that I have done what I know to be wrong. I have done exactly what I thought right at the time, and I am more than ever certain that you and the pernicious life you are leading, are a poison, from which it is my duty to protect the children in every way, now and always.

It is true that we can not again work together, upon any ground. You have successfully blotted yourself out of our life—mine and the children's—and nothing can reconstruct it again, not even your complete repentance. I hope that may come, but in any case, you are no longer a possible factor in my happiness, and never can be.

Happiness, like health, is coming back to me in leaps and bounds, and is based on things so big and permanent, that it makes you seem a mere speck on the distant horizon.

I hope, for the sake of your own soul, and the relief of society in general, that some new wholesome life can grow up in you, and conquer the rot you are walking in now, and I hope that time may come soon.

My utter lack of respect for you today, does not prevent my love and gratitude for the life that was ours when you were a man. I miss that, just as I should have missed you, if you had died three years ago, but I am spending no time dwelling in the past.

Instead, I am completely absorbed in the present and future of the boys and my work, and I shall have no time for any more of your Pharisaical letters.

In January 1910, Mr. Merriam brought another suit against Hartley for refusing to pay the family grocer, Mr. Glover. Upon hearing this, Hartley explained the "matter" to Glover before the suit could come to court, leaving it "to his sense of honor" not to pursue the matter further—"with all chances that by doing right he might lose." For Hartley "would give no promise" that he "would settle the bill." Unfortunately, noted Hartley, Mr. Glover "did not dare to halt it lest he lose his money"—something which Hartley simply could not understand. So against Hartley's wishes, Annie O. Dennett, who could not be terribly proud of her son, paid the bill.

In June 1910, Hartley was sued by Jordan Marsh for non-payment of another bill. Again, as in the 1909 custody trial, Hartley refused to hire an attorney, allowing no one to speak for him but himself. Indeed, he was not even allowed to testify, for after his last experience with Mr. Merriam, Hartley had decided to make a "conscientious objection" to taking the oath.

> *I cannot rightly contract beforehand to tell the whole truth when it is not desired by the lawyers or permitted by the Court; or even to tell the truth where, as I have found, a truthful answer to the question becomes by the subtle suggestion of the lawyers part of a false structure beyond the control of the witness, who has been the innocent partner in its construction though by no means its real author. I know by experience with my wife's attorney, who is by no mere coincidence the attorney of this plaintiff, the nature of the question "have you stopped beating your mother-in-law?" and I cannot undertake to tell the truth under conditions in which I know I shall be thwarted in my effort.[371]*

Hartley's "conscientious objection" gave the hearing a farcical quality. Aunt Lucia and Mary were both present in the courtroom. A delivery boy from Jordan Marsh identified the purchase slips. Hartley was given a chance to cross-question, but refused. Then, because he would not take the oath, Hartley was not allowed to make a statement. By default, the case went to Jordan Marsh (and Mary's lawyer), John Merriam.

It did not end there, however. Hartley still refused to pay the bill. So he was removed to poor debtor court, where he attended one session. But as he refused to answer many questions there, as well, he was given another date on which to bring proper replies. This time, Hartley "decided to state at once to the Court" that he "would not claim to be a poor debtor but simply could not morally pay the judgment of the Court." But as he had already refused to take the oath, he was unable to say even that! So the case went by default again—with an order for Hartley's imprisonment issued to John Merriam.

Under court order, Mr. Merriam was able to remove about eighty or ninety dollars from Hartley's Old Colony Trust Company bank account for part settlement of the Jordan Marsh debt. Outraged upon discovering this, Hartley would not open a bank account in Boston again, "since I am not allowd [*sic*] to determine the disposition of my money—and as another result I gave up money earning for the same reason."[372]Consequently, Hartley became a "farmer."

He wrote a letter to Eben Jordan attacking the Jordan Marsh Company for its part in the "conspiracy" against him. Indignant that Jordan Marsh would bring him to court over such a "small loss," he criticized the company for standing by its collection policy. Hartley asserted, "By this decision the Jordan Marsh Co. accepts the position of chief instrument in a personal persecution. . . ." Quoting the General Manager—who had told Hartley, "All we want is our money"—Hartley continued, "'I cannot yet believe that this statement that 'all we want is our money' represents the last word of a house that must have been built up on honor as well as on profits." Hartley asked Jordan Marsh to withdraw from the fray as "my wife has ample legal power to continue her harrassment of me openly and in her own name."[373]

In the meantime, Hartley, who was now living with the Chases, tried to entice Carleton and Devon to come live with him by offering them frequent gifts of toys and candy. But he continued to balk at paying for their food and coal—leaving Mary to scrape for the essentials for herself and the children. Said Mary, "Naturally little children appreciate baseballs, books and candies more than they do coal and bread and clothing, and they did not know that their father was giving them the one and refusing them the other. They did not suffer, so why should they see?"[374]

Mr. Merriam advised Mary to ask the court to limit Hartley's right to visits and correspondence for the children's own welfare. By September 1910, the insurance policy for the Framingham house had expired and Hartley wouldn't pay the $4.50 due C.S. Adams & Co. The Jordan Marsh bill for $138.20 was still unpaid, and Hartley was found to have defaulted in the municipal court. Another order for his arrest was issued. But Hartley successfully evaded the constable and managed not to serve the order.

Mary was forced to pay mounting insurance bills. Taxes piled up. It was not until a full year later, on 29 September 1911, that Mary finally paid the balance of the Jordan Marsh bill—with provisions to allow the court to collect from Hartley and pay Mary back, if it could do so.

To meet her financial obligations, Mary had found a salaried position with the Massachusetts Suffrage Association. By 1910, she was beginning to gain nationwide status as a suffragist, and she was asked to take over as corresponding secretary of the National Woman Suffrage Association (NAWSA)—fourth on the masthead. Little Devon appeared on the front page of *The Woman's Journal*, a newspaper founded by Lucy Stone and Henry B. Blackwell, carrying a placard which read, "I WISH MOTHER COULD VOTE."[375] The President of the NAWSA, Dr. Anna Howard Shaw, personally requested that Mary relocate to New York City to take over the coordination of the Literature Department and organize the branch offices of the nation's largest suffrage organization. Mary hesitated, unwilling to make such a drastic move away from her children for she did not want to uproot them away from their home. But Dr. Shaw, Jane Addams, M. Carey Thomas, and others framed the invitation in terms of Mary's "duty to the cause." They even offered Mary a higher-paying salary than the one she had received in Boston. That did it. Mary was broke. She accepted the position, and in April 1910, she moved to New York.

In Manhattan, all Mary could afford was a tiny walk-up studio on the fourth floor of the Dearborn, on 350 West 55th Street. The rent was reasonable, but the room, with kitchenette, was so small that if both boys visited her at the same time, one would have to stay across the street at the Mills Hotel: 25¢ a night; lights out by 10 PM, vacate the room by 6:30 AM The small room would be her home for nearly a decade. And the separation from her children was difficult—Mary went up to Framingham every few weeks to spend weekends with them, and during the summer she took off an entire month.

To make ends meet, Mary rented the Framingham house to her childhood friend Kate Ware Smith and her family. Kate moved into the Framingham house in the fall of 1909. At first, Carleton and Devon went under the care of Mary's sister, Clara, who was then living in Holliston, a town near Framingham. And Aunt Lucia and Uncle Ned took an active interest in them as well, visiting their grandnephews often. But before long, Kate offered to watch over the two children.

Mary enrolled Carleton, and later Devon as scholarship students at the newly founded Danforth School, a boarding school in Framingham Center primarily for young boys between eight and sixteen. Living with the Smith family, Carleton and Devon began as day students. Carleton was the school's first pupil. In September 1910 he became a boarding student, and in September 1912, Devon enrolled as a boarder as well. The master, James Chester Flagg, was an old family friend of the Dennetts and a Dartmouth graduate formerly connected with the Hackley School and Milton Academy. At Mary's request, Mr. Flagg assiduously protected the boys from any knowledge about the newspaper notoriety of their parents' separation.

During the time Carleton and Devon were in Kate's care—about two and a half years—Hartley made nine or ten visits to the children.[376] After each of Hartley's visits, Kate observed a partisan spirit in the children, a sort of free discussion of which side was right, showing the matter had been put up to them. Even Kate's own son told her Hartley had explained to them that everybody was mistaken, and that he, Hartley, was wholly right.

Kate also noticed that Hartley was affecting her own efforts to teach the children parental obedience. One day, when Kate Smith came home, she found her own child, Edmund, who was the same age as Carleton, gone. Looking for him at Vaughan's shop, about a half a mile from the house, she found Edmund there with Hartley and several other people. Hartley greeted Mrs. Smith as she came in and asked her not to be too hard on her son Edmund. She said, "but he has disobeyed me and I shall have to punish him."[377] On the way back to the house, Edmund ran on ahead as Hartley and Kate talked.

Hartley said he was not responsible for Edmund's disobeying his mother because he had given Edmund free choice—and every child should have the right to choose between right and wrong. Knowing full well that some would consider him crazy, Hartley said, "I told Edmund that he must decide for himself whether he would disobey you or not." Kate spoke with Hartley about his dealings with the children. She told him that she thought it was very unwise to offer such a decision as he offered her son, that he ought not to discuss problems between him and Mary in front of the children. Hartley claimed that children ought to be taught from earliest childhood to decide those points. Kate said, "when you talk these things over with them you are taking an unfair advantage; they are too young; it excites them; they are too young to judge; they are not able to."

Then Kate told him she had to have some sort of assurance that if she were to take care of his children, he would not take them away if ever he happened to come in her absence. Hartley said he would give her no assurance, not with any children, particularly his own children. When they arrived at the house, Kate's husband George came home, and Hartley laughingly said to George, "Kate has been trying to persuade me to compromise with the devil, but I won't do it."[378]

Hartley also told Kate that he deplored the dilapidation of the Dennett home, saying it was a "great" and "keen" grief to him that he was unable to do anything to help maintain a place which he loved. Kate said, "You know perfectly well you are at liberty to help, and why don't you help Mary keep up the place if you feel that way?" Hartley explained that in appealing to the court, Mary had "gone against her conscience" and had "made it absolutely impossible" for him to cooperate any further with her. He explained that any financial contribution from him would amount to "taxation without representation" and he could submit to "no slave labor."[379]

Meanwhile, as Hartley and Margaret lived together in Alstead, Dr. Chase stayed in Brookline—emerging as Hartley's personal champion. In December 1910, the doctor visited Edwin Mead at his office, walking in with a "lofty and scolding" demeanor. Wanting to discuss Hartley, Dr. Chase asked to open with prayer. The request seemed totally out of place. Noting the doctor's pose soon wore out, however, Ned decided he was "a serious, suffering man, struggling, through appalling obfuscation, to get at some right course."[380] Mead found him pitiable, and told him so. But Dr. Chase wrote a letter to Mary in New York City, claiming that "Mr. Mead and I" mutually felt that Mary was the one to blame for "continuing the present condition."

If that weren't bad enough, Uncle Ned soon heard reports about the doctor spewing even worse sentiments about Mary. The doctor had called Mary a "she-devil" and an altogether "shrewish, artful, jealous, and offensive" woman who was herself responsible for the estrangement between her husband and herself. When the slurs reached the his ears, Edwin Mead was incensed. Provoked to write "the sharpest letter I ever wrote to anybody," Mead told Dr. Chase he was "desperately and intolerably wicked" and it made no difference whether he was "simply reflecting the feelings of your wife and repeating words which she has put into your mouth" or if he was "talking in this nefarious way on your own initiative, trying to excuse your wife by blackening the character of the woman she has so foully wronged."

Uncle Ned put it clearly. "I consider you unworthy of the society of gentlemen," he said, "You told me that no word was to be said against Mrs. Dennett's character. You boasted that you "judged" nobody, although I have seldom heard more bitter or reckless judgments of people expressed in a brief time than by you in your call here the other day."[381] Before long, Uncle Ned decided that Dr. Chase had lost his mind. Dr. Chase denied ever having made the "she-devil" remark—even though it was corroborated by two reliable witnesses. Sputtered Dr. Chase, "If I had done so, would Mr. Cummings have listened to me or spoken with me another moment? No Sir! Or would I have wished to write or see Mrs. Dennett? No Sir! Or would Mr. Cummings have thought it possible for me to speak with Mrs. Dennett's uncle after such remarks, if made? Of course not." Dr. Chase painted a completely ludicrous picture of Hartley's "suffering":

> *Last evening the big constable, with his loaded revolver, called here again to arrest and put in prison your nephew, Hartley. The constable came to try to do so by force a stupid, wicked thing that is called by some "legal"! A thing that you and your niece and your lawyer deliberately worked for and still are working for, tho' using the Jordan Marsh Co. to hide behind in your persecution of your nephew, whom* you *know* in your soul, *is as* pure *and honest and* true *now as he always has been!*

Dr. Chase closed his letter melodramatically, "Oh, Friend Mead, in the words of Tolstoy, ere it is too late,—'Bethink you!'"[382]

In Edwin D. Mead's opinion, as a result of "his interminable wanderings in a morass of falsehood and masquerade," Dr. Chase had "lost all power of telling the truth, of reporting anything accurately, or even of remembering what he said half an hour back."[383] Said Uncle Ned, the "trouble now is more with his wornout brain than anything else."[384] When Mary got wind of the situation, she penned a personal response to Dr. Chase as well.

> *Dr. H. Lincoln Chase,—*
>
> *I do not care to have any talk whatever with you.*
> *You had your chance in the beginning to be a man, but you lacked either the courage or the intelligence or both to act like one, and now you and others are reaping the consequences of your criminal weakness.*
> *You and you alone could have saved it all; and when you wake up and realize that, it will be all the punishment you will ever need.*
>
> *Mary Ware Dennett*[385]

Away in Alstead, Hartley still thought about his sons. "I long so to watch you grow.... A boy can become each year so much braver and stronger, and so steady and true. That is what I want you to be.

It is good to be called true; it is better to be true. Sometimes you have to choose which it shall be."[386] And in another letter, "We must love each other and remember each other. Tell Carleton about me, and tell him I love him."[387] Hartley longed to be there with his children. "I think of you a great deal and I love you as a father and a big brother."[388] Asking for the details of their lives—were they breaking windows with baseballs? Eating cake with candles?—He wanted to make an imprint on their lives. "Don't forget your drawing. I want bye and bye to teach you to make houses—you and Carleton might make them together."[389]

Over the years, Hartley celebrated special days like his own birthday and Christmas by writing to his children. He attempted to counsel his sons, constantly writing to them of Jesus Christ—"that Wonderful Conqueror, of lowly birth and outcast life and despised death"[390]—with whom he so clearly identified. Carleton's birthday fell two days before Christmas, which helped prompt Hartley to write. "The birthday of the wonderful man who is said to have begun his life in an old inn-stable, who preached and lived in such sincerity that his neighbors, and even his family and friends, were angry at him, yet held himself true and fine even among pharisees and those others called sinners; and finally died despised and rejected except by a little handful of humble hearts." Feeling sorry for himself, Hartley connected his own plight with the martyrdom of Jesus Christ. "Ask your mother to tell you about him, and someday I want to talk to you of him too,—he is so much in my mind, and the things he said and did have come to be so very real to me." And he sent a little note to Mary.

Dear Mary—

I get up this morning with thoughts all of you and of our little children. On this day I want to send you my love and my blessing.

Always,

Hartley[391]

But he had made his choice. Living with Margaret as a farmer in Alstead, supported financially by Dr. Chase, hiding from the constable who was after him to pay child support—Hartley had succeeded in alienating his wife and all those connected with his children. For not only did Kate Smith disapprove of him, but headmaster James Flagg had lost all respect for Hartley as well.

Hartley was not welcome at the Danforth School. The only way he could see his children was to arrange his trips to Framingham so that he would be on the same car as the students when they returned home from school. And Devon reported that Hartley had asked him to slip off without its being known at home and join him in Alstead. When Mary found out, she was unnerved. She asked Devon what he had said, and he answered, "I told him I couldn't, 'cause Auntie Kate expected me at home."[392]

When confronted, Hartley denied the accusation. "I have never tried to persuade either of my children to go to East Alstead with me. They listen eagerly when I tell them of East Alstead, and I hope they understand that my arms are open for my children. If an order of exclusive custody could carry with it annihilation of a father's love for his offspring, this crime of the State against the family would indeed come to its own."[393] He defended the meetings as "natural associations" with his own children "under most trying conditions, with their mother in full possession of her exclusive legal control, and jealous of my least communication with them."[394]

Boarding students most of the year at the Danforth School, Carleton and Devon spent vacations at the home of their Aunt Clara Hill in Newton Highlands and at their great Aunt Lucia's in Boston. Kate Smith was planning to move, and the Framingham house would soon stand empty. Consumed by her work in the suffrage movement, Mary began to be concerned about Hartley's influence on Carleton and Devon. Ordinarily, the Court permitted a father to visit his children, and such matters were frequently regulated by decree upon application of either parent. The 1909 probate court ruling of the Dennett case was silent on this matter, however. Scrimping to provide for her two sons, Mary would not lose the children she had almost sacrificed her life to bear. On 11 May 1912, she filed for a divorce from Hartley and sued for permanent exclusive legal custody of Carleton and Devon.

CHAPTER EIGHT

The Trial

he divorce hearings, which started in February 1913 and lasted exactly one month, fascinated the press. Both the Chases and the Dennetts were well known in the Boston area. Their friends and families were all prominent Bostonians involved in progressive social causes. And the custody battle four years earlier had placed an indelible stamp of notoriety in the minds of the public. Divorce was almost unheard of among the middle and upper classes in the early part of the century, and the particular scandal connected with the Dennett-Chase case did more than just raise New England eyebrows. "Yellow journalists" flocked to the courthouse where a story was readily played out for them. Mary had always been sensitive about the idle talk of friends—never mind sensationalist newspaper stories. For her, the nightmare would prove numbing.

Dr. Chase was introduced as the fifty-year old society doctor, whose prominence in Brookline had "won him entry to society on every hand." Providing physical details to satisfy the readers (some of which were created by imaginative copywriters), he was described as slim, over six feet tall, with red whiskers and a mustache. Hartley was portrayed as the doctor's forty-year-old "best friend" (he was actually forty-two), well built and of medium height, who was regarded by his friends as a "brilliant conversationalist." Margaret, the siren, was the thirty-five-year old brunette (she was really forty-five) living in a sumptuous home that had served as "the gathering place of society." And Mary, the ageless wife of the architect who was bringing the charges, was characterized as being "very prominent in the club life among women." A few newspapers added, "She has long been regarded as one of the most zealous of the militant suffragists and has been a member of the 'flying wedge' band that toured Massachusetts recently."[395]

As the Dennett-Chase debacle reached its final chapter, the 1913 trial of *Dennett v. Dennett* brought out extreme passions on all sides. Judge Hall, who had been assigned to the case, asked former senator

F.W. Dallinger to act as "referee" at the hearings in deciding who would be the better parent. Ordered to get to the real truth of the matter, Mr. Dallinger was given "full authority to investigate in any way he saw fit." In addition to the traditional courtroom hearing, Dallinger could and did make use of oral and written statements as well as personal visits. Margaret did not make a statement, and she was also the only one of the four who declined to testify in any of the hearings. As for personal visits, Mr. Dallinger went so far as to visit the Danforth School in Framingham, Clara Hill's home in Newton Highlands, the Mead home in Boston, the Chase home in Brookline, the Chase farm in Alstead, and even a little one-room schoolhouse in Alstead where Hartley proposed to send the children.

In addition, Edwin D. Mead mustered up all his influence as former editor of *New England Magazine* and current director of the World Peace Foundation to ensure that Hartley would not only be denied custody but also be legally prevented from having *any* access to his children at all. Before the proceedings even started, Mr. Mead wrote a personal letter to Dallinger arguing that Hartley's influence was so pernicious that even a few weeks with him and Margaret in Alstead "would be detrimental in the highest degree" and that the "whole beneficial training of the year would be fatally prejudiced in the contrary influences of a few summer weeks." Calling Hartley's "whole course from beginning to end...a course of lawlessness," Mr. Mead insisted that Mary be granted a divorce and given full exclusive legal custody of the children on the grounds of desertion.[396]

Not to be outdone, Hartley issued a statement "for the enlightenment of the Court" (which he also made available to the newspapers) to announce that the real nature of his marital difficulties had never appeared in court. Basically repeating his earlier arguments in a rambling treatise of excuses, he rejected what he called "the technical ground of desertion" by explaining that Mary's "unfriendly" and "scornful" "atttitude and behavior" had forced him to "remove [him]self" from a "morally impossible relationship."[397] He claimed that Mary objected to his conduct not on grounds of immorality, but because she felt left out. The question was chiefly one of "individual sovereignty," he claimed, as opposed to "the marriage contract selfishly interpreted." Weaving in and out of a variety of fantastical assertions,[398] Hartley claimed it was a case where "a mother's desire for control" had come "to look, as it were in a mirage, like a father's infidelity." Not really saying anything new, he finally "revealed" moral incompatibility to be the real ground for divorce rather than the "untrue and technical one of desertion."399

John Merriam was the counsel for Mary Ware Dennett. Fred L. Norton was the counsel for William Hartley Dennett—for Hartley had finally relented enough to hire an attorney.400 The question before Mr. Dallinger was: Who would be the better parent, Mary or Hartley?

Mary herself was the first to take the stand. She gave the facts, as plainly as possible, neither embellishing her statements nor leaving out pertinent particulars. Next came Dr. Frank W. Patch, a Framingham resident for twenty-five years and a long-time intimate of both Dennetts. Formerly president of both the Massachusetts and the national homeopathic medical societies, a professor at the Boston University School of Medicine, and owner of a sanitarium called "Woodside Cottages" in Framingham, Dr. Patch testified that "there could be no possible criticism of [Mary's] character as a mother."401 Mr. Dallinger interrupted the questioning to inquire whether she was a "womanly woman?" and a "domestic woman?" And Frank Patch answered to both, "Thoroughly so."

Then came Edwin D. Mead, who took special care to point out that Mary's case was not one of simple "marital incompatibility." Instead, said Uncle Ned, Mary was suing on "a gross case of desertion, of desertion for another woman."402 Unwilling to let Hartley pretend it was anything less, he praised Mary's mothering, saying, "Her whole attitude has been heroic and saintly."403 Unasked, he gave his own little speech in court, emphasizing that Hartley had failed to contribute "one cent to the care of the children" at a time when Mary, "weakened by sickness...threw herself into the breach and with a devotion unparalleled has taken care of those children of hers." Uncle Ned declared, "I never knew two boys more profoundly affectionate toward each other or two boys whose devotion to their mother was more of a religion. To separate those boys from each other and from the mother would be cruelty incredible."404 In case the court did not understand, Edwin Mead managed to get in a last word. "The question is, what would be the alternative; where would they be placed? He is living with this woman up in New Hampshire. Are they to be taken into the charge of this woman for whom he has deserted his wife?"405

Mary's remaining four witnesses—friend Katharine Ware Smith, mother Vonie, reformer Anne Withington, and schoolmaster James

Chester Flagg—each explained their part in the scenario in like manner. Kate Smith, Vonie, and Anne Withington described their conversations with Hartley; Mr. Flagg talked about the Danforth School and its suitability for children. Recalled for additional questioning, Mary spoke about the negative effects of Hartley's visits on the children. Mr. Dallinger then injected, "After the decree of the Probate Court what, if anything, has Mr. Dennett done toward paying for the maintenance and education of the children?" Mary could only answer, "Nothing whatever." And she also emphasized she was not claiming that Hartley had been "guilty of sexual immorality with Mrs. Chase."

Unsurprisingly, the picture that emerged was that of a husband who had flagrantly deserted his wife and children at a time when the wife was in ill health. Despite the efforts of friends and family, the husband was unremorseful and would not be called back to his home. It became quite clear that Mary had been quite an able mother and wife. The Dennetts, by all accounts, had shared an "ideal home." Even Hartley's attorney, Mr. Norton, was not able to— and did not try to— make any negative contentions about Mary's character. Hartley's only defense was to make it appear that the couple's differences were simply a difference of opinion, "a difference similar to that in religion between orthodoxy and heterodoxy, between Congregationalism and Unitarianism."[406]

In order to make this point, Mr. Norton introduced Hartley's witnesses—of which there were about a dozen, almost twice as many as Mary had. But unlike Mary's witnesses, most of Hartley's witnesses had little involvement in the entire affair. With the exception of Dr. Chase and Hartley himself, few had known Hartley for very long, and almost none had ever even met Mary. Hartley's own mother and brother did not support him. Instead, just about every single one of Hartley's witnesses was an acquaintance he had met in the course of his association with Margaret, a servant in the Chase household, or employed by Hartley for work.

Of note, Robert Bakeman described himself as having been "very intimately acquainted" with both Hartley and Margaret for about four years.[407] A frequent houseguest at the log cabin, Bakeman considered the Alstead camp an "ideal place for children."[408] Asserting that Hartley behaved with children exactly as he wished he himself could behave as a father, Bakeman noted as did other witnesses that Hartley was extremely attentive and interested in children, and that children responded by constantly looking to

Hartley for advice. Bakeman declared that if anything should ever happen to him, next to going to the sister of his wife, he would love for his two children, a four-year-old girl and a two-year-old boy, to be brought up by Hartley Dennett. Under cross-examination, Bakeman refused to condemn Hartley's living with a married woman. He hinted at some basic philosophy, but he could not give it. He did not give any straight answers, and instead said he could only answer in a long discussion—of which he had apparently had many with Hartley.

Hartley's next witness was also a former houseguest. Yet Alfred S. Edwards, state secretary of the Socialist Party of New Hampshire, admitted that he only had interacted with Hartley and Margaret for a total of about a half dozen times. Upon cross-examination, Mr. Merriam asked Edwards, "Has it ever occurred to you that the situation in the home in Alstead as you have seen it is at all abnormal?" Edwards answered, "I should say that the situation is different."[409] Edwards went on to elaborate on his feeling about the "conduct" between Hartley and Margaret, saying that "under the circumstances," he felt their cohabitation was "absolutely proper."[410]

As the witnesses followed, one after another, each testified to Hartley's engaging quality with little children, and denied the immorality of his life with Margaret Chase. Two of the witnesses had only known Hartley for a matter of months: Ada E. Chevalier, a Brookline teacher boarding in the Chase home, sixteen months; Claude C. Smith, boys director of the Young Men's Christian Association (YMCA) in New Bedford, Massachusetts, eighteen months. One witness, Claude Smith, hedged in his testimony upon learning of Hartley and Margaret's mutual profession of love for one another.

Hartley's witnesses who had known him for longer periods of time were all superficial business acquaintances. There was a grocer who had never even seen Hartley and Margaret together and who had never had any extended or particularly intimate conversation with Hartley about his family affairs.[411] All he knew was that as Hartley worked on his house, the architect would often say that he could not allow his personal liberty to be dictated.[412] A hydraulic sales engineer who had visited Hartley about eight or ten times on short business calls had seen Hartley with the two Chase children. This was enough for him to testify that Hartley's influence on the children had to be "unquestionably good," since the children seemed to like him.[413] Finally, Henry H. Adams, a carpenter and builder employed by Hartley for nearly a decade, took a "mind-my-own-business" approach to the relationship between Hartley and Margaret. "That is for them to say; not me. I lay no law down for anybody; I live a law unto my own self and they should do the same." He continued, "I give everyone their own privilege of doing as they like, good or bad."[414]

Then Dr. H. Lincoln Chase took the stand. At first, Dr. Chase was very cavalier. He emphasized that Hartley only moved into the Chase home "when legal proceedings were taken up against him; when the attitude was positively hostile...."[415] Calling the relations between Hartley and Margaret morally pure and proper, he asserted, "there is no suspicion."[416] The "love" between Hartley and Margaret was "true" and "deep," he said, it did not describe a "sexual affection" but an "intellectual friendship."[417]

He then began to ramble on somewhat incoherently about "our little country place."[418] Testifying that he was "glad" to have his children under Hartley's care, he admitted that his own children, Heman and Mary, seemed to "think almost as much of [Hartley] as they do of me, possibly more;—he is with them more."[419] Very piously, Dr. Chase claimed that Hartley was teaching his children the two essential ingredients for success in life: self-control and self-support. This was a particularly ironic statement given that Dr. Chase was, in effect, supporting Hartley's new life as a farmer. Overlooking this fact, however, he blamed Mary again and again for bringing about litigation. Dr. Chase stated, "I...tried as hard as any man could to bring about a peaceful and honorable arrangement for all concerned...."[420]

When Mr. Merriam went on to question the doctor about Hartley's love for Margaret Chase, Dr. Chase would not answer without prepared notes, saying only, "Love has different interpretations to different minds." Mr. Merriam then went on to read "the notes," in which Hartley described his "love" for Mrs. Chase as "a very very real and splendid thing in my life"—something that "exists today" and was still growing.[421] As Mr. Merriam questioned Dr. Chase again and again, reading aloud Hartley's words, reminding him of Hartley's exclusive association with Margaret, Dr. Chase began to have trouble giving straight answers until he couldn't even answer the questions at all. Cracking under pressure, Dr. Chase's responses grew increasingly mechanical and unconvincing.

Mr. Merriam threw Kate Ware Smith's testimony, in which she stated Hartley had plainly told her he felt he had the right to have sexual intercourse with Margaret Chase, in Dr. Chase's face. Asking

Dr. Chase whether or not he still approved of the relationship between Hartley and Margaret, Dr. Chase tried to avoid an answer, saying that he knew that was not a complete statement of Hartley's views, that he knew what Hartley's views were, even questioning that Hartley may have said such things. Mr. Merriam insisted upon an answer, yes or no. Finally, forced to respond, Dr. Chase could only say, "Yes, sir; I do." Mr. Merriam then questioned Dr. Chase about Hartley's habits and whereabouts after the probate court hearing, in which he declined to provide for the maintenance and education of his children. Dr. Chase would only admit that Hartley had not "technically" complied with court order.

Hartley's attorney, Mr. Norton, tried to rescue Dr. Chase by pointing out that although they had lived together, Hartley and Margaret could have slept in different rooms. He also pointed out that by the word "love," Dr. Chase meant "simply...a good, warm friendship between two people," and not "sexual affection, desire or passion." Relieved, Dr. Chase was quick to reiterate over and over again Hartley's talent for "friendship." Said the doctor, "It means it shows his attitude towards all with whom he comes in contact. He even loves his enemies, the few that he has."[422] And the doctor insisted that Margaret was as stainless as Hartley. "Why, it means very much the same as Mr. Dennett does, a good, pure, warm affection, active kindness toward other persons that she expresses it toward; absolutely upright."[423]

Given a second chance to defend his "best friend," Dr. Chase insisted that two married persons had no right whatsoever to have sexual intercourse with other people. He explained away Hartley's conversation with Kate Ware Smith by imagining new words coming from Hartley's mouth, and then he rambled on about various medical reasons why even marital partners should not engage in intercourse, citing examples. At this, even Mr. Dallinger had to tell the doctor that he was avoiding the issue.[424]

When Mr. Norton mentioned Hartley's statement about "if the question as to his having a right to have a child by Mrs. Chase should arise he thought he might feel that he had that right—" Dr. Chase interrupted, saying, "There is an *if* there." Unwilling to even admit the possibility of Hartley's saying such a thing, Dr. Chase went on to claim that Hartley and Margaret were in Alstead alone "with the approval of both families." Even more incredible, the doctor claimed that Hartley and Margaret had been in Alstead on the advice of Mary's mother Vonie! Excusing the obviously ludicrous nature of his claim, the doctor said, "that is my recollection."[425]

By this time, Mr. Dallinger, amazed by the human capacity for denial, tried a fresh tactic. Mr. Dallinger himself proceeded to ask Dr. Chase a few "hypothetical" questions describing the scenario precisely but taking names completely out of the picture. Dr. Chase made several attempts to change details in the "hypothetical" situation, and he insisted that children had a right to two parents. But ultimately, he was forced to concede the need for certain rules—among them, the laws of marriage and obedience to a higher authority.

The final witness for Hartley Dennett was Hartley himself. Hartley's testimony was the epitome of avoidance and evasiveness. Even for the most simple questions, Hartley would not give a straight answer. When asked repeatedly how long he had known Margaret Chase, he could only say he did not know. When asked whether or not he or Mary had ever been at the Chase camp in East Alstead, he would only admit, "Yes, so I understand it."[426] As before, he asserted, "The case is a case in the fight for a higher morality—in marriage and the other relations of the sexes."[427]

The only facts Hartley was clear about were the following: Since 1909 he had been at East Alstead a large portion of the time, Mrs. Chase had also been there a large portion of the time, and he had also been at Brookline at the Chases' house at various times. Hartley was also secure in his claim that he was not having intercourse with Mrs. Chase.

On the issue of child support, Hartley acknowledged that the court had told him he "was supposed to be responsible for the support of my children." But he claimed that under the order, he was not called upon to make any specific provision until Mary asked for it—and Mary had explicitly told him she would not receive anything from him. He claimed that the bill of the Jordan Marsh Company was incurred after the separation, and even after the commencement of the proceedings for separate support, although he conceded, "I am not positive on that subject."

Hartley also went on to deny the incident which caused Edmund to disobey his mother, Kate Ware Smith. Claiming a memory lapse, Hartley could only say "I don't remember," "I don't know" and "I am not sure" about various details of the situation. What he did offer, however, was a new twist, saying he would have cautioned Edmund that it was "a serious business to disobey his mother" for which he would have to be responsible.

When asked to account for the incident in which Carleton was greatly frightened by news from the Tuckerman children that Mary was sending Hartley to prison, Hartley's memory failed him again. Indeed, he finally placed the burden on Carleton, saying, "Kate Ware Smith explained to me at one time, or several times, that Carleton was extremely excitable and that the slightest thing disturbed him. He is considered a very nervous child."[428]

Hartley's goal was custody of his children. "I think one of the children should be in my custody and one in the mother's custody, and I should surely expect that there would be free access to both children and both parents. I think the terms should be absolutely equal. For my part I should have no desire to separate either child from the other or from the other parent."[429] Ideally, he was "willing" that Mary should be of the same family and the same household of himself and the Chases. When asked whether or not he would comply with court order, however, or consider allowing the boys to remain in the Framingham schools, Hartley would make no promises.

As to his finances, Hartley claimed he would be more than willing to support his children—should he have custody of them. Whereas he had once claimed poverty, now he asserted that he had earned as much as seventy-five hundred dollars in a year—although he admitted he had "temporarily discontinued" his profession to devote himself "almost entirely to farming."[430] But, he reassured the court that if he were given care and custody of either or both of the children, he would devote himself to earning a living "sufficient" to secure "a reasonable amount for their proper support."

At this point, Mr. Dallinger decided to question Hartley to find out *why* Hartley had turned away from Mary. Very quickly, however, he found that Hartley had nipped that question at its bud. Despite Mary's pain, hurt, and suffering, Hartley would not admit to having done anything less than the utmost to forward marital harmony. Hartley claimed he had not the "slightest feeling" of "hostility or hatred" toward Mary. As if to confirm that he felt no remorse at seeing Mary suffer, he explicitly denied that he gave Mary less affection, less time, or less attention than before the troubles began. He agreed with Mary's witnesses in saying that the Dennett home had once been "ideal," but he would not admit that his relationship with Margaret Chase had anything to do with its disruption.

What bothered Hartley, evidently, was that his wife would have the audacity to limit his freedom in any way at all. According to his and Margaret's philosphy, freedom was the guiding rule for all in life. Blaming Mary for her "lack of sympathy" for his freedom, he stated her closed-mindedness as the sole reason for the failure of their marriage. Hartley had convinced himself that he loved Mary nonetheless, and that he did not in fact love Margaret any the greater. That his actions betrayed his words seemed not to matter to him at all. That was only *perception*, he would justify, not *reality*— for he and Margaret wished to define their own reality. Hartley would not let himself be pinned down, for he was a man who felt himself to be above the law. "I have no doctrine; I have no theory on the matter. I believe each man should do the very best he can under the circumstances which present themselves."[431]

When Mr. Dallinger asked Hartley about Spirit Fruit, Hartley merely claimed, "I don't have any particular interest in any cult." For by this time, the Spirit Fruiters—who despite their oddities, were really rather gentle and well-intentioned people—had disowned him and Margaret, remonstrating them for abusing the Spirit Fruit name. Shunned by all, he and Margaret had truly become spiritual anarchists, uninterested in following any law or principle except their own, letting their own self-oriented consciences dictate the way. Said Hartley, making a complete mockery of religion and sacrifice, "as I remember it seemed like a wholesome sort of article.... something on 'Faith' in there; something to the effect that Jesus said about...how faith sometimes requires serious sacrifices."[432]

When he was finished, Mr. Norton announced that Hartley "declined" to be cross-examined, insisting that he would be misrepresented. John Merriam demanded the *right* of cross-examination. But Hartley adamantly refused. After consulting with Judge Hall, Dallinger decided it was not within his power to compel witnesses to submit to cross-examination. Hartley was not the only one who "knew his limits." Margaret refused to appear in court at all. She was willing to make a statement to Mr. Dallinger privately—and even answer any questions he had—but she would not submit herself to testifying "in the presence of counsel or of the parties." To this, Mr. Dallinger merely answered that he would accept a written statement, but "did not care to hear the testimony in the absence of counsel or the parties."[433] So Margaret attempted a written statement, but she claimed she was not able to finish in time.[434]

In contrast to Margaret's reticence, Mary came into court yet again to offer her rebuttal. She handed the judge her already completed statement in writing—"simply because I can save your time and mine."[435] Yet she had one request. "I may say, please, that I am not putting this statement in with the idea that it shall be handed over to the court and that the newspapers shall have access to it as they were to Mr. Dennett's statement." She was insistent: "I have done my best to protect my children in every way possible in this matter. I am perfectly willing you should read it but I do not wish it turned over to the court."[436]

In it, she succinctly illustrated the behavior leading to the break-up, as well as the effects of Hartley's visits on the children. Furthermore, she pointed out that with the exceptions of Hartley himself, Dr. Chase, and Harry Adams, a carpenter and builder who had been employed by Hartley for the last decade, none of Hartley's witnesses had known him longer than two or three years. Several had interacted with him only a couple of times in their lives—and almost none had any acquaintance with Mary at all.[437] As to Dr. Chase's claim that Hartley was teaching the Chase children "self-control and self-support," the statement was laughable given Hartley's own utter lack of self-control regarding his marriage and his own inability to be self-supporting.

Mr. Norton had only one question for her in cross examination: "is it a fact that you have told, either told or written, your husband that you would not receive support from him in money?" And Mary answered, "I am perfectly willing to have my letter read. It expresses my views perfectly on the subject." Said she, "I refused to accept personal gifts of money. I told him his obligation to support his family was a permanent one and I stand by that, but I absolutely refuse to accept personal gifts from him."[438] Then the judge asked Mary whether there was any alimony. Mary answered, "No; I would not ask for any." All she wanted was child support. The judge asked whether Mary would change her position on personal gifts. She answered, "No. Never. I have been absolutely consistent through it all. He never offered to pay the bills or to hand me money to pay the bills. What he offered to do was at intervals according to his own judgment to hand me out as a personal gift anything he chose to decide upon."[439]

When the hearing was over, Mr. Dallinger asked Hartley to submit a statement to answer several of his questions. In this statement, Hartley reiterated Hartley and Margaret's view of their relationship and responded to the implication that he and Margaret were sexually unchaste.

The sex question appears to be the pivot on which this case now turns.
Since John Merriam has so persistently insinuated sex impurity into it,

the case has quite changed color. I wish to make clear my convictions on the sex question:

I believe that the sexual organs are organs of reproduction and that their only proper use is for procreation. I call "sexual prostitution" the use of these organs for other purposes, and I believe that what is prostitution outside of marriage is prostitution inside of marriage. . . .

I believe that the established notion that there is a male necessity for sexual indulgence and that there is only an obliging passivity in the female, is false, and pervision of social purity. I believe that in both sexes there is a sex life—an active creative instinct—that is convertible, and that is normally converted, into all forms of creative power, and that there is no shame in sex, but only in its prostitution. And I believe that disease is a reasonable reaction to prostitution, and a social menace in proportion to the extent of prostitution in and out of marriage.

I believe that the natural goal is purity, not impurity, and that an honest facing of the facts of life is necessary to a pure life and an education in purity.

Believing and living this as I have has made me growingly realize the absolute about-face it means in all the relations of the sexes. A "bed," for example, has not to me the sinister significance John Merriam's mind attaches to it; and against his suggestion I squarely assert my belief that once prostitution, legal and illegal, is dropped from the ideas of sexual intercourse, men and women can lie down together and associate freely together without sin and without shame. Children have no longer to be lied to. . . .[440]

The point was irrelevant. For Mary had never accused Hartley and Margaret of sexual infidelity. To the contrary, Mary believed that the pair had never engaged in actual intercourse. But, as her Uncle Ned put it, even if she had "never charged impure relations," the affair was still "a prostitution of the mind and of the soul—and that is the worst kind of prostitution."[441]

Mr. Dallinger was very careful about making his final decision. He visited the school in East Alstead as well as the Danforth School. Given the special claims which Hartley was making, and given the widespread media attention, he wanted to be above reproach. At the end of April 1913, after visiting both Framingham and East Alstead, Mr. Dallinger finally reached a recommendation for Judge Hall.

Mr. Dallinger recounted the facts: There was still a warrant for Hartley's arrest attached to the unpaid Jordan Marsh bill; Mary received an annual salary of $2,500 for her services at the National Woman Suffrage Association; Hartley's only occupation was that of a farmer, living with another man's wife, kept by that same man. Trying to be gracious, Mr. Dallinger spoke to the refinement, high education, and culture of Hartley, Margaret, and Mary; in his second report (revised to be more "palatable" to Hartley), Mr. Dallinger found Hartley and Margaret to be not guilty of adulterous relations (although he also pointed out the "average person" might believe otherwise). Clearly, Mr. Dallinger wanted to appear fair. Yet he stated, "It is evident from all the facts in this case that Margaret Chase, a talented and forceful woman, has been able by the force of her personality to monopolize the affection of Hartley Dennett, another woman's husband, and at the same time to retain the affection of her own husband, who apparently is content to enjoy the society of his wife only on these comparatively rare occasions when she sees fit to permit him to do so."[442]

After evaluating all the evidence, Mr. Dallinger found Hartley Dennett, "as disclosed by his acts and by his own testimony…not a fit person to have the care and custody of either of his children"; Mary Ware Dennett he found, "in every way a fit person to have the custody of both of her children"; and finally, "the comfort, happiness and future welfare of the two children of Mary Ware Dennett and Hartley Dennett demand that they remain in the exclusive custody of their mother."[443]

Reaction was swift. Margaret's mother wrote to her daughter chastising her for breaking up the Dennetts's marriage, and to Mary offering her congratulations. Hartley's mother wrote to Mary apologizing for her son's wantonness. Even Vaughan Dennett, Hartley's brother, wrote to Edwin D. Mead, saying, "I shall always welcome any opportunity to run counter to Mrs. Margaret Chase or any of her machinations."[444] Only Edith Chase Newton, Dr. Chase's sister, supported Hartley and Margaret. A Seventh-Day Adventist, Edith felt Mary had "lost faith" in Hartley's honor.[445]

Not a very good loser, Hartley found his genteel refinement was beginning to wear thin. Complaining that John Merriam had resorted to dirty and uncalled-for character insinuations, Hartley claimed that Mary had tried to bribe some of his witnesses against testifying. He said, "she has shown that if either parent were to be deprived of the care of the children it should be herself, not I."[446] By the end of April, he was desperate. He criticized Mr. Dallinger. "He should begin from the fact that I am a parent and a citizen & with rights belonging to those estates, perhaps even the right to remain innocent until I am proven guilty."[447] Hartley ignored that over the past four years he had relinquished his rights as a parent by refusing to support his family and he had relinquished his rights as a citizen by flagrantly defying the law. Furthermore, he did not seem to realize that during the entire trial he had been presumed innocent but was proven guilty and unfit.

On 28 April 1913, Mary received a formal document awarding her exclusive legal custody of the children, "with reasonable opportunities" for Hartley to visit. As the children were in Mr. Flagg's care at the Danforth School, Mr. Merriam advised Mary to let Mr. Flagg determine Hartley's visits. Since Mr. Flagg was a trusted friend, this would relieve Mary from having to decline Hartley's visits, and it would also spare her details of Hartley's visits. Cautioned Mr. Merriam, "I think it desirable to avoid any dispute with him at present, and would caution you against any correspondence calculated in any way to invite controversy."[448]

Fascinated by the sensationalism, reporters took advantage of the soapopera–like qualities of the 1913 trial of *Dennett v. Dennett*. The Hearst papers had a field day, and even the New York *Times* picked up the story. Hartley became "the young Harvard graduate of 'soulmate' fame." The New York *Tribune* mistakenly reported, "Mrs. Bennett Gets Children." The divorce of a prominent suffragette and a Brahmin free lover tickled popular imagination. Dr. Chase became a curiosity as well. His guiding principle in the coming years would be to "do as Jesus would have done." The doctor was quoted as saying, "Mr. Dennett is so Christian-like as to be more than earthly. Mrs. Dennett has wronged him. It is regrettable."[449] Reporters couldn't resist. What in the world were these free-thinking Arts and Crafts people doing? On and off for the next few years, the Dennett story would grace the tabloids. A new age of relationships had begun.

THE
POLITICAL
YEARS

PART II

CHAPTER NINE

Suffrage

ith her personal life in shambles, Mary sought to plunge herself into a livelihood that was as different as possible from what she had done before. Sublimating her emotions like a true Yankee, the missionary fervor that had characterized her actions since childhood emerged again in full force. The ideals of Arts and Crafts were too tied up with her ex-husband to be pursued, but there were other causes, other ways for her to express her idealism. Beginning anew, she sought refuge in the company of women. And in the progressive circles of the day, the voice of woman was heard first and loudest in the burgeoning movement for women's suffrage.

Many of the men and women closest to Mary were active in fighting for women's enfrachisement. In 1901, Mary Hutcheson Page had organized the Boston Equal Suffrage Association for Good Government. In 1903, Mary's Aunt Lucia Ames Mead had been elected president of the Massachusetts Suffrage League. Edwin D. Mead and George H. Page were among the suffrage husbands who organized and delivered addresses to promote the vote for women at Massachusetts rallies. Other prominent suffragists in the state included Julia Ward Howe, Alice Stone Blackwell, Maud Wood Park, and William Lloyd Garrison—all nationally recognized figures.[450] Before the breakup of her marriage, Mary herself had been casually sympathetic to the movement, but Hartley was silent. So peculiar was this contrast, particularly between a supposedly progressive couple, that later historians would mistakenly assume that it was suffrage—not her husband's misguided "spiritual" path—that had caused the demise of the Dennett marriage.[451]

In reality, it was the other way around. The wife had never alienated the husband with unpleasantly shrill "feminist" demands. Rather, it was the specter of marital disintegration that had consequently pushed her to seek ways to alleviate her anguish. Mary would later confess to a colleague, "I went into suffrage work, as perhaps you know, because I needed an anaesthetic at the time, and suffrage was the nearest thing at hand which was unconnected with my previous work."[452] When she became field secretary of the Massachusetts Suffrage Association in 1908—a salaried position—she threw herself into her new cause.

In Springfield, Massachusetts, amidst much newspaper publicity about suffrage activities, Dennett had organized a whirlwind week of events. At suffrage headquarters, there were talks every day at noon; on warm evenings, speaking was done from doorways to the crowd on the sidewalk. Suffragists served luncheon at popular prices, and in the afternoon between four and five, they offered a "suffrage tea" with light refreshments. In addition, they held an open-air rally, social affairs, suffrage speeches, and moving pictures at two vaudeville theaters, and special meetings at all sorts of clubs. Anne Withington spoke to the Socialists and the Central Labor Union; Max Eastman, secretary of the New York Men's League for Woman Suffrage, spoke to the Board of Trade. On Sunday morning, the Reverend Ada C. Bowles spoke to ministers and church workers, preaching a suffrage sermon at the Universalist Church. Mr. Staples, the minister, was reportedly "most enthusiastic in making arrangements."[453]

Mostly, Mary spoke to the "hard sells," the conservatives, such as the members of the Springfield Woman's Club, a "typically conservative body of earnest, intelligent women who were plainly afraid of the subject—so much so, that it required two meetings of the executive board before they were willing to add this small suffrage subject to their day's program." Yet after hearing Mary speak, some of them admitted themselves converted. She also spoke to some officers and residents of the Young Woman's Christian Association, again invading a very conservative field. Even there, however, she convinced a number of people in the audience to sign enrollment cards.

Dennett's entire argument was based on the simple principle of the equality of men and women. Voting, she declared, was a natural right protected by the United States Constitution. "Our basic principles that 'governments derive their just powers from the consent of the governed'. . . undeniably imply the right of women to direct representation by the vote, since women are governed and women are people."[454] Without equal suffrage, the standard upon which the nation was founded was mere hypocrisy. Recognition of the equality of men and women was necessary for the progress of the entire human race. "While it is true that votes for women will not bring the millenium," said Dennett, "it is equally true that without votes for women, the millenium can not come."

The Springfield campaign was a turning point in the way suffrage activities were organized in Massachusetts. In one week, it was roughly estimated, about thirty-eight meetings were held, six thousand people were reached, and fifteen thousand flyers were given away. Membership in the Springfield League increased 100 percent, with one hundred fifty enrollment cards signed and about fifteen dollars' worth of literature sold. At the end of the week, the Springfield suffragists pledged to organize by political districts and to engage regular headquarters that would be kept open daily from that time on. Dennett was recognized to be the driving force behind it all. Her organizational skills had so revolutionized the way suffrage activities were conducted in Massachusetts that a special brochure was put together to detail the methods of her success.

In late August 1909, Mary organized a "Votes for Women" trip to gather signatures for a statewide petition. The packed itinerary consisted of stops at three towns a day for ten days straight. "It was one long scramble from beginning to end, sleeping, eating, travelling, speaking,—speaking, travelling, eating, sleeping, with hardly a chink anywhere for so much as a fresh...shampoo." The pace was anything but monotonous. "We lodged in every sort of a place, from stuffy wooden country hotels, to swell ones of the city sort, and we ate in hotel dining-rooms full of ebony automatons, or in cheap restaurants where the waitresses had marvellous yellow coiffures, or in tea rooms, or night lunch carts as it happened. We got so we could eat anything from a table-d'hote dinner to a Frankfurter sandwich with equal relish." The suffragists reached an average of seven hundred people a day, gaining a great deal of newspaper publicity.

The regular procedure was to drop off in the busiest part of the town, unfurl the banner (jointed to fold like a fishing pole), unpack the leaflets, and find a nearby drugstore where they could leave their suitcases and have a soda, and sally forth. While one woman hunted up the chief of police, the rest would distribute literature to pedestrians and surrounding shops. They were often met by reporters, who usually began "Are you the...er...er...suffrage ladies?" If it was a mill town, the suffragists learned to station themselves at chief exits just before twelve.

> ... *as the whistle blew and the living stream poured out, we dealt out leaflets as fast as we could and re-iterated "speaking here, after dinner,"*

until the last one had hurried by. Then about twenty minutes before one,
they would come drifting back, shy and curious, and would listen till the
warning bell or whistle sent them scurrying.[455]

Many of the workers asked for extra literature. Some who looked
unfriendly would often sign petitions if asked. In one case, the gate-
keeper of a big mill helped the suffragists win an interested audience by urging the workers as they went home to "hurry up and
eat dinner and come back and hear the ladies!"[456]

When it was not a mill town, the suffragists often had to begin
by speaking to thin air, or to a few loafers or children, but a crowd
always gathered. In the evening, when people were off work and
ready for any kind of diversion, they were able to gather the largest
audiences. All the curious bystanders would quickly come together,
including "young folks just out for fun." Serious listeners would
close in tighter and tighter after the "froth" drifted away, making a
compact mass that would listen to four successive speeches for an
hour, never budging until it was over. If the circumstances were
difficult, the suffragists responded with creativity. Prevented from
picketing at a beach, for example, they took up their banner and
waded into the water! Often, the women were rewarded with spontaneous applause.

Encounters with "antis" only made them work harder. One
vehement anti turned up her nose in a drugstore, refusing to hear
the suffrage argument, remarking it was "highly improper for any
lady to think of voting." Another run-in with a "pompous youth"
"full of book information" and "the mere *method* of argument"
convinced them they were dealing with "the worst possible product
of a college education." In general, however, the women were
encouraged by the positive response of many of their audiences.

I am more and more impressed by the fact that it is not necessary to talk
down or foolishly or rhetorically to an average street crowd, in order to
win either their attention or respect. They respond beautifully to just an
ordinary presentation of justice and democracy, which has certainly rein-
forced our faith in "the plain people" in a very thorough sort of way. They
do not need to be jollied or scolded or coddled or bullied in order to see
that equal suffrage is a natural and necessary evolution of modern life.[457]

By the end of April 1910, the National American Woman Suffrage
Association was begging Mary to leave Massachusetts and join them
in New York City at the National headquarters. The NAWSA was

experiencing turmoil, and its leaders wanted to pull in Mary as the new corresponding secretary of the country's umbrella suffrage organization. M. Thomas Carey, president of Bryn Mawr College and the College Equal Suffrage League, an NAWSA auxiliary, asked Dr. Anna Howard Shaw, President of the NAWSA since 1904, "to urge and if possible to insist on Mrs. Dennett's taking hold at once in New York." She proposed that Mary commute between Boston and New York during a month of transition, spending four and a half days each week at headquarters and the other two days in Boston "arranging her affairs to move to New York." A substantial salary raise, Thomas argued, would put Mary in a much better position to support herself and her two sons—even considering weekly travel expenses on the Boston–New York Merchant's Limited commuter train. Disregarding its inconvenience to Mary, she was forceful. "Please tell Mrs. Dennett that we think it is her duty to do it for the cause."[458]

Mary agreed to move, but upon arrival, she immediately found herself in the ugly throes of partisan politics. Since 1896, the suffragists had failed to win a single state campaign. In 1904 Anna Howard Shaw became the fourth president after Elizabeth Cady Stanton, Susan B. Anthony, and Carrie Chapman Catt. Shaw had bitterly hoped to become president in 1900, when Susan B. Anthony had retired, but because of Carrie Chapman Catt's reputed genius for organization "Aunt Susan" had chosen Catt to succeed her instead. When Catt resigned in 1904, due to an illness in her family, the prize for Shaw came four years too late.[459] Shaw inherited a period that would later be remembered in suffrage history as the doldrums.[460] By 1910 the National organization had become mired in organizational infighting and was facing a deepening crisis that came from the absence of a clear-cut policy able to furnish direction and impetus to a growing number of suffragists clamoring for action.[461]

Critics increasingly blamed Anna Howard Shaw. Ordained as a protestant Methodist minister in 1880 (after her own church refused to ordain a woman), Shaw had given up her Cape Cod parish at age thirty-five to study medicine.[462] Upon receiving her M.D. in 1885, she had worked with impoverished women in Boston slums in a dual role as preacher and physician. But her experiences convinced her that neither her religion nor medicine alone could solve the problems of women. She began to lecture for the Women's Christian Temperance Union, one of the country's largest women's organizations in the late 1800s, and became a close friend of its leader, Frances Willard. Liquor was an important issue for women, because drunken men beat women and children, gambled away earnings, and otherwise behaved in ways that caused the destruction of family and society.[463] Many feminists felt very strongly that alcohol was the source of much societal evil. Before long, the Massachusetts Woman Suffrage Association engaged Shaw to speak about suffrage and, unmatched in eloquence and effectiveness, she decided to give up other causes to make winning woman suffrage her life's work.[464]

Anna Shaw's devotion was complete and her gifts were many, but administrative ability was, unfortunately, not among them.[465] Her brilliant oratory was not matched by organizational skill. Throughout her tenure, the NAWSA was plagued with problems. One major issue was that the members of the National executive board were scattered across the country—usually meeting only once between conventions—forcing almost all business, including voting and consultations, to be conducted by mail. In addition, Dr. Shaw was known to be "easily prejudiced or aroused to hostility," making correspondence "voluminous, inconclusive, and irritating to all parties."[466] Under such circumstances, differences of opinion became personal and highly charged. A strong-willed woman who was ineffective at conciliation, Shaw was often unable to see issues that were at stake and commonly reduced major policy disagreements to petty personality clashes. Needless to say, such a situation was not conducive to much activity.

In 1910 the situation reached a head at the NAWSA Annual Convention, where there was an open rift among the membership and strong charges against the president. Not only did delegates witness the resignation of several National Board members like Harriet Taylor Upton, Rachel Foster Avery, and Florence Kelley, but the withdrawal of these women showed more than personal antagonism. There was a growing dissatisfaction with the cumbersome machinery of the organization and Dr. Shaw's tendency to greet any and all signs of awakening initiative in the ranks as "potential insurgency." Conflicts arose regarding the exceedingly modest pace of the enfrachisement campaign. Aside from a handful of state campaigns and some fruitless efforts in other states, the only visible action among the suffragists was a petition asking President Theodore Roosevelt to recommend woman suffrage in his annual message to Congress.[467] After all, between 1896 and 1910, not one state campaign had succeeded in enfranchising women.

Unwittingly, Mary had stepped into a hornet's nest. While she tried to gain her bearings in the new post, she was bombarded with letters of congratulations. It seemed as if every suffragist of note was trying to curry her favor; many did so by attacking their president. Abigail Scott Duniway, president of the Oregon State Equal Suffrage Association, actually threatened to have Shaw arrested if she crossed the state border! Duniway blamed Oregon's repeated campaign failures on the "Anna Shaw methods, which have never yet succeeded anywhere except in pandering to her love of display, and for *herself*."[468] Mary Grey Peck, whose adoration for Carrie Chapman Catt bordered on obsession,[469] said of Anna Shaw, "As age grows on her, the congenital defects of a vehement temperament become more palpable, but they have had exercise in the past as everybody knows."[470] A supporter of the "insurgents" leaving office, Peck was unabashed in her attempts to influence Dennett and set her "right."

> *I think it is a crime to let a wrong state of things continue for the sake of putting up a show of harmonious righteousness to the world. You may thank your lucky stars that you came into that office after people who had not been educated in the suffrage school of "harmony." We resigned because we could not stand it. We were accustomed to mutual and self respect. We brought the latter away with us! You will profit by our successful struggle to establish the authority of the officer in charge of headquarters . . . No, my dear Mrs. Dennett,—Long live the Insurgents! Nice people like you will gain by our rows every time. I am waiting to hear your views on the future of the National Association, after a few months in the office! Will you give them to me under pledge of secrecy?*[471]

M. Thomas Carey, who had been instrumental in bringing Dennett in, advised Shaw to make a total purge at headquarters. "A clean sweep should be made of *every* one there except of course your secretary and stenographer if you are sure of their loyalty to you.... But everyone employed in the other office must go." Constantly suspicious of "disloyalty," Dr. Shaw was susceptible to those like Carey, who claimed to be "the chief means of rallying to your support, against the powers of darkness, the loyal and true women of the convention."

In response, Mary immediately made it her policy to refrain from taking sides in past disputes. To Carey, she said, "The *work* is tremendously interesting and inspiring, but the difficulties, by the way, are not. . . ."[472] As Corresponding Secretary, all matters concerning the National had to go through her. Motivated by a great distaste for friction, she was unimpressed with the factionalism.

Quickly, Mary developed a talent for appeasing all egos while maintaining strict neutrality. With great diplomacy, she met each appeal by expressing appreciation for the petitioner's "sincerity" and "progressive spirit"—commending the "fine idealism" which she was certain motivated it. She carefully avoided partiality and made it quite clear she would be unresponsive to any "personal grievances." Instead of indignancy or exasperation, she cultivated an attitude that demonstrated kindness and understanding, patience and sympathy.

Finding a way to praise the "candor and frankness" of all entreaties—no matter how inappropriate—Mary set a tone that was a complete departure from the previous administration's. The new atmosphere discouraged backbiting about the elected leader, Anna Howard Shaw. Indeed, Mary actually took a stance of deference to Dr. Shaw, making it a point to cater to Shaw's schedule, always making sure the chief was comfortable. "I have arranged to take my vacation so that I shall be back by the middle of August, when Miss Shaw comes and then we can do the whole thing together. I have a vision of having things in apple-pie order for her comfort . . ."[473] By reestablishing esteem for the elected figurehead, Mary was able to restore a semblance of order at headquarters. Quite wisely, she realized that chaos and disintegration were the only possibilities in an environment without basic respect for the system.

Miraculously enough, in a matter of months, Mary created peace at the NAWSA. Her faith in the essential goodness of her colleagues had helped to bring out their sense of humanity. By treating them with dignity and respect, she had encouraged them to rise to their noble natures. Mary developed a reputation for fair-mindedness and level-headedness. Hearty in her approbation and lavish in her praise, she found that other suffrage leaders were beginning to lavish *her* with praise. All were relieved that the NAWSA had finally found the "right person." Anna Shaw became one of Mary's strongest defenders, repeatedly stating to others, "Mrs. Dennett is simply perfect." Even Harriet Upton Taylor, a former board member who had resigned in protest, was able to write Mary a letter of congratulations.

> *I do want to thank you for suffrage sake for the splendid spirit you have manifested in Headquarters and the unusual work you have done. Of course, you yourself know what you have done and in a certain sense are satisfied, but, of course, it must be gratifying to you to have me tell you that with all the letters I receive from all the word I get from hundreds of*

people I never have heard anything but the kindest things said of you and the position you have taken. Just a letter last night spoke of you as being just and capable. Seems to me that those are two pretty good words for anybody to apply to another written out of the real depths of their heart.[474]

With the beginnings of order established at headquarters, Dennett set herself to the task at hand: getting the vote for women. As corresponding secretary, she furnished facts, handled the media, ran the data department, headed the literature department, wrote propaganda, advised campaigning suffragists, served as office manager, and functioned as central clearinghouse for all that came out of the NAWSA. On speaking tours much of the time, Dr. Shaw was not around very often to oversee the organization of the suffrage movement. That left Mary in charge at headquarters, engaged in the "endlessly detailed work of advising suffragists at every step of their progress, from parlor meetings to final victory at the polls." In one day, she received about fifty pieces of mail—each asking for detailed (and sometimes obscure) suffrage facts, speakers, and literature. Under her direction, the National headquarters became the "central point for receiving and dispersing information."[475]

Although unrecognized today, Mary Ware Dennett was the turning point for the NAWSA. After her arrival, the reach at headquarters grew massively. She saw to it that an enormous amount of information was compiled and distributed "to the four points of the compass on almost every subject mentioned within the lids of Webster's unabridged."[476] No-nonsense to the extreme, she felt no compunction about dismissing people whose work she found to be below par. Her intimate involvement with various local suffrage campaigns gave her a broad-based vision of what was possible. She deluged the country with propaganda; she fed the voracious media machine with suffrage news. The arrival of Mary Ware Dennett at National's headquarters signified the end of the "doldrums." In 1910, the Washington state suffrage campaign succeeded in enfranchising women.

Swept in soon after Mary was another new board member, Jessie Ashley, who would serve as treasurer of the NAWSA. Ashley was a wealthy New York attorney and Socialist who soon became one of Dennett's closest "comrades." Addressing Mary as "dear Little Lady" instead of the traditional "Mrs. Dennett," Jessie stood in stark contrast to the other suffragists, most of whom were middle-aged and respectable. For example, while the other suffragists tried to distance themselves from "free love" so as not to alienate male voters, Jessie Ashley openly proclaimed that she did not believe in marriage, nor did she like children much—her lover was "Big Bill" Haywood of I.W.W. fame, the leader of the Wobblies! One historian of the I.W.W. described the unusual couple:

> *Jessie and Bill were the oddest combination in the world—old Bill with his one eye, stubby roughened fingernails, uncreased trousers and shoddy clothes for which he refused to pay more than a minimum; Jessie with her Boston accent and hornrimmed glasses, a compromise between spectacles and lorgnette from which dangled a black ribbon, the ultimate word in eccentric decoration.*
>
> *Jessie was one of the most conspicuous of the many men and women of long pedigree who were revolting against family tradition. She was the daughter of the president of the New York School of Law...and one of the first women lawyers in New York....A Socialist in practice as well as in theory, she spent large portions of her income getting radicals out of jail....Nevertheless, her appearance at strike meetings were [sic] slightly uncomfortable; class tensions rose up in waves.*[477]

Anxious to win votes for women, Dennett and Ashley would soon grow to see themselves as lone voices at headquarters, social outcasts fighting for justice. Impatient with the pace of the national movement, the pair was eager to see circumstances at headquarters change. In England, militant suffragists led by Emmeline Pankhurst were making transatlantic headlines by deliberately provoking violent police reprisals. Hoping to embarrass party leaders to point where they would feel compelled to do something about woman suffrage, Pankhurst followers threw stones, broke windows, poured acid into mailboxes, and attacked members of government with whips or their bare hands. Many were arrested, and from prison they complained of poor treatment, engaging in prolonged and widely publicized hunger strikes.[478] Whether or not their tactics were appropriate, they were effective in getting the attention of the Parliament, which had hitherto ignored or laughed off disenfranchised—and politically powerless—women.

In the United States, the suffragists had been similarly brushed off by male legislators. Without the right to vote, women who peaceably presented their case were told that a "petition bearing the names of 20,000 women was of no more significance than one bearing the names of 20,000 mice."[479] Looking to the Pankhurst group for answers, Dennett and Ashley soon realized one of the chief differences was not just the militancy, but the amount of money spent. In one year, Mrs. Pankhurst's Woman's Social and Political Union (only one of seventeen English suffrage associations), had spent $172,500 as compared to the NAWSA's piddling $35,000; in a country of 41 million the WSPU employed 110 paid workers while the NAWSA, in a country of 93 million, paid only seventeen of their workers. Indeed, the chairman of the NAWSA's Congressional Committee, who was responsible for presenting the federal Susan B. Anthony amendment to Congress every year, was given a paltry $10 for all her expenses—and she refunded change at the end of her term![480] Arguing that the amount of money spent was a good indication of the amount of activity conducted, Jessie, as treasurer, pushed for a major fund-raising drive to raise $75,000.[481]

The efforts of the newcomers paid off. In 1911, California, one of the largest states in the union, voted to enfranchise women. Despite the victory, however, Mary knew that the National organization still had problems that required fundamental structural changes. When she tried to call meetings, she was confronted with the inefficiencies of a scattered executive board that conducted its business by mail. With definite conceptions of what it took to be successful, she pointed to the English suffragists as a model. When Mrs. Pankhurst had visited the United States, Mary Hutcheson Page, chairman of the National Advisory Committee, had asked the Englishwoman how often their executive committee met. Mrs. Pankhurst had replied: "All the time."[482] Immediately recognizing the need for centralization, Dennett decided the National organization itself needed to be reformed.

As ranking member of the executive board at national headquarters, Mary called together a Committee of Revision to draw up a new NAWSA constitution to be presented at the 1911 Annual Convention. Composed of Jessie Ashley, Harriet Burton Laidlaw, Katherine Houghton Hepburn, Henrietta W. Livermore, and Mary Ware Dennett, chairman (Mary always printed her name last, if she printed it at all), the committee called for sweeping changes. First, it moved to shorten the name of the NAWSA to the National Woman Suffrage Association. Second, it wanted to open up membership to the NAWSA to local suffrage organizations, who previously could only be represented through official state leagues. Third, it moved to limit the executive board to those women who lived near headquarters.[483]

Women, however, proved to be just as resistent to constitutional amendments as men. The suggestion to change the NAWSA's long and cumbersome name, for example, was quickly dropped after Alice Stone Blackwell, editor of *The Woman's Journal*, pointed out the full name had been the result of a difficult merger between the National Woman Suffrage Association (formed by Elizabeth Cady Stanton and Susan B. Anthony) and the American Woman Suffrage Association (formed by Blackwell's mother, Lucy Stone). To drop the *American*, she stated flatly, would be an affront to history.[484] At that, other suffragists chimed in to say a name change might also legally endanger bequests and legacies left to the NAWSA.

Opponents of the open door policy feared admitting new groups into the National association would subvert the power of official state societies. When Harriet Burton Laidlaw, chairman of the Manhattan Woman Suffrage Party, made a broad appeal for "unity with diversity," pleading that no matter what the differences, "let us pray that never may that last silver cord of unity be broken between any two suffrage organizations," Madge Patton Stephens, M.D. answered, "It is a universal law, 'in unity there is strength,' but this unity must begin at home, in the State." She stressed, "The full value of any National organization is the 'tie that binds' the individual club to the county, the county to the State, the State to the National."[485] Using another tactic, Katherine Houghton Hepburn, member of the National advisory committee and president of the Connecticut Woman Suffrage Association, tried to save the measure by pointing out there were about twenty-eight thousand women enlisted in the thirty-seven official state associations, while the New York Woman Suffrage Party alone counted forty thousand members—none of whom could join forces with National according to the present constitution.[486] By limiting its ranks, she pointed out, the National was cutting itself off from potential membership *dues* as well as vital suffrage workers.

Centralization was an even more sensitive issue. Typical was the argument of Catherine Waugh McCulloch of Illinois:

> *If all the officers should be selected from near New York, the other sections of the country, being unrepresented by women of their own type, would lose their interest in and forget their allegiance to the National. The National would then drift into being a New York City society, working on a level with the other excellent societies already covering that ground."*[487]

At this, Susan W. FitzGerald of Massachusetts retorted that there were only nine states represented on the National Executive and Advisory Boards anyway, making so-called "state" representation a figment of the conservative imagination. Furthermore, she said, "There is no question to my mind that whatever the theoretical function of the members of the present board, their actual work is little more than advisory only with the exception of the few that are in close touch with headquarters." Under the new system, the National Board would consist of hands-on suffragists present at headquarters, and the advisory committee would consist of the president of every state association and who would be empowered to call meetings—a change that would actually give greater true representation and power to the states.[488]

Holding fast to states' rights, however, Laura Clay of Kentucky accused the revision of having "the purpose of excluding all women except those in the vicinity of New York from its official *honors*" [emphasis added]. Ever vigilant of those who sought prestige rather than service, Dennett pounced on Clay's words, calling them "an extraordinary confession."

> *Can it possibly be that our association elects its Board for any other purpose than to secure the services its members can perform? Or worse yet, can it be possible that any member would willingly allow herself to be elected for the honor she might receive instead of for the work she could do?*

Unusual in her sincerity, Mary's only aspiration was to live her own life according to "principle." She sought no glory, credit, or recognition—and received none. Already at the center of the national coordinating work, she simply wanted the National board to meet every month—or even every week—instead of once a year. As Hepburn pointed out, "It would be very desirable to have the board members come from different parts of the country and live near headquarters in order to do their work, as do the members of our National Government." Driving home the point, Dennett declared, "...those who oppose the new constitution almost unanimously hark back to the past, fear any change in the future, and conjure up all manner of bogies, which haven't as yet scattered our forces to the four winds, but which they think might."[489]

Opponents, however, stood firm. At the 1911 Convention, the revised constitution was voted down. The institutional stagnation was discouraging. With her personal life in disarray, Mary began to question whether her energies were being best spent at the NAWSA. Her interest in suffrage work had developed from a perception that it had "big possibilities...to make it vitally related to present-day fundamental social problems." She wanted the suffragists to "branch out...into all the forms of radicalism which have any connection with citizenship and personal freedom." But she began to realize the kind of work she and Jessie Ashley were attempting to do was not necessarily wanted at National. Rumors began to fly that Mary "might be open to an offer from the Massachusetts W.S.A."[490] Dennett did feel the "only hope" for the suffrage movement was a strong National board but, she asked, "if that is timid and helpless also, what is there left to depend upon?"

In August 1912, Mary made a clear statement to Dr. Shaw:

> *I* want to get out. *Whether I shall or not depends entirely upon circumstances. If I were personally free and my movements did not affect the children's welfare, or if I had strength enough to work and worry both at the same time, I should decide at once to drop suffrage work after November.*

Saying the suffragists were "conservative and unconstructive and they have successfully suppressed anything that wasn't," Dennett declared the work "just a *bore* unless it is on a background of big inspiring progressive and fundamentally important work! I am not thrilled by it per se one single bit...."[491] She and Ashley decided to resign together. Like her involvement in the Arts and Crafts movement, Mary's interest in suffrage had grown out of the hope that it could regenerate humankind. Like others of the era, Mary was looking for the key that would bring about the complete transformation of human society. But the suffrage movement, although it was a step in the right direction, did not seem to be enough.

Recognizing that Mary Ware Dennett was the reason for the recent turnaround in state campaigns, the suffrage leaders did not want Dennett to leave. From Massachusetts, Alice Stone Blackwell, the same editor of *The Woman's Journal* who had vetoed the name change, tried to discourage Mary from leaving New York.

> *I feel so strongly the importance to the National of having at Headquarters a woman with good sense, discretion, and a sweet temper...I hope you will allow yourself to be re-elected. I thought the National made a ten-strike when they got you, and I should be proportionately sorry, as one of the National officers, if we had to lose you. The position is an important one, and difficult to find the right person to fill.[492]*

Hepburn pointed out that since Mary's arrival, suffragists across the country had begun to leave "behind the propaganda and educational stage to enter the stage of practical politics and final achievement." Anna Shaw was simply a mouthpiece. But even Shaw was distraught at the prospect of Mary's departure, for if Mary left, what would happen to the NAWSA? Mary Ware Dennett had drawn local as well as state societies directly to National.

> *I wish I could beg of you to hold fast by every thing, until the National convention. Do not let go your hold of anything. Let us keep as we have it the plan for next year in our hands. Then if the National does not stand by us but I know it will, we can arrange differently. Don't be in a hurry to reform and reconstruct a whole nation of people. We don't know what will happen until we get to the convention, and the cutting down just now for a while will not hurt us ultimately.[493]*

No longer simply "marking time in the performance of routine duties," the National was "rising to the demands made upon it by the great recent increase in suffrage activities."[494] One suffragist wrote to Dennett saying she "rank[ed]...with Carrie Chapman Catt, our greatest."[495] In 1912, three more states won woman suffrage: Oregon, Arizona, and Kansas. The tide was turning. The time had come to enfranchise women. And Mary Ware Dennett had made herself indispensable.

At the 1912 Convention, the NAWSA elected to take a new approach to winning woman suffrage. Alice Paul, a suffragist who had been jailed with Mrs. Pankhurst's group in England, was appointed chair of the Congressional Committee of the NAWSA. Impatient with the slow state-by-state approach of the National organization, Paul wanted to focus completely on passing a federal amendment. She wanted to step up the pressure on Congress and skip individual state campaigns altogether. Determined to have woman suffrage become a reality as soon as possible, Paul felt no compunction about creating tension to accomplish her ends. Advocating methods such as picketing the White House and ousting the political party in power, Paul was unabashed about increasing the stridency of the American movement. If men would not relinquish the vote graciously, then women should force the issue.

Although unsupportive of some of Paul's more militant moves, Mary, who had decided to give the suffragists another chance even though Jessie Ashley, her closest comrade, was gone,[496] was impressed with the efficiency of Paul's federalist approach. Now the executive secretary, Mary renewed her efforts to give direction to the NAWSA. In charge of the propaganda used by the NAWSA, she wrote a leaflet called "The Real Point," which became the National's most widely used piece of suffrage literature. She devised a popular "suffrage map," which clearly illustrated in which states woman suffrage was legal and in which it was not. And in 1913 she collaborated with Anna Shaw to produce a seven-month series of suffrage articles called "Woman Suffrage," which was published in a magazine called *The Trend*. Drawing up a contract between them, the two women agreed to split the writing and the money, but Dr. Shaw would receive the full byline—and all the credit.[497]

Mary ultimately wrote the majority of the articles in the series even though her name never appeared. In one month, for example, the suffrage series featured photographs of many leading suffragists—most of whom were below Dennett in rank and importance—but Mary's photograph was conspicuously absent. Another month, Dennett wrote and illustrated the *entire* series of articles—and Anna Shaw contributed nothing—yet Mary received no acknowledgment at all. And in still another month, someone with the initials "E.B." described the roles of the top two suffragists in the NAWSA, the president and the executive secretary. While the president was clearly identified as Dr. Anna Howard Shaw—and her duty was summed up in one sentence—the executive secretary was referred to anonymously only by title—even though the description of her functions took up two full pages. Not once was Mary Ware Dennett's name mentioned.

Out of countless suffrage articles published during the period, all except one suppressed any overt mention of Mary Ware Dennett. This single article, a newspaper story entitled, "American Parenthood from the Viewpoint Of a Suffragette Mother: Mrs. Mary Ware Dennett Tells How She Trains Her Children and Says She Thinks the Father Ought to Give Hours of His Time Daily to the Youngsters While the Mother Is Away"[498] included a very flattering photograph of her. Involved in a high-stakes, sensationalized custody battle throughout her tenure at the NAWSA, her widespread anonymity would seem to suggest she was carefully cultivating her public persona. After all, the average American did not look kindly upon "suffragettes"—the word was a derogatory form for *suffragist* and used interchangeably with the term *feminist*. To retain custody of her children, Mary had to prove that giving women the right to vote would *not* bring about the downfall of the family. To keep her family, she had to challenge the prejudice that women with brains made bad mothers.

In the newspaper article, Mary put forth a philosophy of child rearing that was based on the importance of education. Stressing the need for education "to fit persons for the duties and responsibilities of parenthood," Mary emphasized that this kind of moral education was "just as necessary to the young man as to the young woman." Obviously preferring the word "parental" to "maternal," she said that in order to achieve a better balance within the family, men had to learn how to be better fathers and women had to gain a certain amount of self-subsistence. For so long as one spouse remained wholly dependent upon the other, rhetoric about equality remained empty talk. Said Dennett, "I think that most informed and progressive people are agreed as to the necessity of economic independence for the married woman." Proposing a "five hours on, five hours off" working day, in which the mother and the father would alternate "five-hour periods of work with five hours in the company of their children," Dennett felt that the full development of each spouse in all spheres of life would greatly improve the raising of children.

> *The average mother is apt to get too close to her children to know how best to satisfy their needs other than the purely physical ones. Her sense of perspective is destroyed. You often hear mother complaining because father, who comes home and plays with the children before going to bed, won't understand how naughty they really are. But if she could get away from her youngsters now and then she would lose her nervously exaggerated sense of their deficiencies.*[499]

Far ahead of her time, Dennett's attitude toward child rearing was focused on creating a more just, orderly, and peaceful society. Until the reality of equality between woman and man was fully established, the highest social development of mankind would not be possible. And woman would not be able reach equality with men in the social and political spheres until men strove to develop themselves in the domestic sphere. Mary's prescription for living was based on her belief in the uplifting effects of self-control. "The parent should direct every effort toward showing the child the value of temperance in all things. But if at the moment the little one's desires are so strong that he is unable to see the beauty of temperate self-control, the parent should exercise restraint over him until he learns better." The medicine for social illnesses lay in giving children a true spiritual education. "I do feel that one of the flaws in the American system of education is the emphasis laid upon material achievement, rather than on beauty of character. The common educational ideal is that the boy be taught to 'make good,' that is, to achieve a tangible value in dollars and cents. This is often acquired at the expense of unselfishness and a sense of beauty. We ought to teach our children to shun rather than seek this type of success."[500]

Mary's fears of losing custody of her children were not unfounded. Prior to woman suffrage, few states had equal guardianship laws. Children were the legal "property" of the father. Even after the father's death, the state could and did take children away from their mothers—particularly if the father had named a guardian other than the mother in his will. Certainly in the rare instance of divorce, children almost automatically went to the father. A mother had little opportunity to earn a living, so the reasoning went, and what meager salary she could scrape together was rarely enough to cover expenses for herself—never mind dependents. Given tradition, Mary must have been terrified of losing custody of Carleton and Devon. It was no wonder that she kept a low profile. Not only could her activism in the suffrage movement have been used easily as a weapon against her, but she was up against the full force of institutionalized sex discrimination.

Under Mary's leadership, the literature department of the NAWSA reached central importance from a propaganda standpoint. In 1913, two more states, Illinois and Alaska, enfranchised women. Illinois, in particular, was a watershed, for it was the first state east of the Mississippi River to write woman suffrage into law. At the 1913 convention, Mrs. Raymond Brown suggested that the literature department be incorporated into the National Woman Suffrage Publishing Company. With Dennett in charge, the literature department had become more and more of a business. The suffragists hoped the department might not only become self-supporting, but it could even become a source of revenue as well. Convention delegates became so enthusiastic over Brown's proposal that attendees enthusiastically pledged $10,000 worth of stock in ten minutes. Initially supportive of the idea, Dennett became head of the entire operation.

It was not long, however, before Mary began to feel the incorporation of the literature department was an enormous mistake. The National Woman Suffrage Publishing Company was not making money and even worse, the NAWSA had to close down its data department and let go of several paid workers. In April 1914, Mary became disgusted over the way the money was being spent. Sending several memos to board members for review, outlining the waste, she became frustrated when the budget remained unchanged. Convinced that wealthy woman suffragists were having far too much influence on suffrage work, she accused Shaw of following impractical initiatives and yielding to irregular plans. Instead of abiding by the board-approved budget, which Dennett felt all the faithful officers of the association were bound to carry out, Mary felt that the National was unfairly yielding to what she called the "money power."

Flinging accusations at Anna Shaw, Mary stated, "When I first began the work, people told me you had yielded to the money influence, and I refused to listen to the tales or to believe them. Then later, I saw you do it myself, at the instance of Miss Thomas, and I tried to forget it and to believe that it could never happen again. Now it *has* happened again. And I can't shut my eyes and pretend it isn't so. I am oh so sorry!" Writing to Dr. Shaw, Mary rhapsodized about the ideals she wished to see maintained in leaders.

> *I don't believe you realize what it means to some of the younger genera-*
> *tion of devoted suffrage women, to have to reach this point of seeing and*
> *admitting what seem to them such serious flaws in the great leaders. It is*
> *a real hurt, which can not be wholly healed by their gratitude for the big*
> *things the great women have done.*
>
> *The responsibilties and burdens of leadership are tremendous, of*
> *course, and it can't be expected that there should be no shortcomings*
> *and slips in the lives of the leaders, but one can't help wishing them to be*
> *slips from overwork, nerves, poor judgment, anything on earth rather*
> *than slips in making clean clear decisions between right and wrong.*
>
> *We do want to keep our faith.*
> *We don't want to have a bit of saw-dust in our dollies.*[501]

Little by little, Mary became more and more persnickety and nit-pickish. Using phrases such as "dishonesty" and "misappropriation of funds" to describe decisions with which she did not agree, she began to chip away at the peace she had created. Before long, Harriet Burton Laidlaw was moved to write Mary about her "apparently, now, chronic attack upon the board" that was "a footless, peevish going over the old ground in a way suggestive of that telling colloquial metaphor, of 'chewing the rag.'" Laidlaw warned Mary:

> *Now either you should stop sulks, disloyalty, unwillingness to abide by the*
> *vote of a majority,—without which no action could ever be carried out—*
> *or;—if you continue to treat the action of the board in readjusting*
> *national business, not as a difference of judgment and opinion, but*
> *rather as an act of moral torpitude and rash dishonesty,—then you*

should sever your connection with a body whose moral judgments you abhor, whose decisions you flaunt and whose measures you as an officer are unwilling to accept and will only grudgingly carry out. Has it occurred to you that any of this much talked of honesty is involved in your own position. Hasn't honesty call for your loyalty and your cooperation or your severing of connections with a board of which you said categorically this afternoon, "they are all wrong and I am right!" Of course there is nothing personal in this. From long association you know how ready I have been to accede to your judgment, and what a privilege I have thought it to have the aid and inspiration of your keen insight.— That is why your present behavior causes me such keen regret! Of course something must be done, people cannot be asked to work under such conditions and in such an atmosphere as you are quite wantonly creating. Why won't you act like a business woman?[502]

From April to November 1914, Mary waged a campaign against her fellow board members that took on a tone of self-righteousness and complete moral superiority. Blind to her own faults and shortcomings, her entire attitude was reminiscent of Hartley's tone toward her. When the other board members rebuked her, she played the role of martyr. Impervious to criticism, she responded to all comments as "slurs upon the propriety of my convictions."

Finally, Mary tried to resign as head of the publishing company, but the board members responded by voting to make the executive secretary head of the publishing company. At this, Mary felt she had no choice but to resign from the NAWSA entirely. The resignation was a bitter one. Mary wasted no time in hurling open criticisms at the president and trying to prevent the board from carrying out its decisions. Shaw warned Mary, "Having resigned your office, I think you should permit those of us who are responsible to conduct ours according to our best judgment." Saddened by Mary's change in temperament, she attempted to remain affectionate. Denying any desertion, Mary told Dr. Shaw that "what you have evidently wanted from me is *personal* loyalty, regardless of anything else." What could Anna Shaw say in response? Saddened, she took some time to answer her former co-worker.

A lady said to me some time ago when you were being criticised and I, as usual, was defending you, "Why do you always defend Mrs. Dennett, even when you know she is wrong, as you have several times at the National Conventions, even when you knew it would injure you?" I said, "Yes I have done that but I have always believed her mistakes were honest mistakes and no one is free from them." She replied "Some day you will find her out and rule or ruin is always her way." I said "I do not believe it." Then she said sometime you will offend her by not doing what she wants you to, then look out she will turn on you. I replied "I do not believe it." I owe the lady an apology.

I have placed your letter in the packet with Mrs. Upton's to Dr. King and Mrs. DeVoe's to Mrs. Duniways; it belongs in that group. And yet you are the last woman in the world who had any reason for writing me such a letter.

I shall try to forget it and remember only the many splendid things you have done for our cause and others you have tried to do, and personally, the many kindnesses you have shown me, and I am glad they are so many.[503]

The resignation of Mary Ware Dennett was the end of another relationship. Like her relationship with Hartley, it had started out with high expectations and ended with a bitter crash. Under Dr. Shaw's ambiguous and faltering direction, suffragists passionate about their beliefs had been disunified. Campaigning on partisan tickets, supporters of one faction were continually trying to oust loyalists from another. Efforts to achieve stable leadership were foredoomed to failure with the NAWSA embroiled in perpetual dispute, and the turnover rate of the National board had been high. Mary, however, had managed to jumpstart the suffrage movement. She had brought about unity—at least temporarily—and under her direction, nine states had won their suffrage campaigns. It would take the return of Carrie Catt, the campaigns of Alice Paul, and the leadership of other notable women to make full woman suffrage a reality. Now, however, Mary Ware Dennett was on her own. A divorced mother of two without alimony or child support, she was out of a job.

CHAPTER TEN

Bohemia

ortunately, Mary had created a support system for herself after moving to New York City. Although she had no paid employment lined up for herself to cover her departure from the NAWSA, she was confident that she would be able to find a better job. Five years as a professional suffragist had granted her a reputation as a top-notch organizer and speaker. Involved in a variety of progressive movements, it did not matter to her that most of her other activities drew no income. If the suffragists had become too conservative for her tastes, it was partly because she had discovered an alternative way of living. In the years before the First World War, New York was alive with everything new and modern. Flamboyance, not subtlety, was the rule. Possibilities were endless. Plunging forward with complete faith in the future, Mary Ware Dennett seemed to possess an indefatigable optimism and idealism.

In the same Fifth Avenue building as the NAWSA, Mary had been involved with the Twilight Sleep Association, a group that promoted the use of anesthesia to make possible painless childbirth. Highly controversial, twilight sleep, or *Dammerschlaf*, consisted of using a scopolamine-morphine mixture to induce a condition of mind that would allow a mother to remain perfectly conscious during childbirth, yet lose knowledge of events once the birthing process was over. Developed by professors Bernhard Krönig and Carl Gauss at the Women's Hospital in Freiburg, Germany, the method caused instantaneous forgetfulness of pain, which, as the mother experienced it, was the equivalent of complete insensibility to pain. This amnesia meant that painful sensations would not be stored in the memory to haunt the mother after childbirth, thereby eliminating the shock and exhaustion that usually followed.[504]

As one of the group's founders, Mary had served as acting president from 1913 until 1914, when a president was found, and then as first vice-president after that. The idea of twilight sleep must have held great personal appeal for her. In a brochure she put together, she cited statistics stating that in over five thousand cases over ten years, infant mortality decreased over fifty percent and the use of forceps and other operations were reduced—diminishing both the incidence of lacerations and the dangers of infection.[505] For Mary, it may have seemed like a miracle science cure that might have saved her marriage. Not only had all of her childbirths been extremely difficult—her second child had died within a month of being born and she herself had almost died after the third child.

Despite the sentimental glorification of motherhood, childbirth was at that time a serious risk for women. In 1913 more women between the ages of fifteen and forty-four died in childbirth than from any other cause except for tuberculosis, and the mortality was three times that of typhoid fever.[506] In an age in which childbirth regularly threatened a mother's life and health—yet left the father physically untouched—it could be difficult for many husbands to understand the apprehension with which some wives approached sex and possible pregnancy. As the literature of the Twilight Sleep Association put it, "Childbirth with its attendant agonies, horrors, fears and possible blessings, has been the predominant thought of women for centuries...."[507]

Mary was also a single-taxer almost religious in her belief that private property was the cause of much social ill. In 1913, she had been chairman of the Committee of New Voters, speaking at dinners, aiming to create as many single tax converts as possible. A fervent supporter of Henry George's theory of social reconstruction, she wanted to return the land to the commonwealth, rent it to the people, and then use that tax on the land as the only form of income for the state—thus eliminating all other taxes which served as a barrier to industry.[508] Believing that the root of economic evil was land monopoly, which gave landowners an unearned advantage over others, she argued that taxation could be manipulated to force landowners to put idle land to use.[509] The hope was that single tax would bring about a new social order based on human values, with the message: "Use your land or get off it."

In the vanguard of radicalism, Mary had found a culture beyond the suffragists. Marked by a willingness to test limits, this newfound culture found its zenith below Fourteenth Street. New York's Greenwich Village, in the years immediately preceding the First World War, was the center of the progressive world. The Village was the heart of America's literary and artistic bohemia. Intellectuals doubling as social reformers radiated out from the blocks surrounding Washington Square Park. Teahouses, bars, and restaurants served as anchoring points for residents of the community. In moments of gaiety, women danced naked in the fountain of the square; some were rumored to attend masquerade balls "wearing" largely painted—not cloth—costumes![510] Throughout the 1910s, Greenwich Village set the tone for radicals in New York City. For Mary Ware Dennett, it was the perfect hideaway.

In the Village, artists and writers mixed with students, professors, social workers, and journalists in a self-conscious attempt to create an insular radical community. Intellectuals and professionals began to take on the traditionally erratic personal relationships of the artists; artists began to develop philosophical justifications for their living arrangements. Many of the new Villagers were young; they were often poor; and some were strikingly bizarre. Revolting against what they considered the moral hypocrisy and provincialism of American life, they expressed their emancipation loudly and openly. The women wore sandals and long earrings with smocks of "artistic" shades—bilious yellow-green or magenta-tending violet. Female hair, as one contemporary observer noted, was arranged in either a "wildly natural bird's-nest mass or boldly clubbed after the fashion of Joan of Arc and Mrs. Vernon Castle."[511] Tense little faces and slender arms were surrounded by fashionable clouds of cigarette smoke. The men, wearing collars that were either low and rolling or high and bound with black silk stocks, dressed in the style of a bygone day. Too busy with their ideals to cut their hair, Village men were marked by their studied indifference.

In the Village, rooms were available and rents were low. Pulled in by images of a stimulating and unorthodox culture, newcomers wandered in to find a community where deviant behavior—such as writing poetry, painting, living together without religious sanction, or espousing anarchism—would be cherished rather than condemned. Dedicated to acting out against all traditional taboos—boundaries that had enabled people to live with each other for centuries—they lived without regard for consequences.

Among these bohemians there was a real sense of comradery. Never in danger of getting rich and becoming philistines—for they were not cheap, and they had a genius for hospitality[512]—they formed new ideals of "comradeship," which placed high value on loyalty, trust, generosity, endurance, self-reliance, courage, tenderness, ingenuity, craft, irreverence. Striving to live completely "in the present," they valued absolute candor in behavior and speech.[513] Congregating at places like the Liberal Club on MacDougal Street, a self-proclaimed "meeting place for those interested in New Ideas,"[514] intellectuals made a place for themselves where they could meet, fight, and pass out. During its short pre-WWI heydey, the activities at the club were varied and intense: there were birth-control lectures, all-night dances (to which uncorseted women were admitted!) that were the shock of uptown, plays of young dramatists like Sherwood Anderson, anarchist talks by Alexander Berkman, and the latest cubist art from Paris. Rules stipulated that members could bring friends—if not brought too often—and at times that seemed to mean the entire Village population was packed inside the Liberal Club's two parlors.

One member, Henrietta Rodman, possessed free love ideas that included birth control, which she preached to her public school students. A strong-willed feminist, Rodman protested the Board of Education's policy of dismissing women once they were married. In the fall of 1913, Rodman's endorsements of free love inspired one married member of the Liberal Club to take a mistress, who then moved in with him and his wife to the dismay of other members. Then Rodman insisted Liberal Club members admit blacks, something many members resisted. Eventually, Rodman established her own, separate Liberal Club.

In January 1911, a new Village journal called *The Masses* appeared, whose staff lived at the Liberal Club. Max Eastman was elected editor in 1912, without pay. Aiming to publish "what is too naked or true for a money-making press," the publication voiced the revolt of the young and their hopes for the future. The radicalism of *The Masses* appealed greatly to the radical intellectuals, and Mary Ware Dennett was an avid subscriber.[515] Contributors (seldom paid) included Upton Sinclair, Carl Sandburg, Sherwood Anderson, Jo Davidson, Susan Glaspell, and Pablo Picasso.[516] Radical, witty, and slick, *The Masses* had a style and polish that would set the stage for its apolitical successor, *The New Yorker*.

In January 1913, Village intellectuals began gathering at the home of Mabel Dodge, a wealthy heiress who befriended numerous struggling artists, labor organizers, and anarchists. Typically dressed in a silk gown and great floppy hat, Mabel welcomed everybody to her Wednesday evening salons. During each gathering, a cross section of society gathered together to explore the social and political implications of sexual, artistic, and economic change, with discussions focused around politics, art, sex, and literature. Afterward, Dodge offered a scrumptious midnight buffet. Guests included the poor, the rich, laborskates, scabs, strikers, unemployed, painters, musicians, reporters, editors, swells.[517] One gathering offered one of the earliest public discussions of psychoanalysis. Socialism and workers' rights were hot topics. Sexual equality and free love were the subjects of several gatherings, and one night ended with a Villager named Babs embracing sexual equality by announcing her availability to any man present.[518]

Indeed, the radical intellectuals were deeply influenced by the European sex theorists such as Havelock Ellis and Sigmund Freud. Ellis, an English sexologist whose multi-volume *Studies in the Psychology of Sex* presented a view of sex as a healthy human experience, broke with the Victorian sexual code that presented sex as an evil temptation to be performed hastily for procreative purposes only. Calling sex "all that is most simple and natural and pure and good,"[519] he proposed that part of the "art of love" involved the actual cultivation of desires through a "discreet blend of license and abstinence."[520] In "The Erotic Rights of Women" and "The Objects of Marriage," two essays published together in *The British Society for the Study of Sex Psychology*, Ellis placed women as subjects in the sexual equation whereas before they had only been the objects of male desire. Attacking the Victorian idea of female asexuality, he elevated sex from a base animalistic passion to a spiritual pursuit. "For through harmonious sex relationships a deeper spiritual unity is reached than can possibly be derived from continence in or out of marriage."[521]

Presenting sex as a necessary adjunct to feelings of love, he advocated pre-marital sexual experimentation as well as post-marital sexual variety. He advocated masturbation as an initiatory form of sexual behavior and pleasure. With J.A. Symonds, Ellis undertook a painstaking study of different kinds of male and female homosexuality, theorizing that "sexual inversion," as he termed homosexuality, was congenital—that is, an inborn character trait not acquired through socialization. Presenting a broad survey of of sexual practices that he hoped the world would come to accept and understand, Ellis departed in his views from those of the Victorian sexual paradigm.

It was around this time that Sigmund Freud's theories about human sexuality began to circulate among intellectual and artistic circles. Freud, in his work with hypnosis and the interpretation of dreams, had newly theorized the existence of an unconscious that consisted of hidden inner thoughts that motivated human behavior without subjective awareness. In his *Three Essays on the Theory of Sexuality*, first published in English in 1910,[522] Freud went on to propose the existence of an unconscious sex drive or instinct, termed the *libido*, which he posited was the driving force in a person's life; if left repressed, according to Freud, it would find alternate means of expression. Furthermore, he developed the shocking idea that the libido was present throughout one's life—from birth onward. Infants, then, as well as adults were motivated by this unconscious sex drive (albeit in different forms). Finally, presenting the idea that human beings were "polymorphously perverse," Freud suggested that anything could become the object of sexual desire— not just the opposite sex or even other humans—and that it took an act of conscious will for a person to progress toward so-called "normal" sexuality.[523]

Freud's theories first hit American intellectuals and professionals at a Clark University lecture in September 1909. The radicals went on to portray a distorted view of Freud to a receptive audience. When Freud stated that repression of the libido led to pathological symptoms of "neurosis," the bohemians took this to mean that the libido demanded regular and constant expression in explicitly sexual terms—with no limits set. Repression led to illness; mental health required an active sex life. As psychology replaced religion as the new arbiter of human behavior, mental health and illness became the new metaphors for good and evil. Thus, to be "good," one had to be mentally healthy, and to be mentally healthy, one had to be sexually active. Since human beings were polymorphously perverse, sexual activity did not have to be limited to traditional heterosexual intercourse. This take on Freud burst asunder all past restraints. The new morality demanded that sex become an acceptable topic for public discussion and consumption.

In an attempt to break with her past, Mary was trying to change her persona. She was reading Ellis and Freud, who convinced her that the problems of her "neurotic" aunts and uncles were due to their uneven sex lives. She named the Meads, among other relatives, as particular examples of sexually repressed people she knew—perhaps in an effort to distinguish herself from their Bostonian strictness.

Actually, it was about this time that Mary would carry on a very intense, if brief, love affair with a man in her political circle.

Unknown to her family—particularly her sons—the affair gave her life new, if fleeting, energy. All the emotions she had kept suppressed came tumbling out, eager for release. Unlike Hartley, this new man was interested in suffrage and her other struggles as well. Unfortunately, he was also married. Ultimately, their relationship would mean much more to Mary than it would to her lover (who would remarry someone else). At the end, they would part as "friends," leaving Mary hugely disappointed.

Evidently, her lackluster love life was not so drab after all. In addition to a brief fling, one of Mary's colleagues from Twilight Sleep, Marie Smith, was infatuated with Mary—much to Mary's irritation and dismay. Mary wrote to her mother:

> Marie has been a perfect little fool; she insists on being emotional over me, and it has reached the point of positive erotic degeneration in her. I have tried to cure her by being a brute to her, hoping to make her angry at me for once—and then it would be all over—but she only goes through tragic tearful stormy scenes and ends by licking my boots. It makes me sick and disgusted. Why will people do so! I wish to Heaven some wholesome man would come along and marry her. That's what she needs. I'm almost afraid it will wreck our friendship to cure her of this idiotic infatuation, but it's got to be done—for her own sake. It is fearfully unwholesome to let it go on.[524]

Mary had little patience for her colleague's crush. For despite the weakening of extramarital sexual taboos, the sexual revolution was almost exclusively heterosexual. In a small-scale study of 2,200 college-educated women conducted in the early twentieth century, findings indicated that lesbian activity did not seem to increase for women born after 1890. Women of the nineteenth century often engaged in intense emotional relationships, but physical expressions of affection were not defined sexually. It was common for women to write and speak to each other "in words of passionate endearment," and they also hugged and kissed and slept in beds together without sexual implications.[525]

Yet Mary did not want to be considered a prude. Given the circumstances of her divorce, such a thought must have haunted her. The women in Mary's circle had come a long way from the covered piano limbs of the Victorian age. No longer was it necessary to have a husband and children; experiments with companionate marriage were *de rigeur*; in fact, marriage itself was not even really "in." Indeed, Mary's friend Jessie Ashley believed that the day would soon come when the family unit would dissolve—and "good riddance."

And as for Mary herself, in speaking of her love life she would not admit to anyone that she had one, only saying that there was "nothing which could be all-absorbing."

Like many radicals, Mary was beginning to accept a "modern" view of sex which admitted a purpose for human sexuality in addition to reproduction. In particular, sex was now not only legitimized by procreative intent, but also by love, pleasure, and desire. The new ideas gave rise to a new woman, who was beginning to claim some of the sexual freedom that had long been taken for granted in men. Without question, women's sexual behavior was changing, and it was these changes in women that constituted the very essence of the sexual revolution. Indeed, as the sexes moved toward a single sexual standard in which both men and women were more likely to engage in extramarital sex,[526] the prostitution trade weakened significantly between 1910 and 1920—*not* because of a rise in the standards of men but because of a relaxing of the standards of women.

In the aftermath of Mary's divorce, Greenwich Village became a place for Mary Ware Dennett to lose herself. In the 1910s, the new bohemians gobbled up new thought with remarkable speed, going through phase after phase. They embraced studio life and poverty, labor and anarchy, futurist fads, free-love cults, masquerade balls, psychoanalysis, tea shops, Arts and Crafts, playacting, and more. Though Mary lived and worked in midtown, the Village ethos did not escape her. She created her own dress code, wearing long flowing costumes and draping herself in beads. She cut her wavy blonde hair chin-length and held it in place with a headpiece around her forehead—rather Grecian-looking. She sported pince-nez, made her own sandals and dresses, yet somehow managed to keep her look elegant. In her new look, her love of art and beauty took free rein.

When she sought escape, she headed downtown to meet her compatriots, the radical feminists of Heterodoxy. Heterodoxy was a kind of sorority which served as haven to women of widely divergent political views. Beginning in 1912 with a coterie of twenty-five women who gathered together in a show of sisterhood (membership eventually grew to seventy-five before the club disbanded in the early 1940s), members poured their energies into developing "Unity" and "Fellowship" among a little group of free-willed, self-willed women. Every other Saturday, they debated the social and cultural issues of the day while lunching on good, cheap food. Donning the "garment of comradeship and loyalty, courage and charity, trust and faith and love," Heterodites valued a hearty sense of humor, and they prided themselves on their joyous community.

In a letter to their leader, the Heterodites described themselves as "a little band of willful women, the most unruly and individualistic females you ever fell among." They referred to "this hydra-headed Heterodoxy, with its...eating and smoking...imperviousness to discipline and its strange incapacity for boredom" as "something no prudent woman would have ever put her head to." Professionally, the women covered a wide range of occupations: authors, lawyers, journalists, stockbrokers, theatrical managers, physicians, playwrights, radio commentators, motion-picture scriptwriters, and actresses. Their personal lives and relationships ran the gamut from conventionally married heterosexual women (several of whom kept their maiden names after marriage) to free-love advocates and scandalously divorced women (like Mary) to a rather large number of never-married women, a few of whom were lesbians involved in long-term relationships.

Seemingly hard-boiled on the outside, Heterodites considered their true natures to be tender. "For beneath our obstreperous body you know our soul to be profoundly amenable. The real Heterodoxy is a warm and friendly and staunch spirit, in which our conglomerate personalities all have a share...." They loved their "little Order, seemingly so loosely held together, so casual, so free." Members included some of the most renowned women of the era: Charlotte Perkins Gilman, Mabel Dodge, Crystal Eastman, Elizabeth Gurley Flynn, Rose Pastor Stokes, among others. Charlotte Perkins Gilman composed a tribute to their leader, Marie:

> *To Queen Marie*
> *Who gathers folk of warring creeds*
> *And holds them all as friends,*
> *Who ministers to social needs*
> *And strives for social ends—*
> *All praise to her for her high deeds*
> *And the great gifts she spends*
>
> *Loud talk*
> *And simple feasting:*
> *Discussion of philosophy,*
> *Investigation of subtleties*
> *Tongues loosened*
> *And minds at one.*
> *Hearts refreshed*
> *By discharge of emotion!*

Collectively, the Heterodites felt their spirit to be "one of the emotional treasures of life which all women desire, many of them fear, some of them seek, and a few of them find." Counting themselves among life's lucky "finders," they liked to quote Antigone, who said, "It is the aim of women not to hate, but to love one another."527

Their meeting ground was Polly Holladay's famous MacDougal Street restaurant. Synonymous in many minds with the Village itself, Polly's was considered to be "so obviously vital to the Village as to be easily overlooked."528 Not outwardly original or striking in any way (clean, bare, with paper napkins), Polly's offered such amenities as long waits between courses that were conducive to the onset of philosophic, idealistic, anarchistic, and aesthetic debates. The food was excellent—once it arrived. Formally listed in the telephone book as the Greenwich Village Inn, Polly's was notorious for its arrogant headwaiter-cook-dishwasher, Hippolyte Havel (who was also Polly's lover). Havel gained quick fame among Villagers for his ability to spot uptowners as soon as they entered—after which he would denounce them loudly as "bourgeois pigs" while taking their orders. When Polly Holladay's moved to Sheridan Square in 1921, the parlor floor became the Whitney Gallery, one of the precursors of the Whitney Museum.529

Mary circulated among the progressive circles, picking up snippets of free love, free speech, socialism, and even anarchy. A single-taxer with strong socialist tendencies, Mary stood somewhere on the right of the extreme radicals. Falling in with Jessie Ashley and her lover Big Bill Haywood and Crystal Eastman and her brother Max, Mary disavowed the John Reed school of martyrdom that held that everyone should go to prison. It was a heady time for rebels—divided between revolutionaries and reformers. Revolutionaries believed in overthrowing the social system, rash acts of militant protest, and were romantic (if a bit unrealistic) in their politics. They made the most of newspaper publicity by shunning the bourgeoisie and allying themselves with the working class. On the other hand, reformers worked to change the established social system, adhered to reason and logic, and rallied for progress through orderly means. They were a lot more rational, a lot less emotional. Mary was a reformer. Part of her would have liked to have been a revolutionary. She wanted to be a free spirit. She felt a "general kick against anything and everything that tends to *institutionalize* one's mind" and claimed "a distaste for organizations as such"—yet she would eventually help to organize four, act as director of a half dozen, and serve as a member of some fifteen executive boards.

One Saturday in 1914, Mary went down to the Village for a luncheon gathering of the Heterodites at Polly Holladay's. When the radical feminists of Heterodoxy banded together for lunch and serious discussion, good food and drink were plentiful, but the real prize was free-flowing debate on everything modern and unorthodox: from free love to collective childrearing, divorce, and anarchy. Seating arrangements were democratic; members jostled against each other on benches alongside long wooden tables. Meetings could border on bedlam, as hotly contested political opinions were shouted back and forth—order was maintained by the bang of a gavel.

The topic that day was birth control, a cause that was still not quite respectable. At least as far back as 1912, while she was still at the NAWSA, Mary had come across a publication from England called *The Freewoman*, a radical journal that championed such taboo topics as unwed mothers, prostitution, and birth control. She well knew that without artificial contraceptives, women lived in fear of uncontrolled fecundity—a condition that could kill them, destroy their health, or leave them with more children than they could properly care for. She also believed true union between a husband and wife was dependent upon both spirit and body; complete abstinence in marriage did nothing to further the bonds of love. Yet the withholding of sexual favors put a wife in jeopardy of losing her husband, for it was not unusual for a man to seek physical fulfillment elsewhere when he was dissatisfied with his sex life at home.[530] Given the circumstances of her divorce, these issues must have pierced the very soul of Mary Ware Dennett.

Contraceptive information was relatively hard to obtain during Comstock's era. One had to know the channels. It took courage to give and to get and even to tolerate the distribution of information about birth control. In an age when motherhood was considered to be a woman's only destiny, disseminating information about limiting births was a criminal offense. Folk remedies could be passed down from mother to daughter for those who were lucky. For the rich and well-educated, private doctors might be convinced to impart information at personal discretion. But the broadcasting of any such knowledge was strictly illegal—and violators could be and often were prosecuted under the Comstock Act of 1873. The subject itself was disreputable as it was felt to go against the very foundations of human civilization. Rebels were few and unorganized.

As early as 1893, Emma Goldman, anarchist, feminist, and champion of the poor, began the fight for birth control after her release from Blackwell's Island when she began using her prison training as a practical nurse to practice midwifery among the working classes. Jumping from theory to reality for the first time, she was shocked by the haggard, worn-out bodies of poor and ignorant women, who kept giving birth to sickly babies at near-yearly intervals. She noted, "It was incredible what fantastic methods despair could invent; jumping off tables, rolling on the floor, massaging the stomach, drinking nauseating concoctions, and using blunt instruments."[531] In 1900 she attended a secret Neo-Malthusian Congress in Paris, returning to the United States with a stock of contraceptive literature and supplies. In 1908 she met her future lover Ben Reitman, a radical bohemian medical doctor, who helped her win new audiences beyond the foreign-born radicals, helping her share her views with a broader general audience of native-born Americans. By 1910, birth-control had become a staple on Goldman's lecture tours as she determined to open up the issue among newspaper and magazine editors.

At the same time, Dr. William J. Robinson, a rather eccentric physician "remarkably free of anxiety about his own respectability" began his own pioneer work for birth control from the medical standpoint. A medical journalist and muckraker, he published his ideas about sex in his journal *Medico-Pharmaceutical Critic and Guide*, which was "a compendium of the main sexual attitudes in the liberal parts of the medical profession." In an age when science was replacing religion, physicians were becoming the purveyors of the new sexual morality. With the power to determine who did and who did not deserve contraceptive information, many saw themselves as guardians of society. And the society the mostly-male medical profession envisioned was a traditional one in which a woman's place was to produce babies. In 1912, Robinson convinced Abraham Jacobi, the president of the American Medical Association who is known as the father of pediatrics, to endorse contraception in his presidential address. Even then, however, most medical doctors remained skeptical about the practice.

Through the efforts of radical feminists on one side and liberal medical professionals on the other, the cause of birth control began to gain attention. Heterodite Elizabeth Gurley Flynn recalled a 1913 meeting when I.W.W. organizer Carlo Tresco painted a glowing picture of a future economic commonwealth to women strikers, promising them "More babies!" His appeal fell like a dead weight. At this point, Jessie Ashley's lover Big Bill Haywood interjected, "No, Carlo, we believe in birth control—a few babies, well cared for!" And the women burst into laughter and applause. Among the women listening was a nurse named Margaret Sanger, who had been writing about sex matters for the New York *Call*. Deeply influenced by the free love and anarchist ideas of Emma Goldman, Sanger was impressed by the attention birth control commanded. When Sanger sailed for Paris with her husband and children that fall, she began to learn more about contraception—guided by Bill Haywood, who was also in France.

Indeed, Margaret Sanger was the speaker before the Heterodites on that Saturday in 1914. After returning from France, Sanger had decided to start a radical feminist newspaper called *The Woman Rebel*. Jessie Ashley and Mabel Dodge had agreed to loan her money, and with subscription money from almost a thousand women who thought the journal would contain contraceptive information, Sanger had plunged ahead. In the paper, she proclaimed "A Woman's Duty: To look the whole world in the face with a go-to-hell look in the eyes, to have an ideal, to speak and act in defiance of convention." In another issue, she announced, "Rebel women claim the following Rights: The Right to be Lazy. The Right to be an Unmarried Mother. The Right to Destroy. The Right to Create. The Right to Live and the Right to Love." Running lengthy diatribes against marriage, the YWCA, and John D. Rockefeller—all because they represented to her the "oppressor"— Sanger went on to contrast the church and religion unfavorably with cannibalism. Like other unthinking people, whether liberal or conservative, Sanger was myopic and intolerant. Surpassing even the militant I.W.W. in advocating direct action, for example, she printed an article defending assassination solely to rile up her readership.

Brought before the Heterodoxy, Sanger hoped the women would back her on the birth-control issue. The Heterodites joked about their "marriage customs," dividing themselves into "*monotonists, varietists* and *resistants.*" In a parody of themselves, they wrote, "Most of the *monotonists* were mated young and by pressure of habit and circumstance have remained mated. The *varietists* have never been ceremonially mated but have preferred a succession of matings. The *resistants* have not mated at all. These classes are not at all arbitrary. Some monotonists have practiced variety secretly. Some varietists would like to become monotonists because the marriage union label is useful in some lines of professional work.

Many of the monotonists wear rings to show that they have passed through the ceremonial and are nominally the exclusive possession of some male. The scientific observer, however, should not be led astray by outward totems because I have discovered several instances of ring wearing which are deceptive—rings not having been given by the ceremonial mate. Some of the varietists distinguish themselves by short hair, but again, this is not an infallible sign for one or two varietists wear switches or even transformations."[532]

Indeed, many of the members experimented with alternative lifestyles. Of prime importance for almost all in Heterodoxy was economic independence. They prided themselves on their "taboo against taboo." These women were self-sufficient; they did not rely on men for identity or subsistence. The appeal of birth control was obvious, since an unplanned pregnancy could mean long years away from a woman's life work—even a permanent end to her life dreams—and make earning her own living very difficult indeed.[533] Given this, the Heterodites must have seemed likely to be a naturally appreciative natural audience. Yet after her presentation, Sanger did not receive the response she sought. While many of the women of Heterodoxy sympathized with the birth-control cause, they questioned whether or not Sanger had the organizational skills necessary to carry a major campaign.

Outside of Heterodoxy, Emma Goldman and Dr. William J. Robinson, who had been fighting for birth control for over a decade before Sanger, were already leery of the new woman. Robinson would later write a book review of Sanger's autobiography, *My Fight for Birth Control,* in which he criticized "Margaret's expertness in beating the drums and blowing her own horn," saying that "from the very beginning, Mrs. Sanger wanted to be the whole pooh-bah." Calling her account "unfair, false and lopsided," he pointed out, "It was not she who went on the hunger strike, and it was not she who spent years in prison for her birth control and radical activities. On the contrary, her B.C. activity paid her very well, very well indeed."

Sanger's fame had grown recently in direct proportion to her militant and frenzied emotions, but her self-aggrandizement and lack of discipline was alienating to many potential backers. After the publication of *The Woman Rebel,* it had become clear that Sanger's purpose was mostly to stir up female revolt. Shrill and hysterical, Sanger had been losing much of her support. Ashley and Dodge had refused to loan her more money. Max Eastman called Sanger's writing "over-excited…the blare of rebellion for rebellion's sake." Almost half of her subscribers wanted their money back, as two out of the first three issues had been suppressed by Comstock and had contained no practical contraceptive advice. (The mere defense of contraception and abortion was enough to provoke Comstock, not to mention Sanger's personal attacks and insults against him.)

Out of desperation, Sanger had sent press releases to the mainstream newspapers, hoping to be backed as a heroine for free speech; instead, she was denounced and ridiculed. Then on 14 August 1914, she was served with a subpoena indicting her on three counts—two for publication of lewd and indecent articles and one for incitement to murder and riot. The assassination article had pushed her over the edge. After some hard thinking, however, Sanger had decided to appear in court alone, without a lawyer—a dramatic gesture in the tradition of radical anarchists. Brought before the judge, she affected a charming and demure manner to secure a six-week grace period. During this time, Sanger undertook the project she had previously avoided: she put out a pamphlet giving practical birth-control information and signed her name to it. Called *Family Limitation*, the tract recommended douches, condoms, pessaries, sponges, and vaginal suppositories.

Interestingly enough, Caroline Nelson, a Socialist friend who had just returned from Europe, had recently given Sanger the latest birth-control information translated from French and Swedish. A few days later, Sanger had returned the information to Nelson, saying, "I have shown them to a doctor, but he says they are no good." When Nelson reached Portland, Oregon, on her way home to California, she was surprised to receive a bundle of Margaret's *Family Limitation* pamphlets—containing the same "no-good" information she had sent Sanger.[534] Upon confrontation, Sanger cut off all ties with Nelson.

Indeed, Sanger's name was slowly becoming synonymous with the words birth control. Still often credited with coining the term—a false attribution she did nothing to discourage (indeed she often claimed the credit for it herself)—Sanger actually took the phrase from Robert Allerton Parker, "a professional journalist who had come East from San Francisco to try to become a playwright like his friend, Eugene O'Neill, but hadn't made it." Inflicted with polio, Parker was studying yoga in an effort to rehabilitate his partly paralyzed hand. At a meeting called by Margaret Sanger, he and others had tried to come up with a better way to say contraception than the euphemistic "preventative means" or "conscious generation." Parker thought the idea of "control" so prevalent in yoga might also work with birth. Sanger and her friends liked the term, and it stuck.[535]

Through various means, however, Sanger did manage to draw attention to the birth-control cause. Listening to Sanger speak at Heterodoxy, Mary Ware Dennett decided to pursue the matter further. Acting president of the Twilight Sleep Association at the time, Dennett invited Sanger to a tête-à-tête at her tiny one-room apartment on West Fifty-fifth Street. A leading figure in the suffrage movement, Dennett had already had significant amounts of organizational experience by the time she came across birth control. Still, she was curious to learn more about this new cause from her luncheon guest.

Sanger often spoke passionately about the ill effects of withholding birth-control information from women. History does not record their conversation, but Sanger's style was to appeal to emotion. She often spoke of her longing to lift women from the weight that crushed them under years of uncontrollable childbearing. She frequently explained that she had wanted to become a nurse after hearing "hundreds of poverty-burdened mothers pray that their babies be born dead." It was the poor, she would always insist, that needed birth control the most.

From a working-class Irish Catholic background, Sanger liked to claim personal knowledge about the need for birth control, since it gave her a feeling of moral superiority over the ladies of the sheltered upper class. Perhaps she told Dennett the oft-repeated tale of Sadie Sachs, an impoverished tenement wife of uncertain origin[536]who had begged her doctor for the secret of birth control. The doctor's only advice had been, "So you want to have your cake and eat it too, do you? The secret is, tell Jake to sleep on the roof." Soon pregnant again, as the story went, Mrs. Sachs bled to a gruesome death trying to abort herself. Or perhaps Sanger pointed to her own story, recounting how she had watched her mother die of overwork after bearing eleven children. Playing the role of victim very well, she found it never failed to garner sympathy and support. Her dramatic flair held powerful force. Dennett would later recall that Sanger had captured her attention.

Although she would never publicly speak about it, Dennett herself had a story to tell. Despite her blueblood lineage, Dennett had almost no money. Her divorce had left her impoverished—a single mother wholly responsible for the welfare of herself and her two sons. Every cent she earned either went toward meeting simple living expenses or funding her various crusades for social reform.

Modest in conduct, Dennett didn't talk about her personal affairs. She kept the pain of her divorce inside, only confessing years later to a "suffering so deep that nature mercifully blotted out my memory of some of it." Throwing herself into one social reform after another, her friends and family saw only her positive do-good activism. Yet Dennett was intimate with the dangers and sadness childbearing could bring. Unlike Sanger, Dennett had personally suffered through three painful childbirths, all of which had almost killed her. Not one of the three doctors she had consulted had ever offered her the slightest information about contraception.

Listening to Margaret Sanger, Mary Ware Dennett must have reflected on her own situation. For rich and poor alike, the mostly male medical establishment let out the secret of contraception only at its own discretion. The resulting ignorance held all women under its yoke—the perils of childbearing did not limit themselves to the poor alone. The complications of childbirth knew no class boundaries.

After the luncheon, Dennett may have realized that birth control held staggering possibilities for improving the lives of all women. But the notoriety that Sanger relished struck Mary as an inevitable consequence of any leadership position in this revolutionary movement, and Dennett had a deep-seated aversion to publicity. Besides, she still had her children's welfare to consider. Her attorney, Mr. Merriam, had helped her sell the Framingham house, as she completely lacked the means to maintain it—and there was no point now anyhow, as she and Hartley had built it together and neither had any desire to occupy it alone. Ever since she had moved to New York, she tried to visit her sons once every six to eight weeks or so, and she sent them frequent letters and care packages of food and clothing. Nevertheless, they never knew if there would be enough money to make it to the next semester. Hartley refused to contribute any money at all. And he provided no emotional support either. Reserving judgment of Hartley for herself, she had tried to keep her children blissfully ignorant of precise details. Haunted by the sensationalism of her divorce, Mary wanted to avoid the spotlight. Unwilling to risk further damage, Mary Ware Dennett decided to hold off on this new cause.

CHAPTER ELEVEN

Birth Control
and Sex Education

eanwhile, in August 1914, as Mary was breaking with the NAWSA, the unthinkable had happened: War broke out in Europe. Immediately, many in her circle gathered together to plan a protest—Anna Howard Shaw, Carrie Chapman Catt, Harriot Stanton Blatch, among the suffragists; Charlotte Perkins Gilman and Crystal Eastman, among the Heterodites. Drawn together in their desire to express their horror of war and to sympathize with the suffering in Europe, the women had no specific agenda and no explicit platform. Feeling the urgency of making a timely protest, they were simply united in their need to demonstrate the revulsion they felt as bearers of children, givers of life, to the necessary death and destruction of war.

Within weeks, fifteen hundred women dressed in black were marching somberly down Fifth Avenue, accompanied only by the beat of muffled drums. Crowds gathered to watch, breaking the silence with applause when leaders of the procession revealed their peace flag: a large white banner with a dove carrying an olive branch in the center. The dramatic protest by the women was the beginning of a new round of activities among the radicals. For Mary Ware Dennett, who came from a family of peace activists and who had two sons approaching the age of conscription, the issues were familiar. Her uncle Ned had resigned as editor of *New England Magazine* in 1901 to become director of the World Peace Foundation and a vice-president of the American Peace Society; Aunt Lucia was likewise devoted full-time to peace activities as a director of the American Peace Society.[537] With the outbreak of war in Europe, Mary would be pushed toward pacifism.

Initially, Mary responded by wielding her pen against war. Disturbed by the American tendency to teach young people to privilege brawn over brains, she was unwilling to see her two sons become cannon fodder. In October 1914, she wrote to the editor of *Everybody's Magazine*: "It is a crime against youth to poison their minds with the pernicious theory that organized killing is patriotism while individual killing is murder, or that economic questions (the root cause of all war) can be *settled* by fighting. Fighting settles only who is rich, strong, cruel and physically brave, but it can never settle who is right, intelligent or morally brave. As a remedy for wrongs, it is fundamentally a mistake...it is indulging in temper instead of using brains."[538] Arguing for immediate disarmament, she proposed a plan to flood the press of the country with propaganda. Suggesting that the rich should be responsible for paying for the war through conscription of income, she pointed out, "If the Government has the right to ask some men to fight and give their lives to their country, it certainly has the right to ask other men to give their surplus wealth to the nation's cause."

In December 1914, the editor of the *Woman's Home Companion* asked several prominent men and women to respond to a proposal made by Ida M. Tarbell, a well-known economist, that American women support the "Great Patriotism" by halting all purchases of foreign products and buying only American. While most respondents, male and female, agreed with Tarbell's recommendation, Dennett rejected the appeal. Her belief was that the world had become so interdependent that economic disturbances in one country would affect all. "If we do it with an 'America-for-the-Americans' air, or if we do it with the feeling that we could be willing to take away, wholly or permanently, from our sister countries in Europe commercial opportunities they had legitimately built up, the results will be bad. They will in the long run hurt our national character far more than they may temporarily benefit our industries." Instead, Mary sought to guide readers to "the higher Patriotism, the kind which raises a country's standards and efficiency, without hurting those of any other country. It is the Patriotism which is in line with the great ideal—'My country is the world, my countrymen are all mankind.'"[539]

Before long, Mary had become involved with the Woman's Peace Party, a new peace organization arising out of the activity of the Woman's Peace Parade. Presumed to be naturally inclined, by instinct and temperament, to be the nurturers of children and of human life in general, the solidarity of these women indeed came from their biological status as potential childbearers. Suffragists, in particular, emphasized the particular contributions that women could make to the cause of peace. Drawing upon female workers and leaders largely ignored by established peace organizations, the group insisted upon the "special mission of women." Unafraid to champion unpopular causes—as peace was wont to be in a time of war—the women rallied around an issue that could help them come together as a distinct political entity. As feminists, women had just been politically born, and the Woman's Peace Party would become one of the most influential elements of the peace movement.

The purpose of the Woman's Peace Party was to "enlist all American women in arousing the nations to respect the sacredness of human life and to abolish war—to bring about 'a condition of organized living together among nations.'" The women sought to call an immediate convention of neutral nations to seek early peace, limit armaments, organize opposition to militarism, educate youth in the ideals of peace, place diplomacy in democratic control, extend the franchise to women, develop a "Concert of Nations" to supersede the old "Balance of Power," create a worldwide judicial system, substitute economic pressure and sanctions for armies and navies, and to call upon the government to appoint a commission of women and men to promote international peace.[540] The leaders of the Woman's Peace Party wanted to use their influence to try to persuade President Wilson to call an official conference of neutral nations.

Backing the "Wisconsin Plan," an idea formulated by Julia Grace Wales, an instructor at the University of Wisconsin, the women campaigned for a group of experts representing the neutral nations to form a continuous mediating body that would submit satisfactory proposals to the belligerent powers until a mutually satisfactory solution was reached. Expert representatives would not have to commit neutral nations to action; they would only have the "scientific" function of formulating proposals. In addition to the Woman's Peace Party, the "Wisconsin Plan" had the support of the Wisconsin state legislature and the endorsement of Fola La Follette's father, Wisconsin Senator Robert M. La Follette.

Ever mindful of her sons, Mary encouraged them to become activists as well. On the anniversary of the Star Spangled Banner, she let Carl and Devon be the first signers of a historic peace petition from the children of America to the leaders of the world.[541] Counseling her boys about patriotism, she advised them, "our country is in no position to criticize others, when it is allowing such an awful state of affairs as is going on in Colorado where state soldiers and hired detectives and murderers are killing the miners and women and children too, just because they are demanding as much pay and as good conditions as the miners have in Montana and other states."[542] And on other fronts, when a friend started a Junior

Suffrage Corps in New York, she asked the boys whether or not they might want to start one in Massachusetts.

In January 1915 Mary decided to try to reestablish contact with Hartley, reminding him that they had married each other fifteen years earlier. Claiming that she was "now past the pain" and that her new life was "full & vibrant," she asked of him, "How is it for you?"[543] When she received an unsatisfactory response, Mary wrote a rather pathetic short story that would later be published in *The Century* under the pen name "I.C." From a literary point of view, it was lacking—clearly, her strength was in analytic, not narrative, writing. Transparently autobiographical, it was about a jilted woman who took back her philandering husband upon vanquishing the "other woman." The piece was revealing, however. Despite her insistence that excessive sentiment was "idiotic," Mary still harbored fantasies of winning back Hartley. Whether or not she would admit it, her love for him had not diminished.

Indeed, despite the new sexual mores of her friends, disappointment had failed to destroy Mary's faith in the institution of marriage. After the divorce, Mary had told Hartley she would mourn him "as if he were dead." They had cut off communication almost entirely. But even in 1912, Mary had felt strongly enough about marriage to rebut a letter published in *The Freewoman* written by a woman who claimed, "Only the women who are courageous enough to bear and rear healthy-minded and healthy-bodied illegitimate children, and to educate them so that the jeers of semi-civilized society only rouse their pitying contempt, will really assist the movement."[544] In response, Mary had written, "This can be understood, sympathized with and accepted by almost any woman who dares to think below the surface, but after her first deep breath of relief all the freedom from all the galling complications of married life as most of the world has known it, will surely come the conviction that this is a plea for an abnormal individualism that is permissible and necessary just as hospitals and vacations are necessary as remedial and temporary measures, but cannot be a proper or permanent basis for a normal life."[545]

Feeling that the natural state of human beings was in togetherness—and not separation—Mary yearned for the companionship she had once shared with her ex-husband. Yet pride and an overdeveloped sense of decorum prevented her from communicating her feelings to him directly. Instead, she made a detached and intellectual call for the paternal presence in the hypothetical family. Writing in defense of fatherhood, she said that she had "been waiting for some one to speak a definite word for improving the status of men."[546] She argued that it was even more important for men to be present as fathers in the family than for women to be present as mothers— for no matter what, men could never make up for their inability to bear children. Said Mary, "let the fathers personally 'do' for the children as mothers have always done, but let them do *more* of it— far more…. let men have more of the direct care of the children as state employees—more, even, than the woman, and make it enough more to counterbalance the child-bearing."[547]

Praising past contributions of men in childrearing, she pointed out, "Already men have made excellent preparation for this phase of their evolution. It was men who established the kindergarten idea, men who have mostly developed educational systems, men who have invented labor saving household devices, men who have devised improved housing methods, and even men (physicians) who have perfected the science of infant feeding; so it is not a complete affront to their natures. It is simply a logical next step in their development."[548] Said Mary, "They can do it as amateurs in their own homes, as mothers have always done, or they can do it as professionals in the creche, the kindergarten, and the school, as women will presently do; but do it somehow they must if they are to become complete human beings instead of mere males, if children are to have the benefit of fathering as well as mothering, and if there is to be real equality between the sexes."[549]

As a single mother, Mary was feeling the strain of raising two sons on her own. By January 1915, fourteen-year-old Carl was beginning to ask questions about sex. And Mary, as conscientious in her child rearing as she was in her social activism, wanted to do her best to answer them. Regarding sex, she told them, "[Children] need help from older people about this. Remember to save all your questions and ask me. I will tell you *everything*. I don't want you to be able to grow up and say 'Why didn't my mother tell me these things!'"[550]

Researching over sixty pieces of sex education literature for children, Mary found them all unacceptable. Hunting through bookshops, the New York Public Library, and the library of the American Social Hygiene Association, she found all available "social hygiene" works to be incomplete, lacking in factual detail, completely ignorant of the emotional side of sex, and, worst of all, heavily laden with negative value judgments about sex. In one, she felt the author had a "very old-fashioned stupid idea about women that makes me indignant! He talks as if women were made to be *taken care of*, and not as if they were the *partners* in life with men." Then there was another thing she didn't like. The literature all talked "as if the sex relation was *in itself* a *wrong* thing—to be suppressed or ashamed of. It *isn't*. It is the very greatest physical and emotional pleasure there is in the world. It is only bad when it is *misused*."[551] She protested that she had found no piece of sex education literature that seemed to "explain carefully enough *just what* the sex act is. [The writer] takes it for granted that people know what it is and how it should be done and when etc. but they don't."[552]

Carl's questions set Mary's mind working. She had already written much of the literature for the NAWSA, and she had published other articles as well. Feeling that her own upbringing had been woefully inadequate in the arena of sex education, she wanted to protect her sons against what she considered to be "very misleading and harmful impressions." Unwilling to let her own children grow up to be as ignorant as she had been about sexuality, she decided to remedy the problem herself. As she put it, "no matter how sane and wholesome the family environment may be, children are bound to encounter in their school and wider environment many evidences of the unclean and unscientific attitude of mind regarding sex which is to this day one of the most serious of human disabilities."[553] A born New Englander, she felt most comfortable addressing the subject through writing. So in 1915, Mary Ware Dennett wrote an essay for her two sons in an attempt to demystify sex and sexuality so as to leave no lingering questions. Straightforward, honest, and comprehensive, she called the work *The Sex Side of Life: An Explanation for Young People*.

Hoping to be frank and free of embarrassment, Dennett began by addressing sex in terms of physiology. Unlike much of the "expurgated literature" of the time, she included the proper terminology for the sex organs, avoiding euphemisms. She believed that an adult could not assume that a child would know exactly what the sex act was, so she included a full description of sexual intercourse. She described how semen contained the "male part of the germ of life," which met with the ovum, or the "female part of the germ of life," to create a baby, and then she explained labor and childbirth. Demystifying the menstrual cycle, she explained its purpose in reproduction and assured her sons that the menstrual bleeding girls would experience was not an illness but "only a slight inconvenience." She also spoke of seminal emissions, making it quite clear that, in moderation, they were harmless and natural incidents for boys. She went on to reassure them, "Sex union is the very greatest physical pleasure to be had in all human experience, and it helps very much to increase all other kinds of pleasure also."

Going on to explain sex from the point of view of "natural science," Dennett made a conscious decision to emphasize the *differences*—rather than the similarities—between human beings and the plants and animals. Although she recognized that humans had much "in common with the lower orders," she felt it was in recognizing the distinctions that would help "solve the sexual problems of maturity" and make "wise decisions when...grown." She pointed to the amoeba as the "lowest form of life" saying, "it produces its young by merely separating itself in two. One part drifts off from the other part and each becomes a separate live being. There is no male and no female and they didn't *know* they were doing it." In this, she seemed to suggest that the amoeba was lowly precisely because it reproduced by splitting off, not by joining together in union. Next there were plants, in which there *was* a male and female that *did* join together—but "not by coming to each other, or because they *know* they belong together, but quite unconsciously, with the aid of the bees and other insects and the wind..."

When it came to the higher forms of animal life, Dennett explained, there was not only a male and a female, but the male was able to do his own physical traveling to impregnate the female. Sex was unconscious, taking place during "the mating season...usually in the spring." Said Dennett, "The mating season happens once a year among most of the higher animals, like birds and wild cattle, but to some animals, it comes several times a year as with rabbits..." Not only was reproduction automatic and dictated seasonally, but animals tended to be indiscriminate. "Many of the animals make no choice at all in their mating. Any near-by female will do for the male."

In ordering sex and reproduction in terms of how selective the organism was, Dennett was implicitly suggesting that it was the mind—and its capacity for reason and free will—that set human beings apart from plants and animals. That is, human beings could make choices about how they wished to behave. Despite "a certain amount of instinct," the actions of human beings were ultimately within their control. This was not the only distinction. Judging solely by outward behaviors, it could appear that animals were, for example, discriminating in their mating patterns. Wrote Dennett, "But among some of the higher animals the male has a special instinct for a certain female, and the female will not tolerate any but a certain male. Most of the animals have different mates every season, though there are a few kinds where the male and female, once having mated, remain mates for years, sometimes even for life."

Therefore, Dennett believed that among human beings there was an additional feature in sex and reproduction along with conscious will that distinguished them from animals.

Introducing human emotion, she explained that "the sex impulse among finely developed people is far more the result of their feeling of love for each other than mere animal instinct alone." She insisted that "it is *only human beings* whose mating is what we call 'falling in love,' and that is an experience far beyond anything that the animals know." And what exactly was this feeling of love? "It means that a man and a woman feel that they *belong* to each other in a way that they belong to no one else; it makes them wonderfully happy to be together; they find they want to live together, work together, play together, and to have children together, that is, to marry each other; and their dream is to be happy together all their lives. Sometimes the dream does not come true, and there is much failure and unhappiness, but just the same people go right on trying to make it a success, because it is what they care most for." Obviously writing from personal experience, she went on further to elucidate, "The sex attraction is the deepest feeling that human beings know, and unlike the animals, it is far more than a mere sensation of the body. It takes in the emotions and the mind and the soul, and that is why so much of our happiness is dependent upon it."

In human beings, then, sex had a purpose *in addition* to reproduction. While the primary purpose of sex was unquestionably the perpetuation of the species, it was elevated and even ennobling when accompanied by "love." Without love, the sex act was stripped to an unmindful action befitting an animal. She went even further, saying that the mere physical sex act without love was degrading to a human being. Wrote Dennett, "People's lives grow finer and their characters better, if they have sex relations only with those they love. And those who make the wretched mistake of yielding to the sex impulse alone when there is no love with it, usually live to despise themselves for their weakness and their bad taste." Using this concept of love, Dennett struck down on prostitution—which had been so rampant in the Victoria era. She wrote, "Sex relations belong to love and love is never a *business*. Love is the dearest thing in the world, but it can not be bought."

Dennett went on to address a few other subjects that were controversial at the time. Regarding masturbation, she reflected the mood of the day when she wrote, "Boys and girls both sometimes get the bad habit of handling their sex organs so as to get them excited. This is called masturbation or self-abuse. Such handling can be made to result in a climax something like that of the natural sex act, but there is real danger in making a habit of doing this. It is unnatural and sometimes has a shockingly bad result on the boy or girl in producing self consciousness, unusual timidity, an unwholesome mind, flabby muscles and a weak will. When carried to great extremes it has even been known to lead to insanity."

Touching on a still more controversial subject, venereal disease, Dennett mentioned two varieties in particular, syphilis and gonorrhea, saying that they were "both very infectious and at times difficult to cure." She related methods of transmission, emphasizing that they were diseases usually acquired from an infected person, but occasionally from "using public drinking cups, towels, water-closets, or in any way by which an infected moist article can come in contact with one's skin or mucous membrance when it is broken." Describing them as "invisible enemies" that even when asymptomatic could creep "farther and farther into the body, making serious results that hang on for years," she then went on to emphasize that diseased men "frequently give the infection to their wives, sometimes causing them to be so ill that surgical operations are necessary, by which their sex organs are so crippled that they can never be mothers; and, worst of all, innocent unborn babies are infected and come into the world sick or deformed or blind."

Using the subject of venereal disease to again advise against promiscuous sexual relations, she emphasized that the primary cause for venereal disease was widespread prostitution. Indeed, venereal disease was a serious problem at the time. In 1914, one expert estimated that over half of all American men had been infected with gonorrhea. The double sexual standard had led many innocent women to be infected by their husbands—a favorite topic of Charlotte Perkins Gilman in several of her short stories. And as one feminist historian puts it, "Medical discoveries of the consequences of syphilis and gonorrhea showed that they were even worse than had been previously understood."[554] Nevertheless, seeking to eliminate an *irrational* fear of venereal disease, Mary consciously decided to defy moralists by stating that such diseases were becoming curable.

The other controversial topics that Dennett mentioned were twilight sleep and birth control. Saying that doctors were learning more about how to lessen the pain of childbirth for women, she dismissed any suggestion that pain was or should be a necessary adjunct to childbirth. Saying that in the future people would also be able to understand "how to have babies *only* when they want them and can afford them," she also implied that indiscriminate and uncontrolled fecundity was unwise. Not mentioning birth control by name, she merely hinted at her disapproval of the legal prohibitions against contraceptive knowledge, saying, "Unfortunately, there are still many laws which make it a crime to give people information as to how to manage their sex relations so that no baby will be created unless the father and mother are ready and glad to have it happen. However, these laws are less and less enforced, as knowledge spreads."

Ultimately, Dennett's goal was to eliminate fear and shame about sex. Recognizing the dehabilitating effects that prudery could have on a marital relationship that was ideal in every other way, she hoped to protect her sons from the pain that she had once suffered. Said she, "We have contented ourselves by assuming that marriage makes sex relations respectable. We have not yet said that it is only beautiful sex relations that can make marriage lovely." In an effort to steer her children away from cheap and vulgar information acquired from ignorant playmates, she counseled them, "Don't ever let any one drag you into nasty talk or thought about sex. It is *not* a nasty subject. It should mean everything that is highest and best and happiest in human life." The eternal idealist, Dennett wanted to give to her children the "self-control that is born of knowledge, not fear, the reverence that will prevent premature or trivial connections, the good taste and finesse that will make their sex life, when they reach maturity, a vitalizing success."

While she was working on the essay, Mary learned about a competition being offered by the Metropolitan Life Insurance Company through the American Social Hygiene Association for the best pamphlet on sex education for adolescents between the ages of twelve and sixteen. About five hundred papers were submitted in hopes of winning the $1,000 prize. Realizing her work was progressive, Dennett did not expect to win the money, but the contest led her to frame her essay in a form that would make it useful to children other than her own. For weeks, she delved into the materials of the Academy of Medicine and elsewhere for accurate descriptions and scientific explanations. Surprisingly, she found that no simple diagrams of the sex organs existed. So again, she decided to do it herself, drawing her pictures to illustrate the basic form of the organs and their relation to each other. Showing the manuscript to Dr. Parmenter, the family doctor, for an accuracy check, she was surprised when he said he would "not change a word." According to Mary, he also added "that for the first time he had read something that he would be willing to commend to his patients in response to the frequent request of parents, 'What shall I give the children to read on sex?'"⁵⁵⁵ After completing the essay, Mary sent a copy of it off to Carl, saying she "hoped it would be of some use, by way of supplementing what he already knew."

Meanwhile, Mary kept active in public life, desperately trying to forget her private life. Blocking out the pain of her divorce, she denied having any sentimental feelings at all. After her failed love affair, she tried to avoid what she called "entanglement with other people's lives." While everyone else was throwing caution to the winds, she remained terribly discreet. Her outward excuse for avoiding love relationships was her distaste for media sensationalism: she hated her "celebrity" status as the ex-wife of a free lover. She had no desire to hit the newspapers once again.

But in early 1915, her fears about renewed newspaper publicity were realized. Newspaper reporters revived the "soul mate" story which she thought had ended with her divorce trial two years earlier. Apparently, Hartley and the Chases were announcing the prospect of a reconciliation with Mary. First *The World* called, then the Boston *Globe*, then a reporter from the Syndicate. Mary refused to speak with any of them. Nevertheless her phone kept ringing until she was afraid to answer it. And despite her refusal to cooperate, the papers made up a story anyhow.

> *The invitation of Dr. H. Lincoln, his wife and her soulmate, Hartley Dennett, who make up the Golden Rule triangle at Mount Plato, near East Halstead, N. H., to have Mrs. Mary Ware Dennett, who divorced the soulmate in 1909, adopt the creed of harmonious love and form a quadrangle, was turned down to-day.... Mrs. Sarah Christopher, author of "The New Freedom," who lives at 123 Wadsworth Avenue, and who is familiar with the tenets of the members of the Golden Rule colony, said it was quite possible, under the circumstances, that "Mount Plato" would prove a success. "The woman is to be envied," said Mrs. Christopher. "She has a double portion, while most of us only have a half portion. The soul mate caters to her sentimental nature. Under the high cost of living a woman needs a poet to quote Browning to her and a meal ticket—one who will hew and carry."⁵⁵⁶*

Again, she saw her name liberally splashed about in newspaper stories across the country. The publicity wore down her nerves. Now that she had quit the NAWSA, the papers connected her name with the Twilight Sleep Association. Mary may have wanted to reunite with Hartley, but not on these terms.

Already, Mary felt that she "ought to resign" from the Twilight Sleep Association. Earlier, the president of the association had approached Dennett in "great agitation" and said, "Mrs. Dennett, we must be exceedingly careful what *kind* of woman we add to our Executive Committee. We must have no one who has had any *shadow* on her life. There is already one woman on the committee about whom people raise their eyebrows, and we must be *sure* not to let it happen again." When Mary replied, "Do you mean me?" The president looked amazed and said, "Why *no*—I mean Mrs. Dorr, why *should* I mean you?" After telling the president about her divorce, Mary wrote to her mother and insisted, "you can see what effect this sort of thing has. It makes no difference *who* you are, or what you have *really* done or left undone, you are *branded* just the same."

In a state of self-induced panic, Mary sent a note to a newspaper man to "see if something couldn't be sent out about the [Twilight Sleep] Association of a *very newsy* interesting sort featuring *lots* of people and leaving me out of course, so as to somewhat make up for the damage already done." Obsessed by the fear that her reputation had been destroyed by her sensationalist divorce, Mary lashed out at Hartley for letting the press take over. "To go through the world *branded* as a notorious woman—whether or no—is as near unbearable as anything need be. And just now, particularly, when I must start in with some new work. I wish I didn't think it stood in my way, but I know it does. How Hartley can *let* those Chase fools prattle to the papers is more than I can see. He must have lost every shred of delicacy or good that he ever had—not to mention any sense of fairness toward me. He must now [*sic*] how intolerably hard it makes it for me to have the New York papers full of this stuff. The degeneracy of his character is about all the proof any one would need of the validity of his theories."[557] Mary seemed to feel that by wiping out her name, she would clear her record. Hating attention of any sort, she interpreted the publicity as "scandal." Yet her affair paled in comparison to other scandals filling the news.

After being indicted for the *Woman Rebel*, Margaret Sanger had claimed she sought a test-case to challenge the Comstock prohibition against contraception. When she realized that the charges against her were for different violations of the obscenity law and, even worse, for incitement to murder and riot, Margaret realized that, if convicted, she faced a lengthy prison sentence. Unwilling to accept such consequences, she jumped the bail some friends had raised and fled to Canada. Once there, she secured a forged Canadian passport under the name Bertha Watson and sailed to England. But while she was in England, Margaret's husband William was arrested by Anthony Comstock himself for handing out a copy of *Family Limitation*.

The arrest came at an inconvenient time for Margaret. William Sanger, like William Hartley Dennett, was an architect by profession. From the moment he had met Margaret, he was doting and adoring, and had literally carried her off to be married against her will. Interested in radical politics, he had introduced his wife to socialism and anarchism—ideas she had grown to find more interesting than her husband. In particular, she had been profoundly influenced by Emma Goldman, who argued strongly for free love. Goldman called marriage "a vicious institution which made women into sex-slaves just as capitalism made men into wage-slaves." Goldman told Margaret that if she were to be emancipated, she had to repudiate marriage.

This was fine with Margaret, who had never taken very well to domesticity. She had been bored with traditional home life and had convinced William to sell his dream house, which they had designed and built together, for a fraction of its worth. Her three children had never interested her much. "She declared she was seized with a mysterious 'nervous malady' whenever she had to take care of them and clutched at the first outside interest that came along." Their clothes were held together with safety pins, as she had no interest in sewing.[558] Her eldest son was eleven when she enrolled him in the Modern School, an anarchist school, and it was the first time in his life that he had ever gone to school. He would later recall, "Since it was an anarchist place they let us do anything we liked, so I did nothing, I just fiddled around or played ball all day." Then he realized, "I don't want to be a dumbbell. That means I'll have to learn to read and write."[559] So he insisted on being transferred to a Christian Science school where he was soon reading alongside other children.

For Margaret's interest was primarily sex. Mabel Dodge recalled in her memoirs: "Margaret Sanger was a Madonna type of woman, with soft brown hair parted over a quiet brow, and crystal-clear brown eyes.... It was she who introduced us all to the idea of Birth Control and it, along with other ideas about sex, became her passion." Continued Dodge, "She was the first person I ever knew who was openly an ardent propagandist for the joys of the flesh."560 She was tired of her husband. His adulation was not particularly welcome. On New Year's Eve, he had received a letter from his wife asking for a divorce. For Margaret, emotion was a higher force than reason. "Emotion is that which urges from within, without consciousness of fear or of consequences." Wrote Margaret in her 1914 journal, "I love being ravaged by romances."561

Indeed, while she was in England, avoiding her court date, Margaret had found other interests. Havelock Ellis, noted sexologist, had taken an instant liking to Margaret and had taken her under his wing—beginning a relationship with her that would devastate his wife Edith. In addition, Margaret met another lover, a married Spaniard named Lorenzo Portet, with whom she traveled around Europe. This was not the first time Margaret had been associated with other men. In the past, when her husband had protested, she had advised him to find a mistress of his own. He had insisted, "I will let my name be associated with no other woman.... I would be amiss to all the fine emotion that surges within me if I fell from grace.... It cannot be, that's all." But when he was forced to face her anarchist philosophy of free love, he could only say, "To all this I have no answer."562 Now that he had been arrested for handing out a copy of Margaret's pamphlet, William Sanger seemed to believe that he might have found a way back into her life. Instead, Margaret was merely annoyed that he was receiving the publicity that she felt was due *her.* And she was none too eager to return to the States—she wanted to find out what would happen with his court case first.

The capture of William Sanger proved to be a catalyst that crystallized a good deal of dormant sentiment among radical men and women about birth control. Several groups independently and spontaneously gathered together to "do something" about the arrest. Mary went to a meeting of an informal committee called to raise a defense fund for William, and then later, to a meeting at the home of Clara Gruening Stillman. At the beginning of March, Dennett wrote to her mother about an upcoming meeting of people who wanted to work to repeal the state law prohibiting the dissemination of contraceptive information. "I'm crazy to get in and help actively, for I think it is the biggest single help that can come to women, but I can't do that. I can't afford the time, nor the chance that my name would again get tangled in awful newspaper tales. A leddy 'with a past' is awfully handicapped!"563

Yet a week later, after the meeting had taken place, she wrote to her mother again. Not only were a group of radicals attempting to raise a defense fund for William Sanger, but they had felt that the time was ripe to repeal the Comstock Act, the law that made it a felony to give away birth-control information. For this, they had formed a plan to call another special meeting to obtain one hundred reliable sponsors who would let their names be used, and launch a real organized move to repeal the law. Later the group was known as the Committee of 100. Wrote Dennett, "Two things are very astonishing—up to date—one, that no one yet—whether man or woman, radical or conservative has said a word in honest opposition to the necessity for information on birth-control; and the other that very few people want to come out in the *open* and help. Everyone is scared." The more Dennett considered it, the more she realized birth-control was "like any other area of reform." She told her mother, "But I'm inclined to think that when the ice is once broken everyone will wonder why it wasn't done long ago."[564]

While she hesitated, Dennett soon noticed that besides Margaret Sanger only a handful of people were willing to come out in the open to help the birth-control cause. Most of the suffragists, for example, would not go near the subject. Birth-control was beyond their realm. The same was true of the single taxers, many of whom were men who felt no resonance with the birth-control issue. And even among the twilight sleep crowd, the goal was to make childbirth more pleasant—not control its occurrence. For implicit in the message of birth control was the acceptance of non-procreative sex, a subject that was still "not quite nice" outside of bohemian and intellectual circles. Before birth control could become a popular movement, it was necessary to overcome fundamental problems of fear and embarrassment about sexuality.

By the end of March 1915, Mary Ware Dennett decided to cast aside her fears and organize the first birth-control organization in the country, the National Birth Control League, which was formally founded at the home of Clara Gruening Stillman by Dennett, Jessie Ashley, and Stillman. Dennett made a rousing speech at the founding meeting. She pointed out that despite disparate opinions about the tone of the birth-control movement, there was "marked unanimity on one point, that is, the absolute conviction of each individual that covert information about birth control should be freely available." Furthermore, she declared, it was "an encouraging fact that this conviction seems to be held by all kinds of people—from the most cramped conservative to the freest radical." What prevented action, she was convinced, was a "certain timidity" among both radicals and conservatives which seemed "to be born of a fear that the sensibilities and prejudices of others must somehow be protected."[565]

Dennett claimed that this was a false bogey. "Just *what* others no one seems to exactly know. They are mythical elusive people just round the corner who disappear when we really hunt for them. All we can find are people who say, 'Of course personally, I entirely believe in it, but I am sure that it wouldn't do to say so just yet in any but a purely private way.' Now since almost nobody can be found except perhaps Comstocks, who will say for his or her own self—'I think the present law is right', the rest of us only need to simultaneously shed our 'buts' and 'ifs' which we have been holding for the benefit of the indiscoverable other people, and join together to push for the change we all believe in."[566]

Like a true Bostonian, Dennett appealed to the nobility and dignity of man. "For the highly developed civilized human being there is no such thing as natural sex relations, that is, in the animal sense. We do not—after the simple manner of the animals—have a mating season. We do not have an animal baby. It would be anything but ideal to do so. But instead we expand our creative impulses into other channels which are more beneficial and enjoyable for the race. We find creative scope in the whole wide field of science, art, and community life. And along with this expansion we are developing a conscious and unashamed appreciation of the invaluable reactions upon the individual of the sex relation apart from the question of children. This faculty of appreciation—that evolved use of the sex function seems to be peculiar to the human race—an evidence of its higher development and actual progress."[567] Having suffered through her own ordeal, Mary realized birth control needed to be rescued from the taint of indecency.

In the view of Mary Ware Dennett, social reform was mandated from top to bottom. While Sanger broke laws, Dennett wanted to change them. This meant eliminating the law which made birth control a legal obscenity and repealing the legislation which made distributing birth-control information a crime. Under the Comstock Act, the distribution of birth-control information was a state and federal crime punishable by a $5000 fine or five years in prison or both—for a *first-time offender*. No mere misdemeanor, the crime could theoretically subject the guilty to a loss of citizenship rights. This technicality gave Sanger little worry. Part of Sanger's reputation was made by her deliberate flaunting of the law—both to help women gain access to birth control and to help herself gain access to the media. Constantly in the public eye, Margaret Sanger would make sure her name became synonymous with birth control. But Dennett would develop a significantly different approach to birth-control. She wanted to give women the *legal* right to birth-control information. Unlike Sanger, whose hysterical outbursts early in her career had alienated so many, Dennett was an experienced reformer. As secretary of the newly formed NBCL, Mary began the long process of collecting and distributing facts to educate the public about the legal status of birth control. From the start, she decided that the trick was to do something about that "old sneak Comstock."

The League drafted a statement of endorsement to put pressure on New York state legislators to take birth control out of the obscenity laws. The statement addressed the two most common objections against birth control, namely, that "'the discussion and regulation of this matter would be contrary to the will of God and the laws of Nature,' and secondly, that 'to allow free distribution of information in regard to Birth Control would lead to greater immorality.'"

Refuting the first argument, the NBCL answered that it was "unreasonable to assume that the world is better, because of children born through accidental and irresponsible procreation, resulting inevitably in the birth of many thousands who are diseased, deformed or defective, than it would be if fewer children, and healthier ones, were born into homes ready to welcome them and properly prepared and able to care for them." Making clear the importance of reason and the human mind, the document stated, "The whole history of civilization is based on the subordination of natural laws and forces to human reason and intelligence. By guiding, regulating and intelligently directing Nature we have produced more beautiful fruits and flowers, finer and stronger animals; why not better, stronger, healthier and happier human beings?"[568]

In response to the immorality argument, the League argued that the certain good that would result from the use of birth control would be much greater than the possible harm. Believing that fear was not a very good way to restrain sexual relations, the NBCL argued that birth control would remove "temptation to criminal abortion," reduce the "birth of the unfit (from which class our prisons, reformatories and insane asylums are largely filled)," reduce illegitimacy, preserve women from "too frequent pregnancy (which leads to shattered nervous and physical condition both in mother and child),," give economic relief to the poor, and encourage earlier marriages—which they also believed "would tend to reduce the evils of prostitution."

The framers argued that the abuse of knowledge was less to be feared than the abuse of misinformation and ignorance, saying "it is no more indecent to discuss the anatomy, physiology and hygiene of reproduction in a scientific spirit than it is to discuss the functions of the brains, the heart or the lungs." Finally, the statement asked signers to endorse the belief that "whether or not, and when, a woman should have a child is not a question for physicians to decide—except when the woman's life is endangered—or for the clergy or the state legislators to decide, but a question for the individual family concerned to decide."[569] Seeking to unite disparate sectors of activists interested in social welfare, the League determined to bring together radicals and conservatives, rich and poor. birth control was a subject that transcended class boundaries, and to overcome a tradition of prejudice against it, Dennett understood it would have to be given widespread appeal.

Meanwhile, Carl had received the "Sex Side of Life" essay. Being a boy of few words "to whom letter writing came hard," he did not respond by mail. But when he arrived in New York to visit his mother at the summer's end, Mary was not kept waiting for a response—even though she knew better than to bring it up herself. Coming home from his trip to the San Francisco Expo, Carleton greeted his mother, then jumped into the shower to wash off the grime of a transcontinental flight. Before long, Mary heard her son call out. Sticking his wet blond head out of the door, he grinned, "Hi, mother that paper you sent me was all right." Asked the ever-concerned mother, "Did it fill the bill?" And Carl repeated, "It *sure did.*"[570] From that point on, Mary would loan the manuscript frequently to her friends with adolescent children. Said Mary later, "That remark spoke volumes, and I would far rather have had those few words from him than all the thousand-dollar prizes in the world, or the approval of any sex-hygiene jurors, no matter how academically distinguished."

Indeed, despite her involvement in public affairs, Dennett took the role of parent very seriously. At a school debate, Carl argued for woman suffrage, and Mary sent her support: "hooray for you and 'justice'! May your side win!! Here are some leaflets to help you prepare. Get in and dig, and remember that the strongest answer you can give your opponents when they say that women don't *need* it, don't *want* it, aren't *fit* for it, etc. is that men vote whether they need it, or want it, or are fit. Just remind them *what* the qualifications for voting are in this country—a government 'of the *people*,' and that women are *people*. That's really all there is to it." And then she added, "One more point—remember that voting is a *social* function, not a *sex* function."[571]

Dennett was still looking for a way to support herself and her two sons. Continuing to write, she began to take advantage of her former position with the NAWSA to make commentaries on the suffrage movement. In an article called, "What the Ballot Will Not Do," she established her unwillingness to stand for any intellectual compromise when it came to suffrage. A purist, she felt that if woman suffrage were to be won, it should be on the principle of equal rights alone. Sweeping away false sentimentality, she rejected the idea that woman was man's moral guardian. Pragmatic to the core, she dismissed the idea that there could exist a solid women's vote. Women were as diverse as men, and therefore a woman's vote could not win miracles for society. Women should be able to vote, but only because they were human beings. No other reason would do.[572]

Many other suffragists made their plea by discussing grave social abuses and injustices with fervor and emotion, drawing vivid pictures of the sufferings of the victims of these wrongs and implying, if not actually stating, that all would be altered once women received the vote. But Dennett was inflexible. Regarding the connection between poverty and woman suffrage, for example, Dennett proclaimed, "Poverty cannot be easily or quickly legislated away, no matter how much the newly enfranchised and tender-hearted women of the country may wish it to be. It is no such direct and simple matter as passing a city ordinance that a street cross shall stop on the near side of the crossing." Or regarding equal pay, she had this to say: "Equal pay can come only when public opinion and economic considerations demand it, when women come to be considered stable factors in the industrial world, when a woman's marriage does not almost always mean that she quit her job, when women are organized as well as men, and one might better say when they are organized along with men."

> *Before equal pay can really prevail women must be economically independent, even though married: but you know you cannot legislate women into wanting to become economically independent, much less legislate men into wanting them to be so....These matters are quite beyond the scope of laws. They are the results of education and experience....*[573]

Dennett abhorred such false promises that claimed the ballot would enable women to cure all social ills. In suffrage as in other causes, it would become her trademark to reject all arguments of expediency.

By 1915, Mary Ware Dennett was engrossed in a wide variety of activities, and she was unprepared when Margaret Sanger returned to the States in the fall of 1915 to see the words *birth control* blaring back at her from the same newspapers and magazines that had previously avoided "her" issue. While Margaret had been away, public consciousness had shifted dramatically. Instead of wiping out the small pockets of birth-control activity among the radical elements of society, as Comstock officials had hoped, the arrest of William Sanger had spawned a new movement. Spearheaded by Mary Ware Dennett, a cause that had previously been supported only by scattered anarchists, socialists, and eccentric physicians was now quietly but deliberately being translated to arouse the mainstream conscience.

Welcoming Sanger back into the fold, Dennett invited Margaret to serve on the executive committee of the NBCL. Sanger refused. It was bad enough that her husband was receiving the media attention that she felt was due her, but who was Mary Ware Dennett? Sanger viewed Dennett as a rival who, while she had been away, had usurped her rightful place as head of the birth-control cause. Dennett, however, simply felt committed to another vital reform movement.

CHAPTER TWELVE

Radical Politics

I n December 1915, Mary was asked by Winthrop D. Lane to help form and join the Civic Club, a "democratic" social club for men and women actively interested in public affairs. Located in Greenwich Village, at 14 West Twelfth Street, the Civic Club was a center for relaxation and social mingling but its purpose was service. The hospitable, old-fashioned house a few doors from Fifth Avenue was far enough off the beaten track to insure quiet and promote leisure. Members were encouraged to come singly or in groups, to read, talk, and hold informal discussions. The restaurant was excellent, inexpensive, and popular. Tea in the lounge was a daily institution. There were club nights for dancing, plays, games, and other diversions. The club conducted regular Sunday afternoon conferences and monthly or more frequent dinner meetings at which timely topics were discussed by men and women of distinction. There was also a continuous art exhibition in its gallery to encourage the production and ownership of original work, and to provide a direct connection between artists and the public and pave the way for a civic art gallery.

Many of the members were men and women that Mary would work with on committees over the years: Crystal Eastman, Max Eastman, Walter Lippmann, Amos and Gertrude Pinchot, Ida Rauh, Henrietta Rodman, Rose Pastor Stokes, Ida Tarbell, Jessie Ashley, Marie V. Smith, Harriet Stanton Blatch, Henry Chung, W.E.B. DuBois, Londa Fletcher, Mrs. Borden Harriman, Fola LaFollette, Mrs. Thomas Lamont, Winthrop D. Lane, Margaret Sanger, and Oswald G. Villard, among others. Mary worked with activists of both sexes, and in movements such as single tax or international free trade she was often the only female presence on the executive board. Her interests were broad; she was always involved in many organizations at once.

Still seeking regular employment after her break with the NAWSA, Dennett was not idle as she threw herself into various reforms. In October 1915, Dennett had loaned the Twilight Sleep

Association $150 toward meeting its deficit—despite her own precarious financial situation. Without a regular income, however, she had to recognize that she could not afford to conduct a volunteer educational campaign on the cause of women's health. To complicate matters, Marie Smith was writing Dennett constant letters of adulation, and Marie would not stop making lesbian advances toward her.[574] Finally, Mary, who was essentially a moderate woman, was not eager to be associated with something as controversial as twilight sleep. On 6 January 1916, Mary announced her wish to be relieved of the vice-presidency, since there was again no president—and she didn't want the position.[575] It was not long before Dennett, who had become the driving force of the organization, moved to dissolve the association altogether.

Mary was also beginning to make a presence in the field of sex education. The essay she had written for Carl and Devon was making its rounds among her friends. Since 1916, Dennett had been writing to various book publishers hoping to find someone willing to print and market her essay. In letter after letter, however, the publishers wrote back saying that although they admired her work very much, the essay was too short to be profitable.

Simultaneously, in her pursuit of world peace, she had to face the mounting signs that the president was not going to cede to the demands of the Woman's Peace Party to sponsor an official conference to mediate terms of peace. The women had come up with an alternative proposal for an "unofficial" conference of neutrals, in hopes that "the people" would be able to represent themselves instead of being represented by unrepresentative professional diplomats. Even this modest proposal had begun to fade, however, when word reached the women in November 1915 that Rosika Schwimmer, an "irrepressible Hungarian," had somehow persuaded Henry Ford to support a conference of neutrals. Offering solid financial support for the central initiative of the Woman's Peace Party, Ford chartered a ship to carry American delegates to an unofficial conference. Jane Addams was among those chosen to go as a delegate; Mary Ware Dennett was offered a place on the Ford Peace Ship as a reporter.

Unfortunately, despite high hopes, the Ford Peace Ship's "shipload of pacifists" promptly plunged the Woman's Peace Party into public ridicule. On 15 November, Wilson had called for a program of "reasonable" military preparedness that included increased shipbuilding and the creation of a new reserve army of 400,000 men.

The country was drawing closer to war, and the cause of peace was growing increasingly unpopular. The movement away from established diplomatic ties could only lead to a gradual alienation of the Woman's Peace Party from majority opinion in influential circles, particularly on the eastern seaboard. At the January 1916 annual convention, Jane Addams denied any official connection between the Woman's Peace Party and the Ford Peace Ship, but the damage had already been done. Active peace programs were declining "precipitously in popularity," and if the women wanted to retain any influence, they would have to gear their major efforts to less unpopular domestic campaigns.

Indeed, several leaders of the Woman's Peace Party had already begun to complain of the radical leadership of the New York branch. Mary's Aunt Lucia "warned that Crystal Eastman was 'such an extreme socialist that she cannot greatly help the movement...'"[576] In addition, the Massachusetts contingent was concerned about the predominance of several I.W.W. sympathizers in strategic positions in the New York organization. On nearly every issue from an uncompromising suffrage plank to an uncompromising opposition to military preparedness, the New York group took the radical position while New England members, led by the Massachusetts branch, pleaded for less controversial stands.

As part of the New York branch of the Woman's Peace Party, Mary Ware Dennett looked at things differently from her aunt. A group of social workers had organized the "Anti-Militarism Committee" in November 1915, changing its name to the "Anti-Preparedness Committee" in January 1916, and then to the "American Union Against Militarism" in April 1916. The initial structure and proposed methods of the AUAM were to provide information and coordinate the activities of various militant peace groups. Membership was limited to a small devoted group of "high-class experts," who planned a "truth squad" to follow President Wilson on his "Swing around the Circle" for preparedness. Wilson had challenged opponents of increased military preparations to hire their own halls and answer him. In response, the AUAM had decided to organize mass meetings against preparedness in eleven major cities. Seeking a "prize agitator," they sought to enlist a figure from the woman suffrage or prohibition campaign to carry out the propaganda campaign.[577]

In March 1916, Mary Ware Dennett was engaged as field secretary to embark on the "Truth about Preparedness Campaign." Paid a salary of $50 a week plus expenses, she worked as Eastern Organizer managing a series of big mass meetings in five cities: Buffalo, Cleveland, Detroit, Cinncinnati, and Pittsburgh.[578] Quickly, she developed a routine. Going into a town for the first time, she telegraphed ahead to a contact person to gather together a group of prominent local people to organize a committee. Upon arrival, she jumped into a taxi, went to her hotel, telephoned locals to let them know she had arrived, asked them where to meet, and then sent off a few telegrams—about four a day—dictated letters to the public stenographer, and then went off to meet the people. At the meeting, she would meet with the people, argue out their doubts, whoop things up and then get them to elect officers for an organizational structure. After personally visiting with well-known people in town, she would meet with newspaper editors and send a report off to AUAM headquarters. Said Mary, "the nights I can sleep in a bed instead of a sleeping car, I call myself lucky. I average every second night on the train."[579]

The AUAM declared its intention to "throw…a monkey wrench into the machinery of preparedness" and to "stop the war" through a conference of neutrals. Said the Reverend John Haynes Holmes, "every lover of civilization and servant of human kind—the social worker first among them all—must be a *peace fanatic*" and must strike at the roots of commercialism and militarism, and reject the "dilettante, academic, pink-tea, high-brow" approach of the old organized peace movement.[580] With nothing personal against Wilson, most of the AUAM actually felt that his instincts were sound on domestic issues. Perfectly happy with his administration's previous record, they convinced themselves that they retained sufficient personal influence with Wilson to gain his sympathetic attention at this crucial moment.[581]

In April 1916 the AUAM added more objectives to their program. They wanted to keep military training out of schools, resist conscription, and impose income and inheritance taxes to meet costs of any increased military expenditures. Crystal Eastman offered Dennett the job of executive secretary of the local New York City branch of the AUAM and acting secretary of the National while Eastman herself went on summer vacation. Perpetually engaged in payment disputes, however, Dennett refused. Feeling like she was doing most of the work, Mary was unwilling to accept even vacation pay or any other money for work not performed. Unable to come to an agreement, Mary Ware Dennett resigned in July 1916.

In need of a new source of income, Mary turned again to writing. In a May 1916 article called "The Right of a Child to Two Parents," Mary expanded on her ideals of family. Starting off with an image of a "padonna and child"—a young father tenderly holding his little baby in his arms—she emphasized the importance of shared parenthood, saying, "Child-rearing and home-making should be human work, not limited to either sex, but undertaken jointly and equally by both. If bringing up children is really a serious, inspiring work, as we are assured it is, then by all means the men should not be barred out from its beneficent reactions. It is not possible for the selfsame work to be broadening and beautifying if women do it, and petty and inconsequential if men do it. When really pushed to be consistent on the subject, men are apt to resort to expounding about how women are specially fitted for the work, can do it gracefully, have a God-given faculty for it, etc. But really just all there is to it which is God-given is the physical ability to bear the children. All else is the result of practice, moral character, and love, three things which are human and not sex acquirements, and in which men can be quite as proficient as women if they will, and which, if God-given, are bestowed upon men and women alike."

Unbeknownst to Mary, Hartley saw this article and recognized himself as the proud and loving father in the idyllic domestic scene. In a letter to Margaret Chase, he wrote, "Beloved... The introducing skit in the article on 2 parents refers to me, as you may imagine." Having picked up the *Century* article while on a short business trip in Massachusetts, he decided to send it to Margaret in New Hampshire to show her what the "outside world" was thinking about. One can only imagine the thoughts that may have run through his head. Did he feel any wistfulness or longing for his real family? Or did it merely provoke more resentment toward Mary, reminding him that she, not he, had full custody of their children? Certainly, it would have taken real honesty, integrity, and humility—not to mention moral courage—for him to admit to any feelings of the former, and perhaps he did not see the point as he had already hurt his ex-wife so badly. Mary had become the great unknown—their relationship was not necessarily repairable; Margaret was the new constancy in his life. In any case, the article did make him think. He made reference to it in at least two letters to Margaret, and she was wise enough to acknowledge receipt of the article—without making a big fuss about it—a week later.[582]

Indeed, in many ways, Mary's article was revolutionary. Defining a new set of family values, she argued that it was necessary for a mother to be economically independent, "for the sake of the soundness of family life." Rejecting the notion of a male breadwinner and a female housekeeper, she felt it was not enough for the man to simply provide materially for the family. "Men have been apt to assume that their responsibilities to women and children were wholly discharged by merely paying over cash, without much personal service. Both men and women have meant well, but the men have been rather stupidly selfish, and the women stupidly unselfish." Dennett was far ahead of her time; it would take decades for feminists to come to a similar conclusion.

Believing in cooperation and equality—not separate spheres—she disapproved of the husband and father who was technically present but functionally absent. "Children are mostly brought up by their mothers, an arrangement which the world has accepted without question for centuries. But now, owing to the social ferment which, whether we like it or not, is disturbing the women's traditional sphere, we find ourselves asking if that scheme of child-rearing is really best for the children, best for the mothers, and finally if it is best for the fathers." Wrote Mary, "Some one has said that 'the greatest effort of civilization up to date has been attaching man to the family.' Very likely, but in many ways the attachment has been bad for him and bad for the family. It has developed in him a pernicious type of pride which has led him to deem women and children as possessions—a pride no less false when sugar-coated with sentimental or chivalrous talk of the 'my wife, my mother, my sister, my children' variety. Men's families have been for the most part either a source of this false pride or else a millstone round their necks; sometimes both. Most middle-class men are hopelessly dulled and stupefied by mere grubbing to get the family bills paid." She concluded: "The moment both parents take a proportionate share in the earning and in the tending, the normal balance is struck immediately."

Still unable to address Hartley directly, Mary could not know that he read her article on a train in Boston and recognized the opening "skit" as referring to him.[583] Stubborn, Mary possessed that fatal human flaw: the need to be "right." Unfortunately, self-righteousness, even if justified, was a quality born of ego, and one that could never bring happiness. On 21 July 1916, desperate to re-establish contact with her ex-husband, but still unwilling to compromise,

Mary wrote a letter to Hartley that began, "It is possible that I shall not live much longer. If, presently, I find that to be a *probability*—rather than a *possibility*,—it will, of course make a good deal of difference in my plans concerning the immediate future of the boys."[584] Taking on the tone of the proud but martyred mother, she then attacked the father.

> *My wish for them, so far as you are concerned, is that you will help them, financially, from a distance, until they are out of college, and that until then, you will not attempt any closer personal relations with them than now exist. After that, let happen what will. They will be mature enough then, to be able to judge with reasonable fairness, as to the value of your point of view about personal life and responsibilities, and I have no fear for their conclusions. It might even be that they would be much benefitted by friendship with you, and I am sure you would find their friendship—if you could win it—a well of inspiration and pleasure.*
>
> *My own attitude has very considerably altered since you knew me,—and the boys know, in a general way, what my later views are. They know that I have no criticism to make about your love for Margaret and your relations with her. They know that my present criticism is only for your unjust and ungenerous treatment of them and me at a time when I was too undone to make an immediately successful struggle economically. They know, too, how sorry I have been that you gave up your profession and your growing place in the world. So far as the matter has been talked of at all,—which is very little,—the tendency of my influence has always been for them to wait till they are grown before they try to wholly understand.[585]*

Of course, Mary did not die, and Hartley did not respond to her melodramatic attempt at pathos with great remorse. Instead, he wrote back telling her that she was absolutely wrong in separating the boys from their father.

> *I am sure your life under this regime which you have brought into being and kept alive by main strength, is anything but a paradise, and I have told you that in my part as father of our two boys I am practically prevented by it from expressing in action my love and care for them. When you ask me to express in my action your love for them I can only answer that I have love of my own that I wish to apply, and that it is in your power, and it is your duty, to so undo your work that I can do so; and I dare say the sum of your care and mine is a better and bigger care than yours alone, no matter what reinforcements you are able to bring to bear.[586]*

At a stalemate, Mary continued to struggle with subsistence living, hoping to support herself and her two sons through her freelance work. "The Sex Side of Life" essay was enjoying an increasingly brisk circulation among her friends, fueling hopes that it might eventually be published. As copies of the essay came back to her dog-eared and worn, Mary continued to write to book publishers hoping to find a distributor. Activities in the birth-control cause were picking up as well, as the NBCL had chosen Dennett, Elinor Byrns, and Paul Kennaday to act as a legislative committee. As its driving force, Dennett organized followers to harangue lawmakers in Albany about legalizing birth control. The motto of the NBCL was "The first right a child should have is that of being wanted."

On 16 October 1916, Sanger and her sister, Ethel Byrne, opened the first American birth-control clinic in Brooklyn, New York. Sanger showered Italian, Jewish, and other neighborhoods with pamphlets advertising the clinic. For ten cents, the two of them announced, they would show women how to use pessaries, condoms, and other contraceptives.[587] Many of Sanger's patients were poor. "Sex was one of the few luxuries their husbands had, and these men refused to limit their own enjoyment."[588] The clinic lasted for ten days before it was closed by the police for violating the Comstock Act. Immediately Ethel Byrne, whose trial came up before her sister's, was sentenced to a month in jail on Blackwell's Island. To gain publicity, Byrne decided to go on a hunger strike.

Birth-control supporters were quick to respond. The group of women that would later be known as the Committee of 100 was attempting to find one hundred reliable sponsors who would let their names be used to launch a concerted move to repeal the law. These women were willing to overlook some of Sanger's indiscretions because of her charismatic personality, but they preferred to find a legislative solution to the birth-control problem.[589] Rich and powerful, at just one "parlor meeting" they were able to raise $700 simply by passing around a hat![590] Composed of women, however, the committee was wary of doctors and legislators: "We believe that the question of whether or not, and when, a woman should have a child, is not a question for the doctors to decide, except in cases where the woman's life is endangered, or for the state legislators to decide, but a question for the woman herself to decide." This official credo was drafted by Juliet Rublee, a Chicago heiress whose husband served on the Federal Trade Commission as a Wilson appointee.

The Committee of 100 held a rally at Carnegie Hall with Margaret Sanger as featured speaker. The event attracted three thousand supporters and raised $1000. Working-class women filled the

upper gallery seats, which sold for 25 cents, and they offered a
sharp contrast to the "richly dressed" society types in the boxes
below. Several days later, a delegation from the Committee of 100,
afraid that Byrne might actually die of malnutrition, arranged for
Sanger to meet with New York governor Charles Whitman. He par-
doned Byrne, but when Sanger's trial came up she was sentenced to
thirty days at another correctional institution. Sanger did not
attempt a hunger strike, and Byrne's acclaim brought to a head a
long rivalry festering between the two sisters. Instead of bonding
them together in a common cause, the incident caused a permanent
rift between the siblings, and, unfortunately, Sanger saw that it
effectively ended Byrne's participation in the movement.

Meanwhile, in the fall Dennett went on to work as executive
secretary of the Women's Committee to Re-elect Wilson. Many of the
AUAM workers were diverting part of their energies to helping reassure his reelection. Convinced that Wilson shared their basic outlook, they pinned their hopes on him as their best chance of keeping
the country out of war. Writing a pamphlet called "What to Do to
Help Re-Elect President Wilson If You Are a Woman Without a Vote
of Your Own," Dennett argued that Wilson's track record on children, labor, unemployment, farmers, business, taxation, and the
postal service, had "begun to make democracy a reality at last."[591]
She coordinated a "Women's National Automobile Campaign" for
Wilson, enlisting women to drive across the country to make
speeches and distribute literature. Pointing out that Wilson had been
the first president to vote for woman suffrage (as an independent
citizen in New Jersey), she then emphasized, "The women of the
country will never cease to be profoundly grateful that President
Wilson has held the nation steady in times of unprecedented international turmoil, has kept us at peace and has preserved our
national self-respect at the same time."[592]

The campaign to reelect Wilson was successful, and it gave Mary
a prestigious new job as executive secretary of the League for
Progressive Democracy, the women's branch of the Democratic
Party. Paid $300 a month and supplied with an assistant, she was
hopeful about working for change from inside the political system.
With renewed belief in democracy, Mary noted the capacities of the
women workers, saying it was "very noticeable" that the women did
not simply have a "vicarious connection with politics, because they
may have chanced to marry Democratic leaders," but instead they
had all accomplished things of importance themselves. Said Dennett,

"The political creed of these women is simple but big. They demand results. Their main interest is not *politics*, but *policies*; not *men*, but *measures.*"

With Elizabeth Bass, chair of the League for Progressive Democracy, Mary hoped "to lift the mass of the Democratic Party through the women to a plane that *no* political party has ever occupied."593 As a self-described radical, what interested her was the opportunity her position would give "for really radicalizing the Democratic Party, via the masses of the independent voting women of the west." With high hopes, Mary felt she had finally found an organization through which she could effect *wide-scale* social reform. Said Dennett, "If we had been free to carry out our plans it would have meant a new era in American political life. We had plans up our sleeve which we never told for publication but which were the soul of the whole enterprise. The women voters were the balance of power in the presidential election (and will be also in the Congressional elections of next year) and so they could force the Democratic Party in self defense to stand for almost any radical policies."594

But in early April 1917, an announcement from President Wilson changed everything: The United States had declared war on Germany. Intellectuals and peace activists plunged into a time of great angst and internal search. Prominent social workers were disturbed, as they knew that an important part of their program was friendly relations with the government. Even the most ardent supporters of peace were forced to reconsider their associations with the peace movement to retain their jobs and influence within the mainstream machinery. They could not expect government cooperation if they drifted into a "party of opposition." An influential minority now sought more "quiet" approaches, arguing they would lose all opportunity for exerting influence if they continued in opposition to American intervention. After all, an aggressive defense of conscientious objectors seemed to border on deliberate interference with the administration's war efforts. Any support of peace activities would mean a move further toward radicalism.

The goals of the peace movement began to split. The New York members of the Woman's Peace Party had begun to see in the peace movement the possibility of its serving as an agent for wholesale social transformation. Taking great pride in having built the party from "a polite society affair into an active democratic, decisive organization," by late 1916 it was actively encouraging the influx of authors and playwrights and others of a radical or bohemian bent.

Crystal Eastman went so far as to suggest revolutionist John Reed as a speaker for a branch meeting. A secretary of the New York branch began to see the peace movement "as not simply an emotional anti-war cause but as part of the fight for freedom for the great masses of people."595

On the other hand, the Massachusetts branch was busy trying to ply its way back into the mainstream. Members participated in various forms of war service and refused to criticize the administration's policies or urge peace initiatives upon it. "Lucia Ames Mead reported that Massachusetts members were disturbed over the appearance of a pamphlet by Randolph Bourne with a Woman's Peace Party stamp, and that they were 'distressed' over the radicalism and flippancy of a New York branch publication entitled *The Fourlights*. Mrs. Mead warned that to prevent a defection of the Massachusetts branch, the party would have to be 'more explicit' in its patriotism, more appreciative of President Wilson's aims. It should declare that 'there can be no peace until the military domination of Prussia is destroyed.' It would be best, she argued, to keep Crystal Eastman off the national executive board as she was 'so conspicuous in more radical organizations.'"596 By 1917, these two branches—New York and Massachusetts—had emerged as the only strong branches, and their positions had become increasingly polarized. Anna Garlin Spencer remarked that Boston and New York seemed to represent "opposite ends of the moral universe."597

New organizations, "mostly microscopic in active membership and radical in tendency," arose almost daily. On the executive committee of the New York No-Conscription Committee, which would merge with the New York AUAM to turn into the Civil Liberties Bureau of the AUAM, Mary lamented, "Life is just one committee after another!"598 The press hurled epithets at the AUAM, and grafitti covered the lobby walls at headquarters announcing each arrival's entrance into "Treason's Twilight Zone."599 Its officers began to desert the ranks, and the AUAM entered into its final stages of disintegration. Among the suffragists, Carrie Catt offered the services of the NAWSA for war duties such as bond selling and taking a military census to prove that women deserved the vote as much as men.

Pessimism, acute frustration, and confusion of purpose filled the air. Many peace activists, liberal and radical, whose activities and connections had bridged two worlds were forced to make a choice— between the world of institutional and organizational connections with the nation's political and social establishment that allowed them to work as respectable reformers from within the system, and the world of radical dissent in which they operated as knowledge-able critics and occasional allies of those bent upon more revolu-tionary methods of change.[600]

The time had come, many activists concluded, to measure the good that could be accomplished through an uncompromising anti-war stance against the good that could be accomplished as a social worker or reformer who preserved at least a modicum of public influence and worked within the system. Between March and August 1917, the overwhelming majority of men and women in the remaining peace organizations resigned or ceased to participate, allowing the organizations to simply atrophy. One by one, almost without fail, when put to the test, they continued to sympathize with the ideals and goals of the peace organizations, but they aban-doned practical activity for other work that often actually contributed to the nation's war effort. Alice Hamilton recalled that although both she and Julia Lathrop were pacifists, "neither of us took a conspicuous anti-war stand, for the same reason—we were deeply attached to our jobs and feared to lose them." Then she added, "I have never been sure I was right in this. Perhaps it would have been better to make an open protest, but I knew I was not influential enough to have that protest count for much, while my work in the war industries counted for a good deal."[601]

Mary Ware Dennett was one of the rare exceptions. The decision of the president to enter the war devastated her. Mary was "utterly nauseated at the action of the National Suffrage Association for sell-ing out the cause by offering war service to the administration," calling them "craven" for "in every way toadying to the govern-ment." Personally, she had always felt herself to be a consistent pacifist. Her campaign for the AUAM was a fight against the pre-paredness program. She claimed she "never swallowed Wilson whole, that she had always had "several very serious reservations," and had "worked in his election campaign only because [she] believed he was the country's best hope."[602] Furthermore, Dennett pointed to "the most unfortunate narrowness of the small group in the Dem. Nat'l. Com. who had direct charge at Headquarters. They had no interest in the women's end of the work and also a certain jealousy and fear as to the power the women might develop. They used the war as an excuse for cutting down the program in all departments, although their effort to minimize the women's depart-ment was entirely obvious before war was declared."[603]

Claiming she was upset not by Wilson's sincerity, but by his judgment, Dennett was disappointed that he did not at least wait to try out the armed neutrality plan, that he did not call the neutral nations together to consult, that he did not offer mediation to the belligerants, that he did not propose to both Germany and England that both countries should call off their starvation blockades, and that he shut his eyes to the great vision of world citizenship that, in her opinion, had made his "peace without victory" speech the greatest utterance from any president yet.[604] Her disappointment was great, for again, reality failed to match up to her ideals. Lamented Mary, "I am so dreadfully sorry about it all! Of all the various things with which I have been connected, this big plan for building up democracy via the women touched me most deeply. It had such glorious possibilities!"[605]

On 15 April 1917, Dennett submitted a long letter to the head of the League for Progressive Democracy, Mrs. George Bass, explaining her need to resign. Wrote Mary, "Neither the reasons for going into the war, as given by the President, nor the program proposed by him seemed to me compatible with the principles of democracy, or along the line of his own proven idealism."[606] Sending her letter of resignation to friends and colleagues, Mary was deluged with letters of support and admiration. Typically, the responses praised her spirit of courage and self-sacrifice. Possibly, many of the men and women envied Mary for taking the moral high ground, while they themselves capitulated to the war interests. Some sympathizers even wrote to Mary with new job offers, asking her to name her salary.

It was the same pattern again. Beginning with high hopes, Mary worked for a short while before becoming disappointed with what she found. When Anna Howard Shaw, Dennett's former boss at the NAWSA, learned of Mary's resignation, she wrote to her former co-worker, "Of course I do not understand any of the real inwardness of the causes which lead you to take the step you did nor do I understand exactly your stand point toward present conditions. All I know is, that whether we want it or not, whether we approve of it or not, the Nation is at war and I believe that before the war is over the horrible results of it will present themselves in this country as well as in the old world." Counseled Shaw, "We may not approve of all the people who are working nor of all the ways in which they are working, but we must remember, Mrs. Dennett, that we have got to work with human beings and that most human beings are a long way from being perfect. They have their faults, their weaknesses, their sins and their vices, but we have got to work with them. We cannot have people made to order to work with in this world at this time and however we may not agree with their methods or their principles or lack of principles, nevertheless we have got to make the best of the world as we find it and do our part."[607]

As much of an idealist in 1917 as she was when she resigned from the NAWSA, Mary made every effort to live her life wholly according to principle. Often impractical, she was perfectly aware that she had the tendency to be "utterly rash" in undertaking work that was precarious financially. Said Dennett, "I have done just this thing nearly all my life, and it proves to be a very expensive luxury for me, especially as living expenses keep on soaring and I shall very shortly have other financial drains beside the whole care of my two boys."[608] Now that she needed a job, foremost in her mind was the desire to earn her living by doing something she was sure was along the line of the "biggest needs of the time." Encouraged by the job offers, she felt she could set her own price at a minimum of $300 a month.

Considering several jobs, however, she found that she really didn't want any of them. The National Birth Control League, upon hearing that Dennett was free, had jumped at the chance to hire her for full-time work. Sending Mary a telegram and several letters, they insisted that their current executive secretary was "not at all equal to position."[609] Offering Dennett $300 a month, the chairperson insisted, "After all you were our first choice & the ideal person for the job."[610] But after considering all the jobs offered her after her resignation from the League for Progressive Democracy, Dennett decided to make peace activities her priority.

On 30 May 1917, Mary Ware Dennett, along with Crystal and Max Eastman, became one of seven original organizers of the People's Council of America, a radically antiwar organization which looked to the Bolsheviks as an example of how American citizens could wrest power from the government and bring it back to the people.[611] Modeled after the Council of the Workmen's and Soldiers' Delegates, the sovereign power in Russia, it hoped to bring about an early general peace in Europe based on terms already announced by Russian Government: "No forcible annexations, no punitive indemnities, the right of nations to decide their own destinies."[612] The very name "council" was a self-conscious attempt at a direct translation of the Russian term "Soviet."[613] The People's Council brought together radicals, labor leaders, and intellectuals.

That summer, Mary was employed by the People's Council to organize and rally up members on the West Coast, paid $8 a day plus
expenses. In eight weeks, the organization, which was made up of
delegates from existing organizations, enrolled 1,800,000 members.[614] The People's Council put together a Washington delegation to
meet with the president, consisting of Dr. Judah L. Magnus, Mr.
Fischer, Dr. Lindley Keasbey, Job Harriman, and Mary Ware Dennett.
The president declined to receive the committee.[615] Unlike both the
Woman's Peace Party and the AUAM, the initial organizers of the
People's Council made great strides in correcting the middle-class
provincialism of earlier phases of peace movement, and the Council
was able to marshal impressive support from organized labor. The
aim was to have a majority of delegates come from the progressive
trade union locals, the single-taxers, the vigorous socialist locals, the
Granges, the Farmers' Co-operative Union, and other agricultural
organizations.[616]

From the beginning, national leaders of the Socialist Party played
crucial roles in organizing the People's Council: Morris Hillquit,
Algernon Lee, Socialist candidate for governor of New York, James
Maurer, Socialist candidate for president of the United States.
Single-taxers such as Daniel Kiefer and Bolton Hall were prominent,
as were communists such as Benjamin Gitlow, Juliet Poyntz,
Elizabeth Gurley Flynn. In addition, New York City artists and
intellectuals long involved in radical causes also gave the venture
varying degrees of support: John Reed, Randolph Bourne, historian
Charles A. Beard, Sara Bard Field, James Waldo Fawcett, Charles
Rann Kennedy, Edith Wynne Matthieson, Rose and Ann Strunsky,
and Fola La Follette. Finally, A.W. Ricker, editor of *Pearson's
Magazine*, Art Young, cartoonist for *The Masses*, Max Eastman, and
members of the staffs of *New York Call* and *Appeal to Reason* offered
to send out leaflets explaining the purpose of the new organization.

In a press release, Mary stated "that after three months of the
paralyzing mental numbness which the declaration of war induced;
there is now coming the chance to join a great practical movement
for the application of democracy to the war situation." She called
the People's Council a "second Wind" started by an indomitable
group "who have all along refused to be hypnotized by the deaden-
ing remarks heard on every hand that begin,—'But now that the
war is here, I suppose the only thing to do is to see it through, etc.,
etc.'" Dennett stated, "Those who are now the nucleus of the
People's Council believe in the democracy of the people, not the

democracy of the diplomats. They believe that every single bit of real democracy that the United States has achieved up to date, must be kept alive and working not only after the war but during the war." Furthermore, she said, "They believe that the United States government must be made to prove literally and absolutely that its one greatest desire is democracy." She claimed, "The People's Council is positive proof that American democracy is real and alive. It is a spontaneous move for a program based on the policies of the people. And the policies of the people, whenever and wherever they become formulated the world over, are wonderfully alike."[617]

Indeed, Mary was one of the few thorough-going pacifists migrating from the earlier peace organizations. The majority, however, were driven by other motives. "Some seem to have been spurred by the excitement of their rapid radicalization to further adventures that would bring them into even more intimate contact with working-class and bohemian radicalism. Others had found a satisfying sense of community in the comradeship of 'that faithful little regiment which...stood firm when the whole world shook....' 'The loyalty, enthusiasm and devotion of those workers created an atmosphere which cannot be described,' Lella Secor later reminisced. 'I have never lived through such a vivid and buoyant emotional experience.'"[618] Margaret Lane called the continued efforts of nonpacifist peace workers a general "revolt against everything grayhaired and respectable."[619] The attraction of People's Council was the way in which it merged domestic radicalism with agitation for peace. "Even among the more experienced peace workers, its appeal was not so much its pacifistic message as the way in which current events in Russia enabled it to combine ostensible pacifism with a vision of a new American revolution."[620] The propaganda stated, "The President has said that it is our purpose to help make the world safe for democracy. We would like to make democracy safe in our own country!"

That fall, several of the members of the People's Council rallied together to campaign for Morris Hillquit as mayor of New York City. Among them were Mary Ware Dennett, Crystal Eastman, Lella Faye Secor, Rebecca Shelly, and Daniel Kiefer. The campaign was not successful, and in December 1917, the Socialist Party ruled out an antiwar meeting for Madison Square Garden and declined to consider other peace meetings.[621] Furthermore, in September 1917, a group of prowar Socialists connected with the government had begun a direct frontal attack against the People's Council. Indeed, the People's Council had hardly been formally constituted when it began to founder. "Nothing could hide the fact that this last, most radical of the wartime peace organizations, was disintegrating."[622]

Mary's salary was again in arrears, and it would not be until February 1918 that the People's Council would pay up her salary and expenses. The war had radicalized Mary irreversibly. The same year, Dennett, along with Edwin S. Potter, became part of a group that proposed the formation of a new political party, to be called the "Radical Freedom Party" or "Liberty Party," which hoped to secure within four months a competent live chairman in every one of the 435 Congressional districts of the country. Ultimately called the "National Party," the party platform recognized "God as the source of all beneficent government" and regarded the declaration of its principles "as a solemn covenant with the American people." Amos Pinchot was the choice for president. Seeking to be a coalition of the radical and liberal elements of American society, the National Party drew enough attention to be critiqued by Henry Ford, who wrote, "The plan, which undoubtedly was to unite all the forward-looking men into one body, was commendable enough, but it did not recognize the fact that not all forward-looking men are of the stuff that party conventions are made of."[623]

From there, Mary kept busy in a hodgepodge of other political organizations. She was involved with the Women's Committee for World Disarmament, the American Proportional Representation League (which was pushing a new way to tally votes in elections), the New York No-Conscription Committee, and a host of other obscure groups. She became executive secretary of the Meeting Committee of the National Civil Liberties Bureau (later to develop into the American Civil Liberties Union), for which she organized mass meetings to protest the war[624] and was elected to the Executive Board of the National Woman's Peace Party. In 1918, she became involved in the launch of *Feminist Magazine*, a magazine that proposed "to break the age-long silence concerning everything that really matters to women," and was incorporated as the Family Publishing Co.

Jumping from one organization to another, or involved in several simultaneously, she was part of a core community of activists who were constantly pushing for progress. Mary's activities throughout the war years ran like a blueprint of many of the progressive era reform movements that existed. She held leadership positions in so many organizations that it was often difficult to keep track of her, and she would continually draw upon the large number of contacts and use the organizational skills she developed throughout her life. From twilight sleep to single tax to peace to birth control, she said of herself, "A much shorter and better description of me—a jack of all trades."[625] Striving to live by high ideals, she threw herself into whatever seemed most important. Despite all of her activity in various sorts of social reform, however, Mary kept returning to the issue of women and family. For there was a deep hurt in her that longed to be healed—and it was to remedying this pain that she would ultimately devote her whole heart and soul.

CHAPTER THIRTEEN

Sanger vs. Dennett

s the campaign for peace fizzled, so did Dennett's prospects for employment. Sensitive to the exigencies of a changing world, Mary found herself, once again, searching for the ultimate cause that could usher in the dawn of a new day. Drawn to an eclectic assortment of clubs and leagues, she found that each promised to fulfill a different facet of an elusive movement toward broad social regeneration. Reconsidering birth control, Mary wondered if it might not have far-reaching consequences. Might not birth control be a panacea for many social ills?

In January 1918, at the age of forty-five, Mary Ware Dennett agreed to take the position of executive secretary of the National Birth Control League. As she had in 1915, Dennett made eliminating the obscenity laws her first priority. Drawing upon her connections in other areas of social reform, she gathered together radicals and conservatives who were working toward social progress. Convincing the wealthy to lend their names and money to the cause, she put together an organized effort to take birth control out of the obscenity laws. According to Dennett, it was political action, not direct action, that would make birth control commonplace and acceptable. She felt that until sex itself became a topic that could be discussed with good taste by intelligent people, birth control would be dismissed by the general public as a hysterical grievance of sex-crazed anarchists. While not ceasing all activity in other organizations entirely, she focused her energy to a much greater degree on birth control. Making the most of all the training she had received at the NAWSA, Dennett began a nationwide campaign of education and literature distribution.

Setting to work right away, Dennett put together a "Plan of Work for Birth Control" which she circulated among the members of the NBCL. First, she called for groups of people around the country to form leagues and committees. After researching the laws of each state, she had discovered eighteen states that completely prohibited contraceptive information, twenty-three states that had laws "permitting court decisions that contraceptive information is 'immoral' or 'obscene' and therefore criminal,'" and only five states—Georgia, New Hampshire, New Mexico, North Carolina, and Washington—that were without restrictive legislation.[626] Second, she advised the selection of active committees to secure signatures within two weeks, if possible, from representative citizens to a statement endorsing birth control. She counseled, "Include among the signers, well known physicians, clergymen, educators, editors, social service workers, club leaders, business men, labor leaders, trained nurses, etc." Once a stipulated number of signatures had been collected, she instructed birth controllers to give the statement with the signatures to the local papers, together with the address of a chairman or secretary.

From there, all activities were to be centered around repealing the Comstock Act. Dennett wanted it to become common knowledge that the federal law made it a crime to mail birth-control information, and that most of the states made it a "crime to give it by any means whatever." She instructed "birth controllers" to place paid advertisements with legislative blanks and a further appeal for signatures. "ATTENTION! EVERY MAN AND WOMAN IN THIS TOWN! Which sort of family is the biggest asset for the country in time of war, or peace, the one in which an annual baby is born to deplete the mother's health, the father's earnings, the other children's food and care; or the one in which the babies are intelligently 'spaced' like the vegetables in the war gardens, so that the health and money of that family can be used to the utmost advantage for it's own strength and that of the nation?" Now capitulating to the war interests herself, she sought the widest possible appeal. *"Birth control means race conservation. It means having children as they are wanted and can be cared for, not otherwise."*

By this means, Dennett envisioned small groups of newly awakened birth controllers meeting all over the country—"in private homes, churches, schools, labor unions, clubs, anywhere." She encouraged all supporters and all new converts to join the umbrella organization and raise money for large supplies of literature, which would then be distributed all over town. Said Dennett, "By this time you will have made the subject of birth control 'respectable.' You will have disarmed prejudice and public opinion will be with you. And…you will have done your part to hurry on the day when contraception will be taught in the medical colleges, when clinics can be established in all large cities, and when we can be free to publish and distribute an edition of at least a million copies of a pamphlet giving the very best contraceptive information the world affords."[627]

Hoping to help birth controllers such as Margaret Sanger, Dennett instigated a law-abiding campaign to change the laws which criminalized Sanger's activism in the first place. In the winter of 1917, the National Birth Control League had made its first legislative move in Albany, New York, by pushing for a straight state repeal bill to remove the words "preventing conception" whenever they occurred in the obscenity statutes.[628] The bill was introduced by a Democrat and a Socialist, which quickly proved to be a disadvantage in an overwhelmingly Republican legislature. In addition, Dennett soon discovered that what legislators said in private was very different from they were willing to stand for in public. birth control carried the taint of sex, a subject politicians were careful to stay away from, and publicity from sensationalist arrests and hunger strikes did nothing to reassure the lawmakers. Said Dennett, "No one has offered real objection to the bill,—simply an instinctive aversion to the whole subject as a matter of public concern." To remedy this, it would be necessary to reshape the way in which sex itself was viewed.

Focusing on education, Dennett began to make inroads in reshaping sexual ethics. Her essay, "The Sex Side of Life," was still making its rounds among her friends. Before long, someone had passed it along to the *Medical Review of Reviews*, and in December 1917, the editor, Frederic Robinson, had indicated a willingness to publish the little treatise, saying that "if it created wide interest, we would arrange to get it out in pamphlet form for you." Dennett had been seeking a publisher for the essay for quite some time, but she promptly discovered to her dismay that publication in a professional journal meant that her work would be used without pay. Accustomed to writing to augment her income, Mary balked, saying "I should of course like to have the article published in a way that would be financially advantageous."

Eventually, agreeing to publication without pay, Dennett saw her essay, "The Sex Side of Life," published in the February 1918 *Medical Review of Reviews*. Robinson presented it with the special introduction, "We have come across so much rubbish on this subject that we drifted into the conclusion that an honest sex essay for young folks would not be produced by this generation." He continued, "No editor ever confesses that he reads an article with prejudice, but we will admit that we expected this MS would be 'returned with thanks.' It was reasonable to suppose that a laywoman would not succeed where physicians had failed. Even after we had read the introduction we were not convinced, for we have met several books whose texts do not fulfill the promises made by the preface. But after reading a few pages of the essay itself we realized we were listening to the music of a different drummer. Instead of the familiar notes of fear and prejudice, we were surprised to hear the clarion call of truth." Continuing with an unusual recommendation, Robinson wrote: "Mary Ware Dennett's "Sex Side of Life" is 'on the level.' In the pages of the *Medical Review of Reviews* her essay will be read only by the profession, but we sincerely hope that this splendid contribution will be reprinted in pamphlet form and distributed by the thousands to the general public."[629]

Awaiting a response, Dennett embarked on another publishing venture. In February 1918, Dennett became one of fifteen women to incorporate the New York Women's Publishing Company, a group whose primary purpose was to publish a new publication, the *Birth Control Review*. The Board of Directors included Margaret Sanger, Juliet Rublee, Jessie Ashley, Helen Todd, and Virginia Heidelberg, among others. The goal of the group was to use the *Review* as a way to disseminate information about the activities of the birth-control movement. Sanger was editor of the *Birth Control Review*, but Dennett arranged to have one page of each issue devoted to the details of the NBCL's organizational work.[630] Consistent with her goals as executive secretary of the NBCL, Dennett used the page to organize birth-control workers around the repeal of the Comstock Act.

By October, however, Sanger was beginning to complain that too much space was being taken up by the names of the officers of the NBCL and by the League's legislative blanks. Suggesting that the League confine its page to matters of more general and literary interest, Sanger claimed that there was an "overemphasis" on the NBCL's program for changing the law. At a Board meeting, a general discussion resulted in a group decision to omit the names of the League Committee and to print legislative blanks only at intervals instead of in every issue. Although Dennett emphasized the necessity of using the convictions of the readers of the *Review* for making definite progress toward the repeal of the restrictive laws and felt that the League's page should be used for this purpose primarily, she was overruled.[631]

In response, Dennett continued to try to reformulate the way sex was viewed by the general populace. In one of her most important articles written for the *Birth Control Review*, called "The Stupidity of Us Humans," Dennett laid out her philosophy of sex. Drawing upon her youthful ideals of art and beauty, Mary argued that human beings had four basic functions: to feed, clothe, shelter, and mate and reproduce ourselves. In fulfilling these functions, however, she argued that "unaided nature" was not enough. Reminding the reader that it was the ability to *reason* that distinguished man from the beasts, she called upon human beings to use their *minds*.

Dennett posed the question: "what have we learned to do, in addition to what bare nature does for us?" Again, Dennett went down the list. "As to food,—we do something besides satisfy our hunger. We feed ourselves scientifically and artistically,—that is, we *dine*. We avoid gluttony and intemperance. As to clothes,—we do something besides merely covering ourselves. We try to dress health-fully and to give delight to the onlooker, if we can. We avoid excess and ostentation. As to shelter,—we do something besides merely crawl in out of the weather. We make homes, with beautiful furnish-ings and an atmosphere of charm. We entertain." For these first three, she pointed out, "we have added science and art to natural instinct and need, in order to make these three functions *socially* productive beyond their primary intent. We produce emotional, men-tal, moral and spiritual values from our expanded exercise of these basic functions." Stressing that refinement required human beings to develop their functions beyond a basic animal level, she said, "Each one thus becomes a *double* function. It serves its primary purpose and variously enriches our lives besides. We take pride in this devel-opment. It is, in a large way, the measure of our civilization."

With this idea of civility, Dennett addressed sex. "But as to the fourth great natural function, sex relations,—what do we do, what have we learned besides what bare nature teaches us? Mighty little. We don't know what to do. We flounder." Given that the primary purpose of sex was the production of children, she argued that humans were unwilling to "follow primitive nature's way which is to have an annual baby." Yet at the same time, humans did not "insist that the race shall understand how to improve scientifically upon nature's way, by spacing births with reference to health, income, environment and choice. The law declares it a crime to learn this sci-ence, and tradition, outwardly at least, upholds the law." Furthermore, she protested, regarding the "secondary use of sex relations," there were some people who insisted "that there ought not to be secondary uses of this function at all."

Dennett discounted the "purists" who idealized sex relations as "beautiful, sacred, perfect" when the sole purpose was reproduction, but who claimed that any other purpose was "degrading self-indulgence." She said of them, "They accept sex relations as necessary for parenthood and demand complete suppression otherwise,—and arbitrarily call that *moral triumph.*" Continuing her theme, she pointed out, "These people are relatively few. Yet they have a persistent influence on the majority who do not hold such views. They do not succeed in altering the practice of the majority, but they do make the majority feel somewhat apologetic and shame-faced,—for the simple reason that the majority are ignorant and feel somehow that it is improper to be intelligent on this subject." Wrote Dennett, "The mass of people hardly dare to believe that there are precious and vitalizing results from sex relations which are an enrichment of life and a source of happiness just as children are. They are afraid to assume that there are similar emotional, mental, moral and spiritual values to be derived from the exercise of this function, just as legitimately as from the acts of providing ourselves with food, clothes and shelter." Looking again to uplift the human condition, she said of these purists, "Feeling that perhaps the whole thing may be wrong, they find it hard to determine what temperance and good taste in sex life may be." And what was the outcome of an enforced silence on sex? "There are no standards. There is little open discussion....The mass blunder on in darkness and embarrassment."

Dennett's conclusion was that in order for human beings to rise above the purely physical plane, birth control was necessary. Unlike the animals, human beings possessed intellects by which they could organize and perfect society. Indeed, unlike the animals, human beings possessed minds by which they could and did conquer nature. Speaking of sex, she said, "Here is a great field of human development neglected and weed-grown. When shall we wake up and begin seriously to work upon it?" Birth control would elevate humankind. "Getting the Birth-control question straightened out is the first imperative step: It will open the way for all the rest. And presently it will be natural to apply science and art to sex relations as fully as we now do to the matter of food, clothes and shelter."[632]

The birth controllers had used the war effort to argue that "race conservation in war time makes birth control a necessity." Claiming that only by regulating the size of families in proportion to income would it be possible to take proper care of babies, they campaigned to "avoid the wastage of bearing all these thousands of poor little diseased infants, predestined to die before they are a year old, or if they survive, to become in a majority of cases inmates of prisons, insane asylums, and houses of prostitution, as reliable statistics prove."[633] Reasoning that birth control would decrease infant mortality as well as improve the "stock" of those babies that did live, the argument was that contraception would actually push up the population size.

As executive secretary of the NBCL, Dennett was carefully and diligently taking the skills she had picked up in the other movements and transferring them to birth control. She spoke before women's clubs, medical organizations, and political leagues. In one ten-day trip in New York state, she established five local branches of the National League. The travel was exhausting, but she campaigned hard to effect a repeal of the contraceptive clause in the state obscenity law, sending out about sixty circular letters with literature to doctors, legislators, health authorities, social workers, welfare and civic organizations, socialist locals, and others. The membership of the NBCL increased almost ten times within the year. She raised almost five thousand dollars and oversaw the publication of 135,000 pieces of literature. According to Dennett, the war had inculcated a sense of responsibility for public health that was making work for birth control "relatively easy." Said Dennett, "Success is to be had 'for the asking' if enough asking is done."[634]

Dennett's gains only made Sanger uneasy. Withdrawing from their earlier friendship which had started when Dennett invited Sanger into her home, Sanger began to distance herself. Growing increasingly territorial, Sanger began to subvert Dennett's gains. When Dennett published a cohesive plan of action for the NBCL in the *Birth Control Review*, Sanger had Dennett's page discontinued. Calling together a nationwide conference purporting to represent every element of the birth-control movement, Sanger pointedly did not invite the NBCL, the largest birth-control organization in the community. And at a key meeting where she was to address potential birth-control supporters, Sanger promised to appeal to the audience to back Dennett's bill in the New York state legislature. Not only did she break her promise, but when asked, "What about the work in Albany?" Sanger, who advocated a more hands-on approach, answered, "I believe there are some New York women working there, but it is doubtful if legislative work is worthwhile at present."

Undaunted, Mary moved forward in her birth-control work. She decided that the NBCL needed reorganization. Frustrated by the lack of funds, she noticed that by March 1919, only one thousand dollars more had been raised—most of it by herself—and the executive committee had voted to cut back work to a volunteer basis. Furthermore, Dennett's own salary was two months in arrears. Feeling that the time was "ripe" for a major legislative campaign, Dennett decided to resign from the NBCL to found a new organization, to be called the Voluntary Parenthood League. Drawing from the example of the suffrage movement, Dennett realized that rather than work state by state, it would be much more efficient to attack the contraceptive clause of the Comstock Law at the *federal* level. She argued that "Washington was only two hours further away from the Headquarters than Albany, and that convincing Congress was only a slightly bigger task, numerically speaking, than convincing the New York Legislature." Saying "that precisely the same motions had to be gone through in either case...the great difference was that for approximately the same effort, success in the one case would mean altering the laws of only one state, and success in the other case would mean altering the law which affects the whole nation."

Her argument won. Within six months, the NBCL had collapsed, and most of its members had joined the Voluntary Parenthood League. The goals of the VPL were twofold: to make contraceptive knowledge available by removing the words "prevention of conception" from federal obscenity laws "which now besmirch and degrade the question of intelligent parenthood by including it with penalized indecencies," and to educate parents so that children would be born with "due regard to health, heredity, income, choice, environment and the well-being of the community." Emphasizing "intelligent parenthood," Dennett hoped to elevate the status of birth control so that contraception could become available for rich and poor women alike.

Upon founding the VPL, Dennett again invited Sanger to serve on the executive committee. But again, Sanger turned her down. But the move only served to alienate Sanger further. When Dennett tried to underline the absurdity of Sanger's stance against legalizing birth control by pointing out that Sanger's own birth-control pamphlet, *Family Limitation*, was illegal, she only succeeded in antagonizing Sanger still more. In 1919, for the first time, Sanger showed a slight interest in the legislative end of the movement. Striking out against Dennett's "clean repeal" bill, Sanger approved of a bill to legalize birth-control information for doctors only. It was the beginning of an unbridgeable split.

Before long, the schism began to grow embarrassing. After working to convince legislators to pass a "clean repeal" bill, Dennett now had to explain why there was disagreement within the movement. Issuing a document called "Why Two Groups?" Dennett made three major points. First, she explained that the VPL was against a medical monopoly on contraceptive knowledge. Driving home the point that facts about contraceptives were basic information which should be accessible to all—not just the elite, and not just doctors—Dennett argued that the rich would always have access to birth control. To keep birth control under the brand of legal obscenity would only hurt those who needed help the most. Dennett's VPL wanted to see birth control taken out *completely* from the Comstock laws. In no uncertain terms, Dennett called Sanger's measure which allowed access to birth-control information "class legislation": "The legal restrictions as to contraceptive knowledge operate chiefly against the poor.... The well-to-do, in spite of the laws, get information...." Unlike Sanger, Dennett *refused* to settle for class legislation.

In her second important point, Dennett explained that the VPL considered birth control to be a *humanist* movement, a *parenthood* question, to include both men and women. Since it took two to create a child, she reasoned, the responsibility should be consciously shared by *both*. Honoring both sexes on the VPL board, Dennett believed *on principle* in jointly solving the birth-control problem. On the other hand, Sanger, according to Dennett, pushed birth control as a *feminist* movement, a *motherhood* question, to be solved by women *only*. As Sanger wrote in the *Birth Control Review*, "Birth Control is a woman's problem. The quicker she accepts it as hers and hers alone, the quicker will society respect motherhood." Absolutely against any kind of separatist thinking whatsoever, Dennett believed in *partnership*.

Third, the VPL worked for federal legislation first, and state legislation afterward, because federal action would make possible the circulation of authorized publications everywhere and would also lift the ban on verbal birth-control instruction and clinical service in twenty-four states in one fell swoop; Sanger stood for state legislation first and federal legislation afterward—what Dennett considered "a slow and expensive progress somewhat analagous to winning suffrage a state at a time instead of by federal action." According to Dennett, the federal bill provided the quickest way to make birth-control clinics practicable all over the country, by at once removing the obscenity precedent in twenty-four states, and by setting a most compelling example to the other twenty-four states to repeal their special restrictive laws. Sanger opposed the federal bill in the *Birth Control Review* and at her public appearances—even refusing to give the VPL time at her birth-control conferences to explain information concerning the federal bill, and the results it would bring.

Striking out around the country on a negative campaign, Sanger claimed that she had "once, too, been naïve" enough to think that contraceptive information should be available to all. Sanger declared that her European exile had taught her to rethink her attitudes. Now she believed that "doctors only" should have the right to unregulated access to birth-control information. Sanger's willingness to compromise may have stemmed from a legal loophole that had come about after her arrest in 1915—it allowed doctors small leeway for prescribing contraception. Hypocritically enough, however, Sanger herself continued to distribute contraceptive information as she pleased—despite the obvious fact that she was *not* a physician. The only real effect of Sanger's "doctor's only" stance was that it blocked Dennett's progress. Dennett found Sanger's position untenable. Giving in to the mostly male medical establishment, Sanger's policy would have kept birth-control information out of the control of women. Dennett—unwilling to compromise on birth control rights—pleaded with Sanger to join hands and reconsider. Sanger refused.

Keeping up her connections with the medical editor Frederic Robinson, Dennett tried to cultivate the support of the medical profession for the birth-control movement. In March 1919, Dennett oversaw the editing of a symposium of physicians' opinions on birth control for the *Medical Review of Reviews*. She wrote the foreword, emphasizing that "both the average physician and the average layman have one characteristic in common, namely, a sense of confusion and embarrassment which mostly inhibits the aiding of any procedure calculated to remove the whole subject from legal prohibition and social taboos." Dennett asked a group of physicians their opinions about the morality of birth-control knowledge. "Do you think the widespread knowledge of birth control would result in an increase of immorality by permitting sexual indulgence without the responsibilities of parenthood; or do you think it would tend to decrease immorality by enabling young men to marry without the immediate fear of having to support a family?"

Repudiating Sanger's militant tactics of providing birth-control information to women despite the law, Dennett clung to principle. Sanger was a patent hypocrite. Despite her pious attempts to placate the medical establishment with her "doctor's only" ideas, Sanger handed out birth-control information left and right. Like Margaret Chase, Sanger's words often contradicted her deeds.

Dennett, on the other hand, was firm in her integrity. As a leader in the birth-control movement, Dennett received hundreds of requests from people begging her for information on how to prevent unwanted children. The typical letter was from a married woman in poor health with financial problems and a family of several children. With no idea on how to prevent unwanted children, the woman usually appealed to a eugenicist argument—painting a picture of herself as "unfit" to mother further. In an effort to demonstrate the full extent of Comstock restrictions, Dennett responded to every plea for help with a short statement.

> *It is absolutely illegal to mail any contraceptive information anywhere in the country; and in many of our states, including Iowa, it is illegal to give information by any means whatsoever. The Iowa law is especially drastic.*
>
> *Of course the laws are broken all the time. That is why it is time to repeal them. I hope you will help us accomplish it.*
>
> *You surely have need of the information and I hope you will get it in spite of the laws. Have you asked your own physician?*[635]

This sort of response, typical of Dennett, was of little help to the woman requesting aid. An intellectual purist, Dennett insisted upon keeping within legally prescribed boundaries. Excusing herself by stating that "the League cannot be in the business of breaking laws it is working to change,"[636] Dennett was meticulous in following both the letter and the spirit of the law.

Sanger could not fathom how Dennett could be so heartless. Said Sanger of Dennett's tactics, "I felt as one would feel if, on passing a house which one saw to be on fire and knew to contain women and children unaware of their danger, one realized that the only entrance was through a window. Yet there was a law and penalty for breaking windows. Would anyone of you hesitate, if by so doing you could save a single life?"[637] Conveniently overlooking the fact that she was supporting the very law she was so fond of breaking, Sanger lacked consistency.

Two women more different could hardly be imagined. Dennett was hemmed in by her upper-middle-class background. She did not give voice to her private sorrows—not even her own family would ever know the depth of her emotional agony or the reason for her mysterious operation. In Dennett, a proper Bostonian upbringing had left its mark. Reason and logic ruled her mind. Laws won her respect. As a social reformer, Dennett had been a suffragist before turning to birth control. She believed in political action and legislation. What a far cry from Sanger, who spurned organization and legislation as "bourgeois," "pink tea," "lady-like" efforts. A one-time anarchist, Sanger disdained Dennett's pristine focus on the law. Bitter about her lower-middle-class Irish Catholic origins, her fuel was ire. Publicity photos dressed her in modest feminine attire, but they belied the blazing rebel's fiery temperament. Government deserved only defiance! To Sanger, "direct action" was the only worthwhile work—and this meant breaking laws, not changing them. When it came to birth control, Sanger's cry was to "raise more hell and fewer babies."

Meanwhile, the reception to "The Sex Side of Life" in the *Medical Review of Reviews* had been quite good. Robinson cooperated with Dennett by agreeing to send the article out to a large list of friends and acquaintances for publicity purposes. In June 1918, the essay was reprinted again in *The Modern School*. In 1919, after her efforts to find a publisher proved futile, Dennett decided that she herself would reprint "The Sex Side of Life" in pamphlet form. Putting on a cover price of twenty-five cents to cover printing and mailing costs, she made it available to the public. The circulation of the pamphlet would come primarily through word of mouth. Dennett was about to embark on a grueling crusade in Congress, leaving her with little free time for other matters. With the exception of a tiny notice in the *Survey* in 1920, she made no effort to advertise it in the way other publications were promoted. Nor did she send out any circular letters, with the exception of one occasion when notices were sent to the directors of a few children's summer camps. She hoped it would reach as many people as would find it helpful, but she said she "did not want it to have an artificially stimulated circulation."[638] Regardless, the little essay was surpassing the original purpose for which it was written.

Indeed, Carl and Devon were growing up. Devon was a scholarship student at Brookwood, a progressive boarding school; Carl had graduated in the second class of the Loomis School, and was preparing to attend Haverford College on scholarship. Throughout their school years, Hartley had tried to convince Carl and Devon to join him and Margaret in Alstead, tempting them with images of the bucolic life of a country lady and gentleman. But his sons—already hurt keenly—would have none of it. They resented the fact that Hartley had abandoned them and their mother financially and otherwise. Although Mary never spoke ill of her ex-husband to them, the boys resented their father, calling Hartley a master of circumlocution.[639]

In 1919, Carl, who found letter writing difficult, made a heroic struggle to communicate his private feelings to his father on paper: "What you suggested in your letter about the fact that you are not able to perform your duties as a parent seems to me to be totally wrong. From what I can find in the report of the court proceedings, which I was just shown for the first time recently...you deliberately refused to pay for our upkeep and also refused to pay any family bills. In fact you even returned one which had collected in one of the Boston stores before the actual break came about. Also you left mother in an absolutely helpless position when she was sick which certainly isn't a manly way of separating."

Yet despite his hurt, Carl's desire for a connection with his absentee father remained: "Nevertheless from what I have seen of you and what I have heard of your character makes me want to still have pleasant relations with you altho [*sic*] at present I don't see how it is possible for me to do as you suggest. I can see by just talking with you five minutes what a sweet and gentle and interesting mind you have and I do hate like the very dickens to deprive myself of your company....but I can't with a conscience go far, for we are so utterly at odds about the basis of our relationship."[640] Carl awaited a response from his father. But Hartley never answered.

Then in September 1920, Devon wrote to Hartley asking to borrow money at regular bank interest rates to be able to attend school—the same school that Margaret's own son, Heman, was attending. Hartley, suspecting Mary of putting Devon up to the letter to instill guilt in him, wrote back that it was ridiculous for a son to "borrow" money from his own father. Saying he was willing to finance all of Devon's educational expenses if Mary would give up her full hold on the children, Hartley addressed Mary directly. "In my sight the duty goes with the right,—exclusive custody is exclusive right and exclusive duty,—and I know in all my bones that the legal advantages you have over me are like a poison gas thru which I cannot penetrate to the children. I need not repeat that I am eager to take my proper part in the boys' affairs as soon as you can make it possible for me to do so." Enclosing a copy of his letter to Mary in his reponse to Devon, Hartley attempted to put the matter "clearly" to his son.

A week later, upon receipt of the letter from his father, Devon swallowed lead poison. He was rushed to the hospital unconscious, then discharged soon thereafter. Hartley, in a letter to his "beloved" (Margaret), wrote, "I don't know reason—he got my letter yesterday AM or PM I can't quite get it clear." For her part, Mary requested that all medical bills be sent to her. She wrote, "There is no longer any potency in what you call my 'legal advantage.' While I have always scrupulously avoided anything which might seem like dictation to the boys as to their attitude to you, now that they are small children no more, I have made them understand very clearly that they were entirely free to meet any advances you might make to them, exactly in accordance with their own preferences."

Mary continued, "But it happens that neither of the boys wishes to be "turned over," as you say, to your care. Devon is as free as the air to accept your offer...but he decided unqualifiedly that he didn't want it. Both the boys apparently feel toward you an interest which is friendly, but they do not feel toward you as a parent. That matches my own feeling too. I am not averse to meeting you, as occasion might offer, and am hospitable to any friendship which might develop, but I can no more adopt an attitude of joint parenthood with you than can the boys feel toward you as a father. You invalidated that relationship many years ago." Never very good at blaming others, however, Mary was still able to be somewhat forgiving. She wrote, "The possibilities of friendship are perhaps very rich. The prospect for parenthood looks arid. Why not follow the *open* road?"[641]

Meanwhile, Mary was having another conversation with another family member, her Aunt Lucia. Discussing promiscuity, Mary wrote, "Promiscuity,—I certainly am not pleading for that. It seems to me revolting and unlovely. But I should not try to legislate against it. Laws can not touch it. It can only be controlled by education, and it can not have any hard and fast definition either. It is just as hard to tell where a wholesome sex freedom leaves off and promiscuity begins as it is to tell where a good dinner, full of nourishing food and stimulating conversation, leaves off and gluttony begins. Then promiscuity does *not* lead to 'animalism.'" She wrote, "Sex life is a good deal like food, and the average person needs it not,—not in overdoses, but in comfortable amount and along with exhilarating human companionship. And while it is true that the occasional undernourished person can be a bravely resigned and spiritualized character, there is no general benefit to mankind in being underfed or unattractively fed!"

Drawn deeper into her work, Mary was beginning to find a cause that spoke to both her personal and public life. Continuing to emphasize her conciliatory position, Dennett attempted to win the backing of the New York Academy of Medicine. It was a crucial mistake. Intimately familiar with the pain of trusting doctors to take care of her own reproductive health, she wanted to eliminate the "medical monopoly" on birth-control information. As soon as her purpose became clear, the medical men grew nervous. In a letter to Dennett, they sputtered: "The Committee is unanimously of the opinion that such an amendment is undesirable, on the ground that it would remove every obstacle to the indiscriminate distribution of information relating to and advertisement of methods for prevention of conception. In the opinion of the Committee, such a result is to be condemned." The letter continued: "The Committee believes, however, that it would be wise to amend the federal statute so as to permit only licensed physicians, licensed dispensaries and public health authorities to give information with regard to the prevention of conception in the interests of health."

Dennett refused to give up. In letter after letter, she tried to convince the academy to change its mind. Untiring in her persistence, she organized a birth-control conference at New York's Colony Club and invited seventeen physicians to attend. A few accepted, but when the New York Medical Academy got wind of the event, it intervened. Going out of its way to contact all the doctors Dennett had invited to warn them of the detrimental effects of the VPL's federal bill, the academy's actions produced immediate and disastrous results. A number of physicians who had already signed endorsements of Dennett's VPL immediately wrote to her demanding that their names be removed. Their letters were angry; they felt tricked. Apparently, they had not realized that by supporting Dennett's work they could lose their stranglehold on women's health.

Sanger capitalized on Dennett's misfortune. In the summer of 1921, Dennett had invited England's preeminent birth-control worker, Dr. Marie Stopes, to speak in America under the auspices of the VPL. The topic was to be the smooth and efficient opening of nationwide birth-control clinics. Immediately, Sanger had begun sending Stopes letters attempting to dissuade her from any association with Mary Ware Dennett. Sanger told Stopes that the "VPL hasn't *any* medical backing." Threatening to withdraw support for Stopes' book, *Married Love*, which had been banned by the U.S. Post Office, Sanger warned, "If you are associated with the VPL [legitimate doctors] will not give their names nor have anything to do with anyone or anything associated with it." Sanger told Stopes that Dennett "broke away from the National League in a way not to be mentioned" and then, in a move of outright slander, Sanger wrote, "I personally consider Mrs. D outside the pale of honesty and decency."

Sanger's tactics backfired. On 29 October 1921, Marie Stopes wrote to Mary, saying, "Margaret Sanger is writing indignant protests and other people are doing their best to prevent my coming to you." Dennett's detractors included Sanger's followers as well as physicians in the New York Medical Academy. Stopes warned Dennett: "I have personal evidence that she is following methods which I cannot think are consistent with common fairness, and certainly not with a *reformer.*" Although Dennett still had many pro-birth-control physicians serving on the National Council of the VPL, Stopes went on to ask, innocently, "Seriously, is it true that all your medical supporters have resigned in indignant protest as a result of your conduct of your Society, and is it true that if I appear 'under your auspices' my career is irretrievably ruined?'"

The episode was a turning point. On 13 November 1921, Sanger was arrested at a birth-control meeting held at New York City Town Hall. Dennett, putting aside ideological differences, went to the police station to try to help have Sanger released. Dennett had just held a birth-control meeting at Town Hall on 27 October 1921, with Dr. Stopes speaking, and had little trouble. Dennett's protest of Sanger's arrest was on the grounds of free speech. Dennett arrived at the police station, under considerable personal discomfort, for she was feeling ill. She went at once to to see the officer in charge to insist on the prisoner's release. After all, her own meeting in the same hall had proceeded without any police interference, and by right of free speech, Sanger deserved the same. But the officer she sought was nowhere to be found. So making her way through the throng, Dennett attempted the next best thing—to relay the facts to the press. She waited until Sanger had finished her story, and then began to add hers. At this point, Juliet Rublee, Sanger's henchwoman, who was standing directly in front of Dennett, turned and *struck* Dennett, with a backward swing of her arm. The blow used such force that Dennett would have fallen over had it not been for the dense crowd. Said Rublee to the stricken woman, "This is *our* affair, we don't want you in it."

Certainly unprepared for physical violence, Dennett's mind was on the meeting she had held with Stopes in the same hall two weeks earlier. But Sanger had turned Dennett's own friends against her. Juliet Rublee, Dennett's old colleague from the Committee of 100, who had helped organize the Carnegie Hall rally when Sanger was first arrested, had become an ardent defector. Eternally civilized, Dennett wrote to both Sanger and Rublee after the incident, offering reconciliation. Dennett even provided a polite excuse for their behavior, suggesting that Rublee had acted "under emotional stress." But Sanger was in no mood to apologize. Birth-control workers on both sides were incredulous. Many were so incensed that they wrote to Sanger, demanding an explanation. Sanger issued a letter in response—basically to the effect that Dennett was insane. Denying that she had done anything wrong at all, Sanger insisted, "the more I see the acts of the person in question, the more I am inclined to believe that a sanitarium is the proper place for her."

Years later, one of Sanger's coworkers would say, "As far as her cause was concerned, Margaret Sanger counted 1, 3, 4, 5. She was number one, and there was no number two, she would let no one approach her that closely. When Mary Ware Dennett had the effrontery to claim to be another number one, she became Margaret's enemy who had to be vanquished at all costs."[642] When Dennett scored a coup in 1920, convincing the New York State Federation of Women's Clubs—the largest organization of American women to emerge after suffrage was won—to endorse *her* birth-control plan, Sanger was furious. Sanger called for a "boycott" on births in the *Birth Control Review*, which upset Dennett. Resigning from the board, Dennett founded her own publication, the *Birth Control Herald*, since she had been barred from the B. R. *Review*. After painstaking work to build a broad-based coalition of supporters, Dennett feared Sanger would cause birth control to lose its carefully-cultivated respectability.

Piqued by Dennett's perceived usurpation of the leadership of the American birth-control movement, in 1921 Sanger decided to found yet another organization, the American Birth Control League. Wrestling for ideological control of the nascent movement, the two women began a coldly civil dialogue that lasted throughout the 1920s. Addressing each other as "My dear Mrs. Sanger" or "My dear Mrs. Dennett," the two women never quite seemed to make it to a first-name basis of communication.[643] Sanger was threatened by the thought that Mary Ware Dennett might be moving to the helm of what she considered *her* birth-control movement.

CHAPTER FOURTEEN

Congressional Campaigning

With the formation of the Voluntary Parenthood League in the spring of 1919, active campaigning began for the straight repeal of the words "prevention of conception" from the federal obscenity laws. Drawing upon her experience with the New York State Legislature, Dennett was able to approach the work with newfound savvy. The most memorable impression from the state campaign had been the embarrassment of the men in Albany in dealing with the subject of birth control. In Washington, D.C., she decided to make her first and *only* request to be that the federal legislators cooperate with her to create an atmosphere of dignity and decency. Staying away from any hints of radicalism, she sought out sponsors for the bill who were prominent, well-respected, and even conservative. Insisting that the bill was a simple "correction" to an old Comstock "blunder," she distanced herself as far as possible from the birth-control movement. Despite these precautions, however, Dennett would find that fear and shame about sex ran deep.

In July 1919, Dennett began preliminary interviews with members of Congress to scout out a sponsor for the birth-control measure. Discreetly canvassing the leaders in both houses and members of the two judiciary committees to which the bill would be referred, Dennett scrupulously avoided publicity, as she realized that privacy would be the only basis by which candor from the congressmen would be possible. Publicly, Dennett would claim, "The men in Congress are remarkably like men outside of Congress; practically all believe in birth control. But belief is one thing, doing anything about it in terms of legislation quite another. Almost no downright opponents have been discovered and among those few, several have become convinced and even helpful."

This was not entirely true, however. Dennett was painting an optimistic picture to the outside world. Right away, Dennett ran against the familiar prejudice against sexual subjects. Representative James Robert Mann of Illinois, for example, told her that "all the young people would go to the dogs" without legal prohibitions against birth control. He claimed that all human nature was "inherently interested in 'lewdness,' including those who pretended to idealism," and that "those who were pushing this measure were sexless people with no natural impulses...." A firm believer in legislating morality, he had no faith whatsoever in education. Alternating between courtesy and insult, he was described by Dennett as "declining to argue" whenever he saw a logical conclusion coming.[644]

Others who were uncomfortable with the subject Dennett described in her private notes as "coarse, ignorant, and impatient." She highlighted Senator Knute Nelson of Minnesota as a "particularly stunning specimen." Recorded Mary, "More impossible than I anticipated. So bad as to be a grotesque scream. He is an utter ignoramus. Scolded, denounced, interrupted constantly, undertook to tell me what I *thought* regardless of what I *said*, then denounced me for it. His chief remark, repeated about fifty times, mostly at the top of his lungs was, 'You ought to be ashamed, an intelligent American woman like you, to want everybody to be like the... women who are too stuck up to have children, or just raise a few dudes.'" When Dennett explained that she was also not interested in "selfish, rich, childless women," but in the "great mass who could not make their wages support unlimited children and the mothers who lost their health having babies too rapidly," he replied, "'Nonsense... The women with the biggest families are the healthiest, it does "'em good.'"

Dennett tried to present him with infant mortality statistics, but Nelson would only say, "I don't need to read anything. Don't believe in statistics anyway. You ought to be ashamed, etc. Have you any children? Why don't you stay at home and look after them and mind your own business, instead of disgracing yourself like this?" When Dennett explained that she did have children and that it was becaused she wanted *all* children to have an equal chance at health and education that she was working for the bill, he retorted, "Huh—this education business is overdone. At twelve I was ploughing with a yoke of oxen. That's why I can work and amount to something at seventy-seven. Work is what children need and not education." He kept repeating the importance of letting "nature take its course." His constant answer to all logic and data was to "decline to argue." With smiling tolerance and patient condescension, he kept repeating, "I don't need any facts, I know what you want just reading your bill. You want this country to go to the dogs. You want all the women to stop having children." When Dennett asked him if he would at least read the VPL literature, he replied,

"'I will not, I won't read anything I don't need to, God help the country if all the intelligent women are going to be like you, you better go home and pray for a clean heart.'"[645]

Making her way down the Congressional Directory, Dennett studied the list of congressmen looking for the right sponsor. Taking careful notes immediately after each interview, she recorded who was friend and who was foe. For better or for worse, those she counted as "supporters" were often nothing more than good listeners. Senator Thomas Sterling of South Dakota, for example, knew nothing of the bill, and would not sponsor it, but Dennett recorded him as "fine, dignified, intelligent, responsive," and "exceedingly gentlemanly ... with a wholesome mind."[646] Some, like Senator William E. Borah of Idaho, a member of the Senate Judiciary Committee, were wholly in favor and needed no argument, yet still felt that it would be "all but impossible" to get the bill out of committee. Said Borah, "Congressmen are such cowards.... Just let the newspapers talk a little, and not a man will dare stand for it, no matter what he thinks in private, or what he tells you."[647]

By January 1920, a sponsor for the bill was still nowhere to be seen. Dennett had placed her hopes on various legislators, chief among them being Senator Joseph Irwin France of Maryland, whom Dennett had described as someone who matched "perfectly his reputation for being 'the ideal American gentleman.'" A physician and chairman of the Committee on Public Health, France had absolutely approved of Dennett's "policy of quiet work—no sensationalism—bill not attached to radical movement." Considering it a measure for "health and social stability," he considered introducing Dennett's "clean repeal" bill for months.[648] Indeed, he never actually refused—he simply kept postponing his decision and urged the selection of "someone less involved in other legislative projects, who could act quickly."

In the meantime, Senator Nelson, who had been so adamantly opposed to the measure, had changed his mind. Apparently, he had referred all the VPL literature to his wife and sister, who had pronounced it 'common sense and sound.' When Dennett went to speak to him again in January, he chewed tobacco lustily throughout her talk, asked intelligent questions, and even became deferential. It had dawned on him that birth control could be a "clever way of antidoting 'Bolshevism' to make the wage earner healthy and so contented." Impressed with Dennett's health arguments, he apologized for his previous attitude, saying it was due to his feeling toward "selfish rich women who scorned family burdens and his disgust for 'barren' women and their diseased husbands." As chairman of the Judiciary Committee, he said he felt the bill could be "all right if presented in a 'sane, conservative way.'"[649]

It was not until March 1920 that Dennett finally found a sponsor, Senator H. Heisler Ball of Delaware, formerly a practicing physician. On March 19, Dr. Ball had announced his conversion by the VPL literature, and promised to introduce the bill "within a few days." He reiterated his promises both verbally and in writing again and again from that date until the end of the Congressional Session in June, but still the bill was not introduced. As Dennett put it, "The sponsor had been found, but also found wanting."[650] So the hunt began all over again with the next session in December. Nine senators in succession were asked—a process involving months of 'watchful waiting.' All believed in the bill, but none wanted to take responsibility for it.

Meanwhile, by January 1921 the VPL was undergoing major financial difficulties and Dennett's salary was again in arrears. Suggesting two possible ways of improving the organization, Dennett proposed the election of a president—man or woman—who would be prominent enough to attract more substantial support, and she suggested that another director be elected to replace her as well.[651] When her proposals were rejected, Dennett threatened to resign unless the VPL's liabilities were paid and overhead expenses for the next six months guaranteed.

Frustrated, Dennett decided to try a new approach. As the Comstock Act specifically forbade dissemination of obscene materials through the mails, giving sole and arbitrary authority to determine obscenity to the Postmaster General, Dennett decided to take the question directly to the federal post office officials, as postmaster General William Hays had put himself on record many times stating that the post office should not operate a censorship system. Her first interview took place in August 1921 with Dr. Hubert Work, former president of the American Medical Association and first assistant postmaster general. Dennett began by saying "I assume your recognition of the merit of controlled parenthood as distinguished from haphazard parenthood." Instead of finding a point of agreement, however, the doctor immediately grew red in the face and said he had fixed ideas which could be stated in one sentence, namely, "sterilize all boys and girls who are unfit to become parents, and then let nature take its course unhindered."

When Dennett "reminded him that his individual opinion was exceptional for these days," he immediately announced that he was opposed to the entire subject and that it was useless to discuss it. Saying he had seen some of the VPL's literature before, he told her, "I gave it the once-over and forgot it."

Dr. Work insisted that the purpose of the VPL was to "instruct everybody how to have illicit intercourse without the danger of pregnancy." Dennett then gave him her "customary arguments" about achieving morals through education rather than "unenforced and unenforceable" legislation, inviting him to "have some faith in the ultimate decency of average humans instead of assuming that they were all essentially promiscuous."[652] In response, Dr. Work suggested that Dennett see the third assistant postmaster general, Warren I. Grover, whose department oversaw the actual interpretation of the laws. In meeting with Grover, Dennett found the third assistant postmaster general to be "reasonable and receptive." He admitted that the problematic section 211 was "unenforced and unenforceable," but claimed that prosecutions were made if a complaint was lodged against obscene matter. Saying that he would tell Hays that the law was ineffective if he were ever questioned, Grover suggested that Dennett visit the solicitor of the post office, Judge John H. Edwards, and the postmaster general, William Hays. In particular, Hays was the only one who could actually go to the Judiciary Committee to urge legislation.

Dennett went to see solicitor Edwards the very next day. Met at the office by Horace J. Donnelly, who was assistant solicitor, Dennett waited in the outer office as Donnelly took Dennett's card in to Judge Edwards. While she waited, Dennett noticed that the door to the inner office was left ajar. Seated outside, she was exactly in the line of vision with what was going on inside. When Donnelly handed the judge her card, which stated Dennett's position as director of the Voluntary Parenthood League, the men inside promptly passed the card around "snickering and haw-hawing as they swapped comments." Wrote Dennett, "The expression of face which goes with smutty jokes, once seen, is always recognizable. It needed no words to reveal the character of the remarks they made. They seemed in no haste to end the little episode."[653]

When Donnelly finally returned, he informed Dennett that the judge was "too occupied" to see her, but he offered himself in his place, insisting that he, Donnelly, was the resident expert on the obscenity laws. Dennett decided to test his knowledge. She questioned him regarding the particulars of section 211, and she immediately discovered that he had no idea what she was talking about. He was quite familiar, however, with books that had been suppressed. Asking Dennett about Marie Stopes's book, *Married Love*, he asked her "with an undisguised salacious smile if [she] knew the book and liked it and thought it ought to be circulated." Describing his manner as "decidedly repulsive," Dennett noted that the assistant solicitor "sobered perceptibly" when she replied that she thought the book should be required reading for "every married man in the United States" and that "life would be considerably cleaner, sweeter, more decent and lovely if people were brought up in harmony with Dr. Stopes's ideals."

Dennett would later ruminate, "It seemed probable that it was the first time he had ever met a woman engaged in such a task as asking Congress to renovate laws which deal with sex. He apparently assumed at first that I must be getting some salacious stimulation from the work, and he acted accordingly. But when he sensed the fact that he had blundered, he naturally felt disturbed, and it was easier to feel resentful at me than at himself—which is understandable enough. While he mended his manners as the talk proceeded, I came away feeling that he retained the animosity. Subsequent events perhaps served as reminders and accelerators of the prejudice ..."[654]

Having had little luck with the other post office officials, Dennett finally paid a visit to Postmaster General William Hays himself. Immediately, Hays impressed her "as a cordial, able, open-minded, progressive politician." Hays welcomed Dennett's mission and told her that her timing was perfect as he had just about concluded that he should "go to Congress and get all the sections remodelled which had bearing on the censorship question."[655] Very receptive, he requested a resume of the chief arguments and pertinent data, as well as samples of the birth-control publications that were circulating freely in England. When Dennett informed him that it would break the law under section 211 of the penal code to mail such publications to him, he replied, "Oh no, I wouldn't want that done, send them by express." Dennett then explained that express mail was also forbidden under section 245, so Hays smiled and said, "Well then, by messenger." Duly delivering the material to him in this fashion, Dennett was optimistic about the possibility that he might submit a revision of the Comstock Act to Congress. But then in March 1922, Hays resigned to found the Hays Office, the first major censorship board for the budding motion picture industry.

Toward the end of his term, Hays had begun explaining that it was too late for him to make any recommendations to Congress and that he did not want to embarrass his successor. Unfortunately, Hays's successor was Dr. Hubert Work. Dr. Work lost no time posting a conspicuous bulletin in all the post offices of America stating that it was a criminal offense to send or receive matter relating to the prevention of conception. Within the month, Dennett began a correspondence with solicitor John H. Edwards and assistant solicitor H.J. Donnelly of the United States Post Office, kindly inquiring what methods they proposed to use to enforce the law when "alleged infringements were in first class sealed mail." She also pointed out that many books by medical scientists giving specific contraceptive instruction were circulated by mail or express.

Strung out over the course of four months, the communication between Dennett and the post office solicitors pushed home the point that the obscenity laws were wholly unenforceable and, therefore, absurd. Dennett persisted in heckling the men, albeit politely, asking them again and again to be more "specific" and "detailed" in their responses. Evading the question, the solicitor was finally forced to admit that he was "not in a position" to give the requested facts. In July 1922, Dennett published a taunting article in the *Birth Control Herald*, claiming that the Comstock Act was utterly unenforceable.

> *There are about twenty-five million families in the country and, roughly speaking, ten million of these are the well-to-do—those above the income tax exemption. Suppose a tenth of these can be convicted of having secured by mail or express the contraceptive information on which their own family limitation is based. The authorities would hardly imprison a whole million. It would mean "standing room only in the jails." An alternative would be to fine them. One million law breakers, fined $5000 each would provide Uncle Sam with a handy five billion these days, when the national debt stands at about eight billion. But, like the jail idea, this might be a bit impracticable! What alternative is there then? The million malefactors might be acquitted—but that would make the officers of the law look silly. So,—there it is, a large problem staring at the new Postmaster-General. How will he meet it?*
>
> *Dr. Work's Bulletin says "Ignorance of the law is no excuse." Similarly also, difficulty of enforcement is no excuse for him. So long as the law stands he and the Department of Justice must carry it out, or else be unfaithful and inefficient public servants.[656]*

Calling the talk of enforcing the law a "bluff," Dennett challenged the postmaster to either enforce the law or change it. Within months, Dennett received a response. Coming in the form of an impersonal letter, the answer read as follows:

> *My dear Madam: According to advice from the Solicitor for the Post Office Department, the pamphlet entitled "The Sex Side of Life. An Explanation for Young People," by Mary Ware Dennett, is unmailable under Section 211 of the Penal Code. As copies of this pamphlet bearing your name as the sender have been found in the mails the decision is communicated for your information and guidance.*[657]

Not one to be sidetracked, Dennett ignored the letter. Knowing that obscenity could not be legally defined, she later explained, "As I knew this pamphlet did not reflect any obscene thoughts in my own mind, but could be deemed obscene only because of what was read into it by minds in which sex dirt had previously lodged, I of course would not allow the Post Office decision to affect my actions. I quietly continued to send the pamphlet to all who ordered it, and each year it was more and more gratifying to find that it was helpful to just the sort of people I would most like to have it reach."[658]

Dennett was forced to acknowledge, however, that the alternative plan to alter the Comstock Act via the postmaster general was not going to be viable. Furthermore, the VPL could no longer claim to be the only national *organization* that existed to hold active birth-control workers together in unity. In November 1921, Margaret Sanger had created the American Birth Control League, formally challenging Dennett's VPL. By February 1922, Sanger had issued a written statement, the "Position of Margaret Sanger concerning the Birth Control Review," openly hostile to the VPL in no uncertain terms. The statement explicitly stated that the VPL and its views would be barred from the *Birth Control Review*, which was now obliquely acknowledged to be "exclusively a personal organ of Margaret Sanger."

Said Sanger, the VPL "is not entitled to have any space given in the *Review* to any of its activities or accomplishment, or to any of the views of its members or representatives. Even news items concerning work done by the VPL for Birth Control in general are not considered as of any interest to the readers of the *Review* as such, and hence are not invited nor likely to be used." Furthermore, the VPL position of legalizing birth-control information for all—not just doctors—was "officially held to the *Review* to be adopting an erroneous position; and the *Review* will editorially disapprove of their attitude, and deny to them all privilege of expressing their views..." Wrote Sanger, "Individual subscriptions are welcome from all who care to subscribe; but those advocates of Birth Control defined in paragraphs 2 and 3 are expected to understand that the *Review* is not *their* magazine, and that they are not under any moral constraint to feel that it has a reasonable right to expect their support. If they choose to subscribe, it as only as a Baptist might subscribe to a Roman Catholic periodical, to see what was going on in the ranks of another branch of the Christian church, with which he had a common cause as against heathendom and Atheism, but no closer connection."659

The attack from Margaret Sanger siphoned supporters from Dennett's camp. Not only did this affect morale, but it also affected fund-raising. Determined to run a morally upright organization, Dennett refused to pander to potential large donors. She insisted on complete honesty as well as reliability in paying back bills incurred by the VPL. Dependent only on modest contributions from membership drives, the VPL saw its money arrive in dribs and drabs. By the summer of 1922, the funds were so low that Dennett decided to pay off the largest bills herself, with the understanding that she would be reimbursed at a later date. The eternal optimist, Mary Ware Dennett pushed on.

Tenaciously, Dennett turned back to the lawmakers themselves, trying again to find a leading senator and congressman willing to sponsor a bill to eliminate the contraceptive clause from the Comstock Act. Calculating the average congressional family to consist of 2.7 children, she decided the figure was proof enough "that members of Congress likewise believe in controlled parenthood." With her copy of the Congressional Directory in hand, she approached statesmen known for making progressive stands—but once again she found that no matter how liberated their private opinions, fears about the public discussion of sex were strong. Of Representative Graham from Pennsylvania, Dennett noted he was "for the Bill intellectually, but that it did not stir him emotionally a particle." Representative Israel Foster of Ohio said, "And maybe you will call that political cowardice, and maybe it is, but anyway that is where I stand." Representative William N. Vaile of Colorado said, "I make no bones of saying honestly that my job makes a good deal of difference to me, and to my family....while I am much interested in this question, and approve the idea of the

Bill, I probably don't think of it as nearly such an important matter as you do. And therefore I can not help thinking very hard as to what the effect may be on me." As one congressman put it, her "only problem was to get the men to move beyond the stage where their embarrassment inhibited them."

Indeed, the opposition was harsh, and Mary noted their tendency to "bellow or pound the furniture." Senator Thaddeus Caraway of Arkansas told her outright, "Every fourteen-year-old schoolgirl would get hold of this information and begin experimenting." He insisted, "I'm against your bill from beginning to end. If you want to make everybody prostitutes, then go ahead." Representative Gard of Ohio stated he simply "saw no difference between abortion and contraception." Despite Mary's forthright reasoning, it seemed nobody was willing to risk political suicide by broaching the subject. "Oh, I know damn well that no one man is necessary. The world wags right on, no matter who gets snowed under," said Representative Vaile candidly. "Do I seem unheroic?" One basic problem seemed to be that unplanned pregnancy posed only a limited personal threat to men.

In January 1923, Dennett interviewed Senator Albert B. Cummins of Iowa, an older, dignified man who was also president pro tempore of the Senate. High-minded and upright, he listened carefully as Mary went down the points of the bill. She explained her difficulty finding a sponsor, answered his questions regarding immorality and addressed his fears about the receptivity of other congressmen. Dennett insisted, "we are living in a new age, when science and art and religion are being coordinated as never before, and sex is part of that evolution." As she pursued that trail the expression of his face softened perceptibly, and he said in a very gentle voice, "Well, I'm for it." At this, Dennett thought he had meant that he would vote for it, and responded, "Fine, and what else will you do for it?" But when he said quite simply "Why, what else *can* I do for it?" she realized he was telling her that he would introduce it. Scarcely able to believe her ears, she heard him repeat himself firmly and with simple gentlemanliness. She would later recall, "I had to work hard not to let the sweep of emotion I felt, show too much. I fear my thanks were considerably less dear than my arguments! But I managed somehow and told him he was making *lots* of people happier. We then exchanged a few businesslike words about the draft of the bill which I agreed to have prepared that night, and we shook hands. He smiled and said 'Bless you,' and I felt sure he would not be another Senator Ball."[660]

Her instincts were correct. On January 10, 1923, Senator Albert B. Cummins introduced a "straight repeal" bill in the Senate to remove the words "preventing conception" from the Comstock Act. On the same day, Congressman John Kissel of Brooklyn, New York, sponsored the bill in the House, in answer to a letter Dennett had sent to each member of the House asking a "volunteer" to render the service. After four years of persistence, Dennett had finally found two men willing to sponsor her bill. Yet once it was introduced, she faced her next hurdle. Almost no one in Congress wanted to go on record against it, but they squirmed at going on record for it. The bill had finally been introduced, but neither Cummins nor Kissel could convince the men to vote on it. When they tried to bring the matter up, the men would simply "fade away"—that is, the members of the Committee would either not attend the meeting if they knew that the birth-control bill was going to be brought up; those who did attend would conveniently disappear when it came time to vote. As a result, the winter session of 1923 closed with no action taken.

When Congress reopened, the bill had found a new sponsor in the House, Representative William N. Vaile of Colorado. Despite his earlier hesitation, Vaile would prove to be a brave and outspoken supporter. Yet Dennett realized that neither Cummins nor Vaile would be able to push the bill through on their own. Realizing that if she wanted the bill to pass she would have to lay the groundwork herself, Dennett redoubled her efforts. She spoke with legislators individually, declaring that the obscenity laws were broken consistently by physicians, teachers, and even lawmakers themselves, and for that very reason, she argued, it was "absurd to expect or to demand enforcement." She drove home the point that information about contraceptives was basic medical knowledge which should be accessible to all—not just the elite, and not just doctors. And she called the Comstock Act "class legislation," repeating her arguments that those who are well off get the information anyway.

The most important and generally quoted argument against birth-control was fear of immorality. In particular, fear for the chastity of the teenaged girl came up again and again. Dennett responded, "This presupposes a low standard of morality among young girls. Most of us believe that a positive idealism, rather than a negative fear of consequences, is the restraining influence on most of our young women." Said she, "Gradually society is developing a different attitude toward women. We have come to realize that a passive virtue, enforced by lack of opportunity to do otherwise, is not as valuable to society, nor to the individual, as the building up of character, which, having the choice between good and evil, chooses wisely."661

Trying to remove any doubts and hesitations from the legislators, Dennett attempted to distance the bill still further from the birth-control movement. She advised all VPL members to write to their senators and representatives. She instructed any supporters not to be trapped into discussion about birth control itself, saying that the "main issue of the Cummins-Vaile Bill is the right of the citizen to *access to knowledge*" [emphasis added].

By February 1924, the men were still avoiding action on the bill. Desperate for action, Dennett began to break with her policy of "niceness." She issued a circular letter, signed by the "Executive Committee, Legislative Committee, National Council of the Voluntary Parenthood League, Inc.," informing the legislators that unless the Cummins-Vaile bill came up for action that session, members of Congress would be "held responsible" for the delay. Threatening the Congressmen with "exposure" of their "cowardice," Dennett asked, "Would this sort of public attention be your preference?" Sounding weak and pathetically out of touch with reality, her "threats" were more annoying than fearsome. Instead of receiving the response she had hoped for, indignant congressmen told her she was being "impertinent."

Nevertheless, on 8 April 1924, joint hearings on the Cummins - Vaile Bill were held by the Senate and House Judiciary Sub-committees. Congressman Vaile made opening remarks for the restoration of the "American freedom" to acquire knowledge, saying that it had been taken away fifty years earlier by Anthony Comstock. The United States birth rate was cited as silent "proof" that the majority of people wanted to and did obtain information despite the laws. Economics, eugenics, scientific freedom were all cited as reasons to support the Cummins-Vaile Bill. When the opposition brought up the morality of birth control itself, the wisdom of Dennett's insistence to define the issue as one of freedom of access to knowledge—not birth control—became apparent. Yet despite this, the Committees still avoided issuing a report on the bill and again evaded a vote. The chairman of the subcommittee stated that he was sure that "not a single member of his committee *wanted* to vote on the bill." Entirely agreeable to anything except action, he said, "I don't see the use of trying to make reluctant men act."662

Trying to force the men to come to a decision, Dennett was frustrated when she heard that there was to be yet another delay due to a new hearing called for 9 May 1924. Prepared for the usual rehash of anti–birth-control arguments, she was shocked to discover that the chief speaker for the opponents was one Miss Sarah Laughlin of Philadelphia, a woman who had joined the VPL three years ago as a "devoted sincere enthusiast." A regular dues-paying member, Laughlin had come to see Dennett twice in person and had left saying, "Mrs. Dennett, you have no idea what this has meant to me." Sometime thereafter, confidential reports of VPL work done in Washington had begun appearing in what Mary described as a "wretched little magazine" called *The Woman Patriot*, run by a combination of Catholics and members of a former anti-suffrage group. Realizing there was a traitor in their midst, Dennett had tightened security. She had been puzzled, however, about where the infiltration had come from. Now, said Dennett, "the spy reveals herself."663

Then, seven months later, on 19 January 1925, Dennett recorded, "There is very strong circumstantial evidence that some of the Sanger group lobbied against the VPL bill, toward the end of the last session of Congress. Some of the lobbyists working on the Child Labor Amendment definitely said so. But aside from that, there was a striking co-incidence which I saw myself, viz: I noted that Annie Porrit was registered at my hotel in Washington. Within a few days Senator Spencer announced a brand new excuse for stalling; namely, that the States should act first, before Congress could be expected to. State action first, has been Mrs. Sanger's policy ever since the VPL started Federal work." Dennett would claim that Sanger split the meager ranks of birth-control supporters.

Attacked from all directions, the situation must have seemed hopeless. But just at this point, Dennett received word that the Judiciary Sub-committee of the Senate had reached a unanimous decision to report the Cummins-Vaile Bill "without prejudice."664 The bill could now be brought up for a vote by the *full* judiciary committee. Heartened by the news, Dennett threw all caution to the wind. Beginning in February 1925, she began issuing short daily notes to each committee member, handing out bite-size arguments for the bill. In order to get her own way, Dennett began to insist on a logic that was becoming harder and harder to support. Trying to convince legislators that repeal of the clause was a small and easy matter, she advised the birth controllers, "We must not assume that this is a gigantic job. The Cummins-Vaile Bill should have been passed long ago.... Our long suit is to make the congressmen see that this thing does not take any time. It just needs to be tucked in." Insisted Dennett, "The above points are very important to remember. We must help to create a psychology that this bill is long overdue; that it requires no fussing, that it is one of the easiest things Congress has ever been asked to do."[665]

In utter denial about the nature of the Cummins-Vaile Bill, Dennett refused to admit that it *was* about birth control—not just freedom of access to knowledge—and it *was* a radical step she was asking legislators to take. Refusing to address any questions that directly pertained to birth control per se, she called attempts to frame the bill as one about contraception a "paralysis of the reasoning faculties, induced by the embarrassment of sex consciousness." Unwilling to acknowledge any point of view except her own, she left no room for debate on any grounds other than those she had already defined. Dogmatic to the extreme, she succeeded in becoming a nuisance. She used guilt tactics, blame, criticism—everything she could think of—and was completely unwilling to bend from her position. Mary Ware Dennett was "firm" and "logical" to a fault.

The sense of urgency also came from the pressure she felt from the Sanger camp. Wrote Dennett in her campaign diary, "It is hard to exaggerate the necessity for getting out quickly and widely this clear presentation of the bill and the reasons. For one thing, Margaret Sanger is planning some sort of a scheme for dipping into the federal work, and judging by recent straws and the past, it does not presage co-operation, or anything except an opportunity to mix up the public and Congress. We can win on argument without doubt, if we can get our material to the people. But she has ten thousand a year of her own for publicity work in addition to the receipts of her organization, and with money one can advertise *anything over, regardless of its merit*. Sad, but absolutely true! Her organization has spent nearly $63,000 this last year. If we had had that much, it is a fair guess that our bill would have been passed at the last session. The last number of her magazine announces that in the March number the question of federal legislation will be taken up thoroughly, and it is alluded to as 'this important question.' We have taught her that much anyhow! A few years ago she refused to publish the information we offered the magazine, on the ground, that it was not important."[666]

In February 1925, Dennett still had to contend with Senator Rice W. Means of Colorado who refused to meet with her on the

grounds that she was a woman and he was "old-fashioned."[667]
Senator Cummins, who was beginning to voice hopelessness about
the measure, had asked to be relieved of sponsorship several times.
Said Cummins frankly, "You haven't a chance in the world. They
are all against you. You ought to have seen how completely they sat
on me on Monday. I am utterly disgusted with them." Indeed,
Cummins tried to tell a VPL worker that Dennett had already done
the "impossible" in turning the legislators around in their views on
sex. "When I introduced this bill," he said, "I was denounced in my
home city. Prominent club women protested against the bill. I was
criticized for having introduced it and I was asked not to introduce
it again. To-day women's organizations are holding public meetings
in its behalf, are passing resolutions in favor of it and are telegraph-
ing Congress to pass it. I am receiving such information all the time.
I have seen this change occur in these few years." When the woman
tried to attribute the change to Cummins, he simply said, "No. You
can leave me quite out of it. It had *all* been due to Mrs. Dennett. You
can attribute the change entirely to her fine work."

Very likely this was the case, and by March 1925 Dennett had
utterly worn herself out. Sanger was now openly speaking against
Dennett's bill, trying to convince legislators of the need for doctors
to supervise all contraceptive knowledge. Dennett's final hard-line
approach had not only alienated many congressmen, but many in
the VPL disliked it as well. Furthermore, as she was the primary
VPL lobbyist, most others in the League understood the congressional climate only secondhand, from reports she issued and articles
in the *Birth Control Herald.* By the time the session closed, nothing
had been accomplished on the birth-control bill. Dennett was
dismayed. Fear and shame about sexuality had prevented open discussion among the majority. And among the minority, she felt the
ego of one woman had fractured the meager ranks of birth-control
supporters. A decade's worth of work had just fizzled out.

Announcing her decision to resign as early as 25 January 1925,
Dennett finally stepped down in the spring from her active role as
director of the VPL to become consultative chairman of the national
council. Dennett explained that she needed a reliable year-round
income, which she had not had for ten years, and that resulted in a
personal debt of a few thousand dollars. Much of that came from
the expenses of the VPL.

The financial situation was bleak. Dennett had undertaken most
of the fund-raising herself—to the detriment of the campaign—and

she still had not been reimbursed for the outlay of expenses from the summer of 1922. Furthermore, not only was she owed back salary, there was internal strife over the way she had spent some of the funds, with other VPL members feeling that too much of the money had gone toward the congressional campaign. Indeed, the very fact that the League owed her money made many on the VPL's Executive Committee uncomfortable. Mary was not very popular. And if that weren't enough, now Carl and Devon, who were in their twenties, were insisting that their mother's debts were theirs as well. Never one to thrive in a partisan environment, Dennett decided that she no longer wanted to be a part of the "dirt" of political life. She was broke, and the sparring with Margaret Sanger did not sit well with her. The alternative? After a decade and a half of reform work, Mary Ware Dennett decided that she was ready to return to her first love. She would turn back to art.

CHAPTER FIFTEEN

Slowing Down

In October 1922, the year she had first considered resigning from the Voluntary Parenthood League, Mary experienced an acute bout of loneliness. Living alone for over a decade, she must have replayed the events that had led up to her marital breakup again and again in her mind. Despite all that she had suffered on his behalf, time must have dulled the painful moments while illuminating the joyful ones. Essentially, she wanted her original relationship with Hartley back again. With nothing left to lose, Mary wrote a short note to Hartley.

Dear Hartley:

Do you recall, the name of the paper you used to use sometimes for pencil sketches, —it had a sort of coated soft surface, and you couldn't erase or it smudged? It made wonderfully crisp delicate effects.

I should be very glad to have the name of it, and where it can be bought, if you chance to recall it.

Sincerely,

Mary Ware

Going back to a period in time before her last name was Dennett, when Mary and Hartley were simply two young people deeply in love and committed to the ideals of Arts and Crafts, Mary appealed to shared memories of innocence. She was finally ready to take a chance. Hartley did not respond. Instead, he scrawled on the bottom left hand corner of her letter, "Did not reply. Too absurd."[668]

Yearning for her artisan roots, Mary arranged to borrow money from her sister Clara who, with her husband George Hill, was running a posh crafts store in Beverly Hills, California. Mary dusted off her leatherworking tools, and started pounding out *guadamaçiles* once again. She joined the New York Society of Craftsmen, and then displayed her work at an exhibition celebrating the founding of the Society of Arts and Crafts. In a letter to her Aunt Lucia, Mary wrote, "'*No*' to another part-time job.... I have decided to concentrate on the leather and give it a chance. If I don't do it now, I never shall.... never again shall I try any connection with ideas or ideals, as a means of providing a living income."

No longer in the thick of social activism or immersed in family affairs, Mary found her own children were grown. At age twenty, Devon had married Marie Fleugel, a charming woman nine years his senior. A former rhythms and movement teacher at Smith College, Marie, who was pregnant at the time of the marriage, had suggested abortion. But Devon, very much in love, told her he "didn't think [abortion] would be good for Marie Fleugel." Telling the town hall officials that he was twenty-one years old so that he could get married, Devon also carried with him a letter from his mother to support the new couple. On 28 May 1927, Carl decided to marry Catherine Bronson, a woman he had met through his mother's secretary at the VPL, Sonia Bronson. When Carl and Catherine decided to marry, Mary was in Panama. They told Grandma Ware, Vonie (Mary's mother), that they wanted the Reverend John Haynes Holmes, head of the Riverside Church and well-known reformer, to marry them. Instead, they were married by the assistant to Reverend Holmes, with Sonia Bronson and Vonie serving as witnesses.

At about the same time, on 6 July 1925, Margaret and Lincoln Chase were divorced. Having waited until Dr. Chase's mother had passed away, Dr. and Mrs. Chase at last decided to acknowledge that their marital relationship was nonexistent. Spurred by an incident a few years earlier, in which Dr. Chase had introduced Margaret to a visitor as his "wife," it somehow dawned on Margaret that the term did not quite seem to represent the true situation. Once *she* had decided the time had come to rectify the situation, the Chases formally severed their marital ties. Nothing much changed: Margaret continued to live with Hartley, and Dr. Chase lived nearby—maintaining cordial relations with Hartley and Margaret. A year after the Chase divorce, Hartley and Margaret decided to marry—probably around late summer or early fall of 1926. The union was sparked not so much by a desire for conventionality as by a practical need. As the story went, an insurance salesman refused to sell the two unmarried people insurance because they were "living in sin." As a result, Margaret Chase became Margaret Dennett.

Doing her best to carry on, Mary's emotional state was not high. The marriages of her children had brought her happiness, as had the birth of her granddaughter Sally, Devon's child, but in general, Mary was not feeling well. Devon had initiated a reconciliation with his father upon the birth of Sally. And after his marriage to Margaret Chase, Hartley had drawn up a new will leaving money and property to his children, Carl and Devon. Hartley went to great lengths, however, to insure that nothing from his estate could ever find its way to their mother. Feeling like a failure in both her public and private life, Mary attempted to carry on. By upbringing, she was not a complainer. But she would write to her English friend, Marie Stopes, about her depression.

> *Now a word about my long silence. My six years of stiff worrisome work in the VPL sapped my vitality a good deal; especially did the things which went on behind the scenes tax my endurance. This, combined with some strenuous personal problems broke my resistance. So that this last summer was a total loss in every way but one. I was forced into a long vacation in order to avoid a total and permanent breakdown. I was dead to the world for weeks. Presently however I found a renewal of interest in life, through a revival of my old art work. It was a heavenly respite. And maybe by the end of another year, I shall revert to it completely. I will if I can afford to do so.* [669]

Seeking a salary, Mary had begun to experiment more fully with the ideals of natural living. From 1926 to 1927, she was Special Representative of the American Foundation for Homeopathy. Again, she found herself pitted against the traditional medical establishment as she tried to raise funds and support for homeopathic physicians and hospitals. From 1927 to 1928, she was executive secretary for Dr. Philip Rice's School for Organic Development, which promoted the production and supply of organic health foods. Hearkening back to her Framingham days, she renewed her interest in homeopathy and natural living. If nothing else, at least it provided her with an income.

Despite her stated determination to make a complete break with her reform work, however, Mary Ware Dennett decided to take care of a small matter that had been bothering her since 1922—namely, the ruling by the post office that her pamphlet, *The Sex Side of Life*, was obscene. After its initial printing in pamphlet form in 1919—at about the same time she had plunged into the congressional campaigning work—the circulation of the *The Sex Side of Life* had grown by leaps and bounds. With little effort on her part, the pamphlet had found a large audience. The vice-hunting YMCA, Comstock's original sponsor, had begun selling *The Sex Side of Life* in its bookstores and newsstands nationwide; the Bronxville public school system and the Union Theological Seminary picked it up for use as a primary text in child-care classes; several colleges and universities, such as Wells College and Columbia University, bought it for distribution to their students upon graduation; and doctors, parents, church leaders, social workers, camp counselors, schoolteachers snatched it up by the dozens.

Furthermore, spontaneous letters of endorsement and appreciation kept arriving with increasing frequency. Before long, organization leaders were recommending the pamphlet to their members, and the little booklet came to be listed in various bibliographic works. At age fifteen, Devon had said, "Mother, this thing is good, not so much because it tells a fellow anything absolutely new that he never heard of before, but because of the *way* it is told. It helps you to forget nasty terms and tells the facts the way you like to remember them."670 Throughout their adolescence, Carl and Devon had continued to refer back to it as needed. "Each time they read it," Mary reported, "they seemed to get more understanding and satisfaction."671

Given the widespread popularity of her pamphlet, in the spring of 1925 Dennett decided that it would be a "reasonable assumption" that the obscenity ruling might be lifted. Never one to hesitate, Dennett sent a short note to a number of individuals and organizations that had used and commended her pamphlet, asking for endorsements. She let them know that the pamphlet had been banned, and invited them to join in a request to the postmaster general that the ban be removed. The response was enthusiastic, and many wrote to praise and recommend the pamphlet. Convinced that the post office ban did not reflect "public opinion," Dennett sent a large packet of endorsements and supporting letters to prove popular demand and requested that the postmaster general reconsider.

In June 1925, Dennett received a reply from solicitor Blessing stating that he had reexamined *The Sex Side of Life* and had found it "to contain matter which is forbidden admission to the mails." At this vague letter, Dennett began an extended correspondence with Blessing asking him to identify specific passages which he found obscene. After all, the tract contained no information about abortion or contraception, the only *specific* prohibitions in Comstock Act. But repeated efforts to discover what was wrong with the pamphlet were futile. The solicitor would not or could not identify any objectionable passages. He only suggested that she come to his office to discuss the matter in person. Dennett refused. She wrote him, "A written official statement is what I first requested, and I now request it again, on the ground that any citizen who is notified that he is a lawbreaker has a right to a definite statement in writing from the official who declares his act criminal, as to just what constitutes the crime." When Blessing made a final refusal to comply with her request, Dennett gave up. To keep the pamphlet out of the post office's jurisdiction, however, she decided to change from second-class mail to parcel post.

Unable to convince the politicians to change their minds through reason, Dennett was still intent on somehow changing the obscenity law. She attempted to call an "Informal Round Table Conference" between the American Birth Control League, the VPL, and the Committee on Maternal Health on 6 April 1925, with the ABCL representing Margaret Sanger, the VPL representing Mary Ware Dennett, and the CMH representing Dr. Robert Latou Dickinson, another active birth-control worker. The stated intent of the meeting was for the three organizations to find a way to "work together" or, at the very least, not to duplicate each other's efforts. Called together on Mary Ware Dennett's terms, however, the conference could not expect to succeed. Sanger recognized immediately that the discussions proposed to start "from a position identical in every respect, so far as I can see, with what the Voluntary Parenthood League has always advocated. This, as you know, does not accord with the policy of the American Birth Control League." Saying that she was prepared to discuss a concrete amendment to federal law similar to the doctors-only bill she was presenting to Congress, Sanger decided that the meeting "would simply mean a fruitless consumption of time and energy." Alerting Dr. Dickinson to Dennett's plans, Sanger convinced him, too, to decline the invitation. Incensed, Dennett and the VPL workers immediately blamed Sanger for her unwillingness to cooperate. For months, the VPL circulated memoranda discussing the aborted attempt to "reach a compromise." In reality, however, it was Dennett who was unable to bend.

Still committed to the birth-control cause despite herself, Dennett decided to write a book, *Birth Control Laws*. The book would give the history of the Comstock Act and the congressional campaign to change it. This, she decided, would serve to present her views so that she could enjoy her private life. Once it came out, Dennett felt she could conscientiously decline the numerous speaking invitations she continually received from clubs and organizations interested in the birth-control issue. For without Dennett's congressional campaigning, the public activities of the VPL had largely ground to a halt. A president had been named, Myra Gallert, but she was largely titular. As chairman of the national council, Dennett was still the real woman in charge. When *Birth Control Laws* was published in 1926, Dennett dedicated the book to Gallert, but the promotion of *Birth Control Laws* became the primary focus of the VPL.

A year later, however, the women were still confused about what to do about the 1500 leftover copies of *Birth Control Laws*, which had not proved to be a big seller. Furthermore, they still had $600 in the Treasury, which they thought might be used to advertise the book. Myra Gallert and Vine McCasland, another friend of Mary's, were the only women really involved in promoting the book. Besides the book, the only other activity of the VPL was an uncoordinated letter-writing campaign to prominent people trying to convince them of the efficacy of a clean repeal bill. As there *was* no clean repeal bill in the works, however—only a doctors-only bill sponsored by Sanger's camp—this "behind-the-scenes" letter-writing campaign effectively meant trying to steer people away from Sanger's ideas to Dennett's. Needless to say, the efforts were not very effective. By 1927, Myra and Vine were begging Mary to dissolve the VPL.

Yet dissolution would prove to be more difficult than any of them expected. According to "corporation laws," the dissolution of the League would mean refunding the money, which the women felt should be used instead.[672] Dennett, who felt strongly about the principle of the clean repeal bill over the doctors-only bill, continued to write letters and give a fair amount of time to VPL "activities," but she refused on principle to accept payment for her work. Finally, Agnes Engelhard, the treasurer, insisted on sending Dennett a check of $120 for one year's worth of stamps and letters. She also insisted on reimbursing Dennett the small sum of $10 a month in the future. Besides her work in homeopathy and organic foods, after all, Dennett had little other income.[673]

Nevertheless, Dennett had become a recognized leader in the birth-control movement, which meant she continued to receive a flood of letters asking for practical information about birth control. Mostly coming from poor uneducated women, the letters begged for the "secret" to smaller families. Sick and weakened from a lifetime of serial pregnancies, these women were desperate to stem the unrelenting tide of births. Some of these women had ten, eleven, twelve children—and little means of financial support.[674]

Yet Dennett was still meticulous about following the letter of the law. Essentially a cerebral woman, her relationship to the birth-control cause came across as coldly intellectual. She answered even the most heartbreaking of letters with the same terse, unemotional reponse: "It is absolutely illegal to mail any contraceptive information anywhere in the country. Of course the laws are broken all the time. That is why it is time to repeal it. I hope you will help us accomplish it." She excused herself by stating that "the League cannot be in the business of breaking laws it is working to change."

Such cold advice—to join in an abstract political cause which *might* one day change birth-control laws—was of little practical use to women whose bodies were dying. Yet Dennett was not as heartless as she seemed. Pushed by Sanger to consider the human suffering, Mary began to rethink her policy. While she would still not endanger the fair name of the VPL, by the mid- to late-1920s Mary was beginning to break the law herself. She admitted, "I write to all the poor applicants for contraceptive information, who keep stringing along,—and regret the League's inability to break the law, etc. Then privately and anonymously, I do as I think best! All of which takes time, but I can't bear to leave those worried souls dangling."[675]

But poor women were not the only ones seeking help. Dennett received an assortment of letters from people who did not know where else to turn for advice about sex. These letters revealed the prevailing ignorance that lack of open discussion about sexual matters had caused. For example, there was the Dartmouth student who had received a copy of the *The Sex Side of Life* from his parents. Amazed to learn that it was sexual intercourse that produced babies, he wrote that he and his friends had previously associated sex only with nastiness and prostitutes. In another letter, a pharmacist asked Dennett to explain to him how in the world to use an under-the-counter contraceptive that *he himself sold*!

With the influx of letters, Dennett also received a few letters on subjects such as masturbation and lesbianism. Regarding masturbation, which had long been faulted with causing insanity, blindness, and other maladies among its practitioners, Dennett had altered her position on it in *The Sex Side of Life* from actually believing herself that it caused insanity to advising people that "recently many of the best scientists have concluded that the chief harm has come from the worry caused by doing it." While anxious to relieve undue fears, however, she also stressed the importance of unity between the sexes. "Remember, too, that as masturbation is a wholly one-sided and merely physical action, it can never be an adequate substitute for the mutual union of true mates. This union is so much more than physical that there is no substitute for it."[676]

And regarding lesbianism—as well as male homosexuality—Dennett now possessed the view that there was "relatively little danger in these relationships if they are temporary." She recognized the real value of strong relationships between members of the same sex, saying, "Yes indeed the world is full of instances of high-minded fine-spirited relationships between women and women, and likewise between men and men." She did not feel that such relationships were normal, however, if expressed sexually—but she had no desire to condemn the *people* either. Essentially, Dennett felt that the ideal relationship was heterosexual, and that homosexual behavior could be altered given a change of circumstances or self-examination.[677]

Whether she was addressing masturbation or homosexuality, Dennett's guiding principle was that ideal sexual behavior—like other actions in life—should be purposeful. She believed that the sex act was intended to have a physical, intellectual, and spiritual *purpose*. All three needed to be present for the ideal "mating" to take place. After all, in her pamphlet, she presented a view of sexuality whose *primary* purpose was the perpetuation of the species. Yet despite this primary purpose, she felt that human beings—being of a higher spiritual dimension than animals—could not limit themselves to the physical plane alone. In particular, Dennett believed strongly that there needed to be present the divine concept of love.

When it came to her religious beliefs, Dennett now considered herself a pragmatist. Despite her secular view that political anarchy could only lead to chaos and social disintegration, she no longer felt similarly about anarchy in the spiritual realm. Her experience with Hartley and Margaret notwithstanding, Mary now tended toward spiritual anarchy herself—flatly rejecting all institutionalized religion. Indeed, she herself had become something of a secular humanist. The traditional religious faiths she had investigated had not been able to meet the demands of modern living. Although each contained grains of spiritual truth, when viewed as a whole, each somehow fell short. When it came to religion, she now equated submission to a higher authority with authoritarianism.

No form of churchianity of ecclesiastism appeals to me as necessary or even helpful. I was brought up 'in the fold' and emerged many years ago.

*And the emergence seems to me all to the good. I should say that today I
am a decidedly more religious [read "spiritual"] person than I ever was
when I was under the thraldom of conventional Christianity.*[678]

Perhaps Denett's spiritual anarchism simply mirrored the times.
It was undeniable that the do-it-yourself morality that Hartley and
Margaret had championed was now beginning to show its effects in
popular culture. Values that had once been considered "bohemian"
had spread to become the norm among middle-class youth. No
longer did young couples sing and play the piano together on dates;
they necked in cars. The prosperity of the Coolidge years brought
together flappers and dandies. Prohibition was making liquor more
popular, not less. Glamour meant dancing and drinking in
smoke-filled speakeasies. More young women were dropping into
the big cities—without chaperones. Sexual experimentation was no
longer marginal; it had gone mainstream. Fueled by a growing con-
sumerism, advertisers used sex allure and success to sell products.
More importantly, sexual freedom itself became a commodity.
Popular women's magazines blared out trumpet calls about the dangers of repressing the libido. Newspapers, not specialized journals,
told of the dangers of sexual repression. The decline of public reticence about sex redefined womanhood to include the erotic.

Unlike the prewar bohemians whose sexual experimentation had
been based on a self-conscious rebellion, the sexuality of the 1920s
was marked by conformity. A "predigested social fashion," the
youth of the "roaring twenties" slept around because "everyone
else" was doing it. Sensing the inadequacy and irrelevance of
Victorian sexual standards, they did not attempt to replace them
with new ones. The moral idealism of the Greenwich Village rebels
was missing. As one feminist historian would later write, "In all this
rapid change, women's frequent unhappiness and men's frequent
opportunism were perhaps inevitable. The sexual revolution, like
real revolutions, brought violence and suffering, which must accompany the destruction of any traditional social institutions."[679]
Hutchins Hapgood would characterize the mood of the 1920s as
"sexual demoralization." The new sexuality had a sense of purpose-
lessness, and cynicism became the new faith.[680]

Against this tide, Dennett attempted to provide an alternative. In
March 1928, Mary Ware Dennett—along with others such as
Margaret Sanger and Charlotte Perkins Gilman—was asked to con-
tribute a chapter to a book called *Sex in Civilization*. Its purpose, as

Havelock Ellis wrote in the introduction, was to "treat all the phases of sexology nakedly and in the spirit of science." In her chapter, "Sex Enlightenment for Civilized Youth," Mary envisioned the sex education of the future: "Responsibility in sex living will be developed, as the expression of inner fineness. We shall help young people to apply to sex expression the same courtesy, tact, good taste, fairness, honor and understanding that we do to all other relationships,—instead of trying to safeguard it with merely external fences, such as moral dictums, conventional habits, traditional marriage, etc."

Counseling moderation, she did not propose a new generation "brazenly shouting from the housetops that human beings are animals just like any other animal, and that sex expression should be taken as a matter of course when wanted." She did not wish to see young people "yelping noisily about freedom...ostentatiously showing the world that they dare all sorts of exhibitionism." She differentiated knowledge from *license*: "[Young people] will come to see the wide difference between the attitude of the girl who goes hipping along the street with her coat held tightly around the most purposefully jiggling part of her anatomy, and the open-air girl who plays with gayety and bare-legged freedom in her swimming suit,—or, as time goes on, without it. Both girls may feel equally sex conscious, but one feels wicked and the other feels happy."

Again and again, Mary emphasized the importance of family influence: "The child of parents who have felt shame in regard to their own sex feelings or expression, is often so permeated with this general sense of indecency that, in his later years, it is almost impossible for him to clear it entirely out from his consciousness, and make room for a fresh, wholesome, scientific, poetic, joyous realization of the sex side of life." Yet she offered hope: "And conversely, the child whose parents are lovers who have dragged no weight of shame along with their love, but whose sex life has been untramelled, vigorous, sensitive, reciprocal and glad, unconsciously stores in his mental and emotional being a *sexual health of spirit* that will beautifully see him through all manner of later experiences, which might easily otherwise pervert him. This sort of child carries his own environment with him: it protects him, like an umbrella in a down-pour."

Yet as her activities continued, Dennett began to notice strange things happening to her mail. A regular correspondent with Marie Stopes, the British physician and birth controller whose books had been banned in America, Dennett noticed that some of the mail from Stopes was not making it to her. Items sent in first-class sealed mail seemed to stand a good chance of arriving, but second-class mail or parcels seemed subject to loss. Not wanting to be paranoid, Dennett wrote, "I simply can't think it is anything but a series of most vexing happenings, for it really does not seem likely that there is postal espionage to the extent of watching always what you may send to me."[681]

That was not all. Dennett noted that as demand for *The Sex Side of Life* grew, more and more envelopes reached the people to whom they were addressed empty, or else they never arrived at all. Dennett usually used unsealed clasp envelopes to send the pamphlet. "I did not keep account of the number which thus had to be replaced, but it was surprisingly large. I was patient at first about the losses, for if the Post Office clerks were so hungry for knowledge that they were willing to pilfer it, they must have needed it rather badly. However, as their hunger seemed insatiable and their numbers seemed endless, I presently resorted to mailing the pamphlet in sealed envelopes."[682]

Now in her fifties, Dennett was trying to slow down. Both of her sons were married, and she had recently become a grandmother. With the close of the Progressive era, the pre- and postwar social-reform activities had largely simmered to an end. Although she had given her all to the birth-control movement, the heydey of her political involvement was largely over. Dennett wanted to return to her artisan roots, and to try to live an easier, simpler lifestyle. Well aware of the effects of media sensationalism, she had never wanted to be involved in high-profile activities. Even disregarding urgent pleas for help from people seeking birth-control information, Dennett would not openly budge from her law-abiding policy. To the end, Mary was most interested in one thing only: principle. That is why, when Mary Ware Dennett received a notice in the mail charging her with obscenity, her dilemma was all the more ironic.

Livonia Coffin Ware, c. 1887. At age eighteen, Vonie gave up
her dream of attending college to become "little mother"
to her two younger sisters and one younger brother.
Courtesy of Joanna Dennett

George Whitefield Ware, 1880. Mary lost her "blessedly
good-humored" father to cancer in 1882.
Courtesy of Joanna Dennett.

The three Ames sisters, left to right: Vonie, Lucia Ames Mead, and Clara Ames, c. 1915. Refusing to bow before a human master, each believed that marriage was only one of a woman's many life options.
Courtesy of Sally Dennett.

Mary Coffin Ware, 1884. Bespectacled, with long dark blonde hair,
she looked like a young scholar. Distinctions based upon sex
would never make sense to her.

Courtesy of Joanna Dennett.

Mary Coffin Ware, 1893. Artist's Festival. Mary's circle of young artists
and designers loved playacting, costume parties, and theatrical entertainments.

William Hartley Dennett, 1890. Considered quite fashionable
and debonair, Hartley graduated from the Massachusetts Institute
of Technology in 1892. He and Mary were among the founders
of the Boston Society of Arts and Crafts.

Courtesy of Joanna Dennett.

When Mary discovered that there were no longer any craftsmen making gilded leathers, or *guadamaçiles*, she translated two books from Old French that described the process, had die-stamp tools made, and began creating her own *guadamaçiles*. Before long, Mary had revived a lost art form.

At its peak, the Dennett home was described as "one of the most beautiful homes I have ever known, perhaps the most beautiful, the relations not only of Mr. Dennett and Mrs. Dennett, but their relations towards their friends and towards the community. It was...to everyone who knew them a singularly blessed spot."

Courtesy of Margaret Chase Perry.

A rare family portrait, c. 1906. Mary Ware Dennett with Devon on her lap,
Carleton standing, and Hartley on the right.
Courtesy of Nancy Dennett.

The Chase "camp" was simply magnificent. Nearly everybody knew it
for miles around. One simply had to ask for the log house. And from its
windows, the view overlooking the valley below was spectacular.
Courtesy of Margaret Chase Perry.

Margaret Chase and her husband Dr. Heman Lincoln Chase. Margaret said
she was filled with "certainty" about the strength of her own marriage—about
Dr. Chase and "his devotion to her & her own devotion to him."

Devon Dennett, c. 1909. When Mary's two sons helped their mother with her suffrage activities—handing out fliers, selling tickets, holding placards—passing men would often call the boys names or even spit on them.
Courtesy of Joanna Dennett.

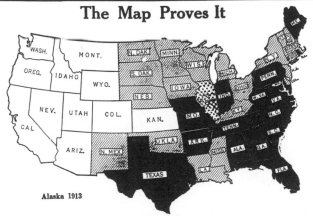

By M. W. D.

Votes for Women a Success

The Map Proves It

Alaska 1913

WHITE STATES; Full Suffrage   SHADED STATES: Taxation, Bond or School Suffrage
DOTTED STATE: Presidential, Partial County and State, Municipal Suffrage   BLACK STATES: No Suffrage

SUFFRAGE GRANTED

1869—WYOMING	1912—ARIZONA
1893—COLORADO	1912—KANSAS
1896—UTAH	1913—ILLINOIS
1896—IDAHO	1913—ALASKA
1910—WASHINGTON	1914—MONTANA
1911—CALIFORNIA	1914—NEVADA
1912—OREGON	

Would any of these States have adopted EQUAL SUFFRAGE
if it had been a failure just across the Border?

NATIONAL WOMAN SUFFRAGE PUBLISHING COMPANY, INC.

505 Fifth Avenue   377   New York City

Mary devised this popular suffrage map, which clearly illustrated states in which woman suffrage was legal and states in which it was not. Although it appeared in articles and even on the letterhead of the NAWSA, Dennett was never credited.

MAY THE HAPPINESS WHICH
ESPECIALLY BELONGS TO
THESE FEW DAYS BE YOURS
THE WHOLE YEAR ROUND!

CARLETON

DEVON

MARY WARE DENNETT
JANUARY FIRST MCMXI

71 WEST 50th STREET
NEW YORK CITY

Mary Ware Dennett, 1912. In a grueling and sensationalist trial one year later,
Mary would win sole and exclusive custody of her two children.

Creating a new life for herself in New York City, Mary would feel her old
spirit coming back to her in "leaps and bounds."

Dennett combined her craftsmanship with her interest in birth control to
create designs for the Voluntary Parenthood League.

DEVON ———— MARY ———— CARLETON

From the Dennetts, big and little,

Dec. 25,   Jan. 1,
1919   1920

Greeting!

    Grateful for the sacrifices she had made for them in childhood, Carl
and Devon would always feel quite protective of their mother. When Mary incurred
debt by paying for the expenses of the Voluntary Parenthood League, her sons, who
were in their twenties, insisted that her debts were theirs as well.

Mary Ware Dennett
Courtesy of Sally Dennett

THE FINAL YEARS

PART III

CHAPTER SIXTEEN

Indictment

On 2 January 1929, after the traditional holiday festivities were over, Mary Ware Dennett picked up her mail—the New Year only bringing back the old routine. Sifting through the many New Year's greetings for 1929, she opened up a peculiar notice. The return address was the Office of the United States Attorney for the Eastern District of New York, Post Office Building, Brooklyn, N.Y. Stamped on it was the title *United States of America vs. Mary Ware Dennett*. The official-looking document notified her that "the defendant" (presumably herself) was required to be in court five days hence to "plead to an indictment heretofore filed, for an alleged violation of the United States Criminal Code." No complaint was stated; no specific charge was named. Beyond the statement that "[i]f defendant fails to attend, a warrant will be issued for her arrest," the notice was vague.[683]

Dennett was puzzled. A strait-laced reformer often attacked by her critics for her uncompromising allegiance to the law, Mary was an old-time New Englander, who could trace her family line back to pre-Revolutionary times. Her history of civic service spanned three decades, from the late 1890s to the present, and now she was fifty-six years old, newly made a grandmother. She lived alone, without the company of husband or children. She could not imagine what she could have done wrong. After letting the shock settle, Mary promptly set about to discover the reason for the indictment. She called her friend, Morris Ernst, a young attorney who was general counsel and a board member of the newly-formed American Civil Liberties Union. Ernst sent over to the U.S. District Attorney's office for a copy of the actual indictment. Nothing. The information was too spotty. But he found out the name of the prosecutor, Assistant District Attorney James E. Wilkinson.

Upon questioning, Wilkinson said he had filed the case on behalf of a Mrs. Carl A. Miles in the Vale of Shenandoah, Grottoes, Va. The charge was the "mailing and delivery, [of] certain non-mailable matter, to wit: a pamphlet, booklet and certain printed matter enclosed in an envelope, which...were obscene, lewd, lascivious, filthy, vile and indecent." Calling the unmentionable item "unfit to be set forth ...upon the records of this Honorable Court," the indictment claimed "said Mary W. Dennett, at the time of such mailing, knew said envelope to contain said pamphlet, booklet, and certain printed matter, which were obscene, lewd, lascivious, and filthy, vile and indecent, against peace and dignity of the United States..." After pressing for details, Ernst discovered that Wilkinson was speaking of the essay Mary had originally written for her two sons. Despite its longstanding acceptance among Americans—it had been written in 1915 and first published in 1918—the author was just now being charged with obscenity. The problem, of course, was the subject matter. Someone had complained about *The Sex Side of Life: An Explanation for Young People.*

The mystery of Dennett's indictment was only the beginning of a series of pretrial problems. The next item was where to obtain bail. Ernst learned from Wilkinson that the court would probably set bail at the astronomical sum of $2,500, a reminder that obscenity, as defined in the United States legal statutes, was no mere misdemeanor. On 6 January 1929 one of Mary's sons contacted William Floyd, a fellow peace activist, to let him know that their mother had been summoned to appear in court at 10:30 the next morning. Floyd had been familiar with the pamphlet since its publication, believed in it, and agreed to furnish bail. On the date of the scheduled court appearance, Dennett, Ernst, and Floyd arrived in court to take care of the matter, but their first couple of bonds were rejected for technical reasons.

After much frustration, Floyd finally went to obtain $2,500 cash from his bank in Manhattan. Meanwhile, Dennett had a chance to observe the workings of the courthouse in detail. The seventh of January was a Monday, and on Mondays the court was filled with liquor cases from the weekend. By the time Floyd left, Mary had already been waiting for a couple of hours, having arrived at the courthouse punctually at 10:30 AM A steady flow of bootleggers and boozers had been streaming before the judge all morning to have their bail and trial dates set. Mary was the only woman among them. When she arrived, all the seats were taken. A U.S. marshal, who had been poking her along by hand, suddenly said, "Hey, some of youse get up and give dis lady a seat." Led upstairs sometime thereafter, she was put into a room with prison bars from floor to ceiling, on the other side of which there was a low wooden rail. The space behind the iron bars was crowded with men; Dennett was the sole woman placed behind the wooden rail. Before long, another woman appeared, "a liquor raid case," to keep her company.

The woman, as it turned out, had been jailed since Saturday night without food. Only those who had money were able to bribe the attendants to go out and buy sandwiches for them. Those without money went hungry. The jailor announced in a loud voice that if they were not able to secure bail by three o'clock they would go to prison. The bonding company runners were active, but many of the people being held had no money with which to pay the inflated fees charged. The woman's bail was $400, but the companies wanted $20 for providing it. She was penniless. At one point the jailer shouted "Dennett" and threw a paper bag at Mary over the railing. The contents consisted of chicken sandwiches that Ernst and Floyd had stopped to buy for her. After one bite, Mary realized she had no appetite. She gave the sandwiches to the woman. Mary would later describe the scenario.

> *The room was high but small. The windows were shut tight, and the air was foul.... The air grew worse. Someone urged that a window be opened. An elderly clerk complied with the request as if it were something abnormal. Soon he felt a "draft" and went back to the airless plan. The only water available was from a tank, below which was one muddy-looking glass tumbler, used by all and sundry. The adjoining toilet facilities were unspeakably horrid—no sex discrimination there—and conditions of ancient dirt were so bad that a description of them would be, in the language of the indictment, "unfit to be spread on the records of the Honorable Court." The irony of being held on the charge of being "filthy," in a place that was positively nasty, soaked into my consciousness as the minutes dragged by.*[684]

After several hours, Dennett was set free and told to come back eight days later for the actual trial.

These inconveniences were only the beginnings of what would seem to her like a long ordeal. The trial would not be held eight days later, nor would it be held the following week. For the next four months, Dennett shuttled back and forth to and from the courthouse, waiting for her case to go to trial. Almost every postponement was made at the request of the judge or the prosecution, not the defense. From beginning to end, Dennett would make thirteen long trips to the courthouse in Brooklyn, wasting "a good half a day each time," usually only arriving to hear her case called and postponed yet again. From the very first frustrating day, Dennett would go home, "feeling as if the day's experience had somehow been a bad dream." Speaking for the prosecution, Wilkinson explained, "This woman has had eleven years in which to find friends for the pamphlet, while I have had only a few weeks to find opponents."[685]

In the meantime, Ernst promptly filed a motion that the indictment be quashed "on the ground that the said indictment fails to state facts sufficient to constitute a crime." He also arranged to exchange advantages with Wilkinson. The original indictment had not identified by name the "pamphlet, booklet, and certain printed matter" that had been found "obscene, lewd, lascivious" etc. Evidently, the "pamphlet, booklet" was intended to refer to *The Sex Side of Life* itself, but Ernst obtained from Wilkinson a written stipulation that the "certain printed matter" was a leaflet of "Representative Opinions" that Dennett customarily included when sending the pamphlet to new readers. These opinions, from people like H.L. Mencken, Havelock Ellis, Goodwin F. Watson, and several dozen others, all highly commended *The Sex Side of Life*. In exchange, Ernst agreed that Dennett would admit to actually mailing the material so as to save the prosecution time and money in bringing Mrs. Carl A. Miles up from Virginia to New York to testify. This way, the defense would guarantee that positive statements about *The Sex Side of Life* could be presented in court, and Mrs. Miles would be spared being called to the witness stand.

For her part, Dennett began making exhaustive adjustments in all areas of her life in preparation for the trial. She made immediate arrangements to cease all mailings of *The Sex Side of Life* pamphlet. By January 15, she had arranged for a form letter to be sent out in response to all incoming orders, explaining that no orders were being filled pending the outcome of the case and apologizing for the delay. By January 20, she had sent out letters to dozens of prominent supporters of her pamphlet to ask them to act as "representative witnesses" in the trial.[686] With the word out that Mary Ware Dennett had been charged with obscenity, letters began to stream in from friends asking what they could do to help. Dennett, in her indefatigable way, took pains to answer every single piece of correspondence.

On January 21, Ernst and Wilkinson appeared in court before Judge Grover M. Moscowitz to make preliminary arguments about whether or not the indictment should be quashed. Ernst presented the document, "Representative Opinions," which not only stated the opinions of thirty-eight prominent people regarding the pamphlet itself, but gave evidence as to the how the pamphlet had been distributed and used. Next, he gave a bit of the history of the essay—how it had been published in *The Medical Review of Reviews*, quoting the editor's introduction, stating its large circulation of about thirty thousand to date. Then Ernst made a case for sex education itself. He pointed out that there were several pamphlets issued by the federal government that urged a similar approach to sex education—"many of which are as frank in detail, and as specific as to terms, as this pamphlet before you." According to government authorities, claimed Ernst, it was only through "general education" that the "prevalent idea of the uncleanness of sex [could] be overcome." Said Ernst, "The pictures of the human body in schools with the genital organs removed, create a secrecy which, according to the leading educators of the land, has a more degrading influence on the young than a clear, simple scientific statement of sexual information…" Ernst argued that Dennett's intentions were pure and the effect was honorable.

> *Above all else the pamphlet is one of sincerity and integrity. There are no dirty words in it. There is nothing in the pamphlet that will create a dirty giggle or a blush. It is sincere and simple and straight-forward. Those are ingredients that do not accompany pornography, obscenity, lewdness and lasciviousness.*
>
> *We are past the period in our education of a natural silence and a taboo on the subject of sex. This pamphlet lifts the veil and does not rend it.… To condemn the pamphlet is to condemn the YMCA, the churches, the Union Theological Seminary and other institutions of that type throughout the country, which have been the distributors and proponents of the pamphlet.[687]*

Ernst compared *The Sex Side of Life* indictment to others in legal history, showing that there were excellent precedents for the dismissal of the case. Taking up the question of the definitions or tests of obscenity, classically carried over from 1868 Hicklin test, he tried to demonstrate that *The Sex Side of Life* could not be considered obscene. The old English formula, saying only "whether or not the publication would have the tendency to deprave or corrupt those whose minds are open to such immoral things," and usually accompanied by the phrase, "and into whose hands the publication might fall," had been modified by recent court decisions in the United States, argued Ernst, and it was now generally necessary to show that "lecherous desires or impure sexual thoughts" had actually been induced. Said Ernst, "There is nothing in this pamphlet that can be deemed to be lecherous or impure. True enough, it deals with sex, but obviously the statute did not mean to imply that all literature dealing with sex would be banned just because some filthy-minded person comes to the conclusion that he procures an impure stimulation from the material."[688]

Judge Moscowitz then tried to ascertain the pamphlet's intended age group. Ernst responded by explaining that Dennett had written it for her two sons, aged fourteen and ten at the time, but that it was unreasonable to ban the pamphlet because of age restrictions. "Adults and adolescents have some rights also, and if we are going to say that the only information that can be spread is such as can be offered to a child of seven, we are by the same token starving the entire rest of the population." Ernst and Dennett then answered a few more questions concerning readership. Said Ernst, "Your Honor knows that children get this information somewhere or other, and it is far preferable to have them get the material in an intelligent, clean way, than to pick it up from somebody whispering a dirty four-letter Anglo-Saxon word, and then have the child snoop around to a dictionary and find out what it means." Trying to drive home the point that sex education was itself necessary, Ernst closed with the words: "If this pamphlet is obscene then life itself is obscene."[689]

Taking up the argument, Wilkinson responded with the attack: "Sex instruction is one thing and perverted sex instruction is another."[690] Students from a girl's school had been visiting the courtroom that day, but they were discreetly herded out before Wilkinson began his comments. Wilkinson began to argue that *The Sex Side of Life* advocated premarital sex and masturbation by putting forth a view of sex and sexuality as something which was healthy, normal, and pleasurable.[691] He took offense at the statement that venereal disease was becoming curable. Then he claimed that *The Sex Side of Life* said nothing about "self-control." Said Wilkinson, "What is the idea, except to show that sex is something that is to be indulged in whenever you feel like it? Is this a book, for instance, that your Honor and I would distribute to the young ladies who were sitting in those chairs to the right of the courtroom this morning." Bringing up the sixteen-year-old girl, he repeatedly stated his concerns. In sum, Wilkinson said, he "felt that young people should retain all their fears in order to keep themselves straight."[692]

Later, Dennett, in her book *Who's Obscene?*, would protest that her pamphlet actually said quite a bit about self-control. From the "Introduction to Elders" preceding the main text, she had written that it was necessary to give young people "the facts" so that they could have "some conception of sex life as a vivifying joy, as a vital art, as a thing to be studied and developed with reverence for its big meaning, with understanding of its far-reaching reactions, psychologically and spiritually, with temperant restraint, good taste and highest idealism." As Dennett emphasized, restraint was "impossible without self-control."[693] In another passage, she wrote, "Only such an understanding can be counted on to give them the self-control that is born of knowledge not fear, the reverence that will prevent premature or trivial connections..."

From the main part of the pamphlet, she wrote, "Our bodies... are more than machines...They are the homes of our souls and our feelings, and that makes all the difference in the world in the way we act, and it makes what we have to learn, not limited to science only, but it has to include more difficult and complicated things like psychology and morality." As she would point out, "Morality is impossible without self-control."[694] Or, in the following passage: "Remember that strong feelings are immensely valuable to us. All we have to do is to steer them in the right direction and keep them well-balanced and proportioned." As she would say, "Steering requires self-control."[695] Finally, Dennett would claim that the following paragraph was entirely about self-control:

> *Remember always that your whole sex machinery is more easily put out of order than any other part of your body, and it must be treated with great care and respect all along. It is not fair to ourselves or to each other to do a single thing that will make us either weak or unnatural. Remember that your sex organs have a very powerful, even if invisible, effect upon your whole being, and up to the time when you are really old enough to love someone to whom you want actually to belong, you must let your sex machinery grow strong and ready for its good happy work when the right time comes.[696]*

Wilkinson, however, had a different interpretation. He argued that Mary was antimarriage, because she wrote the following, "When people really love each other, they don't care who knows about it." What he neglected to mention was that the sentence came from a discussion of prostitution and was immediately followed by this assurance: "They are proud of their happiness. But no man is ever proud of his connection with a prostitute and no prostitute is ever proud of her business." Persistently, he read portions of her text out of context in ways which she felt misrepresented her intentions. Said Wilkinson to the judge, "There is not one word of self-control, with the act of sexual relations described with a rhythmic movement, as she describes the act, if that would not raise in the mind of a fifteen- or sixteen-year-old girl a desire, what is it?"[697]

Unable to decide for himself whether or not *The Sex Side of Life* was obscene, the judge sitting on the preliminary hearing, Judge Grover M. Moscowitz, made a most unusual decision. Unwilling to take on sole responsibility of deciding whether or not to quash the motion, he proposed to hold an open hearing. He invited both sides to invite representatives whose views, endorsements, and criticisms would be given to help him decide where justice lay. He also asked to see Dennett's collection of orders and letters taken from her files to better evaluate how the pamphlet had been used durings its eleven years of circulation. After one postponement, the date was set for January 28.

By this time, the case was beginning to attract public interest. The New York *World* had begun covering the case on January 26 and 27, and many other papers would pick it up as well. When the day arrived, people who had heard about the case crowded into the courtroom. In preparation for the open hearing, Moscowitz had invited three Brooklyn clergymen to share the bench with him: Monsignor John L. Bedford, of the Roman Catholic Church of the Nativity, Rabbi Louis E. Gross of Union Temple, and Dr. George P. Atwater, Rector of Grace Protestant Episcopal Church.[698] The stated object of having the clerics sit beside him was "to aid the conscience of the court."[699] In addition, Dennett had arranged for twenty witnesses of "distinction and importance" to testify on her behalf. They included John Dewey, Dr. Robert L. Dickinson, Dr. Goodwin F. Watson, Mrs. Cecile Pilpel, Rabbi Stephen S. Wise, and the Reverend Eliot White, among others. Dennett had called in her friends from various civic reform circles, as well as prominent representatives from the YMCA, child welfare organizations, and various religious and educational institutions.

At the last moment, however, the judge decided that he would not hear from any of the witnesses who had come to testify. It was an awkward situation for Mary, as all these people were fairly busy and some had traveled long distances to testify at her request, but Moscowitz explained to the assemblage, "To permit the witnesses to take the stand would bring publicity that might affect the minds of the jurymen." Instead, he suggested that the "experts" prepare written statement for submission to the court. Twelve letters or statements, he decided, would be allowed each side.

The letters were due on February 4, and Moscowitz had also set a tentative date for a trial on February 18. Dennett, who had an abundance of supporters who had long used and endorsed the pamphlet, had difficulty narrowing down her choices to a few who would represent a broad sampling of solid public opinion. As a result, she had Ernst submit a "baker's dozen" of thirteen letters from several prominent people.[700] Calling attention to the fact that the letters came from "leaders in practically every field of social contact in the community," Ernst made the case that *The Sex Side of Life* was quite acceptable to mainstream America. He also pointed out that the letters contained more than just opinion—most indicated broad experience with the tract, surpassing a mere statement of non-obscenity to testifying that it was positively beneficial. On the other hand, Wilkinson had difficulty coming up with even a dozen opponents to *The Sex Side of Life*.[701] After some effort, the prosecution finally managed to scrape together eleven letters.[702] Most of these letters consisted of rambling outbursts which showed minimal familiarity with the text in question. A few stated only that Wilkinson had asked for a reading and that, after a quick glance, the author had decided that the pamphlet was useless.

After receiving the twenty-four letters to gauge public opinion, Judge Moscowitz decided to postpone his decision again. Mary updated her notice to people asking for the pamphlet, letting them know of the delay and giving them the option to cancel their orders. More and more people began writing to her, as concern began to be generated that the very legitimacy of sex education was being questioned. The word spread that the judge had asked for letters to estimate public opinion, and letters and telegrams began coming in to him to pressure him to drop the case. Meanwhile, Moscowitz was having difficulties of his own, as there had been charges brought against him concerning his conduct in several bankruptcy cases. He postponed his decision three times, and the trial date was pushed back accordingly. Finally, when he could put off a decision no longer, Moscowitz decided to notify the press that he would not sit on the case due to personal problems.[703]

At this, Ernst conferred with the judge and decided to withdraw his motion to quash the indictment. Instead, Ernst decided to substitute a demurrer which would automatically bring the case before another judge.[704] Before taking this action, however, Ernst had Moscowitz and Wilkinson agree that all twenty-four of the specially permitted letters which Judge Moscowitz had received for and against the case would be made a part of the court record. This would make it possible for the letters to be passed on as evidence to the next judge when the arguments on the demurrer were heard. Written stipulations were drawn up to this effect, and duly signed on March 13.[705]

On March 18, another judge was found, Judge Marcus B. Campbell, who heard both attorneys argue on the demurrer. Ernst and Wilkinson went through many of the same arguments, in briefer form. By this time, the publicity on the case was becoming more widespread. Wilkinson was threatening to sue the *Nation* because of an article by Dudley Nichols that had portrayed him as a fool. Said Mary, he "evidently realized that he better not make such a donkey of himself again, and he was briefer and more restrained than before, but just as vulgar." And Nichols had written to Dennett herself, "Your letter revives my picture of Wilkinson: what a wonderful creature indeed. You wouldn't dare stick him on the stage, for fear of the outcry 'caricature.' He was really wonderful. Poor fear ridden man."[706]

Wilkinson was now referring to Mary as "this lady" as opposed to "this woman," and he had added an extra touch by describing Mary as "this lady" who "opens the window and sticks her head out and beckons in all the neighbors' children" to corrupt their morals.[707] He also selected one of the opposition letters that personally attacked Dennett *herself*, instead of the pamphlet, and read it "with unction." Outside of the courtroom, Dennett did her best to keep up her spirits. "The reaction of the young folks interests me specially. And I am sure they would laugh along with me, to hear the greyheaded Prosecutor solemnly assure the Judge that this pamphlet is guaranteed to send the young folks straight to the devil; and yet he does not produce a single ruined young person to prove it, nor does he even have to show evidence that the ruin occurs; nor will the court allow the defense to bring in the testimony of the hundreds and thousands of young people who have been helped by the pamphlet. The whole thing is pure conjecture. Yet it goes in Court just as if it were proven truth."[708]

After hearing the arguments, however, Judge Campbell announced that he would defer his decision on the demurrer and that, in any event, he would not sit on the case when it came to trial. He explained that if he decided in favor, the prosecution would not want him to sit on the case; if he decided against, he assumed the defense would not want to argue before him. Then he named a new trial date of April 9. On April 5, Judge Campbell notified Ernst that he was going to deny him the demurrer. He also announced that he would not read any of the letters to Judge Moscowitz, which, by signed stipulation, had already been made a part of the court record. Campbell claimed that Moscowitz did not have the right to allow the stipulation which made the letters a part of the record, and so he would not recognize them as such. Furthermore, April 9 came and passed with no trial.

Postponement after postponement marked the next few weeks. Moscowitz's temporary retirement from the bench pending Congressional investigations made it all the more difficult to find a date. There was a glut of cases and a deficiency of visiting judges available from other districts to cover the entire calendar. For one week no jury could sit because there was no judge to preside. Dennett had to make repeated trips to the courthouse, only to hear the clerk announce a postponement. If she did not show up, however, to hear her case called, her bail would be forfeited. Dennett had hoped to be released from bail on personal recognizance, and Wilkinson even agreed to the action. Wrote Dennett to her bondsman, "Evidently Wilkinson deems me at least honest, if not decent."[709] But then on April 10, even that minor request was denied her. As Dennett would put it, "The judge, with his disagreeable grin that prevents any confidence in his sincerity, said no to the proposition for remitting bail."[710]

Meanwhile, the jury was selected and eliminated by awkward publicity. Wilkinson's first sifting process was to inquire whether "any of you gentlemen have read the papers about the case and have formed an opinion."[711] When all twelve men shook their heads vaguely, he then asked: "Have any of you ever read anything by Havelock Ellis or H.L. Mencken?"[712] When two admitted that they had "a little," they were immediately dismissed. Wilkinson's questions caused columnist Heywood Broun[713] of the New York *Telegram* to quip that a more pertinent inquiry might have been: "Have you ever read anything?"[714] For his part, Ernst's primary question was whether any of the men had ever belonged to vice-hunting societies; he also eliminated one man who was found to be a personal friend of Wilkinson. Women, at the time, were not eligible for jury duty. When the jury was finally selected, all but one of the men were middle-aged or elderly, and married with families.[715]

Finally, a third and final arbiter was found to preside over the jurors. Federal Judge Warren Booth Burrows was borrowed from

New London, Connecticut, to serve during Moscowitz's absence. A graduate of the University of Michigan Law School, Burrows had only been nominated for his post a year earlier.[716] Obscenity was a criminal charge, and the government had appointed U.S. Assistant District Attorney James E. Wilkinson to represent Mrs. Miles. For the defense, Morris Ernst, who had been helping Dennett at the outset, decided to volunteer his services. Dennett had read his book, *To the Pure*, and had discussed with him possible ways to change the obscenity laws. In her interaction with him, she had come to know him as someone whose interests she considered "socially constructive as well as legally analytical." Agreeing to take on the case, Ernst would call *The Sex Side of Life* case "the most important in his career."

CHAPTER SEVENTEEN

The Sex Side of Life Trial

On 23 April 1929, after four months of scuttling at the courthouse, *The Sex Side of Life* case finally came to trial. Opening the proceedings, Prosecutor Wilkinson announced that the government's case would be "very simple," because Dennett had admitted to mailing the pamphlet. He simply planned to introduce the contents of the mailing as evidence, read it aloud, and then close the case. Wilkinson emphasized that the question of obscenity as determined by federal law was decided solely by a trial jury, telling the jurors that "you are the exclusive judges of that fact." He then announced that he would only present the first two of three government exhibits: the envelope addressed to Mrs. Carl A. Miles, in the Vale of the Shenandoah, Grottoes, Va., with the return address of M. W. Dennett, 81 Singer St., Astoria, L.I., New York, and *The Sex Side of Life* pamphlet itself.[717] Immediately, Ernst objected to the exclusion of the third exhibit, the "Representative Opinions," referring to the signed stipulations in which they had agreed that the third document would be considered as part of the same parcel as the first two. Wilkinson responded by claiming that the additional material amounted to expert opinion testimony and, as such, refused to introduce it and risk being bound by the contents. Judge Burrows sided with Ernst, and agreed that the provisions of the stipulation were binding.[718]

At this, Wilkinson announced that the government would plead its case against *The Sex Side of Life* based solely on the pamphlet, without calling any witnesses. Giving a dramatic reading of his "evidence" in a "droning low tone, except in those portions which he considered most 'filthy,'" he raised his voice only when he reached the parts of *The Sex Side of Life* that he considered obscene. Calling upon his emotional resources—ostensibly to arouse the proper indignation from his audience—he paused at key moments to let the obscenity of the matter "sink into the minds of the jury." Forced to read the "Representative Opinions" as well, he "rattled through" these "as fast and as monotonously as possible"—doing his best to minimize the effect. With his performance over, so was the government's case. Apparently, Wilkinson felt that there was no need to call upon any witnesses or make any other kind of case. He trusted that *The Sex Side of Life* itself would be proof enough of obscenity.[719]

After Wilkinson presented his evidence, Ernst made one final plea to have the judge dismiss the indictment.[720] Ernst pointed out that the pamphlet had already been distributed for ten years, that it had been "accepted in the community" for the entire time. Indeed, he emphasized that it had first appeared in *The Medical Review of Reviews* in February 1918, that it had been published in 1919 "at the request of the editor of medical magazines," and that it had enjoyed the endorsement of "those people who are identified in our society, with churches, the YMCA, of the Health Departments, the Union Theological Seminary." Furthermore, he pointed out that *The Sex Side of Life* lacked "any of the earmarks of pornography, as laid down in the usual cases before the Courts." That is, the pamphlet openly bore the name of the author herself, the low price demonstrated that it was not published for the sake of profit, and its contents were substantially the same as thousands of other tracts published by the federal government through the Department of Health of the Treasury Department.

Going on to cite various cases that Wilkinson would rely on, Ernst demonstrated that *The Sex Side of Life* was different. He claimed that if *The Sex Side of Life* was indeed "obscene," then the practice by which the YMCA and Union Theological Seminary used the tract as their central text would imply that those two organizations were "corrupting elements."[721] Wilkinson countered by underlining that the opinion of obscenity was for the jury only to decide. It was the trial jury who had to establish "whether the pamphlet does or does not contain matter that is apt to raise lewd and libidinous thoughts in the minds of the young and immature and into those whose hands it may come." It was only those twelve men who would determine whether or not *The Sex Side of Life* was, indeed, obscene. Ernst had made a last effort to stop the proceedings, but the judge responded: "Motion denied."

At this, it was time for the defense to begin its case. Ernst addresssed the jury by announcing ten witnesses, all of whom were prominent community leaders and educators. [722] Hoping to make clear that *The Sex Side of Life* pamphlet was distributed in a sound and legal manner, Ernst sought to remove all suspicion that *The Sex Side of Life* was "surreptitiously sold, that it was sneaked out from under the counter of a soda water or stationery store." Ernst wanted to demonstrate that the tract had been openly displayed and circulated "by churches, educational and charitable organizations" for over a decade. Arguing that obscenity was a construct in the mind of the vice hunter, he concluded by saying that "if people are looking for dirt they can find it anywhere, and if anyone is looking for honest sex instruction, he can find it in this pamphlet."

The first witness Ernst called to the stand was Mr. Abel J. Gregg of the boys Work Section of the National Council of the YMCA. After Gregg identified himself, Ernst asked him "how many hundreds of copies of Mrs. Dennett's pamphlet" he had ordered on behalf of the YMCA for the boys' groups and other affiliated organizations. Wilkinson immediately protested. He pounced, "Objected to as incompetent, irrelevant and immaterial, not within the issues of the indictment." Pushing forward for an advantage, Wilkinson asked to have the jury excused from the courtroom.

Once the jury had filed out of the courtroom, Wilkinson pressed his concern that he did not believe that the defense had the right to produce evidence that might weigh against the case of the prosecution. Said Wilkinson, "I submit, that if we were permitted to...put experts on the stand, there is no question but that we would have a trial here that would be prolonged for two or three weeks on the question of obscenity and the opinion of people on this pamphlet. We are only concerned here as to whether the pamphlet was mailed or not. The jury are the sole and exclusive judges of its obscenity..." He went on to claim that calling experts to the stand would be an indirect way of getting unallowable opinion testimony. Wilkinson insisted that the introduction of "evidence that can have no tendency in the minds of the jury but to confuse them as against the Government's case...and against which the Government can have no redress in the way of rebuttal evidence."[723]

Said Ernst in response, "The basic principle is, will the pamphlet corrupt those into whose hands it is likely to come, and we want to prove into whose hands it did actually come." To illustrate the ridiculous nature of the objection, Ernst went on to state that law books containing detailed description of rape cases and medical books could also be suppressed by Wilkinson's line of reasoning. It was whether or not *The Sex Side of Life* was corrupting, argued Ernst. But Wilkinson shot back, "It is only a question of whether the defendant mailed this pamphlet; and it is for the jury to pass upon the construction of its language."[724]

Wilkinson claimed that Dennett's motives were immaterial. Said Wilkinson, "Here is a woman, if your Honor please, publishing this pamphlet initially for her own children. All right. As soon as that happened, she fulfilled her life's purpose; but for her to call in her neighbor's children, others from around the neighborhood, to tell them about it, that is different." Apparently, Wilkinson felt that sex education should come only from a child's own parents, and the parents could have no outside literature or guidance. When Ernst began to mount a defense, Judge Burrows repeatedly challenged his statements until, in response to Ernst's statements about the pamhlet's distribution, the judge went so far as to say, "Did I understand you to say that twenty-five thousand of them were dumped into the YMCA?" Ernst simply replied, "No, I did not say that, your Honor." The judge relented, "Well, they were sent to them." And Ernst said, "Yes, and I submit that it is our right that the jury have that knowledge; that the YMCA used them in their classes, the Public School System of the State of New York has in part used this pamphlet and I think the jury, if your Honor please, has the right to have those facts before it..."[725]

After hearing Ernst's argument, Judge Burrows sustained Wilkinson's objection by saying that the distribution question was, indeed, irrelevant, and "that the only question before the Court at this time is whether or not that pamphlet which was mailed, is obscene, lewd and lascivious under the statute."[726] When the jury returned, Wilkinson requested that the judge's ruling be made in the jury's presence and that Wilkinson himself be allowed to sustain the objection to Ernst's witnesses. In one swipe, Wilkinson had successfully gagged all of the witnesses for the defense.

Frustrated, Ernst developed a stage ploy that illustrated the suppression to near comic effect. Knowing full well that none of the witnesses would be allowed to speak, Ernst asked that Abel Gregg of the YMCA be recalled to the witness stand and that his rejected questions be recorded by the court stenographer. Then he proceeded with his direct examination.

Q: *Did you use this pamphlet, which is in evidence, that was written by Mary Ware Dennett, in connection with classes conducted by the YMCA?*
MR. WILKINSON: *That is objected to as being incompetent, irrelevant and immaterial and not within the issues joined in the indictment.*
THE COURT: *The objection is sustained.*
MR. ERNST: *Exception.*

Q: *Did you recommend this pamphlet at various meetings of parents?*

MR. WILKINSON: *That is objected to as being incompetent, irrelevant and immaterial.*

THE COURT: *Objection sustained.*

MR. ERNST: *Exception.*

Q: *Did you recommend this pamphlet at various meetings of boys' clubs and adolescents?*

MR. WILKINSON: *I object to that as being incompetent, irrelevant and immaterial.*

THE COURT: *Objection sustained.*

MR. ERNST: *Exception.*

Q: *Do you know of your own knowledge whether or not the YMCA local branches have used this pamphlet in classes for parents and adolescents?*

MR. WILKINSON: *That is objected to as being incompetent, irrelevant and immaterial.*

THE COURT *Objection sustained.*

MR. ERNST: *Exception.*

MR. WILKINSON: *Is that all?*

MR. ERNST: *That's all.*[727]

At that, the witness was excused. Gregg had not been allowed to utter a single word.

Ernst ensured that it was noted on the record that he would have asked similar questions of all the other witnesses. Wilkinson stated that he would have made the same objection, the court affirmed that it would have made the same ruling, and Ernst confirmed that he would have made the same exception. One by one, each defense witness was prevented from speaking. As Ernst read from his roster, the same procedure was repeated. Covering several pages of the Transcript of Record, the suppression of the witnesses for the defense stood out boldly.

With all the witnesses suppressed, Ernst called Mary Ware Dennett herself to the stand to testify. The defendant was allowed to take the stand. Yet as Ernst began his questioning, Wilkinson interrupted almost every one of Dennett's answers—voicing his objection, claiming that Dennett's answers were irrelevant. Dennett tried to explain her motive for writing the pamphlet—that she had found sixty or so other publications to be inadequate, that the manuscript was loaned to friends, that it was published in *The Medical Review of Reviews*, that it was widely distributed, and that it was sold cheaply and without any motive for profit. Wilkinson objected each time, striking her remarks from the record—with the court's approval.

Dennett was not allowed to explain the motive of her writing, only the circumstances under which the pamphlet was written.[728] The point was that her motive was completely "immaterial."

When Ernst asked her if she recalled to whom she distributed the pamphlet, before she could answer, Wilkinson shouted, "Yes or no!" To place the pamphlet in a favorable light, Ernst framed a question about whether or not Dennett still had orders received from "various churches, organizations, both charitable and educational?"[729] Wilkinson objected. Ernst countered by pointing out that Wilkinson had "before said that he would have no objection to Mrs. Dennett testifying as to methods of distribution, but that he objected to the organization representatives testifying that they used it."[730] In response, Wilkinson stated that he had no problem with Dennett's putting on record that she distributed twenty-five thousand copies "but it is immaterial as to how or where. The only question is did she mail this one and is it obscene?"[731]

With the defendant and all of the witnesses gagged, Ernst tried to turn to the evidence. Wilkinson and Judge Burrows had agreed from the start that the "Representative Opinions"—the letter excerpts endorsing Dennett's pamphlet—would be included as part of the evidence. Ernst asked Dennett to produce the originals of the letters, in order to show the jury that they were in fact genuine. When Wilkinson objected, Judge Burrows not only sustained the objection, but interceded and took sides. Said Burrows: "I do not understand that [the "Representative Opinions"] was introduced as anything more than a document that was with the non-mailable matter, and for that only, that it was in the mail. I do not understand that it was for anything else."[732] Calling it "opinion testimony," Burrows judged it inadmissible—even though its admittance had been part of a pre-trial agreement. When Ernst persisted, Judge Burrows said:

> *As I remember, there is no such accusation. The pamphlet itself and these testimonials which accompanied the pamphlet that was mailed, were to be recognized as part of the indictment and on that ground I admitted them; and it was as I recall understood between counsel that I should instruct the jury that they were not to be regarded as testimonials.*[733]

Wilkinson, of course, concurred with the judge.

At this point, Wilkinson began to cross-examine Dennett. Asking her for whom she wrote the pamphlet—zeroing in on the age of her intended audience—Wilkinson began to make insinuations about her motive. Wilkinson requested that Dennett clarify what she meant by "adolescents." Although Judge Burrows had earlier stated that motive was irrelevant, with Wilkinson in command, he seemed to have a change of heart. Dennett simply informed Wilkinson that she "should not be averse to any children reading it but it is written for adolescents."[734] Pressing her for an age, Wilkinson said he wanted her definition. Dennett avoided the question by answering the "dictionary definition." Wilkinson continued to ask questions which were irrelevant as to whether "she mailed the pamphlet in question and whether it was obscene." Inconsistent in his sophistry, Wilkinson tried to paint a personal picture of Dennett as a corrupter of young minds.

Judge Burrows allowed Wilkinson's questioning to ramble on uninterrupted, as the prosecutor painted a personal—if disjointed—picture of Dennett as a corrupter of young minds: "Not one word in this about chastity! Not one word about self-control! Not one word to distinguish simple lust from lawful passion! It described the act as being accompanied by the greatest pleasure and enjoyment. Why, there's nothing a boy could see, on reading this book, except a darkened room and a woman!" He went on: "Where does the institution of honor and family come off if we let a gospel like that go out to the world?"

He vehemently attacked Dennett's views on birth control: "And the author of this pamphlet even suggests that birth control will eventually be practiced. Birth Control!—hitting at the very foundation of government!…What will happen if our national standard falls so low, I ask? Where will our soldiers come from in our hour of need? God help America if we haven't men to defend her in that hour!" Ernst was powerless to stop him. Each time Ernst tried to join in the questioning, Wilkinson immediately objected—with Judge Burrows's approval.

Ernst picked up the age question by asking Dennett whether or not the appropriate age at which a child might receive the pamphlet would be dependent upon personal circumstance—since children varied as to growth and adolescence. Dennett agreed. He asked her the ages to which she had given the pamphlet in the past. She answered between twelve and twenty-five. He then asked at what ages the YMCA and other organizations used the pamphlet. With the Judge Burrows' approval, Wilkinson immediately objected. Bringing up the character of Mrs. Miles, Ernst then pointed out that

Dennett had no idea who Mrs. Miles was or how she would put the pamphlet to use. Ernst renewed his request to put into evidence the other persons to whom Dennett mailed the pamphlet. Not surprisingly, Judge Burrows refused him.

In a last-ditch attempt, Ernst tried another tactic to prove that the pamphlet was not obscene. He attempted to introduce as evidence pamphlets printed and distributed, most of them freely and without charge, whose contents were basically similar to or the same as those of *The Sex Side of Life*.[735] Wilkinson, of course, objected, and Judge Burrows sustained the objection. Indeed, Wilkinson was becoming so confident that he took liberties to make a sloppy blanket statement about the pamphlets' presumed irrelevancy. Obstructing Ernst as he began to present the pamphlets, Wilkinson interrupted Ernst by saying, "I object to any speeches as to what they are identical with. There is a difference between literature generally disseminated by a profit making organization and literature that is disseminated by the United States Government itself."[736] In keeping with his effort to make Dennett appear disreputable, Wilkinson inserted a presumption about Dennett as a "profit making" organization.

Dennett, of course, was not part of a "profitmaking organization." Ernst had earlier attempted to bring in evidence to contradict that very presumption, to demonstrate that she had no profit motive. At that time, however, Judge Burrows had deemed "profit motive" irrelevant. Not only had he been blocked, but now his defense was being shoved backward. Ernst once again moved to dismiss the case "on the ground that it was unconstitutional, that the Government had failed to set forth facts sufficient to constitute a crime, and on the further ground resulting from exceptions taken during the course of the trial regarding the admission of evidence." In what by now had become a predictable ritual, Wilkinson objected, Judge Burrows sustained, and Ernst took exception. Indeed, during the course of the trial, Ernst took a grand total of ninety exceptions.

Finally, Ernst and Wilkinson had the opportunity to sum up their arguments. Ernst appealed to the jurors' sense of reason; Wilkinson to their sentiment and emotion. In a controlled speech, Ernst pointed out: "If the test of obscenity is its capability of suggesting impure thoughts then all literature might be considered indecent."[737] He emphasized the association between sex education and modern science and insisted that the Comstock Law was antiquated.

Wilkinson, on the other hand, delivered an emotional performance that ended in a stormy tirade. Reiterating his opinion that the pamphlet contained nothing about self-control or morality, Wilkinson waxed poetic about the beauty of life and romance— declining to address the actual contents of *The Sex Side of Life*: "There's nothing here about the mighty stars and spaces! Nothing about the flowers, the Savior, about music, poetry, and literature. Why, sir, I am the father of four daughters. But I'd never think of allowing even my twenty-two-year-old daughter who is a school-teacher to lay hand on such filth as this!" He continued, "Would you trust a sixteen-year-old boy and girl in a room alone at night reading this book?" Working himself up to a frenzy, he leaned far over the rail of the jury box and waved the crumpled blue pamphlet in his hand. He declared *The Sex Side of Life* was "pure and simple smut." Like Comstock before him, Wilkinson confused his own prejudice with virtue and patriotism. "If I can stand between the children of this country and this woman who is trying to lead them not only into the gutter, but below the gutter into the sewer," he screamed, "I will feel I have accomplished something!"[738]

The trial concluded with an injunction by Judge Burrows which filled eighteen pages in the Transcript of Record. He informed the jury that Dennett was being indicted for obscenity under the Comstock Act. In quite uncertain terms, Judge Burrows defined the words "obscene," "lewd," "lascivious," and "filthy."

> *Under this statute, the word "obscene" means that which is offensive to chastity and modesty; the word "lewd" means having a tendency to excite lustful thoughts. The word "lascivious" is synonymous with the word lewd. The word "filthy" means foul and unclean.*[739]

Following this, he tossed out the "Representative Opinions," gratuitously questioning their authenticity, and described them to the jury as "things which purport to be the statements of certain persons. Whether they were actually written by those persons or not we don't know, and it is not material to this issue." The judge had, of course, not even allowed Ernst to defend the authenticity of the letters. Having suppressed them earlier anyway, Judge Burrows reminded the jury to disregard them.

The judge then reminded the jury that the law was made to "protect" the "average" person—insinuating that there might be something strange about those who supported *The Sex Side of Life*.

> *...while there may be individuals and societies of men and women of peculiar notions or idiosyncrasies whose moral sense would neither be*

*depraved or offended by the publication now under consideration, yet the
exceptional sensibility, or want of sensibility, of such cannot be allowed
as a standard by which its obscenity or indecency is to be tested.?*[740]

Painting a picture of endorsers of *The Sex Side of Life* as somewhat
abnormal, Judge Burrows asked the jury to consider the "probable
reasonable effect on the sense of decency, purity, and chastity" on
"the family which is the common nursery of mankind, the foundation rock upon which the state reposes."[741]

The court's charge, as made by Judge Burrows, was, practically
speaking, a charge to the jury to seek out and find obscenity no
matter how hidden. His definition of obscenity was so vague as to
be virtually useless, but specific enough to incite a sense of moral
outrage. His questioning of the authenticity of the testimonials overlooked the fact that the defense had attempted to prove their
authenticity by producing the originals. The simultaneous assertion
that only the persons themselves could be questioned conveniently
overlooked the fact that all defense witnesses besides Mr. Gregg of
the YMCA—who had been only allowed to state his name, address,
and occupation—and Dennett herself had been suppressed. The
judge's reminder that the law was formed to protect the "average"
person hinted that anyone who found the pamphlet to be legitimate
was "of peculiar notions or idiosyncrasies" and was perhaps
in "want of sensibilities." This insinuation implied a lack of public
support which was in fact untrue. Had all of the evidence submitted
by the defense not been suppressed, it would have been quite clear
that champions of *The Sex Side of Life* ranged from conservative
groups such as the YMCA and Union Theological Seminary to
avant-garde intellectuals such as John Dewey and Havelock Ellis.
Needless to say, his injunction was overwhelmingly one-sided. Far
from being impartial, the court's charge as set forth by Judge
Burrows was a charge to convict.

Not surprisingly, after a mere forty-two minutes, the jury returned
with a guilty verdict.[742] Ernst immediately moved to have the verdict
set aside and requested a new trial and an arrest of judgment. His
grounds were that the statute was unconstitutional under the First
Amendment, the verdict was contrary to the law, and that all pertinent evidence had been excluded. The Judge agreed to allow Ernst
to make one last plea the following Thursday, April 25.[743]

At this hearing, Ernst made several points. He stated that motive
was always presumed to be relevant and stated ten cases as

precedent. He said that never before had a pamphlet or book been accepted by a community for ten years, and then been attacked and suppressed by the courts. In regard to the testimonials, which had been agreed upon in advance as admissible evidence, he asked Judge Burrows to "re-read your charge to the jury which may have led to the inference that they were falsified and not even honest."[744] Pointing out that the court had gone against precedence to rule out methods of circulation, he reminded Judge Burrows: "Other judges have been compelled out of a sense of decency and respect for law, and after an analysis of opinions, to over-ride juries when they are mistaken."[745] He continued, saying,

> *When men sit in the jury box and are asked to look for pornography, they will find it. Any one who is looking for dirt will find dirt. And I can not fail to call this to your attention. I appreciate throughout the trial your sincerity of purpose, but I venture to make this statement, that your own initial reaction to this pamphlet got so deep into your own sub-conscious that when the evidence was introduced on the stand by the YMCA, you mentioned the word "dumped," "dumped the pamphlets onto the YMCA." It is not a serious thing, but I do not know how important it was to the jury.[746]*

He then added: "Psychologists say there is no such thing as an unintentional slip."[747] Finally, Ernst concluded:

> *This case is important from three angles. One that this precious woman sitting here should not be stamped as a felon, because she disseminated information identical with that disseminated by the Government, and because she had done it at the request of doctors, and for the benefit of the best elements in the community for ten years. But it is important beyond that, because on this case will be predicated further prosecutions, and it is on behalf of this cause that I ask you to find as a matter of law, and as a matter of proof that the pamphlet is not against the morals of the community, that it has been accepted by the decent elements as a matter of fact. And because of the rulings of your Honor during the course of the trial and the unfair and improper charge as to testimonials and on the grave grounds that the case is of real importance, I ask you sir, to take this decision under advisement, and allow me further opportunity to submit a brief.[748]*

Wilkinson then replayed his rambling, disconnected arguments with two new points. First, he claimed that the mysterious "Mrs. Miles" whom he was representing was herself representing a branch of the Daughters of the American Revolution. Second, he read excerpts from two of the eleven letters written to Judge Moscowitz—letters which, when brought forth by the defense, had already been ruled out as evidence! In one excerpt, a Mrs. H.E. Hendrickson, a volunteer social worker and probation officer attached to the Children's Court of the City of New York, told the story of a young girl who loved babies. Upon reading a sex education pamphlet and learning how babies were made, this girl asked a butcher boy to impregnate her—and the fact that the girl felt no guilt was cited as an example that the pamphlet itself was somehow to blame. In another story, an eleven-year-old girl had accused a man of raping her. Describing the entire act of coition in graphic detail, the judges were certain of the man's guilt until the examining doctor reported the girl a virgin. When confronted, the girl admitted that she had lied and that all of her information was based upon a piece of sex education literature—again, somehow the literature itself, instead of the person, was supposed to be blameworthy. Wilkinson's logic was difficult to follow. In neither case was Dennett's pamphlet specifically cited. Instead, he seemed to be making a wholesale argument against sex education in general.

In any case, Wilkinson read his letters with the full blessing of the court—even though the equivalent letters supporting the defense had been quite suppressed. Without stating the stories were bizarre cases that were obviously exceptional, he presented the letters as if they represented the "aggregate" of the community. He did not elaborate on his case, but simply seemed to feel that his personal conclusions were self-evident.

With great aplomb, Wilkinson concluded by saying, "Now I don't see any reason why we should prolong this agony and have this submission of briefs. Your Honor can determine the motion now by denying it."[749] Judge Burrows concurred. He concluded by saying:

> *I believe I conducted the case according to the established principle of law in regard to cases of this character.*
>
> *I believe the jury are the ones who test the sentiment of the community. I believe they reached the right conclusion.*
>
> *I decline to set aside the verdict, and the motion is therefore denied.*[750]

With this, the court adjourned until April 29, when the sentence would be imposed.

CHAPTER EIGHTEEN

Public Outcry

After the verdict was announced, reaction was swift. The Reverend Dr. William Milton Hess, pastor of the Pelham Congregational Church and philosophy professor for fifteen years at Yale University, cornered Wilkinson in the courthouse corridor and told him: "In all my life I have never heard such medieval fatheadism and hot air as you spouted today."[751] Newspapers printed the news: "Grandma's YWCA-endorsed sex pamphlet was found obscene," the "sole evidence allowed was Wilkinson's sonorous reading of the pamphlet, with his flinching at 'lewd' moments," and "quality opinions of Havelock Ellis, Henry L. Mencken, the Reverend Ralph P. Bridgman of the Union Theological Seminary, the Reverend Thomas Eliot Calvert, and others were ordered ignored."[752] Headlines abounded: "Grandmother Found Guilty in Sex Life Pamphlet Trial."[753]

So prevalent were the references to Mary as the silver-haired grandma that she—taking it somewhat personally—actually wrote a series of good-humored letters to protest. "It seems that Dudley Nichols started this elderly woman phrase and it has been more catching than the measles. But he has most charmingly eaten his words, and I know you will when you yourself enter the fifties, and are still lustily jeering at the older generation as I am, and haven't the remotest idea that you have entered the ranks yourself."[754] Ever the earnest reformer, she sent out copies of her resume to show that she had done "a thing or two beside achieve 'silver hair,'" and she also made available photographs to replace the rather ugly drawings that had somehow entered circulation. Wrote Dennett, "I am not doddering yet."

The Mary Ware Dennett case had become a cause celebre. Portrayed as a clash between the old world and the new, sex stood smack in the middle hoping for salvation. The very origins of life itself stood nakedly on trial. How ready were modern man and woman to accept a new definition of civility and refinement that included sex separated from the long-cherished notion of original sin? Or a version of morality that sanctioned the expression of human sexuality beyond its primary purpose of perpetuating the species? The answer from most Americans seemed clear. Newspapers and magazines rushed to show their support for an enlightened view of sex education. *Time, The Nation,* and *The New Republic* all gave the Dennett case extensive and sympathetic news coverage. Letters and telegrams flooded in to Judge Burrows at such a rate that many people assumed the judge would feel under obligation to set aside the verdict as clearly unrepresentative of public opinion— supposedly the basic test in obscenity cases.

At the sentencing, Dennett herself made a statement.

I would invite the attention of the Court and the American citizens to the fact that during the eleven years that this pamphlet has been published and in circulation, no adverse criticism has come to me based on any- thing remotely connected with obscenity. The total number of adverse crit- icisms which I have received by letter has been less than a dozen in eleven years, and all those criticisms were purely of an academic character.[755]

She pointed out that thousands of medical professionals, educators, members of the clergy, parents, woman's club leaders, youth groups, and others endorsed the pamphlet. She drew attention to the fact that, indeed, the pamphlet had been sold all over the coun- try—"in bookshops and in various ways"—for eleven years. At this point, Judge Burrows interjected and brought up a point—which he had just discovered the previous afternoon—that there had been a post office ban since 1922. He said: "I understood during the trial that it had not been distributed through the newsstands but simply had been sent to the YMCA and other organizations.[756] Ernst corrected him and said it was not newsstands but the bookstores of the supporting organizations. The words of Judge Burrows revealed his feeling that the method of distribution was relevant— even though during the actual course of the trial he had said it was immaterial.[757]

Hoping to illustrate Dennett's sincerity, Ernst asked the judge to look at the persistent correspondence that Dennett had initiated with the post office for a complete record of the ban. The judge refused. Instead, Burrows answered by saying: "The sentence of the Court is that the defendant shall pay a fine of $300."[758] Hearing this, however, Dennett promptly stood up in court and declared: "If I have corrupted the youth of America, a year in jail is not enough for me. And I will not pay the fine!" Immediately, Ernst announced his intention to appeal. And some of Mary's old suffrage friends presented her with a bouquet of tulips.[759]

Meanwhile, reporters had managed to uncover a few interesting facts. Wilkinson had told the newspapers that the prosecution was sponsored by the National Society of the Daughters of the American Revolution and the Queens Society for the Prevention of Cruelty to Children. After printing the "facts," the Standard Union received a telegram from the President of the D.A.R., Mrs. Lowell Fletcher Hobart, which stated: "The National Society Daughters of the American Revolution has taken no action whatever regarding Dennett literature."[760] This was followed by a denial from the superintendent of the Queens Society for the Prevention of Cruelty to Children, Mr. John de Leon Sullivan: "Mr. Wilkinson sent a copy of the pamphlet to us and asked our opinion of it....We strongly objected to it, and told him that, but anything we had to do with the case was after it was in the District Attorney's hands. We started nothing."[761]

This was not all. In the face of the denials, Wilkinson changed his tale.

> *A woman in Washington, who is a member of the D.A.R., found a copy of the pamphlet in her daughter's hands. She met the Post Office inspector later and discussed the pamphlet with him and asked that something be done about it. Mr. Dunbar then caused the pamphlet to be mailed to a woman in Grottoes, Va., and started the prosecution.*[762]

Even this, however, was not the full story. It was not long before investigative reporters discovered that there was a reason why Mrs. Miles had never shown up in court: "Mrs. Carl A. Miles" did not exist. Apparently, the post office, in an effort to rid themselves of Dennett's persistent activism, had completely fabricated a non-existent opponent to *The Sex Side of Life.* Piqued by Mary's work, post office officials had rigged up a decoy request—going to the trouble of special-ordering personalized stationery and making up a fake address—in a classic case of Comstock entrapment. The receipt of the pamphlet was supposed to function as post office "evidence." On May 26, 1929, the New York *Telegram* printed the following under the headline, "U.S. Used False Name to Trap Mrs. Dennett":

> *C.E. Dunbar, a Post Office inspector attached to the headquarters staff (Washington) admitted today: "Mrs. Miles is a fictitious character. I ordered one of the pamphlets from Mrs. Dennett, using that name, and when it reached Grottoes, it was forwarded to me here."*[763]

Wilkinson admitted to lying: "Had Mrs. Dennett denied mailing the pamphlet, I would have taken the stand and told the story, but she admitted mailing it and such action was not necessary."[764] The truth was out. Wilkinson's entire story had been a hoax.

Understandably, news of conspiracy only fueled widespread public outrage in defense of *The Sex Side of Life*. The Dennett sex education trial was compared to the Scopes monkey trial, in which modern science sought a place beside traditional religion. The American Civil Liberties Union organized a "Mary Ware Dennett Defense Committee" and contributed facilities for work.[765] A group of people determined to send the pamphlet to President Hoover in defiance of the postal regulations. For his part, the White House disclosed that the president had no intention of being drawn into the controversy raging over the merits of the work.[766] As a result of the favorable publicity, Senator Copeland, one of the legislators Dennett had approached during the VPL congressional campaign, decided to introduce a bill to amend the postal laws as they applied to obscene material. A physician, the senator proudly let himself be quoted in the newspapers.

> There is a conspiracy between the school, the churches, the press and the legislature of this country to prevent the dissemination of sex knowledge.
>
> If there is one thing in the world every man and woman, boy and girl, ought to have it is a knowledge of sex. It is a crime to prevent them from getting it.
>
> Nine-tenths of the blindness, half of the insanity, three-fourths of the troubles necessitating women's operations are caused by venereal diseases, many of them innocently acquired.
>
> There is no reason for keeping general sex knowledge away from anyone. It is more important for young boys and girls to learn about sex than it is for them to learn about geography or history.[767]

Mary Ware Dennett had become a national heroine overnight. Dennett herself stated flatly that she would never pay the fine nor allow anyone else to pay for her. She declared that she would prefer to go to jail as a protest against the folly and injustice of the conviction. Some lawyers and educators believed that a new vice crusade was being waged in a new wave of "sex fundamentalism."[768] Letters of support arrived in bundles from friends and strangers. Dennett attempted and managed to answer each one individually with the help of Carl's wife, Catherine. Overwhelmed by instant fame, she had no idea how to cope with her newfound popularity. Constantly on the telephone, going to Ernst's office or the courts, and battling hopelessly with a cold and sinus trouble, she knew only that she wanted to cling to her ideals.

People hoping to capitalize on *The Sex Side of Life* story proposed all sorts of money-making schemes to Dennett. There were offers to write more books, lecture, do radio and movie clips, and even a vaudeville contract was offered. One agent seemed incredulous when Dennett said she was not considering any speaking engagements at all. Disgusted by the exploitative sentiment, Dennett refused everything. The only exception was a modest proposal by the Vanguard Press to write a book about the trial. Encouraged by Morris Ernst, she agreed—but only on the condition that it be presented as an objective account of the injustice of federal obscenity laws. Dennett felt an extreme aversion to anything that might be seen as personal. Furthermore, by writing a book, she hoped that she would no longer be called upon to appear in public. Like many intellectuals, she placed more stock on the written than the spoken word. Dennett felt it was unnecessary to repeat herself before an audience if what she had to say was already printed on paper.

Others, however, not comprehending Dennett's worldview, wrote to her congratulating her on the riches they assumed would accompany her fame. Acquaintances assumed that she would profit materially from the publicity, and enjoy the attention on top of it. In reality, Dennett was as financially impoverished as ever, and she loathed the notoriety. In fact, the situation was made worse by her feelings of obligation to keep up with her correspondence. Dennett felt forced to employ a secretary and clerk to help answer her large volume of mail, and at the same time she herself had become too caught up in the trial to engage in any form of employment. Dennett had stopped working months before the indictment to devote herself full-time to her *guadamaçiles*. In the interim, her primary form of income had been *The Sex Side of Life* pamphlet, but now that she was prevented from fulfilling mail-orders, even that was largely cut off due to the outcome of the trial. To make matters even more difficult, she was also responsible for the care of her mother and invalid brother.[769]

Too proud to ask for help, Dennett was in dire financial straits. Heaven took pity, however, for days after the trial a letter arrived coming to the rescue. A Mrs. Frances W. Emerson of Cambridge, Massachusetts, wrote to Dennett: "I do not know your circumstances, but I will gladly give $1000.00 if needed to help in this fight for freedom."[770] Unwilling to take advantage of the generosity of a stranger, Mary waited two weeks before replying and even then she would only say timidly "I don't find it easy to answer a message such as yours, simply because it touches me so much; and being an ex-New Englander, I am still more or less the inhibited sort. Will you please read between the lines for me..." Mary then went on to describe the precise financial details of contributing to the National Defense Committee, the book project she was undertaking, the secretary and clerk she had hired, her obligations to her mother and brother, and the loss of a year's work due to all of distractions from the trial.

Mrs. Emerson proved to be a guardian angel. She wrote back, "I liked your letter so much and I read between the lines as you asked me to do, and I found a great deal there. So much in fact that I feel almost like a friend, and therefore emboldened to ask you if you will please keep my check for your own personal expenses. It would give me great pleasure to have you do this, and there is no need to have it known."[771] Hardly able to believe it, Dennett rhapsodized, "It seems like one of those half-awake dreams in which I have many a time fancied how I would—if I could—just send to some one whom I knew to be backed against the wall,—a lump sum that would save the day. And now you have done it to me!"[772] More than happy to fund the reformer that she might have been, Emerson reassured her, "Some stocks that had lain dormant for years suddenly went up, and I have set aside the whole for crusading purposes...."[773]

Before long, Dennett discovered that Mrs. Emerson was the wife of an architect—director of the Department of Architecture at MIT—and that she and her husband were about to set sail for France to examine old brick buildings. It was a funny coincidence. Dennett wrote back wistfully, "Your trip to study red brick buildings sounds so alluring!"[774] Giving her benefactress the names of friends and relatives in the Boston area—all of whose names were familiar, though not personally known, to Emerson—Dennett adopted a gracious, "society" persona in her letters. The irony was unmistakeable. If fortune was a woman, her fickleness was not lost on either lady. This was the genteel life Mary might have led had she stayed married to Hartley; this was the embarrassing poverty Mrs. Emerson could have faced had she lost her favor as her husband's mistress. The lives of women were still in men's hands, and it was the minor twists of fate that determined a woman's final outcome. Wrote Mary, "My husband was an M.I.T. architect, and the Parkers were his clients, as was also president Eliot."[775]

Meanwhile, Hartley wrote a letter from Mill Hollow to his sons and daughters-in-law acknowledging the trial, but stopping just short of expressing any direct feelings of support for their mother.

> *Dear Ones,*
>   *Just a greeting to yez. Saw pictures of my 2 stalwart sons in the paper. The 2 girls ought to have been display'd to show the wise & fortunate matings that come from reading the right literature in adolescence.*
>   *I guess that's all now.*[776]

Hartley, unwilling to admit that he could have made a colossal mistake that had devastated the lives of his wife and children, could only grudgingly acknowledge that Mary's pamphlet was the "right literature." A lifetime earlier Mary had lost her husband because he claimed his wife lacked an enlightened atittude toward relationships. If Mary had wanted to prove to Hartley that she was not backward in sex matters, this trial would have served for her as public vindication.

On 22 May 1929, the Mary Ware Dennett Defense Committee held a mass meeting at the New York City Town Hall. Dr. Edward L. Keyes presided over a number of speakers who represented the Federal Council of Churches, the YMCA and YWCA, and the American Social Hygiene Association. Among the many prominent people who lent their names to the Defense Committee were publisher Roy Howard, Mrs. Marshall Field, and John Dewey, with Dewey agreeing to serve as Committee chairman.[777] Morris Ernst started the proceedings.

> *Now, you may say, why do the people stay humble and supine and stand for it? For many reasons. Few people wish to waste the energy and effort that Mary Ware Dennett has been willing to put into this cause. The book distributors themselves are in business for profit, not essentially for ideals, and they don't want to fight, and furthermore, after the Post Office has banned a book...the cause is practically hopeless to reverse a ban in a civil case, because the Federal Courts are most reluctant to reverse what they term an administrative act of a Government official.*[778]

Dennett's old suffrage friend, Mrs. James Lees Laidlaw, now a director of the American Social Hygiene Association, testified to the beauty of *The Sex Side of Life*. "Reproduction of life is beautiful and wonderful. If we do not approach human life in this way, we are no more than animals, because lack of education and indecent veils of darkness that are lowered, the human mind can be so much worse than the animal. We have seen it."[779] Mrs. Laidlaw told the following story to illustrate the difference between right and wrong sex education.

> *This was many years ago, a child I had educated, very carefully too, so that from the very earliest dawn of thought, she had the right ideas of things. I saw her one day sitting across the lawn with three or four other children. Suddenly they began giggling and snickering and whispering, and they grew red in the face, and I was very disturbed, and I want to tell you men and women the most pornographic thing in the world is the talk of little children who have [been] brought up on evasion and innuendo and low-mindedness, and I saw this little child rise and leave, and she didn't blush at all—she was only seven years old—and after it was all over, she had been listening and not joining in the conversation much, after it was all over and they had gone home, I said to this child, "What were you all talking about?" She said, without hesitancy, that they had been talking in a queer sort of way. I said, "Was it nice?" She said, "No, it was sort of talking about nice things in a horrid way." I said, "Oh, don't you think that is terrible?" "Well, she said, "You know (this without a blush), I wouldn't blame them. I don't believe their fathers and mothers ever taught them 'physiology!'"[780]*

The meeting ended with a set of resolutions which emphasized the need for a permanent agency to study the legal aspects of censorship and its effects on sex education. Emphasizing those cases which affected education and scientific understanding, the committee formed the National Council on Freedom from Censorship.[781]

The appeal was set for January 15, 1930, before the United States Circuit Court of Appeals for the Second Circuit. Speculation mounted about whether or not the case might reach the Supreme Court. Strangers wrote offering legal services. Orders for the pamphlet kept coming in. Banned by the post office in Brooklyn, Dennett realized that she could send them by express from Manhattan. And, of course, the charge against mailing the pamphlet would not prevent her from selling them in bookstores and other such venues. Due in part to the notoriety of the case, *The Sex Side of Life* was selling like hotcakes, with Dennett placing orders of 10,000 at a time. A few admirers were moved to write poetry in Dennett's honor, commending *The Sex Side of Life*. Sympathy, support, and contributions for the defense committee kept pouring in from old suffrage and VPL friends—as well as some enemies. Letter-writers used words like "outrage," "horror," "astounded" to communicate the feeling that Dennett had been "crucified." Even

Margaret Sanger was moved to say a word in support of the Dennett case. Indeed, Dennett's "martyrdom" caused many of the birth-control societies to come around to the VPL policy of a "clean repeal" bill. The new president of the American Birth Contol League (ABCL), for example, Eleanor Jones, who had succeeded Margaret Sanger, read Dennett's book *Birth Control Laws* and was convinced.

It took a year of public mobilization before a verdict was handed down, but on 3 March 1930, in a decision handed down by Justice Augustus H. Hand, cousin of Learned Hand,[782] the verdict of the district court was reversed. The statement in part read as follows:

> *The defendant's discussion of the phenomenon of sex is written with sincerity of feeling and with an idealization of the marriage relation and sex emotion. We think it tends to rationalize and dignify such emotions rather than to arouse lust.... We hold that an accurate exposition of the relevant facts of the sex side of life in decent language and in manifesting serious and disinterested spirit cannot ordinarily be regarded as obscene....No case was made for submission to the jury and the judgment therefore must be reversed.*[783]

Dennett's trial had become a landmark case in censorship law. It swept away the Hicklin test for obscenity, making context a legitimate factor in determining whether or not something was obscene. Dennett's hopes of affecting antiobscenity rulings were realized. After over a year of trial proceedings, Dennett had finally been able to chip away at the Comstock Act. She had faced her fears about public notoriety, and the ordeal was finally over.

The Sex Side of Life was eventually translated into fifteen languages, and it went into twenty-three printings. Dennett agreed to write another book, *Sex Enlightenment for Civilized Youth*, expanded from her chapter in *Sex in Civilization*, as the need for basic sex education continued unabated. Although largely unrecognized today, Dennett had revolutionized the way sex education was taught in America. Indeed, after *The Sex Side of Life* trial, Dennett continued distributing the pamphlet, but she no longer gave speeches or lobbied Congress. In 1930, *The Nation* published a special birth-control number, asking Dennett to contribute an article. Putting aside her work, Dennett agreed—churning out an article in a short period of time. When Sanger learned of Dennett's article, however, she demanded that it be pulled. And indeed it was—even though it had already been typeset—for Sanger had contributed $1,000 to the issue and threatened to withdraw the money.

Tired after the harrowing hype of her trial, Dennett seemed to bow to the opposition. Her campaign to change obscenity laws had brought her many enemies. Internally, she was attacked by Sanger, and externally, by the post office. Finally, in 1931, she appeared to cede control of the birth-control movement to Sanger, but in a letter marked by its eloquence, she begged once more for Sanger to fight for a clean-repeal bill rather than a doctors-only bill:

> *I don't want any de-bunking biographer who may later appear, to have the chance to picture you as a leader whose vision grew dim. People love their popular heroes with wonderful persistence. Don't disappoint them, I beg of you.*
>
> *Forget, please, that you have not liked me any too well. Forget about everything except your big opportunity as a leader. You and I are in totally different positions. I have never had any ambition or bent toward being a public character. You are that by force of personality and the course of events. I shall be only too glad to help you if you will rise to your present chance to be both big and true, and my help will be quiet in proportion as your stand is forthright and steadfast.[784]*

Sanger, of course, turned her back.

Seeking peace and serenity, Dennett tried again to rededicate herself to Arts and Crafts. The ideals of beauty, which had carried her throughout her activist years, demanded full expression. Drawing a small income from her pamphlet and books, Mary held private showings of her *guadamaçile* work. She gave one particularly big luncheon to explain the craft to the women of Heterodoxy, the group of radical feminists who met in Greenwich Village. She had her work displayed on the West Coast with limited success (although one set of Mary's leather bookends was picked up by Marlene Dietrich).

By the mid-1930s, Mary had moved in with her son, Devon, in Woodside, New York. Although much more of an observer now, she could count her membership in a dozen clubs and societies: the Civic Club, the Pen and Brush Club, the Heterodoxy, the Free Trade League, the Voluntary Parenthood League, the City Affairs Committee, the League for Independent Political Action, the Women's Peace Union, the Popular Government League, the Mutual Aid League, the New York Society of Craftsmen, and the Society of Arts and Crafts.

Despite her professed retirement, however, Dennett could not resist some activity here and there. Throughout the 1930s, she continued to work "behind the scenes" for the birth-control movement, continuing a letter-writing campaign to convince prominent people and policymakers to support a clean-repeal bill. Tenacious to the end, Dennett remained a thorn in the side of Margaret Sanger. And her presence was felt on other fronts as well. Although she had grown too weary to work on the front lines of radical politics, Dennett continued to dabble as a peace activist during World War II and became one of the founders of the World Federalists in 1941.

In 1945, Mary moved into a home for the elderly in Valatie, New York. Alone for the last years of her life, she rarely spoke about her marriage, except once, when Devon's wife, Marie, watched Mary chastise herself about her inability to reconcile with Hartley, "I knew you couldn't do it." For his part, before he died, Hartley was heard to say, "I've been a damn fool—those ten years with Mary were the best of my life."[785]

Mary Coffin Ware Dennett died at 2 AM on 25 July 1947. True to her childhood plan, she was promptly cremated. By the following afternoon, all that was left of her were three photographs on her bureau: one of each of her two sons, Carleton and Devon, and one of her ex-husband, Hartley.

Epilogue

WITH obituaries in *Time*, the *New York Times* and other national publications, the passing of Mary Ware Dennett marked a milestone in the realms of birth control, sex education, and censorship law. Half a century after the passage of the Comstock Act, Mary Ware Dennett had managed to make the contraception and abortion clause the focus of intense debates; a full century afterward, the clause would still remain. Split in two, birth control supporters had not been able to remove contraceptive information from its legal classification as a criminal indecency. Neither Dennett's nor Sanger's bill to modify the Comstock Act ever passed. The urgency was greatly reduced, however, in 1936 when Judge Augustus Hand ruled in *United States v. One Package*—also argued by Morris Ernst—that birth control would not have been classified as an obscenity if legislators had known then about the perils of uncontrolled fecundity and the medical usefulness of contraception in saving women's lives. In essence, the ruling allowed physicians to send and receive contraceptive materials through the mails.

Like Hand's 1930 ruling in the *Sex Side of Life* case, the *One Package* decision was a landmark. Although the words remained, the interpretation had changed, making women's access to birth control much easier. Dennett's hope of a "clean repeal" would not be realized, however, for another half century. As she had predicted, with the actual law untouched a woman was still vulnerable in the 1960s when a customs official forced her to throw out her diaphragm upon entering the country. In fact, the contraceptive clause of the Comstock Act was not stricken until 1970, when contraceptives were taken off the obscene list (with some qualifications), and it was not until 1972 that full legal access to birth control was made available for all. True to the vision of Mary Ware Dennett, the Comstock Act had come full circle.

Appendix A

THE COMSTOCK ACT OF 1873[786]

Title 18. Crimes and Criminal Procedure
Chapter 71. Obscenity

Section 1461. Mailing obscene or crime-inciting matter.

Every obscene lewd, lascivious, or filthy book, pamphlet, picture, paper, letter, writing, print, or other publication of an indecent character; and

Every article of thing designed, adapted, or intended for preventing conception or producing abortion, or for any indecent or immoral use; and

Every article, instrument, substance, drug, medicine, or thing which is advertised or described in a manner calculated to lead another to use or apply it for preventing conception or producing abortion, or for any indecent or immoral purpose; and

Every written or printed card, letter, circular, book, pamphlet, advertisement, or notice of any kind giving information, directly or indirectly, where, or how, or from whom, or by what means any of such mentioned matters, articles, or things may be obtained or made, or where or by whom any act or operation of any kind for the procuring or producing of abortion will be done or performed, or how or by what means conception may be prevented or abortion produced, whether sealed or unsealed; and

Every paper, writing, advertisement, or representation that any article, instrument, substance, drug, medicine, or thing may, or can, be used or applied for preventing conception or producing abortion, or for any indecent or immoral purpose; and

Every description calculated to induce or incite a person to so use or apply any such article, instrument, substance, drug, medicine, or thing—

Is declared to be nonmailable matter and shall not be conveyed in the mails or delivered from any post office or by any letter carrier.

Whoever knowingly uses the mail for the mailing, carriage in the mails, or delivery of anything declared by this section to be nonmailable, or knowingly causes to be delivered by mail according to the direction thereon, or at the place at which it is directed to be delivered by the person to whom it is addressed, or knowingly takes any such thing from the mails for the purpose of circulating or disposing thereof, shall be fined not more than $5,000 or imprisoned not more than five years, or both, for the first such offense, and shall be fined not more than $10,000 or imprisoned not more than ten years, or both, for each such offense thereafter.

The term "incident," as used in this section includes matter of a character tending to incite arson, murder, or assassination.

THE SEX SIDE OF LIFE

An Explanation for Young People

BY

MARY WARE DENNETT

WITH NEW DIAGRAMS AND REVISIONS

The illustrative diagrams are based upon accurate measurements of normal human beings. The revisions in the text are in accord with most recent authoritative knowledge of physiology.

PUBLISHED BY THE AUTHOR

INTRODUCTION FOR ELDERS

TO

THE SEX SIDE OF LIFE—AN EXPLANATION FOR YOUNG PEOPLE

In reading several dozen books on sex matters for the young with a view to selecting the best for my own children, I found none that I was willing to put into their hands, without first guarding them against what I considered very misleading and harmful impressions, which they would otherwise be sure to acquire in reading them. That is the excuse for this booklet.

It is far more specific than most sex information written for young people. I believe we owe it to children to be specific if we talk about the subject at all.

From a careful observation of youthful curiosity and a very vivid recollection of my own childhood, I have tried to explain frankly the points about which there is the greatest inquiry. These points are *not* frankly or clearly explained in most sex literature. They are avoided, partly from embarrassment, but more, apparently, because those who have undertaken to instruct the children are not really clear in their own minds as to the proper status of the sex relation.

I found that from the physiological point of view, the question was handled with limitations and reservations. From the point of natural science it was often handled with sentimentality, the child being led from a semi-esthetic study of the reproduction of flowers and animals to the acceptance of a similar idea for human beings. From the moral point of view it was handled least satisfactorily of all, the child being given a jumble of conflicting ideas, with no means of correlating them,— fear of venereal disease, one's duty to suppress "animal passion," the sacredness of marriage, and so forth. And from the emotional point of view, the subject was not handled at all.

This one omission seems to me to be the key to the whole situation, and it is the basis of the radical departure I have made from the precedents in most sex literature for young folks.

Concerning all four points of view just mentioned, there are certain departures from the traditional method that have seemed to me worth making.

On the physiological side I have given, as far as possible, the proper terminology for the sex organs and functions. Children have had to read the expurgated literature which has been specially prepared for them in poetic or colloquial terms, and then are needlessly mystified when they hear things called by their real names.

On the side of natural science, I have emphasized our unlikeness to the plants and animals rather than our likeness, for while the points we have in common with the lower orders make an interesting section in our general education, it is knowing about the vital points in which we differ that helps us to solve the sexual problems of maturity; and the child needs that knowledge precisely as he needs knowledge of everything which will fortify him for wise decisions when he is grown.

On the moral side, I have tried to avoid confusion and dogmatism in the following ways: by eliminating fear of venereal disease as an appeal for strictly limited sex relations, stating candidly that venereal disease is becoming curable; by barring out all mention of "brute" or "animal" passion, terms frequently used in pleas for chastity and self-control, as such talk is an aspersion on the brutes and has done children much harm in giving them the impression that there is an essential baseness in the sex relation; by inviting the inference that marriage is "sacred" by virtue of its being a reflection of human ideality rather than because it is a legalized institution.

Unquestionably the stress which most writers have laid upon the beauty of nature's plans for perpetuating the plant and animal species, and the effort to have the child carry over into human life some sense of that beauty has come from a most commendable instinct to protect the child from the natural shock of the revelation of so much that is unesthetic and revolting in human sex life. The nearness of the sex organs to the excretory organs, the pain and messiness of childbirth are elements which certainly need some compensating antidote to prevent their making too disagreeable and disproportionate an impress on the child's mind.

The results are doubtless good as far as they go, but they do not go nearly far enough. What else is there to call upon to help out? Why, the one thing which has been persistently neglected by practically all the sex writers,— the emotional side of sex experience. Parents and teachers have been afraid of it and distrustful of it. In almost none of the books for young people that I have thus far read has there been the frank, unashamed declaration that the climax of sex emotion is an unsurpassed joy, something which rightly belongs to every normal human being, a joy to be proudly and serenely experienced. Instead there has been all too evident an inference that sex emotion is a thing to be ashamed of, that yielding to it is indulgence which must be curbed as much as possible, that all thought and understanding of it must be rigorously postponed, at any rate till after marriage.

We give to young folks, in their general education, as much as they can grasp of science and ethics and art, and yet in their sex education, which rightly has to do with all of these, we have said "Give them only the bare physiological facts, lest they be prematurely stimulated." Others of us, realizing that the bare physiological facts are shocking to many a sensitive child, and must somehow be softened with something pleasant, have said, "Give them the facts, yes, but see to it that they are so related to the wonders of evolution and the beauties of the natural world that the shock is minimized." But we have not yet dared to say, "Yes, give them the facts, give them the nature study, too, but also give them some conception of sex life as a vivifying joy, as a vital art, as a thing to be studied and developed with reverence for its big meaning, with understanding of its far-reaching reactions, psychologically and spiritually, with temperate restraint, good taste and the highest idealism." We have contented ourselves by assuming that marriage make sex relations respectable. We have not yet said that it is only beautiful sex relations that can make marriage lovely.

Young people are just as capable of being guided and inspired in their thought about sex emotion as in their taste and ideals in literature and ethics, and just as they imperatively need to have their general taste and ideals cultivated as a preparation for mature life, so do they need to have some understanding of the marvelous place which sex emotion has in life.

Only such an understanding can be counted on to give them the self-control that is born of knowledge, not fear, the reverence that will prevent premature or trivial connections, the good taste and finesse that will make their sex life, when they reach maturity, a vitalizing success.

MARY WARE DENNETT.

THE SEX SIDE OF LIFE

An Explanation for Young People

When boys and girls get into their "teens," a side of them begins to wake up which has been asleep or only partly developed ever since they were born, that is, the sex side of them. It is the most wonderful and interesting part of growing up. This waking is partly of the mind, partly of the body and partly of the feelings or emotions.

You can't help wanting to understand all about it, but somehow you find yourself a little embarrassed in asking all the questions that come into your mind, and often you don't feel quite like talking about it freely, even to your father and mother. Sometimes it is easier to talk with your best friends, because they are your own age, and are beginning to have these new feelings too.

But remember that young people don't know nearly so much about it as older people do, and that the older ones really want to help you with their experience and advice; and yet, they, like you, often feel rather embarrassed themselves and don't know how to go about it. I suppose it is because it is all so very personal and still remains somewhat mysterious, in spite of all that people know about it.

If our bodies were just like machines, then we could learn about them and manage them quite scientifically as we do automobiles, but they are not like that. They are more than machines that have to be supplied with fuel (food) and kept clean and oiled (by bathing, exercise and sleep). They are the homes of our souls and feelings, and that makes all the difference in the world in the way we act, and it makes what we have to learn, not limited to science only, but it has to include more difficult and complicated things like psychology and morality.

Maybe I can't make this article help you, but I remember so well what I wanted to know and how I felt when I was

3

young that I am now going to try. And I will tell you to start out with that there is a great deal that nobody knows yet, in spite of the fact that the human race has been struggling thousands of years to learn.

Life itself is still a mystery, especially human life. Human life, in many respects, is like plant and animal life, but in many ways it is entirely different, and the ways in which it is different are almost more important for us to think about than the ways in which it is similar. In all life, except in the very lowest forms, new life is created by the coming together, in a very close and special way, of the male and the female elements. You have studied at school about the plants and you probably have observed certain of the animals, so you know something about what this means, if you do not understand it thoroughly.

But what you want to know most of all is just how it is with human beings. You want to know just what this coming together is, how it is done, how it starts the new life, the baby, and how the baby is born. You want to understand the wonderful sex organs, that are different in men and women, what each part is for and how it works.

If you feel very curious and excited and shy about it, don't let yourself be a bit worried or ashamed. Your feelings are quite natural, and most everybody else has felt just the same way at your age. Remember that strong feelings are immensely valuable to us. All we need to do is to steer them in the right direction and keep them well balanced and proportioned.

Now in order to understand something of why this subject stirs us so, we must notice in what ways we human beings are *different* from the plants and animals. About the lowest form of life is amoeba. It looks like a little lump of jelly, and it produces its young by merely separating itself in two. One part drifts off from the other part and each becomes a separate live being. There is no male and no female and they didn't *know* they were doing it. In the plants a higher stage of development is reached: there is the male and the female

4

and they join together, not by coming to each other, or because they *know* they belong together, but quite unconsciously, with the aid of the bees and other insects and the wind, the male part, the pollen, is carried to the female part—they meet, and at once the germ of a new plant begins to grow.

Then come to the animals. In all higher forms of animal life, the male creature *comes* to the female creature and himself places within her body the germ which, when it meets the egg which is waiting for it, immediately makes a new life begin to grow. But the animals come together without *knowing why*. They do it from instinct only, and they do it in what is called the mating season, which is usually in the spring. The mating season happens once a year among most of the higher animals, like birds and wild cattle, but to some animals, it comes several times a year as with rabbits, for instance. You doubtless know already that the more highly developed the animal, the longer it takes the young one to grow within the mother before it is born, and the longer period when it is helpless to provide its own food and care.

Now we come to human beings, and see how different they are? They have no regular mating season, and while there is a certain amount of instinct in men and women which tends to bring them together, the sex impulse among finely developed people is far more the result of their feeling of love for each other than mere animal instinct alone. Many of the animals make no choice at all in their mating. Any near-by female will do for the male. But among some of the higher animals the male has a special instinct for a certain female, and the female will not tolerate any but a certain male. Most of the animals have different mates every season, though there are a few kinds where the male and female, once having mated, remain mates for years, sometimes even for life. But it is *only human beings* whose mating is what we call "falling in love," and that is an experience far beyond anything that the animals know.

It means that a man and a woman feel that they *belong* to each other in a way that they belong to no one else; it makes them wonderfully happy to be together; they find they

5

want to live together, work together, play together, and to have children together, that is, to marry each other; and their dream is to be happy together all their lives. Sometimes the dream does not come true, and there is much failure and unhappiness, but just the same people go right on trying to make it a success, because it is what they care most for.

The sex attraction is the deepest feeling that human beings know, and unlike the animals, it is far more than a mere sensation of the body. It takes in the emotions and the mind and the soul, and that is why so much of our happiness is dependent upon it.

When a man and a woman fall in love so that they really belong to each other, the physical side of the relation is this: both of them feel at intervals a peculiar thrill or glow, particularly in the sexual organs, and it naturally culminates after they have gone to bed at night. The man's special sex organ or penis becomes enlarged and stiffened, instead of soft and limp, as ordinarily, and thus it easily enters the passage in the woman's body called the vagina or birth canal, which leads to the uterus or womb, which is the sac in which the egg or embryo grows into a baby. The penis and the vagina are of such a size as to fit each other. By a rhythmic movement of the penis in and out the sex act reaches an exciting climax or orgasm, when there is for the woman a peculiarly satisfying rhythmic contraction or throbbing of the muscles of the passage, and for the man the expulsion of the semen, the liquid which contains the germs of life. This is followed by a sensation of peaceful happiness and sleepy relaxation. Sex union is the very greatest physical pleasure to be had in all human experience, and it helps very much to increase all other kinds of pleasure also. It is at this time that married people not only are closest to each other physically, but they feel closer to each other in every other way too. It is then most of all that they are conscious that they belong to each other.

The sex act is called by various names, such as coitus, coition, copulation, cohabitation, sex-intercourse, or the sex-embrace. But all these terms refer to the same thing. The first coitus is apt to be somewhat painful for the woman, as there is a thin membrane, called the hymen, partly closing the vagina which has to be broken through, or preferably gradually stretched. It varies in size and thickness with different women.

Without the sex act, no babies could be created, for it is by this means only that the semen which contains the male part of the germ of life can meet the ovum or the female part of the germ of life. When the two parts come together in the woman's body under just the right conditions, a baby begins to grow—at first so tiny that it could hardly be seen without a microscope, and finally, after nine months' growth in the uterus or womb of the mother till it weighs about seven or eight pounds, it is born, a live human being. The birth process is called *labor*, and it is indeed labor, for it usually means much pain and struggle for the mother, although the baby's journey from the uterus to the world is only a few inches. It takes anywhere from an hour to two days for a baby to be born. Doctors are learning more and more how to lessen the pain, and by the end of another generation it ought to be possible for child-birth to be practically painless for most women. By that time people will more generally understand how to have babies *only* when they want them and can afford them. Unfortunately, there are still many laws which make it a crime to give people information as to how to manage their sex relations so that no baby will be created unless the father and mother are ready and glad to have it happen. However, these laws are less and less enforced, as knowledge spreads.

Now you must understand something about this intricate sexual machinery. Plate I and Plate II show the woman's organs, and Plate III and Plate IV the man's organs. All these illustrations are sections, as if the body were cut in two vertically, with the exception of Diagram B on Plate II. (See pages 14 to 21).

Sometimes it seems very distasteful to us that the sex or generative organs should be placed so near to what we might call our "sewerage system." We do not like to have to connect in our thought anything so sweet and nice as a baby or so happy and precious as the sex embrace with the waste of our bodies, which we want to be rid of with as little thought as possible, as it is disagreeable at best, and we wonder why we were created this way. But we have to remember that the sex organs are very delicate and they are probably placed where they can be best protected from injury. At any rate there they are, and our duty is to understand them as best we can, and take mighty good care of them as our most wonderful possession.

Looking at Plates I and II, you will see the woman's body provides the egg or ovum. These are held, some 3,000 of them, in two small sacs called ovaries, and every little while (usually every four weeks, but not always) an ovum ripens and passes out from the ovary through the fallopian tube (there are two of these, one leading from each ovary) into the uterus or womb, a process which takes about three days. Here it may be met by the male life element, and if so, it becomes fertilized and nests in the lining of the uterus to grow into a baby. This is called fertilization, fecundation, impregnation or conception. But if the egg is not fertilized, it passes from the uterus through the vagina and out of the body.

Every twenty-eight days or so a woman, from the time she is about thirteen or fourteen till she is about fifty, has a slight flow of blood and mucous shreds from the uterus, which is called menstruation. There is a new lining provided periodically for the nourishment, of a baby, but when there is no baby starting to grow, the lining is not needed so it passes away. The flow, menstruation, and the start of the egg on its travels, ovulation, do not necessarily or often happen at the same time. Menstruation lasts from three to five days, and young girls sometimes have pain then and feel languid and "unwell." If so, they should be quieter than usual and avoid cold baths and getting their feet wet. But normal menstruation is not an illness, and a girl in perfect health finds it only a slight inconvenience.

The ovaries not only produce the egg, but they also produce a secretion that is absorbed by the blood and which is most

8

necessary in the development of a baby girl into a woman. This hormone has an almost magical effect in adding the special womanly qualities to the body and character.

Looking at Plates III and IV, you will see the man's sex machinery. The testicles are to a man what the ovaries are to a woman. They are two sacs held in a bag of thin loose skin called the scrotum, and it is here that the sperm cells (spermatozoa) or germs of life grow. The spermatozoa are very tiny and the testicles hold many millions of them. Under the microscope they show a head and tail like a long pollywog. They become very active when released from the testicles and move by a rapid wiggling of the tail part.

Leading from each testicle is a tube called the vas deferens, through which the liquid containing the sperm-cells goes at the time of the sex act on its way to meet the ovum in the woman's body. On the way it is joined by two other liquids, one secreted by the seminal vesicles (of which there are two) and the other by the prostate gland. These three liquids together form the semen, which at the summit of sexual excitement is forced through the penis into the vagina of the woman.

You will notice that the woman has separate tubes for the urine (waste water) and the sex function, but the man uses the same tube for both; that is, in the woman the bladder which holds the urine is emptied by a separate tube, the urethra, while in the man the urethra not only empties the bladder, but it also carries the semen.

The use of the seminal vesicles and the prostate gland is to supply a vehicle and arouser for the dormant sperm-cells, until they reach the ovum, which may take from three hours to two or more days after the semen is expelled into the vagina.

The spermatozoa can only remain alive in an alkaline secretion and the urine is acid, so always just before the penis forces out, or ejaculates the semen, the alkaline secretion from the seminal vesicles and prostate gland is mixed with the sperm-cells to protect them.

9

At the end of the penis is a circular hood or cap of skin, the prepuce, which the doctor often removes or divides. This process is called circumcision, and it is a relief to boys whose prepuce or foreskin is so tight as to make diffculty in keeping the parts beneath clean. All Jewish and Mohammedan babies are regularly circumcised, a custom dating back to early Bible times.

There is a constant internal secretion from the testicles of a man just as there is from the ovaries of a woman, and it has the same beneficial effect on the whole being. It makes a boy what we call manly or virile. The value of the internal secretions of the sex organs in both boys and girls is so great that for that reason, if for no other, the whole sex machinery must be kept in perfect health.

Boys have a certain discomfort to bear which is difficult for them just as menstruation is difficult for girls. But by knowing the meaning of things and taking care of themselves, they need not be seriously troubled by it. Every once in a while as they are growing up, but before they are old enough to really fall in love and marry and have children, boys feel a stirring of the sex organs—sometimes so much so that it makes them quite uneasy and anxious for relief. The thing to do is to keep as calm as possible and keep very busy and very healthy. Vigorous muscular exercise obviates these teasing sensations better than any other means. Then the discomfort will not be too great, and nature will usually bring relief by letting the accumulated semen pass off during sleep. This is called a seminal emission, and is, in moderation, perfectly harmless. Sometimes a vivid sexual dream comes with it, but that too will do no harm, unless a boy lets his mind dwell on it till the excitement grows unnatural. This emission may happen every two weeks or so, but it is not a regular thing. Boys are sometimes alarmed and fear their sex machinery is out of order, but it is a perfectly natural thing, and only means that the organs are relieving themselves of the extra secretions that are not needed till the time comes for the real sex relation.

Boys and girls sometimes get the habit of handling their sex organs in such a way as to get them excited. This is

10

called masturbation or self-abuse. It is also called auto-erotism. Such handling results in a climax something like that of natural sex act. For centuries this habit has been considered wrong and dangerous, but recently many of the best scientists have concluded that the chief harm has come from the worry caused by doing it, when one believed it to be wrong. This worry has often been so great that real illness, both of the mind and body, has resulted. There is no occasion for worry unless the habit is carried to excess. But remember that until you are mature, the sex secretions are specially needed within your body, and if you use them wastefully before you are grown, you are depriving your body of what it needs. So do not yield to the impulse to handle the sex organs in order to relieve the pressure, unless occasionally the feeling is overwhelming and you find that exercise is ineffective, or that nature does not bring you relief during sleep. Remember, too, that as masturbation is a wholly one-sided and merely physical action, it can never be an adequate substitute for the mutual union of true mates. This union is so much more than physical that there is no substitute for it.

Your whole sex machinery is more easily put out of order than any other part of your body, so it must be treated with care and respect all along. It is not fair to ourselves or to each other to do a single thing that will make us either weak or unnatural. Remember that your sex organs have a very powerful, even if invisible, effect upon your whole being, and up to the time that you are really old enough to love some one to whom you actually want to belong, you must let your sex machinery grow strong and ready for its good, happy work when the right time comes. The sex organs during your youth do not need frequent exercise in the same sense that your muscles do. They are active all the time with their internal secretions which strengthen both you and them.

Don't let any one drag you into nasty talk or thought about sex. It is *not* a nasty subject. It should mean everything that is highest and best and happiest in human life, but it can be easily perverted and ruined and made the cause of horrible suffering of both mind and body.

11

There are two very terrible sexual diseases—syphilis and gonorrhea. They are both very infectious and at times difficult to cure. These diseases are usually acquired by sex contact with a diseased person, but they can occasionally be gotten by using public drinking cups, towels, water-closets, or in any way by which an infected moist article can come in contact with one's skin or mucous membrane where it is broken. The worst thing about these diseases is that they are such invisible enemies. After the outside appearance of the disease is gone, they often go reaching farther and farther into the body, making serious results that hang on for years. Men who get diseased frequently give the infection to their wives, sometimes causing them to be so ill that surgical operations are necessary, by which their sex organs are so crippled that they can never be mothers; and, worst of all, innocent unborn babies are infected and come into the world sick or deformed or blind.

Men usually get these dreadful diseases by having sex relations with women who are called prostitutes or "bad women," that is, they are women who, not for love, but for money, sell their sex relations to men who pay for them. Most prostitutes become diseased, and there is, as yet, no way for either them or the men who visit them to be positively safe from infection. But the doctors are making progress in their study of these diseases, and they are finding out how to control and cure them, just as they are in the case of tuberculosis.

But even if some day venereal diseases, as they are called, can be entirely cured and prevented, prostitution will still remain a thing to hate. For the idea of sex relations between people who do not love each other, who do not feel any sense of belonging to each other, will always be revolting to highly developed, sensitive people.

People's lives grow finer and their characters better, if they have sex relations only with those they love. And those who make the wretched mistake of yielding to the sex impulse alone when there is no love to go with it, usually live to despise themselves for their weakness and their bad taste. They are always ashamed of doing it, and they try to keep it secret from their families and those they respect. You can be sure that whatever people are ashamed to do is something that can never bring them real happiness. It is true that one's sex relations are the most personal and private matters in the world, and they belong just to us and to no one else, but while we may be shy and reserved about them, *we are not ashamed.*

When two people really love each other, they don't care who knows it. They are proud of their happiness. But no man is ever proud of his connection with a prostitute and no prostitute is ever proud of her business. Sex relations belong to love and love is never a *business.* Love is the dearest thing in the world, but it can not be bought. The physical side of love is the intensely intimate part of it, and the most critical for happiness, because of its possibilities of blundering and false feeling and wasted treasure; so it is the one side of us that we must be absolutely sure to keep in good order and perfect health, if we are going to make any one else happy or be happy ourselves.

The Plates on the following pages show diagrams or outline-maps of the sex organs.

They are drawn by Dr. Robert L. Dickinson. The author gratefully acknowledges her indebtedness to him for the use of these drawings.

A careful reading of the Explanations will give a clear idea of the function, location and relationship of the sex organs.

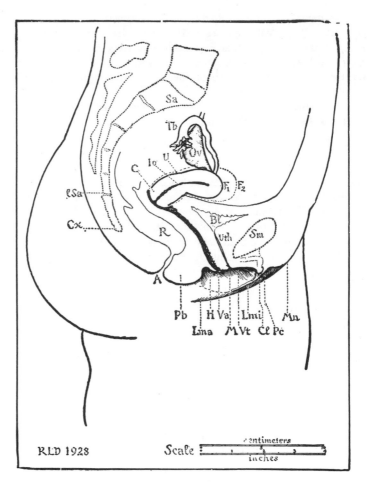

RLD 1928   Scale

PLATE I.

Female Organs, Side View

Copyright from R. L. Dickinson.

Slightly more than one-third size.

A vertical section through the middle of the body. The generative organs are shown in heavy outline; the urinary organs and other parts of the body in lighter outline.

14

PLATE I—EXPLANATION

Bones

The bones are indicated by dotted lines.

Sa—Isa, Sacrum, the largest of the bones at the base of the spine.

Cx, Coccyx, the tip-end bone of the spine.

Sm, Symphysis, the front meeting place of the bony girdle, or pelvis.

Excretory Organs

R, Rectum, which carries away the solid waste matter from the bowels.

A, Anus, the opening of the rectum.

Bl, Bladder, which holds the waste water, or urine. Here shown empty; when full of fluid, it is much larger and balloon shaped.

Uth, Urethra, the tube which carries away the urine.

M, Meatus, or opening of the urethra.

Sex Organs (Internal)

Ov, Ovary in which the egg or ovum grows. There are two ovaries, one at either side and above the uterus.

Tb, Fallopian Tube, which carries the ovum to the uterus. There are two tubes, one leading from each ovary.

U, Uterus or Womb, in which the egg or ovum becomes an embryo and grows into a baby.

*F*1, Fundus, or top of the womb.

*F*2 indicates the increase in size of the uterus, after a woman has had a baby.

C, Cervix, the neck of the uterus, through which the semen has to go, on its way to meet the ovum.

Va, Vagina, or Birth Canal, which leads out from the uterus, and into which the penis fits during the sex act. Here shown at rest or closed, the front and back walls lying almost together, so it looks like a slim tube with irregularly wrinkled sides. During sex union, it is distended and becomes round, with a diameter of an inch and a half or more.

Sex Organs (External)

This group of parts is called the Vulva.

H, Hymen, the membrane which, in the virginal state, partly closes the entrance to the vagina.

Cl, Clitoris, the miniature equivalent of the male organ, the penis. It is mostly hidden under the skin, as indicated by the faint dotted line, but it enlarges when stimulated by the sex act.

Pc, Prepuce, or Fore-Skin of the clitoris. (Plate II.)

Lma, Labia Majora, the rounded outer lips of the vulva, or portal of the sex organs.

Lmi, Labia Minora, the thin inner lips of the vulva. (See Plate II.)

Mn, Mons Veneris, or cushion over the bone *Sm,* symphysis. This cushion is covered with hair which is not shown in the diagram.

Pb, Perineal body. The muscles and tendons which center here hold up all the lower organs, but they relax during the birth of the baby.

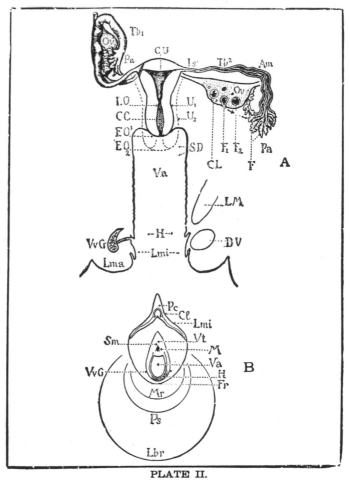

PLATE II.

(A) **Female Organs, Front View**
(B) **Diagram of the Vulva**
Copyright from R. L. Dickinson.
Slightly more than one-third life size.

(A) The ovary and tube on the left side of the drawing are shown in the true position; on the right side they are spread out and cut in two, to show the inside.

(B) The upper part shows the outline of the external genital parts, drawn open. The lower curves indicate the extent to which the vaginal opening can enlarge to permit sex union and birth.

PLATE II—EXPLANATION

(A) *Ov,* Ovary. The one at the left side of the drawing is in natural position and shows the outside. The one on the right side is laid sideways, and cut in two, to show the inside.

Tb1, Fallopian Tube, outside view. *Tb2,* Fallopian Tube, inside view.

F1, Follicle or Sac, from which the ovum or egg has just escaped. The tiny dots behind each arrow indicate its course into the tube. The egg is like the dot on a smaller letter i, just visible.

F2, Follicle, closed, the dot inside indicating the egg which will be freed from its sac a month later.

Cl, Corpus Luteum, or yellow body, the empty puckered sac remaining from the previous month.

Pa, Pavillion, the trumpet-shaped, leaf-like end of the tube, where the egg enters after leaving the ovary. *F,* the fringe-like tips of the tube.

Am, Ampulla, the widened fluted part of the tube.

Is, Ishtmus, the narrowest part of the tube, the inner passage of which is no larger than a bristle, just wide enough for the minute egg to pass. The meeting place of the egg and the sperm cells is between *Tb2* and *A.M.*. The egg is pushed along the tube for three days till it reaches the uterus.

U1, Uterus, showing its virginal proportions.

U2 shows by dotted line the size of the womb after having borne a child. It never shrinks fully back to its virginal size.

CU, Cavity of the Uterus, with front half cut away to show the inside.

IO, Internal Os, or inner mouth, which divides the uterus into two parts. It is in the cavity above this inner mouth that the egg becomes an embryo and grows into a baby.

CC, Cavity of the Cervix, or neck of the uterus.

EO1, External Os, or mouth of the womb.

EO2, indicating size after child-bearing.

SD, Upper part of the Vagina, where the semen is deposited by the male.

Va, Vagina, distended as in sex union.

LM, Levator Muscle, which circles and closes the vagina. There are two of them, only one being shown.

H, Hymen, open as in intercourse.

VvG, Vulvo-Vaginal Gland, which furnishes lubrication during the sex act.

BV, Bulb of the Vestibule, a bunch of veins that, like the clitoris, enlarges from excitement.

Lmi, Labia Minora, the inner lips of the entrance to the vagina.

Lma, Labia Majora, the outer lips.

(B) *Cl,* Clitoris, the small penis-like organ, which enlarges under excitement.

Pc, Prepuce, or fore-skin of the clitoris.

Lmi, Labia Minora, here shown drawn apart.

Fr, Fourchette, or fork, a fold that appears when the vulva is spread open.

Va, Vaginal opening, which leads to the uterus.

H, Hymen, here shown expanded and drawn back. In repose it puckers in and closes, so that the vaginal opening hardly shows.

Vt, Vestibule, a flat triangular space in the middle of which is the

M, Meatus, the opening of the urethra or water-passage.

Vvg, Vulvo-vaginal, or lubricating glands.

Mr indicates the size it may reach in a woman who has had children.

Lbr indicates the expansion when birth occurs. This largest circle permits the passage of the baby's head, which is the largest and hardest part of a new-born baby; the bones of the baby's skull are loosely joined, so that they can be telescoped somewhat during the birth. There is always what is called the "softspot" on top of a baby's head, but as the child grows the joints of the skull become firm and hard.

Sm indicates the position of the symphysis, or front joining of the bony arch of the pelvis, under which the baby's head slips out during the birth process.

17

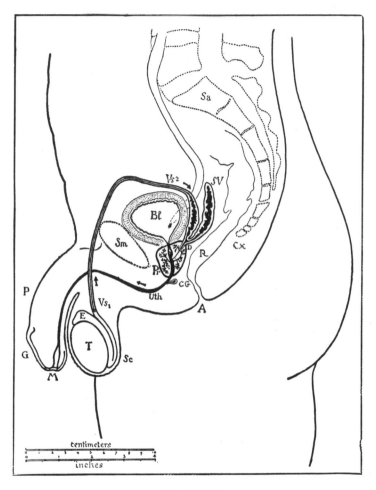

PLATE III.

Male Organs, Side View

Copyright from R. L. Dickinson.

Slightly more than one-third life size.

A vertical section through the middle of the body. The generative organs are shown in heavy outline; the urinary organs and other parts of the body in lighter outline.

18

PLATE III—EXPLANATION

Bones

The bones are indicated by dotted lines.

Sa, Sacrum, the largest of the bones at the end of the spine.

Cx, Coccyx, the tip-end bone of the spine.

Sm, Symphysis, the front meeting place of the bony girdle or pelvis.

Excretory Organs

R, Rectum, which carries away the solid waste matter from the bowels.

A, Anus, the opening of the rectum.

Bl, Bladder, which holds the waste water or urine. Here shown nearly empty. When full it is much larger.

Sex Organs

P, Penis, which fits into the vagina during the sex act; it is here shown relaxed.

G, Glans and Prepuce, or Fore-Skin.

Uth, Urethra, the passage which carries away the waste water of urine, and through which also the germs of life pass during the sex act. The urethra is here shown empty. Plate IV shows it distended.

T, Testicle, of which there are two, and in which grow the spermatazoa, or germs of life. (For an interior view, see Plate IV).

Sc, Scrotum, the bag which holds the testicles.

E, Epididymis, where the spermatazoa are finished and stored. (See Plate IV.)

Vs1 and Vs2, Vas Deferens, which carries the spermatazoa to the urethra. There are two of these tubes, one from each testicle.

SV, Seminal Vesicle, of which there are two, one on either side of the bladder.

Pr, Prostate Gland, cut across to show the inside. The seminal vesicles and the prostate gland each secrete a liquid that forms part of the semen and which acts as a carrier and stimulant for the spermatazoa.

D, Ejaculatory Duct, which expels the spermatazoa at the climax of the sex act.

CG, Cowper's Gland, a tiny gland the function of which is obscure.

Plate IV shows the spermatazoa greatly magnified.

19

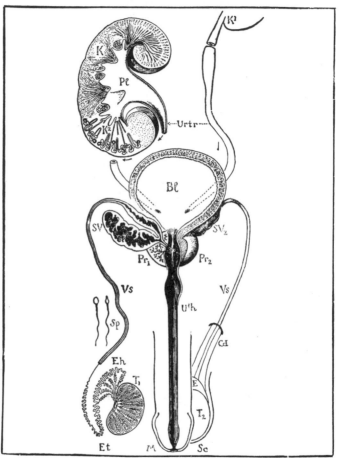

PLATE IV.
Male Organs, Front View
Copyright from R. L. Dickinson.
Slightly more than one-third life size.

The male sex organs and the urinary organs are closely related, so this plate includes the kidneys, which collect the urine or waste water, and the two ureters which convey it to the bladder, where it is held till it is passed from the body.

On the right side of the diagram, the lower part of the kidney is outlined, but to save space is placed nearer to the bladder than it actually is, the ureter being really ten inches long. On the left side the other kidney is shown in its right size in relation to the other organs, but not in its proper place which is ten inches higher. It is cut in two to show the inside.

PLATE IV—EXPLANATION

Excretory Organs

*K*1, outline of the lower part of the Kidney.

K, the Kidney cut open to show the structure.

*K*2, the minute Kidney structure, greatly enlarged.

Pl, the basin where the urine collects.

Urtr, Ureters, which carry the urine to the bladder. They are actually about 10 inches long, but are here shortened to save space.

Bl, Bladder, not distended. The dotted lines indicate the openings of the two ureters.

Sex Organs

Uth, Urethra, shown distended.

M, Meatus, the opening of the urethra, through which both the urine and the semen are passed.

*T*1, Testicle, turned sideways and cut across to show where, in minute ducts in compartments, the spermatazoa are manufactured.

*T*2, Testicle, hanging in place in the scrotum.

Sc, Scrotum.

E, Epididymis. Outside. (See Plate III.)

Eh, Epididymis head. } Inside view, spread out to show structure.
Et, Epididymis tail. }

Vs, Vas Deferens, or Seminal Duct, leading to ejaculatory duct. (See Plate III.) On the left side it is shown cut across to reveal the tiny tube which carries the spermatazoa.

Cd, Spermatic Cord, made up of muscles, nerves and blood vessels in which the vas deferens runs through the opening in the abdominal wall into the interior of the abdomen. The actual length of the vas deferens is about twelve inches. The diagram foreshortens it to save space.

SV, Seminal Vesicle, cut across to show the inside, and pulled to one side to show the form.

*SV*2, Seminal Vesicle, outside view, and shown in its proper place behind the bladder.

*Pr*1, Prostate Gland, cut across to show the inside.

*Pr*2, Prostate Gland, outside view.

Sp, Spermatazoa, front and side views, greatly magnified. Set end to end it would take 500 to span an inch. Over 200 million spermatazoa are released in a single ejaculation.

Appendix C

———————————————— FROM THE DEFENSE ————————————————

From Goodwin F. Watson, of Teacher's College, Columbia University:

Five years ago, as Instructor in Religious Education at Union Theological Seminary, I offered a course in "Work with Young People." Surveying available materials for sex education, Mrs. Dennett's pamphlet, The Sex Side of Life, was chosen by the class as most useful to place in the hands of young people. Since then I have recommended it to other classes at Union, and have used it in religious conferences of ministers, parents, and YMCA secretaries which I have served because of my opportunities as an ordained minister at the Methodist Episcopal Church (Wisconsin Conference), and as Director of Research for the National Council of the Young Men's Christian Association.

From Katharine Bement Davis, head of the Bureau of Social Hygiene and former commissioner of corrections, New York City:

Mrs. Dennett's book presents [sex education] without sentimentality. I know of no better pamphlet of its kind. If this is banned it will undoubtedly result in the banning of all other pamphlets in its class. What is then to become of sex education? Are we going to let our children gain their knowledge through surreptitious and often truly obscene sources, which information moreover is generally incorrect?

From B. S. Winchester, Executive Secretary of the Commission on Christian Education of the Federal Council of the Churches of Christ in America:

I submitted the pamphlet to my wife and, without informing her of the suit, asked her opinion of it. She read it carefully and said she thought it a very fine statement; in fact, she had never seen a more satisfactory one. She seemed surprised that it had been the occasion of this attack. I had asked her to read it having in mind our four daughters and young son.

From Dr. Robert L. Dickinson, Secretary of the Committee on Maternal Health:

For gauging the need of the Dennett pamphlet and the effect of this type of teaching, I have had rather exceptional opportunities. I may qualify as one with an inveterate family-doctor point of view, notwithstanding forty-six years devoted chiefly to obstetrics and diseases peculiar to women; as one who has systematically given instruction prior to marriage and has been honored as father confessor to thousands of women; and as giving, these five years past, his full time without salary to medical investigation of neglected sex problems, with a staff, under a program endorsed by conspicuous medical organizations.

A verdict against the pamphlet would block teaching of doctors and medical students, in medical textbooks and journals, as well as a large part of the printed information on sex matters found essential by lay educators.

From Dr. Louis I. Harris, Ex-Commissioner of Health of New York City:

I do not know Mary Ware Dennett, but I have been familiar with the pamphlet published by her for several years. It impressed me as one of the sanest, sincerest, and most useful monographs of its kind that I have met in my connection with venereal disease control and public health education.

--------------------- FROM THE PROSECUTION ---------------------

From John S. Sumner, secretary of the New York Society for the Suppression of Vice:

There seems to me, no necessity whatever for the plates representing male and female sexual organs. We have found from long experience that pictures representing the human body or vital parts thereof frequently arouses indecent thoughts in the minds of many persons, as indicated by the frequency with which indecently marked advertising posters, and cards are encountered on the platforms and in the cars of transit companies. We have seen this occur in connection with pictures of the most innocent type, displaying the human form. We have seen outline figures of the human form taken from a newspaper indecently marked and deposited in the entry of a girls' institution. It may be said that such things are done by abnormal or subnormal people but their frequency is such that it is evident that there are a great many people of this type. Such plates might be used to instruct persons about to marry if they desire instruction in detail on the physical formation of outer and inner sex organs, but it is not necessary information and is probably sought by very few persons.

From Rev. John Roach Straton, Pastor of the Calvary Baptist
Church, New York City:

*Whether the writer was prompted by commercialism and the deliberate
purpose of stating her thoughts in such a way to stir up a sensational
discussion and thereby enormously enlarge sales, or whether there was
an honest but misguided desire to do service to the human race, is open
to question. In my judgment this book in its practical effect upon children
and young people could not be otherwise than utterly ruinous. Frankly I
believe, because of my observations as a Christian minister, that if this
pamphlet should really be put into the hands of all the young people in
America, as the expressed purpose is, it would go far toward debauching
certainly the weaker elements of the rising generation.*

From J. DeLeon Sullivan, superintendent of the Queensboro Society
for the Prevention of Cruelty to Children, Inc., N.Y.:

*The objections I find to the above pamphlet are as follows: "The
Introduction for Elders" can scarcely be construed as a warning to the
child against sex abuse, and its apparent purpose is to beguile the elders
into permitting the children to retain possession of this pamphlet. The
elders possibly little realizing that in so doing they are accepting for their
children a Communistic doctrine which is foreign to our form of government.*

From Dr. Howard Kelly, Professor Emeritus of Gynecology
in Johns Hopkins University:

*Following our recent soul-racking experiences in the great war, our
nation is obviously at a crossroad: One way leads upward, building up
the family unit by the difficult path of self-control, high ideals, and a pure
Christian faith. The other has a road-house, inviting down into the corruption of the pit, plotting the contamination of youth, with its Mary
Dennetts holding out to the vacillating boy and girl illicit pleasures which
rob the marriage bed of its sanctity and shortly become but apples of
Sodom corrupting the whole life.*

From James M. Kieran, President of Hunter College
of the City of New York:

I understand you would like to have my opinion of The Sex Side of Life,
by Mary Ware Dennett.

*Without at all entering into the motives of the author, but judging
solely by the contents of the pamphlet, my opinion is that it would be
dangerous to the morals of the young to have it get into their possession.*

Notes

1 Mary Ware Dennett, *Birth Control Laws* (New York: The Grafton Press, 1926), pp. 3–4.

2 Madeline Gray (b. 1902), author of *Margaret Sanger*, interview by author, 19 February 1990, Amherst, MA.

3 John M. Blum, Edmund S. Morgan, Willie Lee Rose, Arthur M. Schlesinger, Jr., Kenneth M. Stampp, C. Vann Woodward, *The National Experience Part Two: A History of the United States Since 1865* (New York: Harcourt Brace Jovanovich, Inc., 1981), p. 552.

4 Christopher Lasch, "Mary Ware Dennett," in *Notable American Women (1607–1950) A Biographical Dictionary*, eds. Edward The. James, Janet Wilson James, and Paul S. Boyer (Cambridge, MA: The Belknap Press of Harvard University Press), p. 464. Dennett founded the National Birth Control League in 1915; Sanger founded the rival American Birth Control League in 1921.

5 James Reed, *The Birth Control Movement & American Society: From Private Vice to Public Virtue* (Princeton: Princeton University Press, 1982), p. 336. Although this citation is taken from the main text, Reed makes his most extensive mention of Dennett in a footnote on p. 391.

6 Harry M. Clor, *Obscenity and Public Morality: Censorship in a Liberal Society* (Chicago, The University of Chicago Press, 1969), p. 20.

7 Morris L. Ernst and Alan U. Schwartz, *Censorship: The Search for the Obscene*, with an Introduction by Philip Scharper (New York: The MacMillan Company, 1964), pp. 80–82, 105, 166.

8 C. Thomas Dienes, *Law, Politics, and Birth Control* (Chicago: University of Illinois Press, 1972), p. 89, 105.

9 Alec Craig, *Suppressed Books: A History of the Conception of Literary Obscenity*, with a foreword by Morris Ernst (Cleveland: The World Publishing Company, 1963), p. 133.

10 Samuel Walker, *In Defense of American Liberties: A History of the ACLU* (New York: Oxford University Press, 1990), pp. 84–86.

11 The authors spelled her name "Marie Ware Dennett." James C. N. Paul and Murray L. Schwartz, *Federal Censorship: Obscenity in the Mail* (New York: The Free Press of Glencoe, Inc., 1961), pp. 43–44, 63, 218.

12 George Bernard Shaw as quoted by Robert W. Haney, *Comstockery in America* (Boston: Beacon Press, 1960), 21.

13 Heywood Broun and Margaret Leech. *Anthony Comstock: Roundsman of the Lord* (New York: Albert & Charles Boni, 1927), 15.

14 Broun and Leech, *Anthony Comstock*, 47.

15 *Ibid.*

16 Anthony Comstock, *Frauds Exposed; Or, How the People are Deceived and Robbed, and Youth Corrupted* (Montclair, N.J.: Patterson Smith, 1969 [orig. publ. 1880]), 389.

17 Acts and Laws of the Province of Massachusetts Bay, Section 8 (1792) as quoted in MacMillan, *Censorship and Public Morality* (Aldershot, Hants: Gower, 1983), 345.

18 MacMillan, *Censorship and Public Morality*, 345.

19 The common law was strengthened by statute in three New England states: Vermont (1821), Massachusetts (before 1835), and Connecticut (1834). There was also federal legislation against the importation of indecent pictures and articles (1842) and against the transmission of obscene books and pictures by mail (1865). Alec Craig, *Suppressed Books: A History of the Conception of Literary Obscenity*, with a foreword by Morris L. Ernst (New York: The World Publishing Company), 127.

20 Norman St. John-Stevas, *Obscenity and the Law* (New York: Da Capo Press, 1974), 160.

21 "Beginning about the mid-nineteenth century, the concept of this crime was subtly but significantly changed; the focus shifted from the defendant's personal conduct to the ideas or the content of the expression he was disseminating. Whereas the defendant's public use of obscene creations was once the basis of prosecution, that now became unimportant; obscenity was bad in itself, without regard to conduct or to the actual effect of its previous dissemination, and virtually all distribution was proscribed, regardless of motive, audience reached, or actual harm done. Thus, the law moved, almost unconsciously, into the business of banning books." James C. N. Paul and Murray L. Schwartz, *Federal Censorship: Obscenity in the Mail.* (New York: The Free Press of Glencoe, Inc., 1961), 11–12.

22 *Ibid.*, 12.

23 *Ibid.*, 17.

24 *Ibid.*, 16. This decision implied that even if the overall intent and effect were to be found "laudable," a book could still be judged "obscene."

25 *Ibid.*

26 *Ibid.*, pp. 16–17. Note the ambiguity of the Hicklin test. For a work to be judged obscene, no concrete connection with the young and "weak" needed to be established; no definite negative effect had to be proved. The Hicklin test for obscenity was imprecise to the extreme.

27 Morris L. Ernst and Alan U.

Schwartz, with an Introduction by Philip Scharper, *Censorship: The Search for the Obscene* (New York: The MacMillan Company, 1964), 31.

28 Robert Bremner, "Introduction" to Anthony Comstock, *Traps for the Young*, edited by Robert Bremner (Cambridge, Mass.: the Belknap Press of Harvard University Press, the John Harvard Library, 1967 [originally New York: Funk & Wagnalls, Publishers, 1883, with an introduction by J.M. Buckley D.D.]), xi.

29 Broun and Leech, *Roundsman of the Lord*, 13–14.

30 *Ibid.*, 12.

31 Mary Ware Dennett, *Birth Control Laws* (New York: The Grafton Press, 1926), 30.

32 Mary Ware Dennett Defense Committee, *Sex Education or Obscenity? The Mary Ware Dennett Case* (New York City, n.d.), 3. Folder 481, Box 27, Mary Ware Dennett Papers. Manuscript Collections, Schlesinger Library, Radcliffe College, Cambridge, Mass.

33 That is, it became possible to prosecute a person for giving spoken, as well as written, contraceptive instructions. According to the Voluntary Parenthood League, forty years later eighteen states had laws like New York's, while twenty-two states had modeled their laws on the federal statute.

34 Dennett, *Birth Control Laws*, 31.

35 Mary Ware Dennett, *Who's Obscene?* (New York: The Vanguard Press, 1930), 215.

36 Bremner, "Introduction" to *Traps for the Young*, xvi.

37 The doctors were Dr. J. Bott, Dr. Alex R. King, Dr. Dubois, Dr. Andrews, Dr. Marcus Jacoby, and Dr. C.W. Selden. D.R.M. Bennett, *Anthony Comstock: His Career of Cruelty and Crime* (New York: Da Capo Press, 1971. A Da Capo Press Reprint Series, Civil Liberties in American History. General Editor: Leonard W. Levy. Originally published New York: D.M. Bennett, Liberal and Scientific Publishing House, 1878), 1029.

38 Bennett, *Anthony Comstock*, 1028–1029.

39 *Ibid.*

40 *Ibid.*, 1028–1030.

41 *Ibid.*, 1073–1083.

42 *Ibid.*, 1019.

43 *Ibid.*, 1027–1028.

44 *Ibid.*, 1041–1043.

45 Broun and Leech, *Roundsman of the Lord*, 186–187.

46 Paul and Schwartz, *Federal Censorship*, 45.

47 When the second coming of Christ did not occur as Christians had anticipated, the great expectation turned into the "Great Disappointment." See Michael Sours, *The Prophecies of Jesus* (Oxford, England: Oneworld Publications Ltd., 1991). For a fascinating account of the millennial fervor of the mid-1800s, see William Sears, *Thief in the Night or the Strange Case of the Missing Millennium* (Oxford, England: George Ronald Publishers, 1992).

48 For an overview of America in the 1800s, see Bernard Bailyn, David Brion Davis, David Herbert Donald, John L. Thomas, Robert H. Wiebe, Gordon S. Wood, *The Great Republic: A History of the American People*, Second Edition (Lexington, Massachusetts: D.C. Heath and Company, 1981) 558–585.

49 For an excellent discussion of Bostonians in the 1800s, see Barbara Miller Solomon, *Ancestors and Immigrants: A Changing New England Tradition* (Chicago: The University of Chicago Press, 1972).

50 Information about the decline of the Puritan descendants is taken from Solomon, *Ancestors and Immigrants* and John A. Garraty *The New Commonwealth: 1870–1890* (New York: Harper Torchbooks, Harper & Row, 1968), 4.

51 Note to her grandson Peter Dennett, Folder 9, Box 1, Mary Ware Dennett Papers, Schlesinger Library.

52 John Stuart Mill, "The Subjection of Women," in *Feminism: Essential Historical Writings*, ed. Miriam Schneir, 162–178 (New York: Random House, 1972 [orig. publ. 1869]), 167. Mill wrote his essay in 1861, although it was not published until 1869.

53 *Ibid.*, p. 176.

54 Livonia Coffin Ware to George Ware, shoe box, Warren House, Alstead, New Hampshire.

55 Garraty, *The New Commonwealth*, 13.

56 James Reed, *The Birth Control Movement and American Society: From Private Vice to Public Virtue* (Princeton, N.J.: Princeton University Press, 1983), 7.

57 Reed, *From Private Vice to Public Virtue*, 10.

58 *Ibid.*, 13.

59 *Ibid.*, 6.

60 Nancy Cott, "Passionlessness," in *A Heritage of Her Own: Toward a New Social History of American Women*, eds. Nancy F. Cott and Elizabeth H. Pleck, with an introduction by Nancy F. Cott, 162–181 (New York: Simon & Schuster, 1979), 164.

61 Barbara Epstein, "Family, Sexual Morality, and Popular Movements in Turn-of-the-Century America," in *Powers of Desire: The Politics of Sexuality*, ed. Ann Snitow, Christine Stansell, and Sharon Thompson. 117–130 (New York: Monthly Review Press, 1983), 121.

62 Prostitutes were usually working-class women or women of color. The West Coast had a bustling trade in Asian prostitutes—usually Chinese or Japanese. See Ruth Rosen, *The Lost Sisterhood* (Baltimore: The Johns Hopkins University Press, 1982). In the South, white masters considered black women to be their sexual slaves. See Harriet A. Jacobs, *Incidents in the Life of a Slave Girl*, ed. Jean Fagan Yellin (Cambridge, Mass.: Harvard University Press, 1987).

63 David J. Pivar, *Purity Crusade: Sexual Morality and Social Control 1868–1900* (Westport, Conn.: Greenwood Press, Inc., 1973), 28.

64 For more information on Victorian

anxieties about venereal disease, see Allan M. Brandt, *No Magic Bullet: A Social History of Venereal Disease in the United States Since 1880* (New York: Oxford University Press, 1987).

[65] In England, the prostitute herself—not her male customer—was faulted for the problem. The Contagious Diseases Acts during the 1860s imposed intrusive and humiliating mandatory examinations for all prostitutes. John D'Emilio and Estelle Freedman, *Intimate Matters: A History of Sexuality in America*, (New York: Harper & Row, 1988), 148.

[66] *Ibid.*

[67] Pivar, *Purity Crusade*, 256.

[68] *Ibid.*, 109.

[69] For more information about voluntary motherhood, see Linda Gordon, *Woman's Body, Woman's Right* (Penguin Books: Middlesex, England, 1988), 95–116.

[70] Olive Banks, *Faces of Feminism: A Story of Feminism as a Social Movement* (Oxford: Martin Robertson & Co., 1981), 71.

[71] Information about Mary's early childhood taken from letters between Livonia Coffin Ware and George Ware, shoe box.

[72] For a good sense of Worcester in the mid-1800s, see Joshua Cashan, *Civilizing Worcester: The Creation of Institutional and Cultural Order, Worcester, Massachusetts, 1848–1876*. Ann Arbor, Michigan: University Microfilms International, 1983. University of Pittsburgh, Ph.D. 1974. Copyright 1975.

[73] Mary's own childhood recollections are taken from her personal papers, Folder 9, Box 1, MWD Papers, Schlesinger Library.

[74] George Ware's death and *Titanic* anecdote from interview with Carleton Dennett, 19 May 1992, Santa Cruz, California.

[75] Mary Ware Dennett, hidden manuscript of her private life, uncovered 1995.

[76] Mary Ware Dennett's school papers, Folder 10, Box 1, MWD Papers.

[77] Anecdotes of Mary Ware Dennett's teenage years from her one and only journal, 1888, bookshelf, Warren House, Alstead, N.H.

[78] Mary Ware Dennett's curricula vitae, Folder 9, Box 1, MWD Papers.

[79] Gillian Naylor, *The Arts and Crafts Movement: A Study of Its Sources, Ideals and Influence on Design Theory*, (London: Trefoil Publications, 1990), 8.

[80] Wendy Kaplan, *"The Art that is Life": The Arts & Crafts Movement in America, 1875–1920*, (Boston, Mass.: Museum of Fine Arts, 1987), 102–105.

[81] Kaplan, *"The Art That is Life"*, 219.

[82] Morris as quoted by Lionel Lambourne, *Utopian Craftsmen: The Arts and Crafts Movement from the Cotswolds to Chicago*, (London: Astragal Books, 1980), 22.

[83] Kaplan, *"The Art That is Life,"* 56–60.

[84] *Ibid.*, 301.

[85] *Ibid.*, 78.

[86] *Ibid.*, 303.

[87] *Ibid.*, 218–219.

[88] Later, Dow became an instructor at the Pratt Institute in Brooklyn; in 1904, he was appointed director of fine arts at Teachers College, Columbia University.

[89] *Philadelphia Public Ledger*, 19 October 1894, Folder 179, Box 10, MWD Papers, Schlesinger Library.

[90] Mary Coffin Ware, "Some Foundation Principles," 1894 lecture, Folder 122, Box 7, MWD Papers.

[91] Ibid.

[92] Mary Coffin Ware, "The Study of Decoration," 1894 lecture, Folder 122, Box 7, MWD Papers.

[93] Newspaper clipping, "Where Discrimination Counts," Folder 126, Box 7, MWD Papers.

[94] Mary Coffin Ware, "Theory—Composition etc.," 1894 lecture, Folder 122, Box 7, MWD Papers.

95 Ibid.

96 Ibid.

97 Mary Coffin Ware, "Primitive Ornament," 1894 lecture, Folder 123, Box 7, MWD Papers.

98 Mary Coffin Ware, "Greece," 25 January 1895 lecture, Folder 123, Box 7, MWD Papers.

99 Ibid.

100 Ibid.

101 Mary Coffin Ware, "The Study of Decoration."

102 Mary Coffin Ware, "The Separation of Art and Handicraft," 1894 Lecture, Folder 122, Box 7, MWD Papers.

103 Ibid.

104 Ibid.

105 Ibid.

106 Mary Coffin Ware, "Some Foundation Principles."

107 Ibid.

108 Ibid.

109 Ibid.

110 Mary Coffin Ware to William Hartley Dennett, 30 March 1895, shoe box letters, Warren House, Alstead, N.H.

111 Kaplan, *The Art That is Life,* 209–212.

112 Hartley was descended from Thomas Rogers, who came to the New World on the Mayflower in 1620 and then died a year later in Plymouth, Massachusetts. Copy of letter from J. Vaughan Dennett, 10 March 1935, Margaret Chase Perry archives, Kensington, N.H.

113 Mary Coffin Ware to William Hartley Dennett, 19 October 1894, shoe box letters.

114 Mary Coffin Ware to William Hartley Dennett, undated, probably around 1896, courtship letters, Carleton Dennett collection, Santa Cruz, California.

115 Mary Coffin Ware to William Hartley Dennett, 23 January 1895, show box letters.

116 Mary Coffin Ware to William Hartley Dennett, 11 July 1895, shoe box letters.

117 Mary Coffin Ware to William Hartley Dennett, 29 October 1895, shoe box letters.

118 John M. Craig, *Lucia Ames Mead (1856–1936) and the American Peace Movement,* (Lewiston, N.Y.: The Edwin Mellen Press, 1990), 17.

119 Mary Coffin Ware to William Hartley Dennett, 12 January 1896, shoe box letters.

120 William Hartley Dennett to Mary Coffin Ware, 19 January 1896, shoe box letters.

121 William Hartley Dennett to Mary Coffin Ware, 15 March 1896, shoe box letters.

122 Mary Coffin Ware to William Hartley Dennett, 22 August 1896, Carleton Dennett collection.

123 Annie O. Dennett to Mary Coffin Ware, 17 August 1896, Margaret Chase Perry archives.

124 Marcy Beard to Mary Coffin Ware, 22 November 1896, Margaret Chase Perry archives.

125 Theodora Beard to Mary Coffin Ware, 24 November 1896, Margaret Chase Perry archives.

126 Charles Horne to Mary Coffin Ware, 22 October 1896, Margaret Chase Perry archives.

127 Lucia Ames Mead to Mary Coffin Ware, 1–20 September 1896, shoe box letters.

128 Even today, their descendants know next to nothing about Willie–it's almost as if he never existed.

129 William Hartley Dennett to Mary Coffin Ware, 25 September 1896, shoe box letters.

130 Ibid.

131 William Hartley Dennett to Mary Coffin Ware, 25 September 1896, shoe box letters.

[132] William Hartley Dennett to Mary Coffin Ware, 28 August 1896, shoe box letters.

[133] Mary Coffin Ware to William Hartley Dennett, 8 November 1896, Carleton Dennett collection.

[134] Mary Coffin Ware to William Hartley Dennett, 30 October 1896, shoe box letters.

[135] Mary Coffin Ware to William Hartley Dennett, 27 September 1896, Carleton Dennett collection.

[136] William Hartley Dennett to Mary Coffin Ware, 17 October 1896. shoe box letters.

[137] William Hartley Dennett to Mary Coffin Ware, 29 August 1896, shoe box letters.

[138] Mary Coffin Ware to William Hartley Dennett, 9 November 1896, Carleton Dennett collection.

[139] William Hartley Dennett to Mary Coffin Ware, 24 October 1896, shoe box letters.

[140] Mary Coffin Ware to William Hartley Dennett, 6 December 1896, Carleton Dennett collection.

[141] Mary Coffin Ware to William Hartley Dennett, 23 August 1896, Carleton Dennett collection.

[142] Mary Coffin Ware to William Hartley Dennett, 20 January 1897, Carleton Dennett collection.

[143] Mary Coffin Ware to William Hartley Dennett, 6 January 1897, Carleton Dennett collection.

[144] Mary Coffin Ware to William Hartley Dennett, 8 January 1897, Carleton Dennett collection.

[145] Mary Coffin Ware to William Hartley Dennett, 12 January 1897, Carleton Dennett collection.

[146] William Hartley Dennett to Mary Coffin Ware, 19 February 1897, "Hartley Dennett: Letters to Mary Ware: Italy 1897," compiled by Margaret Chase Perry, Exeter, N.H., December 1986.

[147] William Hartley Dennett to Mary Coffin Ware, 26 February 1897, "Italy 1897."

[148] William Hartley Dennett to Mary Coffin Ware, 1 March 1897, "Italy 1897."

[149] William Hartley Dennett to Mary Coffin Ware, 4 March 1897, "Italy 1897."

[150] William Hartley Dennett to Mary Coffin Ware, 26 March 1897, "Italy 1897."

[151] William Hartley Dennett to Mary Coffin Ware, 26 March 1897, "Italy 1897."

[152] Ibid.

[153] Mary Ware Dennett, undated manuscript (about 1915) of her love life, p. 18.

[154] William Hartley Dennett to Mary Coffin Ware, 23 March 1897, "Italy 1897."

[155] Mary Coffin Ware to William Hartley Dennett, 24 August 1896, Carleton Dennett collection.

[156] Mary Coffin Ware to William Hartley Dennett, 10 December 1896, Carleton Dennett collection.

[157] Mary Coffin Ware to William Hartley Dennett, 7 June 1897, Carleton Dennett collection.

[158] Mary Coffin Ware to William Hartley Dennett, 27 May 1897, Carleton Dennett collection.

[159] Annie O. Dennett to William Hartley Dennett, 11 May 1898, Margaret Chase Perry archives.

[160] William Hartley Dennett to Annie O. Dennett, 13 May 1898, Margaret Chase Perry archives.

[161] Ibid.

[162] Hartley Dennett, miscellaneous love poems, in envelope marked "Before the Change," Margaret Chase Perry archives.

[163] William Hartley Dennett to F.W. Dallinger, April 1913, "On the Petition of Mary Ware Dennett dated 11 May 1912 for Exclusive Custody of the two children of herself and Hartley Dennett," Commonwealth of Massachusetts,

Middlesex Superior Court, Margaret Chase Perry archives.

164 Mary Ware Dennett to Annie O. Dennett, 10 June 1900, Margaret Chase Perry archives.

165 Mary Ware Dennett to Annie O. Dennett, 10 June 1900, Margaret Chase Perry archives.

166 *Ibid.*

167 Mary Ware Dennett to Annie O. Dennett, 10 June 1900, Margaret Chase Perry archives.

168 Author and source unknown, Arts and Crafts article, 175, Margaret Chase Perry archives.

169 Author and source unknown, Arts and Crafts article, 176, Margaret Chase Perry archives.

170 Mary Ware Dennett as quoted in author and source unknown, Arts and Crafts article, 188, Margaret Chase Perry archives.

171 Sarah Farmer's father, Moses Garrish Farmer, was the brother-in-law of Mary's Uncle Charles Carleton Coffin. Moses Farmer was an inventor, and he and Coffin constructed a telegraph line between Harvard College Observatory and Boston together; in 1852, they installed the first electric fire alarm in the world. Craig, *Lucia Ames Mead*, 8.

172 Various reproductions of past Greenacre programs as compiled by Kenneth Walter Cameron, *Transcendentalists in Transition* (Hartford, Conn.: Transcendental Books, 1980).

173 Hartley mistakenly noted that the passage he cut out was translated from the Persian. The passage is from *The Hidden Words of Bahá'u'lláh,* and although there are some *Hidden Words* translated from the Persian, this one was actually translated from the Arabic. The modern-day translation is as follows:

O Son of Spirit!

I created thee rich, why dost thou bring thyself down to poverty? Noble I made thee, wherewith dost thou abase thyself? Out of the essence of knowledge I gave thee being, why seekest thou enlightenment from anyone beside Me? Out of the clay of love I molded thee, how dost thou busy thyself with another? Turn thy sight unto thyself, that thou mayest find Me standing within thee, mighty, powerful, and self-subsisting.

Bahá'u'lláh, *The Hidden Words of Bahá'u'lláh* (Wilmette, Il.: Bahá'í Publishing Trust, 1990), translated by Shoghi Effendi with the assistance of some English friends, 6–7.

174 Greenacre has since grown tremendously, and now offers year-round courses on the history, practice, and beliefs of the Bahá'í Faith.

175 Mary Ware Dennett to Annie O. Dennett, 16 August 1900, Margaret Chase Perry archives.

176 William Hartley Dennett to Mary Ware Dennett, 10 January 1901, Margaret Chase Perry archives.

177 Mary Ware Dennett to Annie O. Dennett, 25 June 1901, Margaret Chase Perry archives.

178 Mary Ware Dennett to Annie O. Dennett, 22 August 1901, Margaret Chase Perry archives.

179 Mary Ware Dennett to Annie O. Dennett, 25 June 1901, Margaret Chase Perry archives.

180 *Ibid.*

181 Mary Ware Dennett to Annie O. Dennett, 22 August 1901, Margaret Chase Perry archives.

182 Kaplan, "The Art That is Life," 212–213.

183 *Ibid.,* 273.

184 *Ibid.,* 273.

185 Among the early participants of the Handicraft Shop were Louis Comfort Tiffany, Gustav Stickley, John LaFarge, and Will Bradley.

186 Kaplan, "The Art That Is Life," 273.

187 *Ibid.,* 273.

188 *Ibid.,* 300.

189 William Hartley Dennett to Mary Ware Dennett, 14 February 1902, Margaret Chase Perry archives.

190 William Hartley Dennett to Annie O. Dennett, 1 September 1901, Margaret Chase Perry archives.

191 *Ibid.*

192 Lucia Ames Mead to William Hartley Dennett, 20 July 1902, Margaret Chase Perry archives.

193 Sarah Jane Farmer to William Hartley Dennett, 14 October 1902, Margaret Chase Perry archives.

194 William Hartley Dennett, "Fourth Report for Class of 1893, Harvard University," 1909, Margaret Chase Perry archives.

195 William Hartley Dennett to Annie O. Dennett, 28 July 1903, Margaret Chase Perry archives.

196 Mary Chase Burroughs, undated, biographical sketch of William Hartley Dennett, Margaret Chase Perry archives.

197 *Ibid.*

198 Kaplan, *"The Art That is Life,"* 300.

199 A.B. Le Boutillier to William Hartley Dennett, 13 April 1904, Margaret Chase Perry archives.

200 Anne Withington, *Dennett v. Dennett*, 47–48, Folder 17, Box 2, MWD Papers.

201 William Hartley Dennett to F.W. Dallinger, "On the Petition of Mary Ware Dennett."

202 Hartley Dennett, miscellaneous love poems, in envelope marked "Before the Change," Margaret Chase Perry archives.

203 D'Emilio and Freedman, *Intimate Matters*, 174.

204 Mary Ware Dennett to Marie Stopes, 1921, Folder 288, Box 16, MWD Papers.

205 William Hartley Dennett to Mary Ware Dennett, around 1901 or 1902, Margaret Chase Perry archives.

206 William Hartley Dennett to Mary Ware Dennett, around 1901 or 1902, Margaret Chase Perry archives.

207 William Hartley Dennett to Annie O. Dennett, 8 December 1906, Margaret Chase Perry archives.

208 Margaret Everett Chase, unsubmitted letter to F.W. Dallinger, 1913, Margaret Chase Perry archives.

209 *Ibid.*

210 *Ibid.*

211 *Ibid.*

212 *Ibid.*

213 William Hartley Dennett to Mary Ware Dennett, 17 July 1906, Margaret Chase Perry archives.

214 William Hartley Dennett to Mary Ware Dennett, 20 July 1906, Margaret Chase Perry archives.

215 William Hartley Dennett to Mary Ware Dennett, 23 July 1906, Margaret Chase Perry archives.

216 There were four members in Mary's Economics Committee: Mary Ware Dennett, Margaret Chase, Sadie Drew, and a Mrs. Shaw. From Margaret Everett Chase, unsubmitted letter to F.W. Dallinger.

217 Kaplan, *"The Art That is Life,"* 298.

218 *Ibid.,* 299.

219 Margaret Everett Chase to Mary Ware Dennett, 22 October 1906, Margaret Chase Perry archives. Hartley Dennett would later own quite a bit of property in the Alstead area.

220 *Ibid.*

221 *Ibid.*

222 Margaret Everett Chase, unsubmitted letter to F.W. Dallinger. The story, if true, is an interesting precursor to Mary's later work in sex education.

223 *Ibid.*

224 *Ibid.*

225 Margaret Everett Chase to Mary Ware Dennett, 1908, Margaret Chase Perry archives.

226 William Hartley Dennett to Annie O. Dennett, 7 June 1907, Margaret Chase

Perry archives.

227 William Hartley Dennett to Mary Ware Dennett, 31 May 1907, Margaret Chase Perry archives.

228 *Ibid.*

229 *Ibid.*

230 *Ibid.*

231 William Hartley Dennett to Mary Ware Dennett, 22 May 1907, Margaret Chase Perry archives.

232 William Hartley Dennett to Mary Ware Dennett, 26 May 1907, Margaret Chase Perry archives.

233 William Hartley Dennett to Mary Ware Dennett, 3 June 1907, Margaret Chase Perry archives.

234 *Ibid.*

235 William Hartley Dennett to Mary Ware Dennett, 3 June 1907, Margaret Chase Perry archives.

236 Margaret Everett Chase to William Hartley Dennett, Margaret Chase Perry archives.

237 Margaret Everett Chase to William Hartley Dennett, 24 May 1907, Margaret Chase Perry archives.

238 Mary Ware Dennett, *Dennett v. Dennett*, 4.

239 *Ibid.*

240 Margaret Everett Chase, unsubmitted letter to F.W. Dallinger.

241 *Ibid.*

242 *Ibid.*

243 Margaret Everett Chase to William Hartley Dennett, around June 1907, Margaret Chase Perry archives.

244 Margaret Everett Chase to William Hartley Dennett, Sunday evening, around June 1907, Margaret Chase Perry archives.

245 *Ibid.*

246 *Ibid.*

247 Kaplan, *"The Art That is Life,"* 361.

248 William Hartley Dennett to Mary Ware Dennett, 25 May 1907, Margaret Chase Perry archives.

249 Margaret Everett Chase, unsubmitted letter to F.W. Dallinger.

250 *Ibid.*

251 *Ibid.*

252 *Ibid.*

253 William Hartley Dennett to Annie O. Dennett, 15 September 1907, Margaret Chase Perry archives.

254 William Hartley Dennett to Annie O. Dennett, August 1907, Margaret Chase Perry archives.

255 William Hartley Dennett to F.W. Dallinger, "On the Petition of Mary Ware Dennett."

256 *Ibid.*

257 *Ibid.*

258 Mary Ware Dennett's rebuttal, *Dennett v. Dennett*, 169–177.

259 William Hartley Dennett to F.W. Dallinger, "On the Petition of Mary Ware Dennett."

260 *Ibid.*

261 Mary Ware Dennett's rebuttal, *Dennett v. Dennett*, 169–177.

262 *Ibid.*

263 William Hartley Dennett, summer 1907, Margaret Chase Perry archives.

264 Book of Matthew, 10:16–23, as quoted by William Hartley Dennett, undated personal notes, Margaret Chase Perry archives.

265 William Hartley Dennett to Annie O. Dennett, August 1907, Margaret Chase Perry archives.

266 William Hartley Dennett to Annie O. Dennett, 3 September 1907, Margaret Chase Perry archives.

267 William Hartley Dennett to Annie O. Dennett, August 1907, Margaret Chase Perry archives.

268 William Hartley Dennett to F.W.

Dallinger, "On the Petition of Mary Ware Dennett."

269 William Hartley Dennett to Annie O. Dennett, 15 September 1907, Margaret Chase Perry archives.

270 William Hartley Dennett to Annie O. Dennett, 19 September 1907, Margaret Chase Perry archives.

271 Margaret Everett Chase to Mary Ware Dennett, 20 September 1907, Margaret Chase Perry archives.

272 Livonia Coffin Ware, *Dennett v. Dennett*, 44.

273 *Ibid.*

274 Margaret Everett Chase to Mary Ware Dennett, 7 February 1908, Margaret Chase Perry archives.

275 Margaret Everett Chase to Mary Ware Dennett, around 7 February 1908, Margaret Chase Perry archives.

276 *Ibid.*

277 Mary Ware Dennett to Margaret Everett Chase, 9 February 1908, Margaret Chase Perry archives.

278 Mary Ware Dennett's personal notes, Margaret Chase Perry archives.

279 Margaret Everett Chase to Mary Ware Dennett, 19 February 1908, Margaret Chase Perry archives.

280 Margaret Everett Chase to Mary Ware Dennett, 19 February 1908, Margaret Chase Perry archives.

281 Margaret Everett Chase to Mary Ware Dennett, 5 March 1908, Exhibit D, *Dennett v. Dennett*, Folder 18, Box 2, MWD Papers. Also draft of letter in Margaret Chase Perry archives.

282 Margaret Everett Chase to Mary Ware Dennett, 5 March 1908.

283 *Ibid.*

284 Mary outlined eleven points of rebuttal in response to Margaret's claims:

1. The fact that you consciously felt ready "for all that misinterpretation and false idealism" could offer—shows that you have not been entirely un-self conscious as you said you had been—the other day—and your actions certainly haven't appeared un-self conscious a good deal of the time.

2. I can't see how it is possible for you to recognize any "degradation" in the situation—unless you suspect in some dim way—that there may be an element of wrong and injustice in it. If you are sure you are all right in this matter—no picture—however vivid—could make any sense of degradation enter you soul.

3. You are right in saying that I felt something nobler and truer in the situation when we ended our talk, but it was due to the very fact that I was convinced more thoroughly than ever that you sincerely *believe* you are right—even though your natural instinct might suggest that perhaps there was *some* wrong mixed in with the right. So long as I am sure of your conscientious sincerity—I can't do anything but respect you and your stand-point—even though I hunger so terribly to have you see the one point—that is so little and yet so big—that would make all the rest natural and helpful— and its beauty vastly increased.

4. I earnestly believe with you, too, "that the gift of a pure love is a priceless treasure—and a light *not* to be hidden—but to be shown." But there is one thing just here that you don't see—and that is that the *expression* of that love—where it demands *exclusive* privacy—that is, a *consciously hidden* expression—is a wrong.

5. There is no *true* parallel to be made between this *exclusive* as "the service that is perfect freedom"—in the red prayer book. The freedom that while it expands and develops to infinite proportions still controls and guides itself—so that no one else's life is prevented from *equal* expansion and development.

6. The expression that you have in mind—as perfectly compatible with the true marriage relation is—I think—much the same thing that I have in mind—but what you actually *do*—by way of expression—is, I think, many times an actual contradiction of your own ideal—without your realizing it.

I believe it is a real danger—for you—as for us all—to assume that because what you want is—in the main—right and fine—that everything you want is necessarily right and fine.

7. Your conception of the true marriage relation—is—I can see—radically different from mine. You lay stress on it as an institution—which has rights, demands, etc. To me, it is not only that, which is its external side, but it is a *life*, a flowing back and forth between a man and a woman of a confidence and mutual dependence; and it is a thing that in its base has no *effort* in it—however much its outer part may be enlarged and developed by conscious effort. The institutional side of marriage is only a fitting and proper manifestation of the external part that the life itself indicates. I am sure that monogamy is as much a spiritual as an economic or physical necessity, and that the best thought and experience of mankind has proved it so.

It is impossible for a man to have exactly the *same* sort of intimacy and privacy with two women at the same time, as that he should rightly have *sexual* relations with two women at the same time. And if this is *not* true, then marriage is *nothing* but a physical and economic institution. And such a conclusion is to me a revolting thought—and entirely contrary to all the highest aspirations I have. If I am not able to explain this so it seems intelligible to you, it simply means that my power of expression is limited, and not that my ideal is base or selfish. I am absolutely *sure* expression of love (which is absolutely the *only* wrong element that I can see in your relation with Hartley.) and the free *open* expression of love that you speak of toward our children—or other friends—or causes—and ideals etc. You can't liken it rightly to a love for the cause of "equal opportunity" because that love wants for itself no expression that *bars out* anything else—but rather it eagerly takes *in* everything else.

Your insistence on this exclusive privacy and intimacy is a contradiction of the idea of equal opportunities rather than an example of it. It is the very essence of equal opportunity that it shall not infringe an iota on the life of another. That is what we all recognize. True marriage life is just as much a separate spiritual identity—and not synonymous with friendship—(although including it) as true social life is an identity—and not simply the adding together of individual lives. And the truest living of both the marriage life and the social life is perfect freedom.

8. You make a most serious mistake if you think my ideal simply means "standing pat" to any out-grown notions of the past. It would be much simpler to think about, of course, if that were the case—for then—you could serenely hope that I would in time progress enough to see your standard—and believe in its truth. And I can understand how easy it is for you to assume that because you have felt a great expansion in your life of late, that *every* phase of your change is an indication of growth in the right direction. It isn't necessarily true that *every* strong impulse is a good one.

9. You speak of my considering you an intruder in my "problem." There is no intrusion there. Whatever problems I may have are another matter, and I have no desire to escape from any problems, however, difficult. But what I do desire to preserve from intrusion is our own personal privacy—Hartley's and mine—and I say *our*—very emphatically—for it is not *mine*. It is not a thing that can exist alone. It is a unity—an identity by itself. It would be utter selfishness for me to expect what you seem to assume I do expect—for myself alone.

10. You can't possibly take from me anything that is mine. If the fullest sort of happiness in life is meant to be mine—it will be mine—anyway—no matter what you do or do not do. The same is true of you—and everybody else. I can not *demand* that Hartley form any part of the unity I know—have long felt—and is a part of me—but it may be that he *can't help doing* so—and that is what I hope—and confidently believe. I can not demand anything. I can only wish that both you and he might be willing to act on the *assumption* that the unity between us is right and thorough in its nature—with no barriers anywhere, and that you could willingly and cordially do—if you only

saw the truth—without of that. There is nothing in the true marriage relation that can either *give* or *forbid* freedom. The freedom is there anyhow. It is a matter of the free flowing out of two spirits into one spirit—not a matter of man-made law. And so, when anything grows up that makes a spot that blocks that free flowing of spirit—in any way—the unity is blighted to just that extent—whether temporarily or permanently—can not be foretold. So long as there is no *exclusiveness* about it—no outside loves or friendships—or interests of *any* sort—can do anything but enrich the unity of the life of married people—but the moment there is any *exclusive* privacy or intimacy with another—a wall is made which must of necessity dam the stream of perfect love.

II. I confess that I find it very hard to be patient with you—when you assume that your insight into Hartley's character and method of growth is truer than mine—and appeal to me to trust my "interests" to his care—as if I were so small or so stupid as to be thinking of my own "interests." It would seem as if it ought to be unnecessary to even say that I could never wish him to do anything else than to be true to his own light. And I find it most difficult to hold myself from emphatic resentment of your insulting assumption of my "degrading 'below-stairs' interpretation of the efforts of a noble soul." I can only hope that your best self will be heartily ashamed of so mean and untrue a thought. I have done you the credit to sincerely believe that you were doing and thinking what you *believed* to be noble—even though I think you have been—in part—self-deceived—and I think it only just that you should do me equal credit. I can not believe that my life, as a whole or even in particular—has been so poor and despicable as to warrant any such criticism as you make. And I assure you, if anything could make me doubt your sincerity, such insults as this last would certainly do it. It is entirely unworthy of you, Margaret. You are too good a woman to indulge in any such talk. It will only hamper you in your effort to work out a true ideal and live up to it.

I have written this under difficulties

and interruptions—and if it doesn't say what I intended, it is my fault—and not the fault of the truth that I know and see—however feebly I express it—or live it.

Sincerely, Mary

[285] Mary Ware Dennett to Margaret Everett Chase, 10 March 1908, Margaret Chase Perry archives.

[286] William Hartley Dennett to Mary Ware Dennett, 14 February 1908, miscellaneous poems, in envelope marked "During the Change," Margaret Chase Perry archives.

[287] In mid-1907, Boston newspapers accused the Reeds of "championing a 'home of spontaneous love' that seduced 'innocent virgins' from neighboring Wellesley College. The allegations were based on a an angry father's accusations over an argument with his daughter. The stories appear to be completely untrue.

[288] H. Roger Grant, *Spirit Fruit: A Gentle Utopia* (DeKalb, Il.: Northern Illinois University Press, 1988).

[289] Jacob L. Beilhart, "Faith," *Spirit Fruit*, February 1901, Vol. 2, No. 9, Margaret Chase Perry archives.

[290] Jacob L. Beilhart, "Faith," *Spirit Fruit*.

[291] *Ibid.*

[292] Spirit Fruit derived its name from the numerous references in the Bible about the "fruit of the Spirit." Christ Himself told His followers how to distinguish true prophets from false, by advising, "You will know them by their fruits." 7:15–20.

[293] William Hartley Dennett, undated, personal notes, Margaret Chase Perry archives.

[294] William Hartley Dennett to Mary Ware Dennett, 21 May 1908, Margaret Chase Perry archives.

[295] William Hartley Dennett to Mary Ware Dennett, 26 May 1908, Margaret Chase Perry archives.

[296] Mary Ware Dennett to Margaret Everett Chase, 19 June 1908, Margaret Chase Perry archives.

[297] William Hartley Dennett to F.W.

Dallinger, "On the Petition of Mary Ware Dennett."

298 Livonia Coffin Ware, *Dennett v. Dennett*, 44.

299 Over time, Edwin Mead would become more and more incensed over the entire affair until he made a general call to Mary's friends to speak out. In a growing confirmation that the New England tendency to keep "private" matters discreet had allowed Hartley and Margaret to continue unchecked, he called the silence of her "friends" an outrage.

300 Edwin Doak Mead, *Dennett v. Dennett*, 16.

301 *Ibid.*

302 *Ibid.*

303 *Ibid.*

304 Edwin Doak Mead to William Hartley Dennett, 28 May 1908, Margaret Chase Perry archives.

305 *Ibid.*

306 William Hartley Dennett to Edwin Doak Mead, 30 May 1908, Margaret Chase Perry archives.

307 William Hartley Dennett to Margaret Everett Chase, 30 May 1908, Margaret Chase Perry archives.

308 Edwin Doak Mead, *Dennett v. Dennett*, 16.

309 *Ibid.*

310 Heman Lincoln Chase in the handwriting of William Hartley Dennett to Edwin Doak Mead, 17 June 1908, Margaret Chase Perry archives.

311 Roberts to William Hartley Dennett, 23 February, Margaret Chase Perry archives.

312 Lucia Ames Mead to Mary Ware Dennett, 19 September 1908, Margaret Chase Perry archives.

313 *Ibid.*

314 Lucia Ames Mead to Mary Ware Dennett, 19 September 1908, Margaret Chase Perry archives.

315 William Hartley Dennett to Mary Ware Dennett, 24 August 1908, Margaret Chase Perry archives.

316 Mary Ware Dennett to William Hartley Dennett, 26 August 1908, Margaret Chase Perry archives.

317 Mary Ware Dennett to Carleton Dennett, 20 August 1908, Margaret Chase Perry archives.

318 Hartley must have hated this. For what he loved about Margaret was her frankness and openness and her ability to tell and share all.

319 Mary Ware Dennett to Carleton Dennett, 24 August 1908, Margaret Chase Perry archives.

320 Carleton Dennett to Mary Ware Dennett, 28 August 1908, Margaret Chase Perry archives.

321 Carleton Dennett to Mary Ware Dennett, 126 August 1908, Margaret Chase Perry archives.

322 *Ibid.*

323 Carleton Dennett to Mary Ware Dennett, 166 August 1908, Margaret Chase Perry archives.

324 Carleton Dennett to Mary Ware Dennett, 23 August 1908, Margaret Chase Perry archives.

325 Frederick Reed to "friend" (apparently William Hartley Dennett), 30 November 1908, Margaret Chase Perry archives.

326 William Hartley Dennett, undated, personal notes, Margaret Chase Perry archives.

327 William Hartley Dennett, undated, personal notes, Margaret Chase Perry archives.

328 Edith Chase Newton to Alice Stone Blackwell, 15 March 1910, Margaret Chase Perry archives.

329 Margaret Everett Chase to William Hartley Dennett, 22 December 1908, Margaret Chase Perry archives.

330 Margaret Everett Chase, undated, personal notes, Margaret Chase Perry archives.

[331] Matthew 10:34–39, as quoted by William Hartley Dennett, January 1909, personal notes, Margaret Chase Perry archives.

[332] Katharine Ware Smith, *Dennett v. Dennett*, 38.

[333] *Ibid.*

[334] *Ibid.*

[335] *Ibid.*

[336] Anne Withington, *Dennett v. Dennett*, 50.

[337] John Merriam's questioning of H. Lincoln Chase, *Dennett v. Dennett*, 50.

[338] Mary Ware Dennett, *Dennett v. Dennett*, 456.

[339] Mary Ware Dennett's rebuttal, *Dennett v. Dennett*, 169–177.

[340] A.A. Merrill to Mr. Page, 8 August 1909, Margaret Chase Perry archives.

[341] *Ibid.*

[342] *Ibid.*

[343] *Ibid.*

[344] *Ibid.*

[345] *Ibid.*

[346] William Hartley Dennett, "Fourth report for class of 1893, Harvard University," 1909, Margaret Chase Perry archives.

[347] Mrs. George Everett to Mary Ware Dennett, 16 August, Margaret Chase Perry archives.

[348] *Ibid.*

[349] When asked when Devon was born, for example, Hartley simply said, "Well, he is four years old now. You can calculate it." Hartley could not remember when he had moved to Framingham, he did not know when he first knew Margaret Chase. His utter dependence on his wife was evident even in court. He casually tossed off the answer to one question, saying, "If you will ask Mary, she will remember." And when Mr. Merriam asked Hartley if Margaret had made "repeated and frequent visits to you in your home in Framingham?" Hartley out and out prevaricated: "I should not have said so; not repeated." Probate Court trial transcript, 22 September 1909, Folder 19, Box 2, MWD Papers.

[350] A week earlier, Vaughan had sent Hartley a "birthday" note apologizing for kicking him out and remonstrating him for not hiring a lawyer.

I had hoped to see you long enough to express my feelings and my convictions regarding your attitude toward your coming hearing. You went with Lincoln to see the Judge; the burden of his song was: be represented by counsel. Later you went to some kind of a preliminary affair and where did you land? Where did you land the day we all went to East Cambridge? This Hellhound of Mary's lays his pipe well and sets his traps. Why are you so simple that you like to be made laughing stock of? They will put it all over you and you are as helpless as a child. For God's sake either keep out of Court or get counsel. Don't make a big newspaper story to please your enemies.

Vaughan Dennett to William Hartley Dennett, 15 September 1909, Margaret Chase Perry archives.

[351] Probate Court trial transcript, 6.

[352] Probate Court trial transcript, 26.

[353] *Ibid.*

[354] John M. Merriam to Mary Ware Dennett, 1909, Margaret Chase Perry archives.

[355] Most likely, this was a reference to Hartley's playful displays of affection. There is little information on precisely how physical Hartley and Margaret's relationship was. Newspaper clippings, 1909 trial, Folder 20, Box 2, MWD Papers.

[356] Parroting something he had been spoon-fed, Lincoln explained Mary's anguish by saying her relatives had badly influenced her. "The result was that they poisoned her mind. Then, with utter disregard to our explanations of the affair, she brought the matter to court." He praised Hartley and Margaret. "My wife and Mr. Dennett are two of the same mind. They

are of the kind that would go to jail rather than pay a fine where principle was involved." Newspaper clippings, 1909 trial, Folder 20, Box 2, MWD Papers.

357 Typewritten note, presumably transcript of some sort, Margaret Chase Perry archives.

358 Probate court trial transcript, 27.

359 Probate Court trial transcript, 28.

360 John M. Merriam to Mary Ware Dennett, 16 October 1909, Margaret Chase Perry archives.

361 John M. Merriam to Mary Ware Dennett, 21 October 1909, Margaret Chase Perry archives.

362 John M. Merriam to Mary Ware Dennett, 16 October 1909, Margaret Chase Perry archives.

363 Mary Hutcheson Page to William Hartley Dennett, 17 December 1909, Margaret Chase Perry archives. Before long, Hartley simply began returning letters to the sender unopened.

364 Mary Ware Dennett, *Dennett v. Dennett*, 58.

365 Mary Ware Dennett to William Hartley Dennett, 18 October 1909, Margaret Chase Perry archives.

366 Mary Ware Dennett to William Hartley Dennett, 18 October 1909, Margaret Chase Perry archives.

367 William Hartley Dennett to Mary Ware Dennett, 24 October 1909, Margaret Chase Perry archives.

368 *Ibid.*

369 William Hartley Dennett to Mary Ware Dennett, 24 October 1909, Margaret Chase Perry archives.

370 William Hartley Dennett to Mary Ware Dennett, 4 December 1909, Folder 18, Box 2, MWD Papers.

371 William Hartley Dennett, *Jordan Marsh Co. v. Hartley Dennett*, June 1910, Margaret Chase Perry archives.

372 William Hartley Dennett, personal notes, June 1910, Margaret Chase Perry archives.

373 William Hartley Dennett to Eben D. Jordan, 29 March 1910, Margaret Chase Perry archives. Obviously, Hartley had degenerated into delusions of grandeur.

374 Mary Ware Dennett's rebuttal, *Dennett v. Dennett*, 169–177.

375 Front page, *The Woman's Journal*, 15 January 1910, Volume XLI, No. 3, Margaret Chase Perry archives.

376 Katharine Ware Smith, *Dennett v. Dennett*, 51.

377 Katharine Ware Smith, *Dennett v. Dennett*, 52.

378 Katharine Ware Smith, *Dennett v. Dennett*, 54.

379 Katharine Ware Smith, *Dennett v. Dennett*, 54.

380 Edwin Doak Mead to Mary Ware Dennett, 29 December 1910, Margaret Chase Perry archives.

381 Edwin Doak Mead to Heman Lincoln Chase, 27 December 1910, Margaret Chase Perry archives.

382 Heman Lincoln Chase to Edwin Doak Mead, 29 December 1910, Margaret Chase Perry archives.

383 Edwin Doak Mead to Cummings, 30 December 1910, Margaret Chase Perry archives.

384 *Ibid.*

385 Mary Ware Dennett to Heman Lincoln Chase, December 1910, Margaret Chase Perry archives.

386 William Hartley Dennett to Carleton Dennett, 15 September 1911, Margaret Chase Perry archives.

387 William Hartley Dennett to Devon Dennett, 27 February 1912, Margaret Chase Perry archives.

388 William Hartley Dennett to Carleton Dennett, 15 September 1911, Margaret Chase Perry archives.

389 *Ibid.*

390 William Hartley Dennett to Carleton Dennett, 22 December 1911, Margaret Chase Perry archives.

391 William Hartley Dennett to Mary Ware Dennett, 1911, Margaret Chase Perry archives.

392 Mary Ware Dennett's rebuttal, *Dennett v. Dennett*, 169–177.

393 William Hartley Dennett to F.W. Dallinger, "On the Petition of Mary Ware Dennett."

394 *Ibid.*

395 Newspaper clippings, April 1913, Folder 20, Box 2, MWD Papers.

396 Edwin Doak Mead to F.W. Dallinger, 5 March 1913, Margaret Chase Perry archives.

397 Hartley would explain, "It is therefore true that...I left my home. But it is not true that I deserted my home or my family: I took up residence at my brother's place, a few minutes' walk from my own home, in order to be at hand to help in the care of the house and of the family." William Hartley Dennett to F.W. Dallinger, "On the Petition of Mary Ware Dennett."

398 Hartley claimed that Mary's earlier "testimony...was I think uniformly witness to my good character and my devotion to my home." That claim and others in his "statement for the enlightenment of the Court" make for some incredulous reading.

399 William Hartley Dennett to F.W. Dallinger, "On the Petition of Mary Ware Dennett."

400 In his statement, however, he reiterated his "conscientious objection" to the oath—indeed, that was part of the reason he submitted a statement. This time, however, the conscientious objection did not prevent Hartley from taking the stand, for his testimony appears on court record. He would, however, refuse to submit himself to John Merriam's questioning.

401 Frank Patch, *Dennett v. Dennett*, 13.

402 Edwin Doak Mead, *Dennett v. Dennett*, 16.

403 Edwin Doak Mead, *Dennett v. Dennett*, 20.

404 Edwin Doak Mead, *Dennett v. Dennett*, 23. Indeed, Carleton and Devon, perhaps the most important mortal judges of all, would never—for the rest of their lives—sway from their loyalty to their mother. Almost a century later, Carleton would remember Mary as just about the best mother a boy could have.

405 Edwin Doak Mead, *Dennett v. Dennett*, 23.

406 Fred L. Norton, *Dennett v. Dennett*, 56.

407 Robert Bakeman, *Dennett v. Dennett*, 73.

408 *Ibid.*, 75.

409 Alfred Edwards, *Dennett v. Dennett*, 85.

410 *Ibid.*, 86.

411 Albert E. Smith, *Dennett v. Dennett*, 100.

412 *Ibid.*, 101.

413 Charles O. Rogers, *Dennett v. Dennett*, 104–105.

414 Henry H. Adams, *Dennett v. Dennett*, 94–95.

415 Heman Lincoln Chase, *Dennett v. Dennett*, 111.

416 *Ibid.*, 117.

417 *Ibid.*, 108.

418 *Ibid.*

419 *Ibid.*, 118–119.

420 *Ibid.*, 120.

421 *Ibid.*, 128.

422 *Ibid.*, 138.

423 *Ibid.*, 139.

424 *Ibid.*, 140.

425 *Ibid.*, 141–142.

426 William Hartley Dennett, *Dennett v. Dennett*, 151.

427 William Hartley Dennett to F.W. Dallinger, April 1913, "On the Petition of Mary Ware Dennett," Margaret Chase Perry archives.

[428] *Ibid.,* 153.

[429] *Ibid.,* 155.

[430] *Ibid.,* 156.

[431] *Ibid.,* 164.

[432] *Ibid.,* 166.

[433] F.W. Dallinger, *Dennett v. Dennett,* 168.

[434] Margaret also wrote a letter to Edwin D. Mead, but ultimately decided against sending it. Margaret Everett Chase to Edwin Doak Mead, undelivered letter, Margaret Chase Perry archives.

[435] Mary Ware Dennett's rebuttal, *Dennett v. Dennett,* 169.

[436] Mary Ware Dennett's rebuttal, *Dennett v. Dennett,* 169.

[437] She continued by pointing out that Hartley's witnesses knew absolutely nothing of Hartley's nine-year marriage—for the most part, they had met him afterwards; indeed, most knew him solely in the context of Hartley's relationship with Margaret. And to further decline their credibility, all of Hartley's witnesses, with the exception of Hartley, Dr. Chase, and Harry Adams, were either employees of the Chases, or former Alstead camp guests. Mary Ware Dennett's rebuttal, *Dennett v. Dennett,* 169–177.

[438] Mary Ware Dennett, *Dennett v. Dennett,* 177–178.

[439] *Ibid.,* 178.

[440] Margaret Everett Chase, undated, personal notes; William Hartley Dennett, statement to court, 17 February 1913, Margaret Chase Perry archives.

[441] Edwin Doak Mead to Reverend Edward Cummings, 2 January 1911, Margaret Chase Perry archives.

[442] F.W. Dallinger, Report to Judge Hall, April 1913, Margaret Chase Perry archives.

[443] *Ibid.*

[444] Vaughan Dennett to Edwin Doak Mead, 7 May 1913, Margaret Chase Perry archives.

[445] Edith Chase Newton to Alice Stone Blackwell, 19 June 1910, Margaret Chase Perry archives.

[446] William Hartley Dennett to Fred L. Norton, March 1913, Margaret Chase Perry archives.

[447] William Hartley Dennett to Fred L. Norton, 25 April 1913, Margaret Chase Perry archives.

[448] John M. Merriam to Mary Ware Dennett, 3 May 1913, Margaret Chase Perry archives.

[449] Newspaper clippings, April 1913, Folder 21, Box 2, MWD Papers.

[450] Ida Husted Harper, *History of Woman Suffrage: Volume 6: 1900–1920,* (New York: Arno & The *New York Times,* 1969), 269–270.

[451] Christopher Lasch, "Mary Ware Dennett," in *Notable American Women (1607–1950) A Biographical Dictionary,* eds. Edward T. James, Janet Wilson James, and Paul S. Boyer (Cambridge, Mass.: The Belknap Press of Harvard University Press), 464.

[452] Mary Ware Dennett to Anna Shaw, 17 August 1912, Folder 211, Box 12, MWD Papers.

[453] Mary Ware Dennett to Mary Hutcheson Page, 24 August 1909, Folder 203, Box 12, MWD Papers.

[454] Mary Ware Dennett, "The Simplicity of the Suffrage Question," Folder 214, Box 12, MWD Papers.

[455] Mary Ware Dennett to Mary Hutcheson Page, 24 August 1909, Folder 203, Box 12, MWD Papers.

[456] *Ibid.*

[457] *Ibid.*

[458] M. Carey Thomas to Anna H. Shaw, 21 April 1910, Folder 204, Box 12, MWD Papers.

[459] Robert Booth Fowler, *Carrie Catt: Feminist Politician,* (Boston: Northeastern University Press, 1986), 25.

[460] Eleanor Flexner, *Century of Struggle: The Woman's Rights Movement in the*

United States, (Cambridge, Mass.: The Belknap Press of Harvard University Press, 1959), 248.

461 Flexner, *Century of Struggle*, 257.

462 Shaw nearly starved through divinity school, because of a sexist rule that subsidized food for male students only. Aileen S. Kraditor, *The Ideas of the Woman Suffrage Movement: 1890–1920*, (New York: Anchor Books, 1971), 8.

463 Flexner, *Century of Struggle*, 182.

464 *Ibid.*, 237–238.

465 *Ibid.*, 248.

466 *Ibid.*

467 *Ibid.*, 249.

468 Mrs. Abigail Scott Duniway [President, Oregon State Equal Suffrage Association] to Miss Dennett, 14 July 1910, Folder 206, Box 12, MWD Papers.

469 Peck wrote Catt many love letters, and her preoccupation with Catt seemed to go beyond mere fondness. See Fowler, *Carrie Catt: Feminist Politician.*

470 Mary Grey Peck to Mary Ware Dennett, 10 June 1910, Folder 204, Box 12, MWD Papers.

471 Mary Grey Peck to Mary Ware Dennett, 12 June 1910, Folder 204, Box 12, M.W.D. Papers.

472 Mary Ware Dennett to M. Carey Thomas, 10 July 1910, Folder 206, Box 12, MWD Papers.

473 *Ibid.*

474 Harriet Taylor Upton to Mary Ware Dennett, 21 November 1910, Folder 208, Box 12, MWD Papers.

475 March 1914, *The Trend*, Folder 222, Box 13, MWD Papers.

476 Mary Ware Dennett, "Report of the Executive Secretary: from Dec. 5, 1913 to Sept. 6, 1914, Folder 214, Box 12, MWD Papers.

477 Melvin Dubofsky, author of history of I.W.W., as quoted in Madeline Gray, *Margaret Sanger*, 39.

478 Flexner, *Century of Struggle*, 251.

479 June 1914, *The Trend*, Folder 222, Box 13, MWD Papers.

480 Flexner, *Century of Struggle*, 262.

481 Jessie Ashley to NAWSA, 1911, Folder 209, Box 12, MWD Papers.

482 "The New Constitution: Arguments For and Against," Reprinted from "The Woman's Journal" for the convenience of delegates, Convention of the NAWSA at Louisville, Kentucky, 19–25 October 1911, 64 pages, Folder 220, Box 13, MWD Papers.

483 *Ibid.*

484 Perhaps hoping to avoid another rupture, a few suffragists then added that to change the name would be to invite legal problems—particularly in reference to legacies and bequests to NAWSA—making the technical difficulties a "practical" justification for keeping the long name, 9 September 1911, from officers at Headquarters, "As to leaving out the word American, that point may well be yielded, since Miss Blackwell has shown that we are under moral obligation to retain it, and Mrs. McCulloch that we endanger bequests if we don't."

485 Madge Patton Stephens, 22 July 1911, "The New Constitution: Arguments For and Against," Folder 220, Box 13, MWD Papers.

486 In Maryland, the official Maryland state association had 780 members, and was a member of National, but the Just Government League of Maryland numbered 3,000 members and the Equal Suffrage League numbered 800 members—neither of which could become members of National. Katherine Houghton Hepburn, member of the National advisory committee and president of the Connecticut W.S.A., 7 October 1911, "The New Constitution: Arguments For and Against," Folder 220, Box 13, MWD Papers.

487 Catherine Waugh McCulloch, 26 August 1911, "The New Constitution: Arguments For and Against," Folder 220, Box 13, MWD Papers.

488 Susan W. FitzGerald, 7 October 1911, "The New Constitution: Arguments For and Against," Folder 220, Box 13, MWD Papers.

489 Mary Ware Dennett, 7 October 1911, "The New Constitution: Arguments For and Against," Folder 220, Box 13, MWD Papers.

490 Alice Stone Blackwell to Mary Ware Dennett, 17 April 1911, Personal, Folder 209, Box 12, MWD Papers.

491 Mary Ware Dennett to Anna Shaw, 17 August 1912, Folder 211, Box 12, MWD Papers.

492 Alice Stone Blackwell to Mary Ware Dennett, 17 April 1911, Personal, Folder 209, Box 12, MWD Papers.

493 Anna Howard Shaw to Mary Ware Dennett, 23 September 1912, Folder 211, Box 12, MWD Papers.

494 Katherine Houghton Hepburn, member of the National Advisory Committee and President of the Connecticut W.S.A., 7 October 1911, "The New Constitution: Arguments For and Against," Folder 220, Box 13, MWD Papers.

495 L. Daniels to Mary Ware Dennett, 18 March 1911, Folder 209, Box 12, MWD Papers.

496 Whereas Dennett, recognized as absolutely vital to the life of the suffrage movement, was under intense pressure from the women of the NAWSA to stay on, Ashley, who was no doubt important in her own right, was let go without much comment.

497 In one issue, Mary actually penned the entire series of articles—even though Dr. Shaw received the full byline.

498 Marguerite Mooers Marshall, "American Parenthood from the Viewpoint Of a Suffragette Mother," New York Evening World, 7 October 1912, Folder 227ff, Box 13, MWD Papers.

499 Ibid.

500 Ibid.

501 Mary Ware Dennett to Anna Shaw, 1 September 1914, Folder 214, Box 12, MWD Papers.

502 Harriet Burton Laidlaw to Mary Ware Dennett, April 1914, Folder 214, Box 12, MWD Papers.

503 Anna Howard Shaw to Mary Ware Dennett, 8 September 1914, Folder 214, Box 12, MWD Papers.

504 The Freiburg Method of Dämmerschlaf or Twilight Sleep; by Wm. H. Wellington Knipe, A.M., M.D., F.A.C.S., New York City, Reprinted from The American Journal of Obstetrics and Diseases of Women and Children. Folder 601, Box 37, MWD Papers.

505 Twilight Sleep Association, First Vice-President, Mrs. Mary Dennett—"Why a Twilight Sleep Association Was Formed," Folder 601, Box 37, MWD Papers.

506 The committee of 100, "The Birth Control Movement," 1917, 23. Folder 238, Box 14, MWD Papers.

507 Twilight Sleep Association, First Vice-President, Mrs. Mary Ware Dennett—"Why a Twilight Sleep Association was Formed," Folder 601, Box 37, MWD Papers.

508 Believing that a single tax would make unemployment disappear forever (Land Values, Journal of the Movement for the Taxation of Land Values, October 1915, 147, "Women's Henry George League [Address of Mary Ware Dennett at the Annual Dinner, New York]. Folder 604, Box 37, MWD Papers.), her "specialty" lay in "presenting the single tax as a great fundamental social idea, rather than as a fiscal reform." (December 14, 1916, Mary Ware Dennett to Miss Estelle M. Stewart of The Joseph Fels Interational Commission. Folder 604, Box 37, MWD Papers.)

509 Professor R.T. Ely, Taxation in American States and Cities. Folder 604, Box 37, MWD Papers.

510 See Anna Alice Chapin, Greenwich Village (New York: Dodd, Mead and Company, 1917), 292–293.

511 Ibid, 210–211.

512 Ibid, 213.

513 Richard Miller, Bohemia: The

Protoculture Then and Now, (Chicago: Nelson-Hall, 1977), 138.

514 Terry Miller, *Greenwich Village and How it Got That Way*, (New York: Crown Publishers, Inc., 1990), 218–219.

515 Edmund T. Delaney, *New York's Greenwich Village*, (Barre, Mass.: Barre Publishers, 1968), 105.

516 Terry Miller, *Greenwich Village and How It Got That Way*, 175.

517 Delaney, *New York's Greenwich Village*, 105.

518 Terry Miller, *Greenwich Village and How it Got That Way*, 120–122.

519 D'Emilio and Freedman, *Intimate Matters*, 224.

520 Reed, *From Private Vice to Public Virtue*, 91.

521 Havelock Ellis, "The Erotic Rights of Women and The Objects of Marriage: Two Essays," 20.

522 First English publication in 1910 in the *Journal of Nerv. and Ment. Dis. Publ. Co.* as "Three Contributions to the Sexual Theory." First German publication in 1905 under the title *"Deuticke."* From Freud, *Three Essays on the Theory of Sexuality* (New York, Basic Books, Inc., 1962), p. ix.

523 That is, penis-vagina intercourse.

524 Mary Ware Dennett to Livonia Ware, 4 March 1915, private Dennett papers.

525 Gordon, *Woman's Body, Woman's Right*, 192–193.

526 "Changes in women's sexual behavior constituted the very essence of the sexual revolution. That fact has been obscured by the tendency of most historians to place men at the center of all large changes, and more specifically by the Kinsey and other reports on sexual behavior which drew attention to changes among both sexes." Ibid., 192.

527 "Heterodoxy to Marie," Christmas 1920, Box 2, Folder 2, Inez Haynes Irwin Collection, Schlesinger Library Manuscripts Collection.

528 Terry Miller, *Greenwich Village and How It Got That Way*, 221–223.

529 Ibid.

530 "The repressions of the nineteenth century had been primarily directed against male philandering; for women, moral, religious, and medical imprecations agaist 'indulgence' were almost unnecessary, so serious were the social, biological, economic and psychological risks, not to mention the frequent lack of pleasure that kept women from yielding to temptation or from experiencing temptation in the first place." Gordon, *Woman's Body, Woman's Right*, 182–183.

531 Emma Goldman, *Living My Life* (New York: The New American Library, Inc., 1977), 185.

532 "Marriage Customs and Taboo Among the Early Heterodites," by Florence Guy Woolston (pseudonym for Inez Haynes Irwin), Reprinted from *The Scientific Monthly*, November 1919, Copyright 1919 by the Science Press. Box 2, Folder 2, Inez Haynes Irwin Collection, Schlesinger Library Manuscripts Collection.

533 Ibid.

534 Caroline Nelson to Mary Ware Dennett, 1 April 1930, Folder 386, Box 22, MWD Papers.

535 Gray, *Margaret Sanger*, 72.

536 There is a question among historians about whether or not Sachs was an actual person or a composite of many women like her. In either case, the poignancy of the tale was real.

537 C. Roland Marchand, *The American Peace Movement and Social Reform* (Princeton, N.J.: Princeton University Press, 1972), 130.

538 Mary Ware Dennett to Erman J. Ridgway, 14 October 1914, *Everybody's Magazine*. Folder 214, Box 12, MWD Papers.

539 December 1914, *Woman's Home Companion*. Folder 222, Box 13, MWD Papers.

540 Platform of the Woman's Peace Party, Folder 637, Box 39, MWD Papers.

541 Mary Ware Dennett to Carleton and Devon Dennett, 13 September 1914, Folder 13, Box 1, MWD Papers.

542 Mary Ware Dennett to Carleton and Devon Dennett, 24 April 1914 , Folder 13, Box 1, MWD Papers.

543 Mary Ware Dennett to William Hartley Dennett, 21 January 1915, Margaret Chase Perry archives.

544 Florence S. Howard Burleigh, letter to *The Freewoman*, March 2, 1912.

545 Mary Ware Dennett to editor of *The Freewoman*, 17 April 1912.

546 *Ibid.*

547 *Ibid.*

548 *Ibid.*

549 *Ibid.*

550 Mary Ware Dennett to Carleton and Devon Dennett, 10 January 1915, Folder 13, Box 1, MWD Papers.

551 Mary Ware Dennett to Carleton Dennett, 10 January 1915, Folder 13, Box 1, MWD Papers.

552 Mary Ware Dennett to Carleton and Devon Dennett, 10 January 1915, Folder 13, Box 1, MWD Papers.

553 Mary Ware Dennett, *Who's Obscene?* (New York: The Vanguard Press, 1930), 4.

554 Gordon, *Woman's Body, Woman's Right*, 204–205.

555 Dennett, *Who's Obscene?*, 5.

556 New York *Evening Mail*, 1 February 1915, Folder 20, Box 2, MWD Papers.

557 Indeed Hartley's own mother, Annie O. Dennett, wrote to her son in dismay, "Why can't you keep your affairs private & out of the newspapers? I'll never be happy again." Adding that even his own brother, Vaughan, "wishes you'd change your name & spare us." Annie O. Dennett to William Hartley Dennett, 1 and 2 March 1915, Margaret Chase Perry archives.

558 Gray, *Margaret Sanger*, 36.

559 Stuart Sanger as quoted in Gray, *Margaret Sanger*, 40.

560 Mabel Dodge as quoted in Gray, *Margaret Sanger*, 58–59.

561 Gray, *Margaret Sanger*, 58.

562 Ibid., 65.

563 Mary Ware Dennett to Livonia Ware, 4 March 1915, Dennett private papers.

564 Mary Ware Dennett to Livonia Ware, 12 March 1915, Dennett private papers.

565 Speech at the meeting which organized the National Birth Control League, March 1915, at Clara Stillman's house, Folder 269, Box 15, MWD Papers.

566 *Ibid.*

567 *Ibid.*

568 National Birth Control League, "An Endorsement of Birth Control," Folder 251, Box 14, MWD Papers.

569 *Ibid.*

570 Dennett, *Who's Obscene?*, 6.

571 Mary Ware Dennett to Carleton Dennett, 15 November 1915, Folder 13, Box 1, MWD Papers.

572 Mary Ware Dennett, "What the Ballot Will Not Do," September 1915, *Woman's Home Companion*, Folder 222, Box 13, MWD Papers.

573 *Ibid.*

574 Marie wrote frequently and explicitly—and often with great passion.

"Dear Mary,

You talk sex and think sex—and psychology too—and meanwhile you let a perfectly good girl who has more genuine friendship for you than all her badness put together—after all—go thru the tortures of the damned because you are cock-sure it's good for her.

There is such a thing as making a morbid and cowardly person see her illness and cowardice finally and set about correcting it—and there is such a thing as outraging and insulting the things in that person for which she herself has respect.

It is a terrible thing I have done—forcing my illness on you—but at bottom it has nothing to do with you and it breaks my heart to think that you *will* consider it that way until we so thoroughly misunderstand that we can't save a splendid friendship.

Your girl,

Marie"

Marie Virginia Smith to Mary Ware Dennett, May 17 1915, Folder 598, Box 37, MWD Papers.

575 Mary Ware Dennett to the Executive Committee of the Twilight Sleep Association 6 January 1916, Folder 599, Box 37, MWD Papers.

576 Marchand, *The American Peace Movement and Social Reform*, 219.

577 *Ibid.*, 240–241.

578 Mary Ware Dennett to Hollingsworth Wood, 18 April 1916, Folder 616, Box 38, MWD Papers.

579 Mary Ware Dennett to sons, 4 April 1916, Folder 13, Box 1, MWD Papers.

580 Marchand, *The American Peace Movement and Social Reform*, 233–234.

581*Ibid.*, 248.

582 William Hartley Dennett to Margaret Chase, 30 April 1915, Margaret Chase Perry archives.

583 William Hartley Dennett to Margaret Chase, 28 and 30 April 1916, Margaret Chase Perry archives.

584 Mary Ware Dennett to William Hartley Dennett, 21 July 1916, Margaret Chase Perry archives.

585 *Ibid.*

586 William Hartley Dennett to Mary Ware Dennett, 5 August 1916, Margaret Chase Perry archives.

587 Reed, *From Private Vice to Public Virtue*, 106.

588 *Ibid.*, 81.

589 Mary Ware Dennett, Jessie Ashley, Rose Stokes, Crystal Eastman, and many others were involved in the Committee of 100.

590 Ellen Chesler, *Woman of Valor: Margaret Sanger and the Birth Control Movement in America* (New York: Simon & Schuster, 1992), 154.

591 Mary Ware Dennett, "What to Do to Help Re-Elect President Wilson If You Are a Woman Without a Vote of Your Own," Folder 636, Box 39, MWD Papers.

592 Mary Ware Dennett, "Wilson or Hughes? The Difference It Makes to The Women," Folder 636, Box 39, MWD Papers.

593 Elizabeth Bass to Mary Ware Dennett, 23 April 1917, Folder 636, Box 39, MWD Papers.

594 Mary Ware Dennett to Miss Charlotte Anita Whitney, undated, Folder 636, Box 39, MWD Papers.

595 Marchand, *The American Peace Movement and Social Reform*, 221.

596 *Ibid.*, 220–221.

597 *Ibid.*, 219.

598 Mary Ware Dennett to "C.T.", 16 November 1916, Folder 634, Box 39, MWD Papers.

599 Marchand, *The American Peace Movement and Social Reform*, 257.

600 *Ibid.*, 294–295.

601 *Ibid.*, 259.

602 Mary Ware Dennett to Miss Charlotte Anita Whitney, undated, Folder 636, Box 39, MWD Papers.

603 Mary Ware Dennett to Mary Fay, 20 June 1917, Folder 658, Box 40, MWD Papers.

604 Mary Ware Dennett to Mrs. Pratt, 12 May 1917, Folder 636, Box 39, MWD Papers.

605 Mary Ware Dennett to Mary Fay, 20 June 1917, Folder 658, Box 40, MWD Papers.

606 Mary Ware Dennett to Elizabeth Bass, 15 April 1917, Folder 636, Box 39, MWD Papers.

607 Anna Howard Shaw to Mary Ware Dennett, 19 May 1917, Folder 655, Box 40, MWD Papers.

608 Mary Ware Dennett to Mary McMurtrie, 20 April 1917, Folder 636, Box 39, MWD Papers.

609 Gertrude M. Pinchot to Mary Ware Dennett (telegram), 13 April 1917, Folder 269, Box 15, MWD Papers.

610 Virginia T. Heidelberg to Mary Ware Dennett, 15 April 1917, Folder 269, Box 15, MWD Papers.

611 Incidentally, in 1917 this work in peace issues gave Mary the occasion to contact Margaret Chase. Folder 648, Box 40, MWD Papers.

612 People's Council Propangada, Folder 657, Box 40, MWD Papers.

613 Marchand, *The American Peace Movement and Social Reform*, 308.

614 People's Council propaganda, Folder 657, Box 40, MWD Papers.

615 Seventh Meeting of the Organizing Committee, 13 June 1917, Folder 657, Box 40, MWD Papers.

616 People's Council Propaganda, Folder 657, Box 40, MWD Papers.

617 Press matter, People's Council, Folder 657, Box 40, MWD Papers.

618 Marchand, *The American Peace Movement and Social Reform*, 305.

619 *Ibid.*, 305–306.

620 *Ibid.*, 306.

621 *Ibid.*, 319.

622 *Ibid.*, 321.

623 Henry Ford, "This Was Not the Third Party", editorial in The *Dearborn Independent*, Folder 645, Box 40, MWD Papers.

624 Mary Ware Dennett to "Dear Friend," 5 January 1918, Folder 619, Box 38, MWD Papers.

625 Mary Ware Dennett to Estelle M. Stewart, 14 December 1916, Folder 604, Box 37, MWD Papers.

626 National Birth Control League, Folder 259, Box 14, MWD Papers.

627 National Birth Control League, Folder 259, Box 14, MWD Papers.

628 Dennett, *Birth Control Laws* (New York: The Grafton Press, 1926), 73. Most members of the NBCL lived in New York, although there were scattered local groups across the country.

629 "The Sex Side of Life," reprinted in February 1918 *Medical Review of Reviews*, Folder 502, Box 28, MWD Papers.

630 28 May 1918, fourth meeting, subseries 2, placement code 65, Sophia Smith Collection.

631 8 October 1918, at the Civic Club, subseries 2, placement Code 65, Sophia Smith Collection.

632 Mary Ware Dennett, "The Stupidity of Us Humans," *Birth Control Review*, January 1919, Folder 275, Box 15, MWD Papers.

633 Gertrude M. Williams, "Race Conservation in War Time Makes Birth Control a Necessity," Folder 269, Box 15, MWD Papers.

634 Report of the retiring secretary of the National Birth Control League. From 17 January 1918 to 17 February 1919, Folder 271, Box 15, MWD Papers.

635 Mary Ware Dennett's response to request for contraceptive information from Iowan woman, Folder 371, Box 21, MWD Papers.

636 Ibid.

637 Dennett, *Birth Control Laws*, 67.

638 Dennett, *Who's Obscene?*, 7.

639 Carleton Dennett, numerous interviews with author.

640 Carleton Dennett to William Hartley Dennett, Carleton Dennett collection.

641 Mary Ware Dennett to William Hartley Dennett, 9 & 15 September 1920, Margaret Chase Perry archives.

642 Gray, *Margaret Sanger*, 145–146.

643 Correspondence with Margaret Sanger, early history (1910–1920, n.d.), Folder 285, Box 16, MWD Papers. Also, Dennett-Sanger correspondence re: Sanger bill (1924–1930, 1931) and newspaper clippings (1931). Folders 399–401, Box 22. MWD Papers.

644 Representative James Robert Mann, interview with Mary Ware Dennett, 30 July 1919, Campaign notes, Folder 302v, Box 17, MWD Papers.

645 Senator Knute Nelson, interview with Mary Ware Dennett, 24 September 1919, Campaign notes, Folder 302v, Box 17, MWD Papers.

646 Senator Thomas Sterling, interview with Mary Ware Dennett, 4 September 1919, 12 September 1919, Folder 302v, Box 17, MWD Papers.

647 Senator William E. Borah, interview with Mary Ware Dennett, 5 September 1919, Campaign notes, Folder 302v, Box 17, MWD Papers.

648 Senator Joseph Irwin France, interview with Mary Ware Dennett, 24 September 1919, Campaign notes, Folder 302v, Box 17, MWD Papers.

649 Senator Knute Nelson, interview with Mary Ware Dennett, Campaign notes, Folder 302v, Box 17, MWD Papers.

650 Mary Ware Dennett, Voluntary Parenthood League talk prepared for Margaret Sanger's Conference, 11 and 13 November 1921, Folder 241, Box 14, MWD Papers.

651 Voluntary Parenthood League Minutes, 31 January 1921, Folder 264, Box 15, MWD Papers.

652 Dennett, *Who's Obscene?*, 15–16.

653 Dennett, *Who's Obscene?*, 17–18.

654 Ibid., 19–20.

655 Ibid., 20.

656 Dennett, *Birth Control Herald*, July 1922, quoted in Dennett *Birth Control Laws*, 52.

657 E.M. Morgan, Postmaster, to Mary Ware Dennett, 2 September 1922, Folder 463, Box 26, MWD Papers.

658 Dennett, *Who's Obscene?*, 34.

659 Margaret Sanger, "Position of Margaret Sanger Concerning the Birth Control Review," 1 February 1922, placement code 65, subseries 2, Sophia Smith Collection.

660 Senator Albert B. Cummins, interview with Mary Ware Dennett, 5 January 1923, Folder 303v, Box 17, MWD Papers.

661 The Committee of 100, "The Birth Control Movement," 1917, 30–31. Folder 238, Box 14, MWD Papers.

662 Dennett, *Birth Control Laws*, 165.

663 Mary Ware Dennett, Campaign Diary, 9 May 1924, Folder 244, Box 14, MWD Papers.

664 Mary Ware Dennett, press release, 21 January 1925.

665 Voluntary Parenthood League Executive Committee Minutes, 24 December 1924, Folder 241, Box 14, MWD Papers.

666 Mary Ware Dennett, Campaign Diary, 13 February 1924, Folder 243, Box 14, MWD Papers.

667 Mary Ware Dennett, Campaign Diary, 12 February 1925, Folder 246, Box 14, MWD Papers.

668 Mary Ware Dennett to William Hartley Dennett, 10 October 1922, Margaret Chase Perry archives.

669 Mary Ware Dennett to Marie Stopes, 27 November 1926, Folder 292, Box 16, MWD Papers.

670 Ibid.

671 Dennett, *Who's Obscene?*, 8.

672 Myra Gallert to Mary Ware Dennett, 17 September 1928, Folder 256, Box 14, MWD Papers.

673 Myra Gallert to Mary Ware Dennett, 9 December 1928, Folder 256, Box 14, MWD Papers.

674 Requests to Mary Ware Dennett for contraceptive information, letters from 1926–28, Folders 370–379, Box 21, MWD Papers.

675 Mary Ware Dennett to Myra P. Gallert, 14 July 1928, Folder 255, Box 14, MWD Papers.

676 Mary Ware Dennett, *The Sex Side of Life: An Explanation for Young People*, published by author.

677 Mary Ware Dennett to anonymous, 24 May 1926, Folder 467, Box 26, MWD Papers.

678 22 April 1930, Mary Ware Dennett to Rev. Wilbur Rand, Folder 422, Box 24, MWD Papers.

679 Gordon, *Woman's Body, Woman's Right*, 196–197.

680 Ibid., 200–201.

681 Mary Ware Dennett to Marie Stopes, 26 April 1927, Folder 292, Box 16, MWD Papers.

682 Dennett, *Who's Obscene?*, 8.

683 Dennett, *Who's Obscene?*, 44.

684 Ibid., 52–53.

685 Ibid., 53.

686 Mary Ware Dennett, form letters, 15 January 1929 and 20 January 1929, Folder 435, Box 24, MWD Papers.

687 Dennett, *Who's Obscene?*, 56.

688 Ibid., 57.

689 Ibid., 55–60.

690 Ibid.

691 Ibid.

692 Ibid., 66.

693 Ibid., 62.

694 Ibid.

695 Ibid.

696 Ibid., 62–63.

697 Ibid., 63–65.

698 Mary Ware Dennett Defense Committee, *Sex Education or Obscenity?*, 5, Folder 483, Box 27, MWD Papers.

699 Ibid.

700 Letters supporting the defense were from the following people: Goodwin F. Watson of Teacher's College, Columbia University; Stephen S. Wise, Rabbi of the Free Synagogue, New York City; Mrs. Cecile Pilpel of the Child Study Association of America; Albert R. Klemer of the National Council of the Young Men's Christian Association of the United States of America; B.S. Winchester, executive secretary of the Commission on Christian Education of the Federal Council of the Churches of Christ in America; Katharine Bement Davis, head of the Bureau of Social Hygiene and former commissioner of corrections, New York City; Dr. Robert L. Dickinson, secretary of the Committee on Maternal Health; Edward J. Allen, director, and five associates of the Seth Low Junior College of Columbia University, Brooklyn; Dr. Edward L. Keyes, President of the American Social Hygiene Association; Professors Harrison Elliot and Arthur J. Swift, of Union Theological Seminary, New York; John Dewey, Professor of Philosophy in Columbia University; Dr. Smith Ely Jelliffe, Neurologist, New York City; and Dr. Louis I. Harris, ex-commissioner of Health of New York City. Dennett, *Who's Obscene?*, 70–102.

701 Dennett, *Who's Obscene?*, 70.

702 Letters supporting the prosecution were from the following people: Rev. John Roach Stratton, Pastor of the Calvary Baptist Church, New York City; George B. Murphy, Chaplain of St. John's Long Island City Hospital, New York; James M. Kieran, President of Hunter College of the City of New York; Dr. G.A. Smith, Supt., and Dr. R.G. Wearne, Clinical Director of Central Islip State Hospital for the Insane, New York; Canon William Sheafe Chase, Rector of Christ Church, Brooklyn, N. Y.; Dr. Howard Kelly, professor emeritus of gynecology in Johns Hopkins University; John S. Sumner, Secretary of the New York Society for the Suppression of Vice; J. D. Dillingham, principal of the Newton High School, Elmhurst, Borough of Queens, New York City; Mrs. H.E. Hendrickson, probation officer, Laurelton, L.I., N.Y.; William Lathrop Love, M. D., New York State senator; and J. DeLeon Sullivan, superintendent of the Queensboro Society for the Prevention of

Cruelty to Children, Inc., N.Y. Ibid., pp. 102–129.

703 Dennett, *Who's Obscene?*, 130.

704 Ibid.

705 Ibid.

706 Dudley Nichols to Mary Ware Dennett, 19 February 1929, Folder 455, Box 26, MWD Papers.

707 Mary Ware Dennett to William Floyd, 22 March 1929, Folder 434, Box 24, MWD Papers.

708 Mary Ware Dennett to Prof. S.L. Millard Rosenberg, 13 March 1929, Folder 464, Box 26, MWD Papers.

709 Mary Ware Dennett to William Floyd, 8 April 1929, Folder 434, Box 24, MWD Papers.

710 Mary Ware Dennett to William Floyd, 10 April 1929, Folder 434, Box 24, MWD Papers.

711 Dennett, *Who's Obscene?*, 132.

712 Ibid.

713 Heywood Broun was one of Anthony Comstock's "official" biographers—"official," that is, in the sense that Comstock himself approved the biography.

714 Dennett, *Who's Obscene?*, 132.

715 Ibid., 133.

716 "Warren Booth Burrows," in *Judges of the United States, Second Edition,* 70, published under the Auspices of the Bicentennial Committee of The Judicial Conference of the United States, 1983.

717 Dennett, *Who's Obscene?*, 133.

718 *U.S. v. Mary W. Dennett,* Transcript of Record, Folder 491v, Box 28, MWD Papers.

719 Dennett, *Who's Obscene?*, 135.

720 Ibid., 160.

721 Ibid.

722 They were Mrs. Larkin, National Committee for Mental Hygiene; Myrtle Le Compte, Teachers College, Columbia University; Mrs. Pilpel, Child Study Association; Frank Kiendl, Attorney, Directory of Boys' Work; Mrs. Clara Savage Littledale, managing director, *Children: the Magazine for Parents*; William A. Jenny, young men's secretary, Prospect Park YMCA; Dr. Max Exner, Educational Division of the American Social Hygiene Society; Dr. Bascom Johnson, the legal director of the American Social Hygiene Society; Abel J. Gregg, of the National Council of the YMCA; Edward J. Allen, acting director of Seth Low Junior College, Columbia University in Brooklyn; Dr. Robert L. Dickenson of the Brooklyn Academy of Medicine and secretary of the Committee on Maternal Health; Mr. Jesse Perlman, director of the Associated Guidance Bureau; Mr. William H. Dewar, executive secretary, Prospect Park YMCA; Professor Harrison L. Elliot of the Union Theological Seminary; and Professor Goodwin Watson of the Teachers College, Columbia University. *U.S. v. Mary W. Dennett, Transcript* of Record, 15, Folder 491v, Box 28, MWD Papers.

723 Dennett, *Who's Obscene?*, 163.

724 *U.S. v. Mary W. Dennett,* Transcript of Record, 18–19, Folder 491v, Box 28, MWD Papers.

725 *U.S. v. Mary W. Dennett,* Transcript of Record, 20–22, Folder 491v, Box 28, MWD Papers.

726 Dennett, *Who's Obscene?*, 166.

727 *U.S. v. Mary W. Dennett,* Transcript of Record, 26–28, Folder 491v, Box 28, MWD Papers.

728 *U.S. v. Mary W. Dennett,* Transcript of Record, 28–30, Folder 491v, Box 28, MWD Papers.

729 Dennett, *Who's Obscene?*, 170.

730 Ibid., 170–171.

731 Ibid., 171.

732 Ibid., 172.

733 Ibid. Later, in his charge to the jury, Judge Burrows insinuates that the testimonials may be forgeries.

734 Ibid., 173.

735 The pamphlets were: *Today's World Problem in Disease Prevention* issued by the United States Public Health Service, Treasury Department, Washington, D.C.; *The Problem of Sex Education in the Schools* issued by the New York State Department of Health, Albany, N.Y., and reprinted by permission from the pamphlet of the Treasury Department, United States Public Health Service; *Sex Education: Symposium for Educators* issued by the Treasury Department, United States Public Heath Service; *Healthy Manhood*, a pamphlet distributed by the New York Department of Health, cooperating with the United States Health Service; *Syphilis, Gonorrhea and Chancroid—Healthy Mothers and Babies*; *Man-Power*, reprinted with permission from a pamphlet issued by the United States Public Health Service, by direction of the Surgeon General; *Sex and Youth* by Sherwood Eddy, published by Doubleday, Doran & Co., Inc.; *The Effectiveness of Certain Social Hygiene Literature* by Paul Strong Achilles, Ph.D., published by the American Social Hygiene Association, by agreement with the United States Public Health Service. *U.S. v. Mary W. Dennett*, Transcript of Record, 41–43, Folder 491v, Box 28, MWD Papers.

736 Ibid., 43.

737 *U.S. v. Mary W. Dennett*, Transcript of Record, 50, Folder 491v, Box 28, MWD Papers.

738 Dennett, *Who's Obscene?*, 177–178. Actual textual quotes corroborated by *U.S. v. Mary W. Dennett*, Transcript of Record, Folder 491v, Box 28, MWD Papers.

739 Ibid.

740 *U.S. v. Mary W. Dennett*, Transcript of Record, 54–55, Folder 491v, Box 28, MWD Papers.

741 Ibid.

742 Mary Ware Dennett Defense Committee, *Sex Education or Obscenity?*, 5, Folder 483, Box 27, MWD Papers.

743 Dennett, *Who's Obscene?*, 183.

744 Ibid.

745 Ibid., 186.

746 Ibid.

747 Ibid., 187.

748 Ibid., 187–188.

749 Dennett, *Who's Obscene?*, 189.

750 Ibid.

751 *New York Telegram*, Folder 496, Box 28, MWD Papers.

752 Newspaper clippings, Folder 494, Box 28, MWD Papers.

753 "Grandmother Found Guilty in Sex Life Pamphlet Trial," *Daily News*, 24 April 1929, Folder 494, Box 28, MWD Papers.

754 Mary Ware Dennett to Heywood Broun, 1 May 1929, Folder 415, Box 23, MWD Papers.

755 Dennett, *Who's Obscene?*, 191.

756 Ibid., 192–193.

757 Ibid., 193.

758 Ibid., 194.

759 Mary Ware Dennett Defense Committee, *Sex Education or Obscenity?*, 5, Folder 483, Box 27, MWD Papers.

760 Brooklyn Standard Union, Folder 497f, Box 28, MWD Papers.

761 Ibid.

762 Ibid.

763 "U.S. Used False Name to Trap Mrs. Dennett," New York *Telegram*, 26 May 1929, Folder 496, Box 28, MWD Papers.

764 Ibid.

765 American Civil Liberties Union, *The Prosecution of Mary Ware Dennett for "Obscenity,"* June 1929, New York City, 6, Folder 481, Box 27, MWD Papers.

766 April 30, 1929, El Paso *Evening Post*, "Sex Booklet Sent Hoover: Urge President to Pass on Work's Merit", United Press Leased Wire, Folder 419, Box 24, MWD Papers.

767 "Sex Booklet Sent Hoover: Urge President to Pass on Work's Merit", *El Paso Evening Post*, United Press Leased Wire, 30 April 1929, Folder 419,

Box 24, MWD Papers.

768 Leland Hazard to *The New Republic*, 7 May 1929, Folder 447, Box 25, MWD Papers.

769 One could not help but wonder whether or not she received any financial support from family members such as the Meads. After all, Mary did not seem to have a regular or dependable salary. The documents to provide such information seem extant, however.

770 Frances W. Emerson to Mary Ware Dennett, 29 April 1929, Folder 431, Box 24, MWD Papers.

771 Frances W. Emerson to Mary Ware Dennett, 20 May 1929, Folder 431, Box 24, MWD Papers.

772 Mary Ware Dennett to Frances W. Emerson, 22 May 1929, Folder 431, Box 24, MWD Papers.

773 Frances W. Emerson to Mary Ware Dennett, 26 May 1929, Folder 431, Box 24, MWD Papers.

774 Mary Ware Dennett to Frances W. Emerson, 22 May 1929, Folder 431, Box 24, MWD Papers.

775 Ibid.

776 William Hartley Dennett to Carl and Devon Dennett, 15 May 1929, Margaret Chase Perry archives.

777 Samuel Walker, *In Defense of American Liberties: A History of the ACLU* (New York: Oxford University Press, 1990), 85.

778 Mary Ware Dennett Defense Committee, Public Hearing on "Sex Education—Freedom or Censorship," Town Hall, New York City, 21 May 1929, Folder 484, Box 27, MWD Papers.

779 Ibid.

780 Ibid.

781 *Maternal Health Committee brochure*, 40, Folder 382, Box 21, MWD Papers.

782 Walker, *In Defense of American Liberties*, 85.

783 *United States v. Dennett. No. 238*, Circuit Court of Appeals, Second Circuit, 3 March 1930, in Edward De Grazia, *Censorship Landmarks* (New York: R.R. Bowker Company, 1969), 83–36.

784 Mary Ware Dennett to Margaret Sanger, 28 February 1931, Folder 399, Box 22, MWD Papers.

785 Marie Dennett, interview by author, 9 May 1992.

786 Ernst and Schwartz, 31–32.

787 Judge Moscowitz [copies of letters written to him on MWD's behalf, 1929]. Folder 453, Box 26. Mary Ware Dennett Collection.

788 Interestingly enough, the Dennett and Chase families are very close friends today.

Selected Bibliography

A NOTE ON SOURCES

IN May 1989, Carleton Dennett, Mary Ware Dennett's eldest son, donated his mother's papers to the Schlesinger Library at Radcliffe College, the largest women's history library in the United States. That spring, I was fortunate enough to win a writing fellowship for my senior honors thesis whose primary stipulation was use of the Schlesinger Library resources. My original proposal fell through, and Schlesinger staff were kind enough to point me to the Dennett collection—despite initial resistance on my part. Insisting that Dennett was the new Charlotte Perkins Gilman, another early twentieth-century feminist "discovered" at the Schlesinger, the archivists felt that the Dennett papers were a treasure trove.

A meticulous filekeeper, Mary Ware Dennett collected an enormous array of material over her lifetime, which amounted to a biographer's dream. After being processed by Anne Engelhart, the Mary Ware Dennett Collection included forty-three file boxes, one card file, five folio folders, five oversize folders, and seven oversize volumes. Later, the Dennett family was generous enough to allow access to additional private papers and photographs. All exceedingly well-preserved, these documents included 125-year-old letters between Dennett's parents, Vonie and George Ware; childhood letters and school papers of Mary dating back to the 1870s; a complete set of courtship letters between Mary Coffin Ware and William Hartley Dennett. In addition, Margaret Chase Perry, granddaughter and namesake of Margaret Everett Chase, happened to be a professional archivist who had privately organized all the family papers of Hartley Dennett and Margaret Chase.[788] Several descendants of some of the major characters in the story graciously allowed themselves to be interviewed for the book. In particular, Sally, Nancy, and Joanna Dennett, granddaughters of Mary, provided letters, photos, and memories. Carleton Dennett, who was in his nineties throughout the project, possessed an excellent memory and was interviewed many times during the last years of his life; Mary's younger son, Devon, had passed away, but his 96-year-old widow was also interviewed several times during the last months of her life.

The discovery of Mary Ware Dennett was pure serendipity. Due to previous unavailability of source material as well as to Dennett's own resistance to publicity, there has never been a full-length biography of her life. Now, however, in addition to untouched archival collections and extensive amounts of secondary research on related subjects, this account has the benefit of colorful anecdotes from the family. Even Dennett herself seemed to help out, providing notes along the way and producing a 499-page manuscript about her private life that turned up months before this book's publication. In many ways delivered on a silver platter, the story of her life unfolded as if Mary Ware Dennett were hoping for a biography to be written about her—despite her trademark modesty.

────────── ARCHIVAL COLLECTIONS ──────────

Hartley Dennett Papers. Private Collection of Margaret Chase Perry, Kensington, NH.

Mary Ware Dennett Papers. Arthur and Elizabeth Schlesinger Library, Radcliffe College, Cambridge, MA.

Margaret Sanger Papers. Sophia Smith Collection, Smith College, Northampton, MA.

Marie Stopes Papers. Wellcome Institute for the History of Medicine, London, England.

────────── BOOKS AND ARTICLES ──────────

Allen, Frederick Lewis. *Only Yesterday.* New York: Harper & Row, 1959.

Bahá'u'lláh. *The Hidden Words of Bahá'u'lláh.* Wilmette, Illinois: Bahá'í Publishing Trust, 1990. Translated by Shoghi Effendi with the assistance of some English friends.

Bailyn, Bernard, David Brion Davis, David Herbert Donald, John L. Thomas, Robert H. Wiebe, Gordon S. Wood. *The Great Republic: A History of the American People.* Second Edition. Lexington, Massachusetts: D.C. Heath and Company. 1981.

Barker-Benfield. *The Horrors of the Half-Known Life: Male Attitudes Toward Women and Sexuality in Nineteenth-Century America.* New York: Harper & Row, Publishers. 1976.

Barnes, Djuna. "Greenwich Village As It Is," originally appearing in *Pearson's Magazine,* October 1916. Reprinted as book, *Greenwich Village As It Is.* New York: The Phoenix Bookshop, 1978.

Baskin, Alex. *John Reed: The Early Years in Greenwich Village.* New York: Archives of Social History, 1990.

Bennett, D.R.M. *Anthony Comstock: His Career of Cruelty and Crime.* New York: Da Capo Press, 1971. A Da Capo Press Reprint Series, Civil Liberties in American History. General Editor: Leonard W. Levy. Originally published New York: D.M. Bennett, Liberal and Scientific Publishing House, 1878. Pp. 1009–1119

Blair, Karen J. *The Clubwoman as Feminist: True Womanhood Redefined, 1868–1914.* New York: Holmes & Meier Publishers, Inc., 1980.

Blum, John M., Edmun S. Morgan, Willie Lee Rose, Arthur M. Schlesinger, Jr., Kenneth M. Stampp, C. Vann Woodward. *The National Experience: Part Two: A History of the United States Since 1865.* New York: Harcourt Brace Jovanovich, Inc., 1981. Pp. 388– 699.

Brandt, Allan M. *No Magic Bullet.* New York: Oxford University Press, 1987.

Briant, Keith. *Marie Stopes: A Biography.* London: Hogarth Press, 1962.

Broun, Heywood, and Margaret Leech. *Anthony Comstock: Roundsman of the Lord.* New York: Albert & Charles Boni, 1927.

Callen, Anthea. *Angel In the Studio: Women in the Arts and Crafts Movement 1870-1914.* London: Astragal Books, 1979.

Cameron, Kenneth Walter. *Transcendentalists in Transition.* Hartford, CT: Transcendental Books, 1980.

Cashan, Joshua. *Civilizing Worcester: The Creation of Institutional and Cultural Order, Worcester, Massachusetts, 1848–1876.* Ann Arbor, Michigan: University Microfilms International, 1983. University of Pittsburgh, Ph.D. 1974. Copyright 1975.

Chapin, Anna Alice. *Greenwich Village.* New York: Dodd, Mead and Company, 1917.

Chase, Heman. *Short History of Mill Hollow: The Early Industrial Center of East Alstead, New Hampshire.* 1969.

Chesler, Ellen. *Woman of Valor: Margaret Sanger and the Birth Control Movement in America.* New York: Simon & Schuster, 1992.

Cheuse, Alan. *The Bohemians,* 1982.

Comstock, Anthony. *Frauds Exposed; or, How the People are Deceived and Robbed, and Youth Corrupted.* Originally published 1880. Reprinted Montclair, New Jersey: Patterson Smith, 1969.

Comstock, Anthony. *Traps for the Young.* Edited by Robert Bremner. Cambridge, MA: The Belknap Press of Harvard University Press, 1967. The John Harvard Library. Originally New York: Funk & Wagnalls, Publishers, 1883. With an Introduction by J.M. Buckley, D.D.

Connelly, Mark Thomas. *The Response to Prostitution in the Progressive Era.* Chapel Hill, North Carolina: The University of North Carolina Press, 1980.

Cott, Nancy F. *The Bonds of Womanhood: "Woman's Sphere" in New England, 1780–1835.* New Haven: Yale University Press, 1977.

_____. "Passionlessness," in *A Heritage of Her Own: Toward a New Social History of American Women,* eds. Nancy F. Cott and Elizabeth H. Pleck. With an Introduction by Nancy F. Cott, pp. 162–181. New York: Simon & Schuster, 1979.

Craig, Alec. *Suppressed Books: A History of the Conception of Literary Obscenity.* With a Foreword by Morris L. Ernst. New York: The World Publishing Company, 1963.

Craig, John M. *Lucia Ames Mead (1856–1936) and the American Peace Movement.* Lewiston, New York: The Edwin Mellen Press, 1990.

Cumming, Elizabeth and Wendy Kaplan. *The Arts and Crafts Movement.* New York: Thames and Hudson, 1991.

Davey, Peter. *Architecture of the Arts and Crafts Movement.* New York: Rizzoli, 1980.

Degler, Carl. *At Odds: Women and the Family in America from the Revolution to the Present.* New York: Oxford University Press, 1980.

Degler, Carl N. *Is There a History of Women?* An Inaugural Lecture delivered before the University of Oxford on 14 March 1974. Oxford, England: Clarendon Press, 1975.

Deglar, Carl N. "What Ought To Be and What Was: Women's Sexuality in the Nineteenth Century." *American Historical Review,* December 1974: 1467–1490.

De Grazia, Edward. *Censorship Landmarks.* New York: R.R. Bowker Company, 1969, pp. 83–36.

Delaney, Edmund T. *New York's Greenwich Village.* Barre, Massachusetts: Barre Publishers, 1968.

D'Emilio, John, and Estelle B. Freedman. *Intimate Matters: A History of Sexuality in America.* New York: Harper & Row, 1988.

Dennett, Mary Ware. *Birth Control Laws.* New York: The Grafton Press, 1926.

_____. *Who's Obscene?* New York: The Vanguard Press, 1930.

Drinnon, Richard. *Rebel in Paradise: A Biography of Emma Goldman.* 1982.

Dye, Nancy Schrom. *As Equals and As Sisters: Feminism, the Labor Movement, and the Women's Trade Union League of New York.* Columbia: University of Missouri Press, 1980.

Epstein, Barbara. "Family, Sexual Morality, and Popular Movements in Turn-of-the-Century America." In *Powers of Desire: The Politics of Sexuality,* ed. Ann Snitow, Christine Stansell, and Sharon Thompson. 117–130. New York: Monthly Review Press, 1983.

Ernst, Morris L., and Alan U. Schwartz. *Censorship: The Search for the Obscene.* With an Introduction by Philip Scharper. New York: The MacMillan Company, 1964.

Faulkner, Peter. *Against the Age: An Introduction to William Morris.* Boston,: George Allen & Unwin, 1980.

Flexner, Eleanor. *Century of Struggle: The Woman's Rights Movement in the United States.* Cambridge, MA: The Belknap Press of Harvard University Press, 1959.

Foucault, Michel. *The History of Sexuality: Volume I: An Introduction.* New York: Vintage Books, 1980.

Fowler, Robert Booth. *Carrie Catt: Feminist Politician.* Boston: Northeastern University Press, 1986.

Freedman, Estelle. "Separation as Strategy: Female Institution Building and American Feminism, 1870–1930." *Feminist Studies 5,* (Fall 1979): 512–29.

Garis, M.R. *Martha Root: Lioness at the Threshold.* Wilmette, Illinois: Bahá'í Publishing Trust, 1983.

Garraty, John A. *The New Commonwealth: 1870–1890.* New York: Harper Torchbooks, Harper & Row, 1968.

Gerard, David. *John Ruskin & William Morris: The Energies of Order and Love.* London, England: The Nine Elms Press, 1988.

Gilman, Charlotte Perkins. *Women & Economics: The Economic Factor Between Men and Women as a Factor in Social Evolution.* New York: Harper Torchbooks, Harper & Row, Publishers, 1966. Edited and with an Introduction by Carl N. Degler. Originally published Boston: Small, Maynard & Company, 1898.

Goldman, Emma. *Living My Life.* New York: The New American Library, Inc. 1977.

Gordon, Linda. *Woman's Body, Woman's Right.* New York: Grossman Publishers, 1976.

Grant, H. Roger. *Spirit Fruit: A Gentle Utopia.* DeKalb: Northern Illinois University Press, 1988.

Gray, Madeline. *Margaret Sanger: A Biography of the Champion of Birth Control.* New York: Richard Marek Publishers, 1979.

Griego, Elizabeth, "The Making of a 'Misfit,' Clelia Duel Mosher, 1863–1940" in *Lone Voyagers: Academic Women in Coeducational Institutions, 1870–1937,* edited by Geraldine Jonçich Clifford. New York: The Feminist Press, 1989.

Haney, Robert, *Comstockery in America.* Boston: Beacon Press, 1960.

Harper, Ida Husted. *History of Woman Suffrage: Volume 6: 1900–1920.* New York: Arno & The New York Times, 1969.

Jalland, Pat. *Women, Marriage and Politics: 1860–1914.* Oxford: Clarendon Press, 1986.

James, Henry. *The Bostonians.* New York: The Modern Library, 1956. With an Introduction by Irving Howe. Originally published 1886.

Kaplan, Wendy. *"The Art that is Life": The Arts & Crafts Movement in America, 1875–1920.* Boston: Museum of Fine Arts, 1987.

Kennedy, David M. *Birth Control in America: The Career of Margaret Sanger.* New Haven, CT: Yale University Press, 1970.

Kisch, Arnold I. *The Romantic Ghost of Greenwich Village: Guido Bruno in his Garret.* Frankfurt: Peter Lang GmbH, 1976.

Kraditor, Aileen S. *The Ideas of the Woman Suffrage Movement: 1890–1920.* New York: Anchor Books, 1971.

Lambourne, Lionel. *Utopian Craftsmen: The Arts and Crafts Movement from the Cotswolds to Chicago.* London: Astragal Books, 1980.

Lasch, Christopher "Mary Ware Dennett," in *Notable American Women (1607–1950) A Biographical Dictionary,* eds. Edward T. James, Janet Wilson James, and Paul S. Boyer. Cambridge, MA: The Belknap Press of Harvard University Press. 463–465.

Leach, William. *True Love and Perfect Union: The Feminist Reform of Sex and Society.* New York: Basic Books, Inc., Publishers, 1980.

Lucie-Smith, Edward. *The Story of Craft: The Craftsman's Role in Society.* Ithaca, NY: Cornell University Press, 1981.

MacMillan, P.R. *Censorship and Public Morality.* Aldershot, Hants: Gower, 1983.

Marchand, C. Roland. *The American Peace Movement and Social Reform, 1898–1918.* Princeton, NJ: Princeton University Press, 1972.

McCann, Carole R. *Birth Control Politics in the United States: 1916–1945.* by Ithaca, N.Y.: Cornell University, 1994.

Mencken, H.L. *The Editor, the Bluenose, and the Prostitute: History of the "Hatrack" Censorship Case.* Edited by Carl Bode. Boulder, CO: Roberts Rinehart, Inc. Publishers, 1988.

Mill, John Stuart. "The Subjection of Women" in *Feminism: Essential Historical Writings.* Edited by Miriam Schneir. New York: Random House, 1972 (originally published 1869), pp. 162–178.

Miller, Richard. *Bohemia: the Protoculture Then and Now.* Chicago: Nelson-Hall, 1977.

Miller, Terry. *Greenwich Village and How it Got That Way.* New York: Crown Publishers, Inc., 1990.

Morgan, David. *Suffragists and Democrats: The Politics of Woman Suffrage in America.* East Lansing, MI: Michigan State University Press, 1972.

Nash, Ogden. *Hard Lines.* New York: Simon & Schuster, 1931.

Naylor, Gillian. *The Arts and Crafts Movement: A Study of Its Sources, Ideals and Influence on Design Theory.* London: Trefoil Publications, 1990.

O'Neill, William L. *Divorce in the Progressive Era.* New Haven: Yale University Press, 1967.

O'Neill, William L. *The Last Romantic: A Life of Max Eastman.* New York: Oxford University Press, 1978.

Oraison, Marc. *Morality for Our Time.* Garden City, NY: Doubleday, 1968.

Paul, James C. N., and Murray L. Schwartz. *Federal Censorship: Obscenity in the Mail.* New York: The Free Press of Glencoe, Inc., 1961.

Pivar, David J. *Purity Crusade: Sexual Morality & Social Control 1868–1900.* Westport, CT: Greenwood Press, Inc., 1973.

Reed, James. *The Birth Control Movement & American Society: From Private Vice to Public Virtue.* Princeton, NJ: Princeton University Press, 1983.

Robinson, Paul. *The Modernization of Sex: Havelock Ellis, Alfred Kinsey, William Masters and Virginia Johnson.* New York: Harper & Row, Publishers, 1970.

Rosen, Ruth. *The Lost Sisterhood: Prostitution in America, 1900–1918.* Baltimore: The Johns Hopkins University Press, 1982.

Ross, Ellen, and Rapp Rayna. "Sex and Society: A Research Note from Social History and Anthropology" in *Powers of Desire: The Politics of Sexuality,* ed. Ann Snitow, Christine Stansell, and Sharon Thompson, 51–73. New York: Monthly Review Press, 1983.

Russett, Cynthia Eagle. *Sexual Science: The Victorian Construction of Womanhood.* Cambridge, MA: Harvard University Press, 1989.

Sanders, Marion K. *The Lady and the Vote.* Cambridge, MA: The Riverside Press, 1956.

Sears, William. *Thief in the Night or The Strange Case of the Missing Millennium.* Oxford, England: George Ronald Publishers, 1992.

Severn, Bill. *Free But Not Equal: How Women Won the Right to Vote.* New York: Julian Messner, 1967.

Schwarz, Judith. *Radical Feminists of Heterodoxy: Greenwich Village 1912–1940.* Lebanon, NH: New Victoria Publishers, Inc., 1982.

Shackleton, Robert. *The Book of Boston.* Philadelphia: The Penn Publishing Company, 1916.

Smith-Rosenberg, Carroll. "The Female World of Love and Ritual: Relations Between Women in Nineteenth-century America," in *Disorderly Conduct: Visions of Gender in Victorian America.* New York: Random House, 1985.

Sochen, June. *Herstory: A Woman's View of American History.* New York: Alfred Publishing Co., Inc. 1974.

Solomon, Barbara Miller. *Ancestors and Immigrants: A Changing New England Tradition.* Chicago: The University of Chicago Press, 1972.

Sours, Michael. *The Prophecies of Jesus.* Oxford, England: Oneworld Publications Ltd., 1991.

Stansky, Peter. *Redesigning the World: William Morris, the 1880s, and the Arts and Crafts.* Princeton, NJ: Princeton University Press, 1985.

Stein, Roger B. *John Ruskin and Aesthetic Thought in America, 1840–1900.* Cambridge, MA : Harvard University Prss, 1967.

Stockman, Robert. *The Bahá'í Faith in America: Origins 1892–1900: Volume I.* Wilmette, IL: Bahá'í Publishing Trust, 1985.

St. John-Stevas, Norman. *Obscenity and the Law.* New York: Da Capo Press, 1974.

Trimberger, Ellen Kay. "Feminism, Men, and Modern Love: Greenwich Village, 1900–1925" in *Powers of Desire: The Politics of Sexuality,* ed. Ann Snitow, Christine Stansell, and Sharon Thompson, 131–152. New York: Monthly Review Press, 1983.

Vance, Carole S. "Gender Systems, Ideology, and Sex Research" in *Powers of Desire: The Politics of Sexuality,* ed. Ann Snitow, Christine Stansell, and Sharon Thompson, 371–384. New York: Monthly Review Press, 1983.

Walker, Samuel. *In Defense of American Liberties: A History of the ACLU,* pp. 72–114. New York: Oxford University Press, 1990.

Ware, Caroline. *Greenwich Village, 1920–1930; a Comment on America.* 1935.

Watson, Steven. *Strange Bedfellows: The First American Avant-Garde.* New York: Abbeville Press Publishers, 1991.

Wilson, John. *Love, Sex, & Feminism: A Philosophical Essay.* New York: Praeger Publishers, 1980.

Wolff, Herbert A. "Morris L. Ernst," in the *1976 Memorial Volume of The Association of the Bar of the City of New York,* pp. 15–18. New York, 1976.

Young, Arthur Nichols. *The Single Tax Movement in the United States.* Princeton: Princeton University Press, 1916.

Index